The Little Big
COOK BOOK

The Little Big Cook Book
was created and produced by McRae Books Srl
Borgo Santa Croce, 8 – Florence (Italy)
info@mcraebooks.com
Publishers: Anne McRae and Marco Nardi

Text: Carla Bardi, Mollie Thomson
Editing: Anne McRae
Photography: Marco Lanza, Walter Mericchi
Art Director: Marco Nardi
Layout: Filippo Delle Monache, Piero Bongiorno
Repro: Litocolor, Florence - Fotolito Toscana, Florence

ISBN 88-88166-22-X

Printed and bound in China, by Tims Printing

The Little Big
COOK
BOOK

McRae Books

CONTENTS

Starters & Snacks 6
Soups 96
Pasta 142
Rice & Risotto 200
Bread 248
Focaccia 284
Pizza & Calzone 322
Savory Pies 368
Eggs 412
Fish & Seafood 432
Poultry 468
Veal & Beef 508
Lamb 542
Pork 558
Vegetables 618
Salads 652
Desserts 696
Crêpes 770
Small Cakes & Cookies 812
Cakes 862
Jams & Preserves 896
Sauces 930
Index 960

STARTERS
& SNACKS

HARD-BOILED EGGS WITH BELL PEPPERS

Serves: 4–6

Preparation: 10' + 30' to chill

Cooking: 25–30'

Level of difficulty: 1

- 1 yellow and 1 red bell pepper/capsicum, finely chopped
- 2 white onions, finely chopped
- 2 cloves garlic, finely chopped
- 1 tbsp finely chopped parsley
- 1 tbsp finely chopped fresh basil
- salt and freshly ground black pepper to taste
- 2 tbsp extra-virgin olive oil
- 6 medium tomatoes
- 1 tbsp white wine vinegar
- ¹/₂ tbsp sugar
- 6 hard-boiled eggs, shelled

Combine the bell peppers, onion, garlic, parsley, and basil in a skillet (frying pan) with a dash of salt and the oil and sauté over medium heat. ❧ To peel the tomatoes, bring a large pot of water to a boil. Plunge the tomatoes into the boiling water for 30 seconds and then transfer to cold water. Slip the skins off with your fingers. ❧ Cut the tomatoes into small cubes and add to the skillet. Cook over medium-low heat until the sauce is thick. ❧ Add the vinegar and sugar, and mix well. Season with salt and pepper. ❧ Remove from heat and set aside to cool. ❧ Cut the eggs in half lengthwise. Remove the yolks, mash, and add to the tomato and bell pepper sauce. Mix well. ❧ Fill the eggs with the mixture and arrange them on a serving dish. Spoon any extra sauce over the top (or serve on slices of toasted bread with the eggs). ❧ Refrigerate the eggs for at least 30 minutes before serving.

NUN'S TOAST

Melt the butter in a small saucepan over medium heat. ❧ Sauté the onion for 3–4 minutes without letting it brown. ❧ Sift in the flour and stir with a wooden spoon for a minute or so to "cook" the mixture. ❧ Pour the milk in gradually, stirring steadily so that no lumps form. ❧ Season with salt and pepper and cook for 2–3 minutes more after the last addition of milk. ❧ Spoon the sauce onto a heated serving dish. Cut the eggs in half and arrange them in the sauce. ❧ Sprinkle with the parsley. ❧ Serve hot, accompanied by hot buttered toast.

Serves: 4

Preparation: 10'

Cooking: 10'

Level of difficulty: 1

- 2 tbsp butter
- 1 medium onion, finely chopped
- 2 tbsp all-purpose/ plain flour
- 4 cups/1 liter milk, warmed
- salt and freshly ground black pepper to taste
- 6 hard-boiled eggs, shelled
- 1 tbsp finely chopped parsley

STUFFED EGGS

Serves: 2–4

Preparation: 10'

Level of difficulty: 1

- **4 hard-boiled eggs, shelled**
- **2 tbsp cream**
- **2 tbsp finely chopped mixed fresh herbs (parsley, mint, marjoram, dill)**
- **4 tbsp mayonnaise**
- **salt and freshly ground black pepper to taste**
- **dash of paprika**
- **lettuce leaves and salad tomatoes, to garnish**

Cut the eggs in half lengthwise. ❧ Scoop out the yolks, being careful not to break the whites. ❧ Combine the yolks in a small bowl with the cream, herbs, mayonnaise, salt, and pepper and mash with a fork. ❧ Use a teaspoon to stuff the filling into the hollow egg whites. Dust each egg with paprika for extra color. ❧ Rinse the lettuce leaves, dry well, and arrange on a serving dish. Place the eggs on the lettuce and garnish with slices of tomato.

EGGS FAIRY⊰STYLE

Cut a slice off the bottom of each egg so that they will stand upright. ⚘ Spread the mayonnaise over the bottom of a serving dish. Set the eggs, upright, in the mayonnaise, not too close to each other. ⚘ Cut the plum tomatoes in half, remove the pulp and seeds, and use the halves to put a "hat" on each upright egg. ⚘ Dot the tomato caps with extra mayonnaise to look like the spots on mushrooms. ⚘ Garnish with the pieces of bell pepper and gherkin and sprinkle with the parsley. ⚘ Refrigerate for 30 minutes before serving.

Serves: 3–6

Preparation: 20' + 30' to chill

Level of difficulty: 1

- **6 hard-boiled eggs, shelled**
- **1 cup/250 ml mayonnaise**
- **3 red plum tomatoes**
- **$1/4$ red and $1/4$ yellow bell pepper/ capsicum, cut in tiny diamond shapes**
- **6 pickled gherkins, sliced**
- **6 tbsp finely chopped parsley**

COUNTRY-STYLE EGGS

Serves: 6

Preparation: 10'

Level of difficulty: 1

- **12 hard-boiled eggs, shelled**
- **8 basil leaves, finely chopped**
- **3 tbsp finely chopped parsley**
- **2 tbsp capers, finely chopped**
- **5 oz/150 g green olives, pitted and finely chopped**
- **1/2 cup/125 g freshly grated Parmesan cheese**
- **1/2 cup/60 g fine dry bread crumbs**
- **3/4 cup/180 ml dry white wine**
- **freshly ground black pepper to taste**
- **4 tbsp extra-virgin olive oil**

Cut the eggs in half lengthwise. ✿ Mix the basil, parsley, capers, and olives together in a bowl. Stir in the Parmesan and bread crumbs. Gradually stir in the wine. ✿ Add the pepper and gradually stir in the oil. The mixture should be thick but still fluid. ✿ Place the eggs on a platter with the yolks facing up. Spoon the mixture over the eggs and serve.

CHEDDAR ONION DIP

P lace the sour cream and cheese in a medium bowl. ❧ Add the soup mix and stir until smooth. Season with the pepper. ❧ Cover the bowl and refrigerate for 2 hours. ❧ Serve with potato chips, crackers, or raw vegetables.

Serves: 3–6

Preparation: 20' + 2 h to chill

Level of difficulty: 1

- 1 (1½ oz/45 g) package dry onion soup mix
- 2 cups/500 ml sour cream
- 3 oz/90 g Cheddar cheese, grated
- 3 tbsp pimento
- freshly ground black pepper to taste

RICOTTA CHEESE WITH FRESH HERBS

Serves: 6

Preparation: 5' + 1 h to chill

Level of difficulty: 1

- **1 lb/500 g fresh Ricotta cheese**
- **16 fresh basil leaves, finely chopped**
- **2 tbsp finely chopped parsley**
- **2 tbsp each finely chopped thyme and chives**
- **3 bay leaves**
- **1 tsp fennel seeds, crushed**
- **1 clove garlic, finely chopped**
- **salt and freshly ground white pepper to taste**

Combine the Ricotta, basil, parsley, thyme, and chives in a bowl and mix well. ❧ Add the bay leaves, fennel, garlic, if using, salt, and pepper and mix again. ❧ Refrigerate for 1 hour. ❧ Remove the bay leaves and serve with freshly baked bread.

CHEESE EGG DIP WITH CRUDITÉS

Serves: 2–4

Preparation: 5' + 1 h to chill

Level of difficulty: 1

- **1 cup/250 g cream cheese**
- **2 tbsp mayonnaise**
- **1–2 tsp spicy mustard**
- **1 tsp Worcestershire sauce**
- **1 tbsp chopped chives**
- **2 hard-boiled eggs, shelled**
- **3 tbsp milk**
- **salt and freshly ground white pepper to taste**
- **2–4 carrots**
- **2–4 stalks celery**

Place the cream cheese in a medium bowl and stir in the mayonnaise, mustard, Worcestershire sauce, chives, eggs, and milk. Mix until smooth. ❧ Season with salt and pepper and refrigerate for at least 1 hour. ❧ Just before serving, rinse and scrape the carrots, then cut into strips. Remove any tough fibers from the celery and cut into strips the same size as the carrots. ❧ Arrange the raw vegetables on a large platter. ❧ Spoon the egg dip into an attractive serving dish and place at the center of the platter with the vegetables.

Try this dip with cherry tomatoes, radishes, and spring onions, or with crackers or potato chips.

PRICKLY CHEESE & CELERY BALLS

Melt the butter in a saucepan over low heat. ❧ Combine the butter and Gorgonzola in a medium bowl and mix well. ❧ Gradually add the oil, lemon juice, and pepper, and stir carefully with a wooden spoon until the mixture becomes a thick cream. ❧ Divide the cheese mixture in two equal parts and shape into balls. Wrap each ball in aluminum foil and refrigerate for 1 hour. ❧ Wash and dry the celery and chop into sticks about 3 in (8 cm) long and $1/4$ in (6 mm) wide. ❧ Remove the foil from the cheese balls and place them on a serving dish. Press pieces of celery into the cheese balls so that they stick out like a porcupine's quills. ❧ Serve cold.

Serve these tasty treats as an appetizer or with salad and freshly baked bread at lunch.

Serves: 6

Preparation: 20' + 1 h to chill

Level of difficulty: 1

- 4 tbsp butter
- 14 oz/450 g soft Gorgonzola cheese
- 2 tbsp extra-virgin olive oil
- juice of 1 lemon
- freshly ground white pepper to taste
- 12 large stalks celery

WILD SALAD GREENS WITH WARM CAPRINO

Preheat the oven to 350°F/180°C/gas 4. ❧ Rinse the salad greens and dry thoroughly. Place on two serving plates. ❧ In a blender, mix 2 tablespoons of the oil with the olives and honey until creamy. ❧ Drizzle the remaining oil over the salads, then season lightly with salt. ❧ Place the Caprino in an ovenproof dish and heat in the oven for 5–10 minutes. ❧ When the cheese is heated through, but not melted, place two in the center of each salad. Spoon the the olive cream over the top and serve at once.

Serves: 2
Preparation: 10'
Cooking: 5–10'
Level of difficulty: 1

- **1–2 cups mixed wild salad greens**
- **3 tbsp extra-virgin olive oil**
- **¹/₂ cup/60 g pitted black olives**
- **1 tbsp honey**
- **salt to taste**
- **4 tiny forms Caprino cheese**

BAKED TOMATOES WITH CHEESE

Serves: 4

Preparation: 15'

Cooking: 40'

Level of difficulty: 1

- **8 medium tomatoes**
- **salt and freshly ground black pepper to taste**
- **4 tbsp extra-virgin olive oil**
- **1 tbsp finely chopped parsley**
- **1 tbsp finely chopped basil**
- **4 tbsp flour**
- **2 cups/500 ml milk**
- **dash of nutmeg**
- **4 oz/125 g Fontina or Cheddar cheese, grated**

Preheat the oven to 400°F/200°C/gas 6. ❧ Cut the tomatoes in half, squeezing gently to remove the seeds. Place in an ovenproof baking dish and season lightly with salt and pepper. Drizzle with 1 tablespoon of oil and sprinkle with the parsley and basil. Bake for 20 minutes. ❧ Heat the remaining oil in a small saucepan over low heat. Add the flour and stir constantly until thick. ❧ Gradually add the milk, stirring constantly, and cook until smooth and dense. Season with salt, pepper, and nutmeg, and stir in the cheese. ❧ Fill the tomatoes with the cheese mixture and bake for 20 more minutes, or until the cheese is lightly browned.

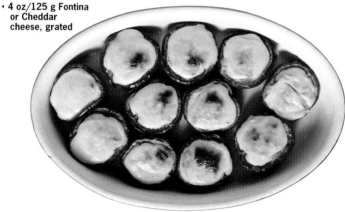

TOMATOES WITH CAPRINO CHEESE

S lice the tops off the tomatoes. Scoop out the pulp using a small teaspoon and set aside. ☙ Place the shells upside down in a colander to drain for 10 minutes. ☙ In a bowl, mix the oil, tomato pulp, olives, garlic, basil, salt, pepper, and cheese until well mixed. ☙ Stuff the tomatoes with the filling and refrigerate for at least 30 minutes before serving.

This dish comes from Italy, where it is served as an appetizer throughout the hot summer months.

Serves: 4

Preparation: 15' + 30' to chill

Level of difficulty: 2

Variation
• For a lighter dish, use 8 oz/250 g of fresh Ricotta cheese instead of the Caprino.

- 12 cherry tomatoes
- $1/2$ tbsp extra-virgin olive oil
- 10 green olives, chopped
- 1 clove garlic, finely chopped
- 6 fresh basil leaves, torn
- salt and freshly ground black pepper to taste
- 8 oz/250 g soft Caprino cheese

FAVA BEANS WITH PECORINO CHEESE

Rinse the beans thoroughly under cold running water. Dry well with paper towels. ❧ Discard any tough or withered looking pods, or any with ugly spots or marks. ❧ Slice the cheese into large dice or wedges. ❧ Arrange the beans and cheese on an attractive platter or dish and serve.

Serve this dish as an appetizer in the spring when fava beans are tender enough to be eaten raw.

Serves: 6–8

Preparation: 5'

Level of difficulty: 1

- 3 lb/1.5 kg raw, young fava/broad beans, in their pods
- 14 oz/450 g Pecorino cheese

STUFFED CELERY STALKS

Serves: 6–8

Preparation: 15' + 1 h
to chill

Level of difficulty: 1

- 8 oz/250 g Gorgonzola cheese
- 4 oz/125 g Mascarpone cheese
- 4 tbsp milk
- 2 cloves garlic, finely chopped
- 1 tbsp extra-virgin olive oil
- salt and freshly ground black pepper to taste
- 10 large stalks celery
- 1 tbsp each finely chopped parsley and chives

Melt the Gorgonzola in a heavy-bottomed saucepan over very low heat. ❧ Remove from heat and add the Mascarpone and enough milk to obtain a dense, creamy mixture. ❧ Add the garlic, oil, salt, and pepper. Mix until smooth. ❧ Cover and refrigerate for 1 hour. ❧ Trim the celery stalks and remove any tough fibers. Cut into pieces about 3 in (8 cm) long. ❧ Fill the celery with the cheese mixture, sprinkle with the parsley and chives and serve.

Health and figure conscious friends will be delighted if you include this dish in a party, picnic, or barbecue spread.

CHEESE FONDUE

Slice the cheese thinly and place in a bowl with enough milk to cover. Leave to stand for 2–4 hours. ❧ Half-fill a saucepan or the bottom pan of a double boiler with water and bring to a very gentle boil. Place a heatproof bowl or the top pan of the double boiler containing the butter in it and leave to melt. ❧ Drain the milk off the cheese, reserving the milk. Add the cheese to the melted butter, together with 3–4 tablespoons of the reserved milk. ❧ Stir continuously with a wooden spoon over the gently simmering water until the cheese has melted and threads start to form. At no point during preparation should it be allowed to boil. ❧ Stir the first 4 egg yolks into the cheese one at a time, incorporating each one very thoroughly before adding the next. The mixture should be glossy and smooth. If it still looks a little grainy, add the fifth egg yolk and stir for 1 minute. Season with salt and pepper. ❧ Transfer the fondue to a fondue pot. Serve with thickly sliced toasted French bread. ❧ The gourmet version of this fondue is served with a sprinkling of wafer-thin slices of white truffles.

Fondue is made throughout the European Alps. This recipe comes from northwestern Italy.

Serves: 4–6

Preparation: 15' + 2–4 h to stand

Cooking: 15'

Level of difficulty: 1

- **14 oz/450 g Fontina cheese**
- **1 cup/250 ml whole milk**
- **2 tbsp butter**
- **4–5 egg yolks**
- **salt and freshly ground white pepper to taste**
- **slices of toast**

CHEESE & ALMOND PUFFS

Serves: 4

Preparation: 10'

Cooking: 30'

Level of difficulty: 2

- 4 oz/125 g almonds
- ²/₃ cup/180 ml cold water
- 4 tbsp butter
- ²/₃ cup/100 g all-purpose/plain flour
- salt to taste
- 3 oz/90 g freshly grated Parmesan cheese
- freshly ground white pepper to taste
- 2 eggs

Preheat the oven to 400°F/200°C/gas 6. ❧ Blanch the almonds and peel them by placing in a bowl and pouring enough boiling water over the top to barely cover. Leave for 1 minute. Drain and rinse under cold water. Pat dry and slip off the skins. Chop coarsely. ❧ Combine the cold water with 3 tablespoons of butter in a small saucepan over medium heat. When the water starts to boil, remove the pan from heat and incorporate the flour and salt, stirring constantly with a wooden spoon. ❧ Return the saucepan to the heat and cook until the dough is thick, stirring all the time. ❧ Remove from the heat and stir in the cheese and pepper. Set aside to cool. ❧ Beat the eggs into the cooled dough one at a time. ❧ Beat the dough vigorously. Transfer to a pastry bag with a smooth tube about ¹/₄ in (6 mm) in diameter. ❧ Butter a baking sheet and dust with flour. ❧ Place marble-size balls of dough on the baking sheet and sprinkle with the almonds, making sure they stick to the puffs. ❧ Bake for 15–20 minutes, or until golden brown. The puffs will swell as they bake. ❧ Serve at room temperature.

PARMESAN
ICE CREAM

Mix the cream with the Parmesan, salt, and pepper in the top of a double boiler or in a heatproof bowl. Cook over barely simmering water until the cheese is completely melted. Remove from heat and set aside to cool. ✿ Pour through a sieve to strain. ✿ Pour the resulting liquid into an ice cream maker and process as directed. ✿ If you don't have an ice cream maker, pour the liquid into a freezerproof container and freeze, stirring at intervals as the mixture thickens and freezes. ✿ After 3 hours in the freezer, take the mixture out and transfer to a food processor. Blend until smooth, then replace in the freezer. Repeat this process after another 3 hours' freezing. ✿ Serve with an ice cream scoop.

Serves: 6

Preparation: 15' + 6 h to freeze

Level of difficulty: 1

- **2 cups/500 ml light/single cream**
- **12 oz/350 g freshly grated Parmesan cheese**
- **salt to taste**
- **cayenne or chile pepper to taste**

HOT CHEESE & HERB APPETIZER

Serves: 4

Preparation: 5'

Cooking: 10'

Level of difficulty: 1

- 4 tbsp extra-virgin olive oil
- 2–3 cloves garlic, lightly crushed
- 4 thick slices fresh Pecorino cheese
- 2 tbsp red wine vinegar
- 1 tsp dried oregano
- freshly ground black pepper to taste

Sauté the garlic in the oil in a large skillet (frying pan) over medium heat until pale golden brown. Remove the garlic and discard. ❧ Place the cheese slices in the skillet in a single layer, increase the heat and cook, turning several times with a spatula. ❧ Sprinkle the cheese with the vinegar, oregano, and pepper. Cover and cook for 2 minutes more. ❧ Serve very hot.

CHEESE CROQUETTES

Serves: 4

Preparation: 20'

Cooking: 25'

Level of difficulty: 1

- 4 tbsp butter
- 5 tbsp all-purpose/ plain flour
- 1 cup/250 ml milk
- 4 tbsp cream
- 11 oz/300 g tasty cheese, grated (sharp Cheddar, Fontina)
- 2 egg yolks, beaten
- salt and freshly ground white pepper to taste
- $^1/_2$ cup/75 g all-purpose/plain flour
- 2 eggs, beaten with $^1/_2$ cup/125 ml milk
- 1 cup/150 g fine dry bread crumbs
- 2 cups/500 ml oil, for frying

Melt the butter over low heat in a medium saucepan. ❧ Add the 5 tablespoons of flour and cook for 3–4 minutes, stirring constantly. ❧ Stir in the milk and continue cooking until the mixture is thick. ❧ Add the cheese and stir until melted, then stir in the egg yolks. ❧ Season with salt and pepper, then set aside to cool. ❧ Scoop up spoonfuls of the cooled mixture and shape into croquettes. ❧ Dredge the croquettes in the second measure of flour, then dip them into the egg and milk mixture. Finally, roll them in the bread crumbs. ❧ Heat the oil in a large skillet (frying pan) until very hot. Fry the croquettes in batches until golden brown all over. ❧ Drain on paper towels and serve hot.

These crispy croquettes will send your cholesterol levels into orbit! But then, once in a while won't hurt.

35

CHEESE BISCUITS OR STRAWS

P reheat the oven to 400°F/200°C/gas 6. ❧ Sift the flour and baking powder into a large bowl. ❧ Rub the butter into the flour, then add the cheese. ❧ Season with salt and pepper and stir in enough of the milk to make a stiff dough. ❧ Roll the dough out into a very thin sheet and use a cookie cutter or small glass to cut into rounds if making biscuits, or a sharp knife to cut into straws. ❧ Place on a greased baking sheet and bake for 10–12 minutes, or until golden brown. Straws will be cooked a minute or two before the biscuit shapes, so do not cook them on the same baking sheet. ❧ Serve hot or at room temperature.

Serves: 8–10

Preparation: 20'

Cooking: 10'

Level of difficulty: 1

- ²/₃ **cup/100 g all-purpose/plain flour**
- **1 tsp baking powder**
- **4 tbsp butter**
- **3 oz/90 g Cheddar or Emmental cheese, grated**
- **salt and freshly ground black pepper to taste**
- ¹/₂ **cup/125 ml milk**

CHEESE & HAM CROQUETTES

P lace the milk, salt, and nutmeg in a medium saucepan and bring to a boil. ❧ Melt the butter in another saucepan. Stir in the flour and cook until thick. ❧ Remove from heat and gradually add the milk. ❧ Return to heat and cook, stirring constantly, until thick. ❧ Remove from heat and stir in the ham, cheese, and two egg yolks. Leave to cool. ❧ Beat the remaining eggs in a bowl. ❧ Shape spoonfuls of the mixture into walnut-sized balls. Dip in the eggs, then roll in the bread crumbs. ❧ Heat the oil in a large skillet (frying pan) until very hot. Fry the croquettes in batches until golden brown all over. ❧ Drain on paper towels and serve hot.

Serves: 6

Preparation: 30'

Cooking: 20'

Level of difficulty: 1

- 2 cups/500 ml milk
- salt to taste
- dash of nutmeg
- 6 tbsp butter
- ²/₃ cup/100 g all-purpose/plain flour
- 4 oz/125 g ham, chopped
- 4 oz/125 g tasty cheese, grated (sharp Cheddar, Fontina)
- 4 eggs
- 1 cup/150 g fine bread crumbs
- 2 cups/500 ml oil, for frying

FRIED MORTADELLA

Serves: 6
Preparation: 10'
Cooking: 20'
Level of difficulty: 1

• 4 eggs, beaten
• 1¼ lb/600 g mortadella, sliced medium-thick and each slice cut in quarters
• 2½ cups/400 g dry bread crumbs
• 2 cups/500 ml oil, for frying
• 2 fresh lemons, to drizzle

lace the eggs in a medium bowl. ❧ Dip the mortadella in the eggs, then twice in the bread crumbs so that they are well coated. ❧ Heat the oil in a skillet (frying pan) until very hot. Fry the mortadella pieces in batches until golden brown. ❧ Drain on paper towels. Drizzle with the lemon juice and serve hot.

FILLED RICE FRITTERS

Cook the rice in lightly salted water until tender. Drain and cool. ❧ Boil the peas in salted water for 2 minutes. Drain and place in a small saucepan with 1 tablespoon of oil and the water. Cover tightly and cook for 4–5 minutes. ❧ Sauté the onion in the remaining oil. Add the veal and cook for 2 minutes over high heat, using a fork to break up any lumps. ❧ Season with salt and pepper. Add the tomatoes and cook for 20 minutes or until thick, then add the peas. ❧ Stir the saffron liquid into the eggs. Mix with the rice and grated cheese. ❧ Place a tablespoonful of the rice mixture in your palm and make a hollow with your thumb large enough to hold 1 tablespoon of the meat filling and a cube of cheese. Cover with another tablespoon of rice and shape into a ball. ❧ Dredge in the flour, dip in the egg, and roll in the bread crumbs. ❧ Deep-fry in very hot oil until golden brown. ❧ Drain and serve hot.

- 1¹/₂ cups/300 g short-grain rice
- ³/₄ cup/100 g fresh or frozen peas
- 3 tbsp extra-virgin olive oil
- 1 tbsp water
- 1 small onion, finely chopped
- 5 oz/150 g ground lean veal
- salt and freshly ground black pepper to taste
- ¹/₂ cup/125 g canned tomatoes
- ¹/₄ tsp saffron, dissolved in 1 tbsp warm water
- 2 eggs
- ¹/₂ cup/60 g freshly grated Pecorino Romano cheese
- 4 oz/125 g Mozzarella cheese, cubed
- 1 cup/150 g all-purpose/plain flour
- 2 eggs, beaten
- 2¹/₄ cups/400 g dry bread crumbs
- 2 cups/500 ml oil, for frying

MEDITERRANEAN FRITTERS

Serves: 4–6

Preparation: 15' + 2 h to chill

Cooking: 35'

Level of difficulty: 1

- 1¹/₂ lb/750 g potatoes
- 6 oz/180 g Feta cheese, crumbled
- 2 cloves garlic, finely chopped
- 4 tbsp finely chopped fresh dill
- 1 egg, lightly beaten
- 1 tbsp fresh lemon juice
- salt and freshly ground white pepper to taste
- 1 cup/150 g dry bread crumbs
- 2 cups/500 ml oil, for frying

Peel the potatoes and boil in a large pan of lightly salted water until tender. Drain well and mash. ❧ Add the cheese and continue mashing, then stir in the garlic, dill, egg, lemon juice, salt, and pepper. ❧ Cool to room temperature then refrigerate for 2 hours. ❧ Shape the mixture into fritters and roll in the bread crumbs. ❧ Heat the oil in a large skillet (frying pan) until very hot. Fry the fritters in batches of 5–6 until golden brown. ❧ Drain on paper towels and serve hot.

FRIED MOZZARELLA SANDWICHES

Serves: 4

Preparation: 15'

Cooking: 10'

Level of difficulty: 1

- **8 slices day-old sandwich bread, crusts removed**
- **8 oz/250 g Mozzarella cheese, sliced**
- **2 eggs**
- **2–3 tbsp milk**
- **salt and freshly ground black pepper to taste**
- **8–10 tbsp bread crumbs (optional)**
- **2 cups/500 ml oil, for frying**

Cover 4 slices of bread with the Mozzarella, making sure the cheese does not overlap the edges of the bread. Season with salt and pepper and cover with the remaining slices of bread. Transfer to a plate and cut the sandwiches diagonally. ❧ Beat the eggs and milk with salt and pepper. Pour over the sandwiches and leave to stand for 2 minutes. Turn the sandwiches over so that they absorb all the egg mixture. ❧ If liked, dredge in the bread crumbs. ❧ Make sure that the edges are well soaked with the egg mixture so that they will set on contact with the hot oil, sealing the Mozzarella inside. ❧ Heat 1 in (2.5 cm) oil in a medium skillet (frying pan) until very hot. Fry the sandwiches 3–4 at a time until golden brown on both sides. ❧ Drain on paper towels and serve hot.

SAVORY PASTRY FRITTERS

Dissolve the yeast in the water and set aside to rest for 15 minutes. ❧ Sift the flour and salt into a medium bowl. Make a well in the center and pour in the lard and yeast mixture. Stir with a fork, gradually working in the flour, adding a little more water if needed. ❧ Transfer the dough to a floured work surface and knead until smooth. Shape into a ball and leave to rise in the bowl, covered with a clean cloth, for about 1 hour. ❧ Roll out the dough into a sheet $1/8$ in (3 mm) thick. Cut into lozenges or rectangles about 2 in (5 cm) long. ❧ Heat the oil in a large skillet (frying pan) until very hot. Fry the fritters in batches until golden brown all over. ❧ Drain on paper towels and serve hot.

Serves: 8–10

Preparation: 40' + 1 h to rest

Cooking: 20'

Level of difficulty: 2

- $1^1/_2$ oz/45 g fresh yeast or 3 ($^1/_4$ oz) packages active dry yeast
- 1 cup/250 ml warm water
- $3^1/_3$ cups/500 g all-purpose/plain flour
- salt to taste
- 4 tbsp melted lard
- 2 cups/500 ml oil, for frying

ONION FRITTERS IN BALSAMIC VINEGAR

Serves: 4

Preparation: 15' + 30' to stand

Cooking: 25'

Level of difficulty: 1

- **4 large onions, thinly sliced**
- **4 tbsp extra-virgin olive oil**
- **4 eggs**
- **salt to taste**
- **$1/2$ cup/60 g freshly grated Parmesan cheese**
- **1 cup/150 g dry bread crumbs**
- **2 cups/500 ml oil, for frying**
- **balsamic vinegar to taste**

Sauté the onions in the olive oil until light golden brown. ❧ Beat the eggs and salt in a bowl, then stir in the Parmesan and bread crumbs. ❧ Add the onions and mix well. Set aside for at least 30 minutes. ❧ Heat the oil in a large skillet (frying pan) until very hot. Drop spoonfuls of the mixture into the oil and fry until golden brown all over. ❧ Drain the fritters on paper towels. ❧ Drizzle with balsamic vinegar to taste. Serve hot.

The superb flavor of the balsamic vinegar blends beautifully with the eggs and onions.

45

FRIED GREEN TOMATOES

Cut the tomatoes into ¹/₂-in (1-cm) thick slices. Discard the first and last slices with skin on one side. ❧ Place four bowls side by side and fill the first with the flour, the second with the eggs and beer, and the last two with the bread crumbs. ❧

This dish comes from Italy, where it is served often throughout the summer months.

Heat the oil in a large skillet (frying pan) until very hot. ❧ Dip the tomato slices into the flour; make sure they are well-coated and shake off any excess. Flour all the slices and set them on paper towels. Be sure not to lay the floured slices on top of each other. ❧ Immerse the slices in the egg, turn a couple of times, drain and pass to the first bowl of bread crumbs. Turn several times until well-coated. ❧ Repeat with the second bowl of bread crumbs. ❧ Place 4 or 5 slices in the hot oil and fry until golden brown. Turn carefully at least twice using tongs or two forks. ❧ Continue to fry until all the tomatoes are cooked. ❧ Drain on paper towels and sprinkle with salt. ❧ Serve hot.

Serves: 4–6

Preparation: 15'

Cooking: 40–50'

Level of difficulty: 2

- **6 large green tomatoes**
- **1 cup/150 g all-purpose/plain flour**
- **4 eggs, beaten to a foam**
- **4 tbsp beer**
- **2 cups/250 g dry bread crumbs**
- **2 cups/500 ml oil, for frying**
- **salt to taste**

BRUSCHETTA WITH TOMATO & BASIL

Toast the bread until golden brown over a barbecue or in the oven (so that it dries out and is very crisp). ❧ Rub the slices with the garlic. Sprinkle with salt and pepper, and drizzle with half the oil. ❧ Cut the tomatoes in half, sprinkle with salt, and set them upside down for 20 minutes to drain. ❧ Chop the tomatoes in small cubes. Arrange them on the toast and garnish with the basil. Drizzle with the remaining oil and serve.

Serves: 4

Preparation: 10'

Cooking: 5'

Level of difficulty: 1

- **4 large slices firm-textured bread**
- **2 cloves garlic**
- **salt and freshly ground black pepper to taste**
- **6 tbsp extra-virgin olive oil**
- **6 ripe tomatoes**
- **8–12 fresh basil leaves, torn**

BRESAOLA
WITH FRESH CHEESE

Serves: 4–6

Preparation: 10'

Level of difficulty: 1

- **5 oz/150 g fresh creamy cheese (Robiola, Caprino, Philadelphia Light)**
- **salt and freshly ground black pepper to taste**
- **2 bunches mixed salad greens, washed and dried**
- **4–6 tbsp extra-virgin olive oil**
- **12 large slices bresaola (or prosciutto)**

S eason the cheese with salt and pepper and stir well with a wooden spoon. ❧ Arrange the salad greens on individual plates and drizzle with the oil. ❧ Spread the cheese on the slices of bresaola or prosciutto. Roll up each slice, and arrange on top of the salad greens. ❧ Serve with thick slices of toast.

49

FLORENTINE LIVER TOASTS

Remove the bile and any connective tissue from the chicken livers. Chop coarsely. ❧ Sauté the onion in the oil in a heavy-bottomed medium saucepan over medium heat. Add the bay leaf and chicken livers. ❧ Brown the chicken livers for 5 minutes, then add the wine and Marsala. ❧ As soon as the liquid has evaporated, add the capers and anchovies. ❧ Season with salt and pepper and cook for 40 minutes. Add a little hot stock whenever the mixture starts to dry out. ❧ Remove from the heat, discard the bay leaf, and chop finely or process briefly in a food processor. ❧ Return the mixture to the pan over low heat and stir in the cream and half the butter. Stir constantly until it begins to bubble, then remove from the heat. ❧ Cut the bread in slices or triangles and spread lightly with the remaining butter. Place on a baking sheet and toast lightly in the oven. ❧ Spread with the liver mixture, arrange on a serving dish, and serve.

Serves: 4

Preparation: 15'

Cooking: 50'

Level of difficulty: 2

- **6 chicken livers**
- **1 small onion, finely chopped**
- **2 tbsp extra-virgin olive oil**
- **1 bay leaf**
- **4 tbsp dry white wine**
- **4 tbsp dry Marsala**
- **1 tbsp capers**
- **4 anchovy fillets**
- **salt and freshly ground black pepper to taste**
- **¹/₂ cup/125 ml chicken or beef stock (bouillon cube)**
- **1 cup/250 ml light/single cream**
- **6 tbsp butter**
- **1 long loaf firm-textured bread (French loaf is ideal)**

SAUSAGE TOASTS

Preheat the oven to 400°F/200°C/gas 6. ❧ Toast the bread in the oven. ❧ Place the sausage meat in a medium bowl. Add the cheese and pepper and mix well with a fork. ❧ Spread each toast with a generous helping of the sausage and cheese mixture and transfer to a large, shallow ovenproof dish. ❧ Bake for 5–10 minutes, or until the cheese has melted and the topping is bubbling. ❧ Serve piping hot straight from the oven.

Serves: 6
Preparation: 10'
Cooking: 5'
Level of difficulty: 1

- **1 long loaf firm-textured white bread (French loaf is ideal), sliced**
- **8 oz/250 g highly flavored fresh sausage meat (garlic, herb, or spicy)**
- **8 oz/250 g fresh semi-hard grating cheese, coarsely grated**
- **freshly ground black pepper to taste**

MOUSETRAPS

Serves: 3–6

Preparation: 10'

Cooking: 10–15'

Level of difficulty: 1

- **6 large slices firm-textured bread**
- **12 slices bacon**
- **2 tbsp butter**
- **6 large slices of sharp Cheddar cheese**
- **6 slices tomato**
- **salt and freshly ground black pepper to taste**

Toast the bread. ❧ Sauté the bacon in a small skillet (frying pan) for 5 minutes, or until half-cooked. ❧ Spread with the butter and place a slice of cheese on each one. Top with a slice of tomato and two slices of bacon. Season with salt and pepper. ❧ Place under a hot broiler (grill) and cook until the cheese has melted and the bacon is crisp. ❧ Serve hot.

SAUSAGE ROLLS

Preheat the oven to 400°F/200°C/gas 6. ❧ Shape the sausage meat into long sausages about 1 in (2.5 cm) in diameter. Cut them into pieces about 2 in (5 cm) long. ❧ Roll the pastry out until very thin and cut into rectangles just large enough to wrap the pieces of sausage. ❧ Wrap each piece of sausage in a piece of pastry and place on a baking sheet, with the join facing down. Brush each one with a little beaten egg and use a sharp knife to cut holes in the top. ❧ Bake for 25–30 minutes, or until golden brown. ❧ Serve hot or at room temperature.

These rolls make perfect party food. Prepare ahead of time and freeze until needed.

Serves: 10–12

Preparation: 20'

Cooking: 25–30'

Level of difficulty: 1

- 2 lb/1 kg sausage meat
- 1–2 rolls frozen flaky pastry, thawed
- 1 egg, lightly beaten

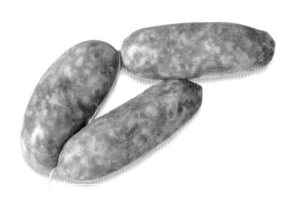

CREAM CHEESE WITH FRESH HERBS

Place the garlic, cheese, bay leaf, onion, basil, thyme, sage, and cream in a food processor and blend until smooth. ❧ Transfer the mixture to a bowl and refrigerate for at least two hours before serving. This will allow the herbs to suffuse the cheese with their subtle flavors. ❧ Spread the cream on toast or crackers to serve.

Serves: 6–8

Preparation: 10'

Chilling: 2 h

Level of difficulty: 1

- 2 cloves garlic
- 2 cups/500 g cream cheese
- 1 bay leaf
- 1 small onion, chopped
- 1 tsp each fresh basil, thyme, sage, chopped
- 2 tbsp heavy/ double cream

FRESH CHEESE & OLIVE TOASTS

Serves: 4–6

Preparation: 20'

Level of difficulty: 1

- **1 cup/250 g fresh cheese (Caprino, Philadelphia, Robiola, etc.)**
- **2 tbsp fresh chives, finely chopped**
- **¹/₂ cup/60 g pitted black olives**
- **2 anchovy fillets**
- **1 tbsp capers conserved in vinegar**
- **2 tbsp extra virgin olive oil**
- **8–10 slices whole wheat bread, crusts removed, cut into squares and toasted**

Mix the cheese with the chives in a medium bowl. ❧ In a blender or food processor, finely chop the olives, anchovies, capers, and oil. ❧ Spread the cheese mixture on the toast and top each with a teaspoonful of the olive mixture.

FRIED POLENTA
WITH MUSHROOMS

Serves: 6

Preparation: 20'

Cooking: 20'

Level of difficulty: 1

- ◆ 2 lb/1 kg fresh porcini or white mushrooms
- ◆ 2 cloves garlic, finely chopped
- ◆ 6 tbsp extra-virgin olive oil
- ◆ salt and freshly ground black pepper to taste
- ◆ 2 tbsp finely chopped calamint or thyme
- ◆ 2 cups/500 ml oil, for frying
- ◆ 6 large slices cold polenta

Rinse the mushrooms under cold running water. Pat dry with paper towels. ❧ Detach the stems from the caps. Chop the mushrooms coarsely, keeping the stems and caps separate. ❧ Sauté the garlic in the olive oil in a large skillet (frying pan) until pale golden brown. Stir in the mushroom stems and cook for 5 minutes. ❧ Add the mushroom caps and mix well. Season with salt and pepper. Stir in the calamint or thyme and cook for 4–5 minutes more. ❧ Heat the oil in a large skillet until very hot. Fry the polenta slices in two batches until golden brown on both sides. ❧ Spoon some of the mushroom sauce onto each slice and serve hot.

This recipe comes from Italy where porcini are common. Try it with other wild mushrooms.

BLUE CHEESE SNACKS

Prepare the pastry and refrigerate for 30 minutes. ❧ Preheat the oven to 350°F/180°C/gas 4. ❧ Melt the butter in a medium saucepan and stir in the flour followed by the milk. Bring to a boil and stir constantly until thick, about 2–3 minutes. ❧ Remove from heat and stir in the cheese. Season with salt and pepper. ❧ Heat the cream and oregano in another saucepan and bring to a boil. Cook over low heat for 4–5 minutes. Set aside to cool. ❧ Beat the cream and egg yolks into the cheese mixture. ❧ Roll out the pastry to 1¼ in (6 mm) thick and cut into disks about 3 in (8 cm) in diameter. Use the disks to line 12 fluted or plain patty or muffin pans. ❧ Spoon the filling into the pans. Roll out the remaining pastry and cut into disks about 1-in (2.5 cm) in diameter and place one on top of each filled pan. ❧ Bake for 25 minutes, or until golden brown.

Serves: 6

Preparation: 25' + 30' to chill

Cooking: 25'

Level of difficulty: 2

- 1 quantity **Plain Pastry (see page 370)**
- 2 tbsp butter
- 3 tbsp all-purpose/ plain flour
- ³/₄ **cup/180 ml milk**
- 4 oz/125 g blue cheese, crumbled
- ³/₄ **cup/180 ml heavy/double cream**
- 2 tsp dried oregano
- 3 large egg yolks
- salt and freshly ground black pepper to taste

MUSHROOM & TRUFFLE TOASTS

Serves: 6

Preparation: 30'

Cooking: 20'

Level of difficulty: 1

- 11 oz/300 g mushrooms (porcini or white mushrooms, or a mixture of the two)
- 4 tbsp butter
- 1 tbsp brandy
- 1 cup/250 ml light/ single cream
- 4 oz/125 g cheese (Stracchino, or grated Cheddar or Emmental)
- 1 small white truffle, fresh if possible, grated
- 12 slices French bread, toasted

Clean the mushrooms thoroughly and chop coarsely. ❧ Melt the butter in a skillet (frying pan) and add the mushrooms a few at a time (giving the moisture they produce a chance to evaporate). Cook, stirring at intervals, until tender. ❧ Sprinkle with the brandy and cook until it has evaporated. ❧ Heat the cream separately in a small saucepan. Add the cheese and let it melt over a low heat while stirring. ❧ When the cheese is completely blended with the cream, remove from the heat and stir in the mushrooms and truffle. ❧ Spread on the toast and serve hot.

If you can't find fresh truffles, use the truffle cream now available in economical tubes.

61

CHEESE FRITTERS

I n a large bowl, mix the two types of flour with the salt and enough water to make a dense batter. Set aside for at least 1 hour. ❧ Stir the cheese and grappa or brandy into the batter. ❧ Heat the pork fat in a large skillet (frying pan) until very hot. Place 2 teaspoons of the batter in the pan for each fritter. Turn to cook on both sides. Drain on paper towels. Repeat until the batter is all fried. ❧ Serve hot.

Serves: 4

Preparation: 10' + 1 h to rest

Cooking: 25'

Level of difficulty: 2

- ²/₃ cup/100 g all-purpose/plain flour
- ²/₃ cup/100 g rye flour
- 1 tsp salt
- about ¹/₂ cup/125 ml lukewarm water
- 8 oz/250 g cheese, thinly sliced (Cheddar, Fontina)
- 1 tbsp grappa or brandy
- 4 oz/125 g pork fat/lard for frying

STUFFED FRIED OLIVES

Serves: 6
Preparation: 30'
Cooking: 45'
Level of difficulty: 1

- 5 oz/150 g each ground beef and pork
- 2 tbsp extra-virgin olive oil
- 2 tbsp tomato paste
- 4 chicken livers, chopped
- 1 day-old bread roll
- 3 eggs
- 6 tbsp freshly grated Parmesan cheese
- salt and freshly ground black pepper to taste
- dash each of nutmeg and cinnamon
- 60 giant green olives, pitted
- 1 cup/150 g all-purpose/plain flour
- 1 cup/150 g bread crumbs
- 2 cups/500 ml oil, for frying

Sauté the beef and pork in a skillet (frying pan) with the olive oil for 5 minutes. Add the tomato paste and cook for 15 minutes. ♣ Add the chicken livers and cook for 5 minutes more. ♣ Soak the bread roll in cold water, squeeze out excess moisture, and crumble into a bowl. ♣ Add the meat mixture, 1 egg, the Parmesan, salt, pepper, nutmeg, and cinnamon. Mix well. ♣ Use the mixture to stuff the olives. ♣ Arrange three bowls, with the flour, remaining eggs (beaten), and bread crumbs. Dredge the olives in the flour, dip them in the egg, and roll in the bread crumbs. ♣ Heat the oil in a large skillet (frying pan) until very hot. Fry the olives in batches until golden brown. Drain on paper towels and serve hot.

HOT AND SPICY GREEN OLIVES

Rinse the olives in cold water and pat dry with paper towels. ❧ Lightly crush the olives with a meat-pounding mallet. ❧ Use the same instrument to bruise the cloves of garlic. Place the olives and garlic in a serving dish. ❧ Remove the rosemary leaves from the sprig and chop coarsely. Add to the olives, together with the mint, oregano, red pepper flakes, and oil. Mix well and cover. Set aside in a cool place (not the refrigerator) for at least 2 hours before serving. ❧ Serve with freshly baked bread.

Serves: 4–6

Preparation: 10'+ 2 h to rest

Level of difficulty: 1

- **11 oz/300 g green olives, pitted**
- **4 cloves garlic, peeled**
- **1 sprig fresh rosemary**
- **1 tbsp coarsely chopped mint**
- **1 tsp teaspoon oregano**
- **1 tsp red pepper flakes**
- **4 tbsp extra-virgin olive oil**

FALAFEL

Serves: 6–8

Preparation: 25' + time to soak and rest

Cooking: 25'

Level of difficulty: 2

- 1 lb/500 g **garbanzo beans/ chick peas**
- 1 medium **onion**
- 2–3 cloves **garlic, finely chopped**
- 1 medium **potato**
- 1 small bunch **parsley**
- 1 tsp **ground coriander**
- 1 tsp **cumin seeds**
- 1 tsp **dried oregano**
- 1 tsp **salt**
- 1 tsp **freshly ground white pepper**
- 3 tbsp **all-purpose/ plain flour**
- 2 tsp **baking powder**
- 2 cups/500 ml **oil, for frying**

Soak the garbanzo beans in a large bowl of water for 24 hours. ❧ Drain and rinse well. ❧ Place the garbanzo beans, onion, garlic, potato, and parsley in a food processor and chop coarsely. ❧ Add the coriander, oregano, cumin, salt, pepper, flour, and baking powder and process until well mixed. ❧ Set aside to rest for 2–3 hours. ❧ Heat the oil in a large skillet (frying pan) until very hot. ❧ Scoop out tablespoons of the mixture and shape into slightly flattened patties. ❧ Fry the patties in batches of 4–5 until golden brown. Drain on paper towels. ❧ Serve the falafel hot or warm as a starter or snack or use them to fill pita bread with salad greens and sliced tomatoes.

TZATZIKI

Place the cucumber, yogurt, olive oil, vinegar, lemon juice, salt, dill (or mint), and garlic in a deep bowl and stir well. ❧ Cover the bowl with plastic wrap and refrigerate for at least 1 hour before serving. This will allows the flavors to deepen and blend.

Serves: 4

Preparation: 10' + 1 h to chill

Level of difficulty: 1

- 1 cucumber, peeled and grated
- 1¹⁄₂ cups/375 g creamy full-fat yogurt
- 1 tbsp extra-virgin olive oil
- 1 tsp white vinegar
- 1 tbsp lemon juice
- salt to taste
- 2 tsp finely chopped dill or mint
- 2 cloves garlic, finely chopped

HOUMOUS

Serves: 6–8

Preparation: 30' +
time to soak

Cooking: 20–30'

Level of difficulty: 1

• 1 lb/500 g
garbanzo beans/
chick peas
• 4 tbsp tahina
(sesame seed
paste)
• 2 tbsp fresh lemon
juice
• 2 cloves garlic,
finely chopped
• salt and freshly
ground black
pepper to taste
• ³/₄ cup/180 ml
water

oak the garbanzo beans in a large bowl of
water overnight. ✿ Rinse well and cook over
low heat for about 50 minutes, or until tender.
✿ Place the garbanzo beans, tahina, lemon juice,
garlic, salt, and pepper in a blender or food
processor and chop finely. ✿ Add enough of the
water to obtain a smooth and creamy dip. ✿
Garnish with parsley, extra garbanzo beans, and a
drizzling of extra-virgin olive oil.

EGGPLANT DIP

Preheat the oven to 400°F/200°C/gas 6. ❧ Pierce the eggplants 5–6 times each with the tines of a fork. Bake for 1 hour. Set aside to cool. ❧ Cut the eggplants in half and use a spoon to scoop out the flesh. Place in a large bowl with the garlic and mash using a fork or potato masher. ❧ Combine the tahina with the lemon juice in a small bowl. Stir in the water and salt. ❧ Stir this mixture into the eggplant. ❧ Refrigerate for 1 hour before serving. ❧ Sprinkle with the parsley and chile pepper, if using, and drizzle with the oil just before serving.

Serves: 6

Preparation: 20' + 1 h to chill

Cooking: 1 h

Level of difficulty: 1

- **2 large eggplants/ aubergines**
- **3 cloves garlic, finely chopped**
- **1 cup/250 ml tahina (sesame seed paste)**
- **freshly squeezed juice of 2 lemons**
- **4 tbsp water**
- **1 tsp salt**
- **2 tbsp finely chopped parsley**
- **1 fresh red chile pepper, finely chopped (optional)**
- **2 tbsp extra-virgin olive oil**

GUACAMOLE

Cut the avocados in half lengthwise. Remove the stones. Use a spoon to hollow out the green, fleshy part. Put the flesh into a bowl and mash with a fork. ⚜ Stir in the lemon juice and salt. ⚜ Add the onion, garlic, and chilies to the avocado and stir well. ⚜ Chop the tomato and add to the avocado. Stir well. ⚜ Serve the guacamole with corn chips as a dip.

This Mexican dish makes a wonderful starter. It can also be served at a cocktail party or buffet.

Serves: 4

Preparation: 15'

Level of difficulty: 1

• **2 avocados**
• **2 tsp lemon or lime juice**
• **salt to taste**
• **2 cloves garlic, finely chopped**
• **1 green onion, finely chopped**
• **2 tbsp finely chopped green chile pepper**
• **1 small tomato**

SALSA PICO DE GALLO

Serves: 4

Preparation: 15' +
12 h to chill

Level of difficulty: 1

- **1 large onion**
- **2 large tomatoes**
- **2 tbsp finely chopped cilantro/ coriander**
- **1–2 fresh green chile peppers, finely chopped**
- **juice of 3 limes**
- **salt to taste**

Chop the onion and tomatoes. Place them in a medium serving bowl with the cilantro. Stir in the chile peppers, lime juice, and salt, mixing well. Refrigerate for 12 hours before serving. Serve with corn chips or as a sauce with meat or fish.

LEBANESE PIZZAS

Prepare the dough. Shape into a ball and place in a bowl. Cover and let rise for 1 hour. ❧ Sauté the onions in the oil in a large skillet (frying pan). Add the meat and sauté until brown. Add the pine nuts, salt, pepper, all-spice, red pepper flakes, and cinnamon. Cook over low heat for 30 minutes. ❧ Remove from heat and stir in the yogurt. ❧ Preheat the oven to 350°F/180°C/gas 4. ❧ Grease 2 baking sheets. ❧ Divide the dough into pieces about the size of an egg. Roll into smooth balls. Cover and let rest for 15 minutes. ❧ Place the balls on the baking sheet and flatten to about ¼ in (5 mm) thick. Spread each one with topping. ❧ Bake for 30 minutes, or until light golden brown.

Serves: 8–10

Preparation: 30' + time for dough

Cooking: 30'

Level of difficulty: 2

- **2 quantities Pizza Dough (see page 324)**

TOPPING

- **4 tbsp extra-virgin olive oil**
- **2 onions, finely chopped**
- **2 lb/1 kg coarsely chopped beef**
- **4 tbsp pine nuts**
- **1 tsp salt**
- **1 tsp freshly ground black pepper**
- **1 tsp allspice**
- **½ tsp red pepper flakes**
- **1 tsp ground cinnamon**
- **1 cup/250 ml plain yogurt**

SPINACH PIES

Serves: 6–8

Preparation: 40' +
time for dough

Cooking: 25'

Level of difficulty: 2

- **2 quantities Pizza Dough (see page 324)**

FILLING

- **2 small onions, finely chopped**
- **1 tsp salt**
- **1 lb/500 g fresh spinach, washed and finely chopped**
- **freshly ground black pepper to taste**
- **2–3 tbsp fresh lemon juice**
- **6 tbsp extra-virgin olive oil**

Prepare the dough. Shape into a ball and place in a bowl. Cover and let rise for 1 hour. ❧ Preheat the oven to 350°F/180°C/gas 4. ❧ Grease two baking sheets. ❧ Sprinkle the onions with the salt. ❧ Mix the spinach with the onions. Work the mixture in your hands until wilted and watery. Squeeze out excess moisture and place in a large bowl. ❧ Stir in the pepper, lemon juice, and oil. ❧ Divide the dough into pieces the size of walnuts. Roll into balls and set aside for 15 minutes. ❧ Roll each piece of dough into a flat disk. Spoon a heaped teaspoon of filling onto the center. Fold the bottom left and right pieces into the middle and seal by pinching, then bring down the top piece to form a triangle and seal. ❧ Brush the tops of the pies with oil. Bake for 25–30 minutes, or until golden brown.

VEGETABLE SAMOSAS

P lace the potatoes, peas, corn, cumin, onion, chile, cilantro, and mint in a large bowl and mix well. Season with salt and lemon juice. ❧ Place a piece of pastry on a work surface. Spoon 1 tablespoon of the filling onto the center of each piece. Fold up the pastry to form a triangle. ❧ Heat the oil into a large skillet (frying pan) to very hot. Fry the samosas in batches until golden brown all over. Drain on paper towels. ❧ Serve hot with a fresh cilantro relish or a chile sauce.

Serves: 4–6

Preparation: 15'

Cooking: 5'

Level of difficulty: 2

- 3 potatoes, boiled and mashed
- 3 oz/90 g frozen peas, cooked and drained
- 2 oz/60 g canned corn, drained
- 1 tsp cumin seeds, crushed
- 1 small red onion, finely chopped
- 2 green chile peppers, finely chopped
- 2 tbsp fresh cilantro/coriander, coarsely chopped
- 2 tbsp fresh mint, coarsely chopped
- salt to taste
- juice of 1 lemon
- 1 package spring roll pastry
- 2 cups/500 ml oil, for frying

Serves: 4

Preparation: 10'

Cooking: 15'

Level of difficulty: 1

- 6 tbsp butter
- 1 medium onion, finely chopped
- 1 clove garlic, finely chopped
- 1 cup/250 g chicken livers, chopped
- $1/2$ tsp powdered mustard
- 1 tbsp brandy or sherry
- salt and freshly ground black pepper to taste
- 1–2 tbsp cracked black peppercorns

CRACKED PEPPER PÂTÉ

M elt the butter in a small saucepan and sauté the onion and the garlic until translucent. ❧ Add the chicken livers and sauté for 5 more minutes, or until cooked through. ❧ Remove from heat and allow to cool slightly before adding the mustard and brandy or sherry. ❧ Place in a blender or food processor and process until smooth. ❧ Season with salt and pepper. ❧ Put into a dish and cover with cracked peppercorns. ❧ Refrigerate until ready to serve.

This pâté is surprisingly simple to make. Serve with hot toast or crackers.

EGG, VEGETABLE, & BACON PÂTÉ

Melt the butter in a heavy-bottomed saucepan over low heat. Stir in the flour and cook for 2 minutes. ❧ Remove from heat and stir in the milk. Return to heat and cook, stirring continuously, until thick. ❧ Clean the

This recipe is from Provence, in southern France. Serve with bread, salad, and a glass of dry white wine.

mushrooms, rinse well, and slice thinly. ❧ Sauté the bacon in a small skillet (frying pan) for 5 minutes. Pour off the fat and set the pieces aside. ❧ Sauté the shallots in the oil for 5 minutes. Pour in the wine and cook until reduced by about half. ❧ Add the mushrooms, tomatoes, and tomato paste and cook for 10–15 minutes, or until reduced. ❧ Season with salt and pepper and add the olives. ❧ Remove from heat and stir into the roux sauce. Set aside to cool. ❧ Preheat the oven to 400°F/200°C/gas 6. ❧ Beat the eggs until frothy and stir them into the cooled mixture. ❧ Stir in the cheese and tarragon and mix well. ❧ Lightly butter two 4 x 12 in (28 x 10 cm) pâté molds. Divide the mixture evenly between them and bake for about 1 hour, or until the mixture is firm to the touch.

Serves: 8–10
Preparation: 45'
Cooking: 1 h
Level of difficulty: 2

- 6 tbsp butter
- ²/₃ cup/100 g all-purpose/plain flour
- 1 cup/250 ml milk
- 5 oz/150 g white mushrooms
- 5 oz/150 g bacon, diced
- 8 shallots, chopped
- 3 tbsp extra-virgin olive oil
- ²/₃ cup/180 ml dry white wine
- 2 lb/1 kg tomatoes, chopped
- 1 tbsp tomato paste
- salt and freshly ground black pepper to taste
- 20 black olives, pitted and coarsely chopped
- 8 eggs
- 5 oz/150 g Edam cheese, grated
- 20 leaves fresh tarragon

78

LIVER PÂTÉ

Remove the bile and any connective tissue from the chicken livers and chop coarsely. ❧ Sauté the chicken and calf's liver together in the butter with the garlic and parsley for a few minutes. Season with salt and pepper. ❧ When the liver starts to dry out, add the Marsala and continue cooking for 5–10 minutes, or until the liver is cooked. ❧ Remove the liver and add the bread crumbs to the juices in the pan. Mix well and remove from heat. ❧ Chop the liver and bread crumbs finely in a food processor. ❧ Place the eggs, yolks, liver, bread crumbs, and Parmesan in a bowl and mix until fairly stiff. If it is too dry or firm, soften with a tablespoon or two of stock made with boiling water and a bouillon cube. ❧ Butter a 4 x 12 in (10 x 28 cm) pâté mold and line with waxed paper. ❧ Spoon the mixture into the mold. ❧ Place the mold in a large pan of boiling water and leave for at least 30 minutes, so that the pâté will finish cooking bain-marie. ❧ Garnish with sprigs of parsley and serve warm or at room temperature with toasted bread and plenty of butter.

Serves: 6

Preparation: 25'

Cooking: 40'

Level of difficulty: 2

- **5 chicken livers**
- **1 lb/500 g calf's liver, coarsely chopped**
- **4 tbsp butter**
- **1 clove garlic, finely chopped**
- **2 tbsp finely chopped parsley + sprigs to garnish**
- **salt and freshly ground black pepper to taste**
- **1 cup/250 ml Marsala**
- **1/2 cup/75 g bread crumbs**
- **2 eggs + 2 yolks**
- **1 cup/125 g freshly grated Parmesan cheese**

CORN & PEANUT FRITTERS

Place the corn, peanuts, scallions, ginger, garlic, and cumin in a blender or food processor. Process until very finely chopped. Transfer to a large bowl. ❧ Stir in the egg and flour and mix well. ❧ Heat the oil in a large skillet (frying pan) until very hot. Drop in tablespoons of the mixture and fry in batches until golden brown all over. ❧ Drain on paper towels. Serve hot.

Serves: 4

Preparation: 10'

Cooking: 15'

Level of difficulty: 1

- **4 oz/125 g canned corn, drained**
- **5 oz/150 g peanuts**
- **3 scallions/spring onions, coarsely chopped**
- **2 tsp finely grated ginger root**
- **1 clove garlic, finely chopped**
- **1 tsp cumin seeds**
- **1 egg, lightly beaten**
- **2 tbsp all-purpose/ plain flour**
- **1 cup/250 ml peanut oil, for frying**

FILLED ZUCCHINI

Serves: 4

Preparation: 40'

Cooking: 10'

Level of difficulty: 2

- ♦ 1¹/₄ lb/600 g squash or pumpkin
- ♦ 6 large zucchini/ courgettes
- ♦ 8 tbsp freshly grated Parmesan cheese
- ♦ 8 amaretti biscuits, crumbled
- ♦ salt and freshly ground black pepper to taste

Peel the squash rind and cut the flesh into small pieces. Cook in a large pan of boiling water for 20 minutes. Drain well. ❧ Preheat the oven to 190°F/375°C/gas 5. ❧ Cut the zucchini in half. Hollow out the center, leaving a thickness of ¹/₄ in (5 mm). Place in a separate large pan of boiling water and cook for 5 minutes. Drain well and pat dry with kitchen towels. ❧ Process the squash and zucchini flesh in a blender or food processor until smooth. Season with the salt and pepper. ❧ Stir half the Parmesan and amaretti into the squash. ❧ Spoon the mixture into the zucchini. Butter a baking pan and place the zucchini in it. Dot with the butter. Sprinkle with the remaining Parmesan and amaretti. ❧ Bake for 10 minutes, or until golden brown.

POLENTA CRÊPES WITH SPICY SPINACH

Place the polenta in a mixing bowl with $1/4$ teaspoon of salt. Make a well in the center and pour in the eggs followed by enough of the water to obtain a smooth, fairly thin batter. ❧ Heat $1/2$ tablespoon of oil in a crêpe pan and add about 3 tablespoons of the batter. Spread evenly over the bottom of the pan and cook until lightly browned on both sides. Repeat until all the batter is used. Stack the crêpes up as they are ready and set aside in a warm place. ❧ Preheat the oven to 350°F/180°C/gas 4. ❧ Cut the chilies in quarters and place in a food processor with the chile oil and water. Blend until peppers are finely chopped. ❧ Add the spinach and process again until the mixture is well blended. ❧ Transfer this mixture into a bowl and add the Ricotta, half the Cheddar, eggs, salt, pepper, and red pepper flakes. Mix well. ❧ Spread about 3 tablespoons of the spinach and cheese filling along the center of each crêpe. Roll the crêpes up and place them in a lightly buttered 9 x 13 in (23 x 33 cm) baking dish. ❧ Sprinkle with the remaining cheese and a drizzle of spicy sauce. Bake for 25 minutes, or until the cheese is golden brown. ❧ Serve hot straight from the oven.

Serves: 4–6
Preparation: 15'
Cooking: 35'
Level of difficulty: 2

- 4 oz/125 g polenta
- $1/2$ tsp salt
- 4 eggs, beaten
- 1 cup/250 ml water
- 8 tbsp extra-virgin olive oil
- 2 fresh green or red chilies, seeded
- 2 tsp chile oil
- 1 tsp water
- 12 oz/350 g fresh spinach
- 8 oz/250 g Ricotta cheese
- 8 oz/250 g Cheddar (or Emmental) cheese, grated
- 2 eggs
- 1–2 tsp red pepper flakes
- freshly ground black pepper to taste
- Tabasco or other spicy sauce

GARLIC MUSHROOMS

Heat the butter and oil in a large skillet (frying pan) over medium heat. Add the mushrooms and cook, stirring frequently, for 15 minutes. ❧ Add the garlic. Continue cooking for 5 minutes more. Stir in the parsley and season with the salt and pepper. ❧ Serve hot.

Serves: 4
Preparation: 5'
Cooking: 20'
Level of difficulty: 1

- 4 tbsp butter
- 4 tbsp extra-virgin olive oil
- 1 1/2 lb/750 g mixed mushrooms
- 2–3 cloves garlic, finely chopped
- 1 tbsp finely chopped parsley
- salt and freshly ground black pepper to taste

MUSHROOM CRISPS

Serves: 4

Preparation: 25'

Cooking: 20'

Level of difficulty: 2

- **300 g mixed wild mushrooms**
- **3 shallots**
- **1 tbsp finely chopped parsley**
- **1 tbsp finely chopped cilantro/ coriander**
- **salt and freshly ground black pepper to taste**
- **2 tbsp extra-virgin olive oil**
- **4 large crêpes (see page 773)**
- **1 apple**

Preheat the oven to 400°F/200°C/gas 6. ❧ Sauté the mushrooms, shallots, parsley, cilantro, and salt in the oil in a large skillet (frying pan) over medium heat until the mushrooms are tender. Remove from heat and set aside. ❧ Lightly oil a metal pudding mold. Fit a crêpe into the mold and bake in the oven until crisp. Slip out of the mold and repeat with the other crêpes. ❧ Carefully fill the crispy crêpes with the mushroom mixture. Garnish with slices of raw apple. Sprinkle with salt and pepper and drizzle with a little extra oil, if liked. ❧ Serve warm.

SEAFOOD SALAD

Serves: 8

*Preparation: 1 h + 1 h
to soak + 30' to chill*

Cooking: 1 h

Level of difficulty: 2

- 1 lb/500 g octopus
- 14 oz/450 g squid
- 2 tbsp salt
- 14 oz/450 g
  shrimp
- 14 oz/450 g clams
- 14 oz/450 g
  mussels
- 8 tbsp extra-virgin
  olive oil
- 2 tbsp finely
  chopped parsley
- 2–4 cloves garlic,
  finely chopped
- 1 tsp red pepper
  flakes (optional)
- 2 tbsp fresh lemon
  juice
- salt and freshly
  ground black
  pepper to taste

Clean the octopus and separate the tentacles and head from the body by grasping the head and pulling it apart from the body. Remove the ink sac from the head. Remove the bony part and clean out the insides. ❧ To clean the squid, cut each one lengthwise and remove the plastic-like internal bone and the stomach. Discard the internal ink sac. ❧ Place the squid and octopus in a pot with 3 quarts (3 liters) of cold water and 1 tablespoon of salt and bring to a boil over high heat. Cook for 45–50 minutes, or until tender. ❧ Leave to cool in the water. ❧ Drain and chop the tentacles and octopus in small pieces and slice the bodies of the squid in rings. Transfer to a salad bowl. ❧ Bring 1 1/2 quarts (1 1/2 liters) of water and 1 tablespoon of salt to a boil. Rinse the shrimp thoroughly and add to the pot. Cook for 2 minutes. Drain and set aside to cool. ❧ Peel the shrimp and add to the salad bowl. ❧ Soak the clams and mussels in a large bowl of water for 1 hour. Pull the beards off the mussels. Scrub well and rinse in abundant cold water. ❧ Place the shellfish in a large skillet (frying pan) with 2 tablespoons of oil and cook over medium heat until they are all open. Discard any that have not opened. ❧ Discard the shells and add the mussels and clams to the salad bowl. ❧ Mix the parsley, garlic, chilies, lemon juice, remaining oil, salt, and pepper in a bowl. Pour over the salad and toss well. ❧ Refrigerate for 30 minutes before serving.

SEAFOOD MORSELS

P lace the slices of bread in a blender or food processor with the chile pepper, basil, cheese, oil, and salt and chop finely. ❧ Stuff the anchovies with the filling, then roll them up. Dredge in the flour, dip in the egg white, and roll gently in the bread crumbs. ❧ Place the mussels in a large skillet (frying pan) over medium heat until they are all open. Discard any that do not open. ❧ Process the pine nuts, capers, and rosemary in the blender until finely chopped. Make a tiny slit in the mussels with a sharp knife and stuff with the mixture. Dredge in the flour, dip in the egg white, and roll gently in the bread crumbs. ❧ Rinse the scallops in cold running water and pat dry with paper towels. Wrap each mollusk in a sage leaf and a piece of bacon. Thread the mollusks in twos onto cocktail sticks. Dredge them in the flour. ❧ Heat the oil in a large skillet until very hot. Fry the seafood morsels in batches until golden brown all over. Drain on paper towels. ❧ Serve hot.

Serves: 6

Preparation: 1 h

Cooking: 30–40'

Level of difficulty: 3

- 2 slices white bread, crusts removed
- 2 cups/350 g dry bread crumbs
- 1 red chile pepper
- 1 bunch basil
- 3 oz/90 g smoked Cheddar cheese
- 1 tbsp extra-virgin olive oil
- 1/4 tsp salt
- 12 anchovies, gutted
- 1 cup/150 g all-purpose/plain flour
- 2 egg whites, beaten
- 18 large mussels
- 4 tbsp pine nuts
- 1 tsp capers in salt, washed
- sprig of rosemary
- 12 scallops
- 12 leaves fresh sage
- 6 small slices bacon, cut in half
- 2 cups/500 ml oil, for frying

SQUID, BACON, & BELL PEPPER SKEWERS

Cut the squid in rings. Cut the bacon and bell peppers into bite-size pieces. ✼ Assemble the skewers by alternately threading the squid, bacon, and bell peppers onto wooden skewers. ✼ Place the basil in a bowl with the salt, pepper, oregano, and lemon zest. Add the oil and lemon juice and mix well. ✼ Place the skewers under a preheated broiler (grill) or in the oven at 350°F/180°C/gas 4. Turn frequently and baste with a little of the sauce. ✼ Serve drizzled with the remaining sauce on a bed of salad greens.

Serves: 6

Preparation: 25'

Cooking: 15–20'

Level of difficulty: 2

- 1¹/₂ lb/750 g squid, cleaned (see page 89 for how to clean squid)
- 14 oz/400 g bacon, in thick slices
- 14 oz/400 g red bell peppers
- 20 leaves basil, torn in half
- salt and freshly ground white pepper to taste
- ¹/₂ tsp dried oregano
- grated zest and juice of 2 lemons
- 6 tbsp extra-virgin olive oil

SALAMI & CHEESE
SKEWERS

Serves: 6

Preparation: 20'

Cooking: 15–20'

Level of difficulty: 1

- 24 thick slices salamis, cut in quarters
- 8 oz/250 g Pecorino cheese, cubed
- 6 pickled gherkins, thinly sliced
- 24 small pickled onions
- 4 slices firm-textured bread, diced
- 2 eggs, beaten

P reheat the oven to 350°F/180°C/gas 4. ❧ Thread pieces of salami, cheese, gherkin, pickled onions, and bread onto 12 wooden skewers. ❧ Dip the skewers in the egg and arrange them in a single layer in a large ovenproof dish. Bake for 15–20 minutes, or until the bread is nicely toasted. ❧ Serve hot.

CHICKEN SATAY

Serves: 8

Preparation: 15'

Cooking: 10'

Level of difficulty: 1

- **4 whole chicken breasts**

SAUCE
- **4 oz/125 g unsalted peanuts**
- **3 scallions/spring onions, coarsely chopped**
- **2 cloves garlic**
- **1 tsp curry powder**
- **1 tsp ground cumin**
- **$^1/_2$ tsp ground coriander**
- **1 tbsp honey**
- **2 tsp soy sauce**
- **1 cup/250 ml water**

MARINADE
- **2 tbsp soy sauce**
- **2 tsp lime juice**
- **2 tsp sesame oil**

Cut the chicken into small cubes. Thread it onto 32 skewers. ❧ Sauce: Place the peanuts, scallions, garlic, curry powder, cumin, coriander, honey, soy sauce, and water in a blender or food processor and chop until smooth. ❧ Transfer to a small saucepan over medium heat. Cook, stirring constantly, for about 3 minutes, or until the mixture thickens. ❧ Marinade: Place the soy sauce, lime juice, and sesame oil in a small bowl and mix well. Brush over the chicken. ❧ Place the chicken skewers under a preheated broiler (grill) and broil for 3–5 minutes on each side, or until well cooked. Brush with the soy sauce mixture while cooking. ❧ Serve hot with the peanut sauce on the side.

SOUPS

VEGETABLE SOUP

Serves: 4

Preparation: 30'

Cooking: 2 h

Level of difficulty: 1

Place the garlic, onion, celery, parsley, sage, rosemary, potato, carrots, zucchini, tomatoes, and kidney beans in a large pot. Add the water, cover, and simmer over low heat for 1¼ hours. ❧ Add the cabbage and peas and cook for 25 more minutes. ❧ Season with salt and pepper. Add the rice and cook for 20 minutes. ❧ Serve hot.

- 3 cloves garlic, finely chopped
- 1 large onion, coarsely chopped
- 4 stalks celery, sliced
- 4 tbsp finely chopped parsley
- 4 sage leaves, torn
- 1 tbsp finely chopped fresh rosemary leaves
- 1 potato, 2 carrots, 2 zucchini/courgettes, 2 tomatoes, all diced
- 1 cup/180 g fresh (or dried and soaked) white beans
- 2 quarts/2 liters boiling water
- ½ Savoy cabbage, coarsely chopped
- ½ cup/90 g fresh or frozen peas
- salt and freshly ground black pepper to taste
- ¾ cup/185 g short-grain rice

Serves: 4

Preparation: 20'

Cooking: 35'

Level of difficulty: 1

- ¹/₂ **cup/75 g diced bacon**
- **1 onion, finely chopped**
- **2 cloves garlic, finely chopped**
- **1 tbsp finely chopped parsley**
- **1 tbsp finely chopped marjoram**
- **6 fresh basil leaves, torn**
- **2 tomatoes, peeled and chopped**
- **4 tbsp extra-virgin olive oil**
- **2 quarts/2 liters cold water**
- **2 cups/450 g pearl barley**
- **salt and freshly ground black pepper to taste**
- **6 tbsp freshly grated Parmesan cheese**

PEARL BARLEY SOUP

S auté the bacon, onion, garlic, parsley, marjoram, and basil in 1 tablespoon of the oil in a large saucepan for 4–5 minutes. ❧ Add the tomatoes, then pour in the water and bring to a boil. ❧ Add the pearl barley and season with salt and pepper. Cook, stirring frequently, for about 30 minutes, or until the pearl barley is tender. ❧ Sprinkle with the Parmesan and drizzle with the remaining oil. ❧ Serve hot.

MINESTRONE WITH RICE

Serves: 4–6

Preparation: 30'

Cooking: 2 h

Level of difficulty: 1

Place the bacon, garlic, onion, celery, parsley, sage, rosemary, potatoes, carrots, zucchini, tomatoes, and beans in a large saucepan. Add the water, cover and simmer over low heat for at least 1 1/4 hours. 🌢 Add the cabbage and peas and cook for 25 more minutes. 🌢 Season with salt and pepper and add the rice. Cook for 20 minutes, or until the rice is tender. 🌢 Serve with the Parmesan passed separately.

- 1 cup/250 g diced bacon
- 2 cloves garlic, finely chopped
- 1 large onion, coarsely chopped
- 2 stalks celery, sliced
- 1 tbsp coarsely chopped parsley
- 1 tbsp finely chopped fresh rosemary leaves
- 2 potatoes, diced
- 2 carrots, diced
- 2 zucchini/ courgettes, diced
- 2 tomatoes, diced
- 1 cup/180 g fresh (or dried and soaked) red kidney beans
- 2 quarts/2 liters boiling water
- 1/2 small Savoy cabbage, coarsely chopped
- 1 cup/225 g short-grain rice
- salt and freshly ground black pepper to taste
- 8 tbsp freshly grated Parmesan cheese

FLORENTINE SOUP

Serves: 4

Preparation: 20' + time to soak

Cooking: 1¼ h

Level of difficulty: 2

S oak the garbanzo beans overnight. ❧ Drain and rinse well. ❧ Place in a saucepan, cover with cold water, add 2 garlic cloves and a sprig of rosemary. Simmer for about 1 hour, or until the garbanzo beans are tender. Season with salt after about 50 minutes. ❧ Drain, reserving the cooking water. ❧ Chop three-quarters of the beans in a food processor, keeping the remainder whole. ❧ Heat half the oil in a large saucepan and sauté the remaining garlic and rosemary for 3 minutes. ❧ Add the tomato paste and cook over medium heat for 2 minutes. ❧ Add the chopped and whole garbanzo beans and the reserved cooking liquid and bring to a boil. If the soup is very thick, dilute with a little stock. ❧ Add the tagliatelle and cook for 8–10 minutes, or until the pasta is cooked. Season with salt and pepper. ❧ Serve hot.

- 2 cups/450 g dried garbanzo beans/ chick peas
- 4 cloves garlic, bruised
- 2 sprigs rosemary
- salt and freshly ground black pepper to taste
- 6 tbsp extra-virgin olive oil
- 2 tbsp tomato paste
- 1–2 cups/250–500 ml *Beef Stock* (see page 140)
- 7 oz/200 g tagliatelle, broken into short lengths

Serves: 4

Preparation: 10'

Cooking: 20'

Level of difficulty: 1

- 4 tbsp extra-virgin olive oil
- 2 scallions/spring onions, finely chopped
- 8 zucchini/ courgettes, diced
- salt and freshly ground black pepper to taste
- 6 cups/1.5 liters *Beef Stock* (see page 140)
- 2 eggs, lightly beaten
- 1 tbsp finely chopped parsley
- 1 tbsp finely chopped basil
- 8 tbsp freshly grated Parmesan cheese

CHUNKY ZUCCHINI SOUP

eat the oil in a heavy-bottomed saucepan and sauté the scallions for 2–3 minutes. Add the zucchini and sauté for 5 more minutes. Season with salt and pepper. ❧ Add the stock and cook over medium-low heat for 10 minutes, or until the zucchini are tender. ❧ Add the eggs, parsley, and basil and stir rapidly. Sprinkle with the Parmesan. Serve hot with croutons, if liked.

HERB & RICE BOUILLON

B ring the stock to a boil and add the rice. ❧
Simmer for about 15 minutes, or until the
rice is tender. ❧ Just before removing from
the heat, add the parsley, butter, and sage. ❧
Season with salt. ❧ Serve hot with the Parmesan
passed separately.

Serves: 4

Preparation: 5'

Cooking: 20'

Level of difficulty: 1

- **5 cups/1.25 liters
  Beef Stock (see
  page 140)**
- **1 cup/225 g short-
  grain rice**
- **4 tbsp finely
  chopped parsley**
- **1–2 fresh sage
  leaves, finely
  chopped**
- **salt to taste**
- **1 tbsp butter**
- **8 tbsp freshly
  grated Parmesan
  cheese**

HOMEMADE TORTELLINI

Serves: 4

Preparation: 1 h + 3 h to rest

Cooking: 2–3'

Level of difficulty: 3

Prepare the pasta dough. Shape the dough into a ball and set aside to rest for 1 hour, wrapped in plastic wrap. ❧ Melt the butter in a skillet and sauté the pork. When browned, chop finely in a food processor together with the Mortadella and Parma ham. ❧ Transfer the meat mixture to a bowl and stir in the egg, Parmesan, nutmeg, salt, and pepper. (The filling can be prepared a day in advance). ❧ Prepare the tortellini as explained on page 145. Spread the freshly made pasta out on a clean cloth to dry for about 2 hours. ❧ Add the tortellini to the stock and simmer gently for 2–3 minutes. ❧ Serve in individual soup bowls.

- 1 quantity *Pasta Dough* (see recipe, page 144)
- 2 tbsp butter
- 4 oz/125 g lean pork, coarsely chopped
- 4 oz/125 g Mortadella
- 3 oz/90 g Parma ham
- 1 egg
- 1³/₄ cups/225 g freshly grated Parmesan cheese
- pinch of nutmeg
- salt and freshly ground black pepper to taste
- 7 cups/1.75 liters boiling *Beef Stock* (see page 140)

Serves: 4
Preparation: 10'
Cooking: 20–25'
Level of difficulty: 1

- 2 lb/1 kg asparagus
- 4 tbsp butter
- 1 cup/150 g all-purpose/plain flour
- 2 cups/500 ml milk
- 3 cups/750 ml *Beef Stock* (see page 140)
- salt and freshly ground white pepper to taste
- 3 egg yolks
- 8 tbsp freshly grated Parmesan cheese
- $^1/_2$ cup/125 ml light/single cream

ASPARAGUS CREAM

Trim the tough bottom parts off the asparagus stalks. ❧ Melt half the butter in a medium pan over medium heat and add the flour, stirring all the time. ❧ Pour in the milk, then the stock. ❧ Bring to a boil and add the asparagus. Season with salt and pepper. ❧ Cook for 15 minutes. ❧ Chop in a food processor until smooth, then return to heat. ❧ Mix the egg yolks, remaining butter, Parmesan, and cream together in a medium bowl. ❧ Pour the mixture into the asparagus and stir until thick and creamy. ❧ Serve hot.

CREAMY PEA SOUP

Serves: 4

Preparation: 10'

Cooking: 25'

Level of difficulty: 1

- **3 tbsp butter**
- **1 small onion, finely chopped**
- **3 cups/450 g shelled fresh peas**
- **4 cups/1 liter Beef Stock (see page 140)**
- **salt to taste**
- **½ quantity Béchamel Sauce (see page 950)**

Melt the butter in a medium saucepan over low heat. Add the onion and sauté until it is soft and translucent. ❧ Stir in the peas and cook for 2–3 minutes. ❧ Add 3 cups (750 ml) of the stock and cook for about 20 minutes, or until the peas are tender. ❧ In the meantime, make the Béchamel Sauce and set aside. ❧ When the peas are cooked, chop in a blender or food processor until smooth. ❧ Return the peas to the saucepan and stir in the Béchamel. If the soup seems too dense, add some of the remaining stock. Season with salt. ❧ Return the pan to medium heat for 5 minutes, or until the soup is hot enough to be served.

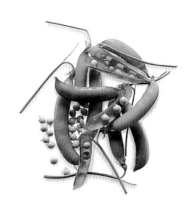

LEEK & POTATO SOUP

Finely chop the onion, parsley, garlic, carrot, and celery together. ❧ Sauté this mixture in the oil in a large skillet (frying pan) for 4–5 minutes. ❧ Add the leeks to the skillet and cook for 10 minutes. ❧ Add the potatoes and water. Season with salt and pepper and add the basil. Cook until the potatoes are very tender, about 40 minutes. Remove from heat. ❧ For a smooth creamy soup, chop in a food processor. ❧ In winter, serve the soup piping hot poured over the croutons. In summer, chill the soup and serve with the croutons sprinkled on top. ❧ Drizzle with extra olive oil before serving.

Serves: 4

Preparation: 20'

Cooking: 50–60'

Level of difficulty: 1

- **1 large onion**
- **small bunch of parsley**
- **1 clove garlic**
- **1 carrot**
- **1 stalk celery**
- **4 tbsp extra-virgin olive oil + extra for serving**
- **6 leeks, sliced**
- **6 large potatoes, peeled and diced**
- **4 cups/1 liter cold water**
- **6 leaves fresh basil**
- **salt and freshly ground black pepper to taste**
- **croutons (cubes of deep fried or toasted bread)**

SAVOY CABBAGE & SALAMI SOUP

Serves: 6

Preparation: 15'

Cooking: 40'

Level of difficulty: 2

- 2 cloves garlic, finely chopped
- 1 white onion, finely chopped
- 6 tbsp extra-virgin olive oil
- 4 lb/2 kg Savoy cabbage, cut in thin strips
- salt and freshly ground black pepper to taste
- 6 cups/1.5 liters water
- 5 oz/150 g salami, diced
- ¾ cup/180 g short-grain rice
- 2 tbsp finely chopped parsley
- 4 oz/125 g Parmesan cheese, in thin slivers

Sauté the garlic and onion in the oil in a large skillet (frying pan) until pale gold. ❧ Add the cabbage and season with salt and pepper. Cook over medium heat for 15 minutes, then pour in the water and bring to a boil. ❧ Add the salami, followed by the rice and simmer until the rice is tender, about 20 minutes. ❧ Sprinkle with the parsley and Parmesan just before serving.

HEARTY LENTIL SOUP

S oak the lentils in a bowl of cold water for 3 hours. ❧ Drain the lentils and place in a saucepan with the onion, carrots, celery, bay leaf, and garlic. Add enough cold water to cover to about 2 in (5 cm) above the level of the lentils. ❧ Cover and cook over low heat for about 45 minutes. ❧ Discard the bay leaf, add the sage and rosemary, and continue cooking, still covered and over low heat, for 5–10 more minutes. ❧ The lentils should be very soft, almost disintegrating. Season with salt and pepper, drizzle with the oil, and serve hot.

Serves: 4–6

Preparation: 10' + 3 h to soak

Cooking: 1 h

Level of difficulty: 1

- 2 cups/450 g dry lentils
- 1 medium onion, finely chopped
- 2 small carrots, scraped and diced
- 2 stalks celery, cleaned and thinly sliced
- 1 bay leaf
- 2 cloves garlic, finely chopped
- 3 fresh sage leaves, finely chopped
- 2 tbsp finely chopped fresh rosemary leaves
- salt and freshly ground white or black pepper to taste
- 6 tbsp extra-virgin olive oil

PEARL BARLEY & VEGETABLE SOUP

Serves: 4
Preparation: 25'
Cooking: 25'
Level of difficulty: 1

Place the beans and sage in a saucepan with enough cold water to cover by 2 in (5 cm). Cover and simmer for 45 minutes. ❧ Discard the sage. Chop half the beans in a blender or food processor with as much of the cooking water as needed to make a fairly dense cream. Transfer to a bowl and stir in the whole beans. ❧ Place the bacon, leek, celery, carrot, Swiss chard, red pepper flakes, and garlic in a medium saucepan. ❧ Add the stock, bring to a boil, and cook over medium heat for 15 minutes. ❧ Add the pearl barley and half the oil and cook for 15 minutes. ❧ Add the beans and cook for 15 more minutes. ❧ Season with salt, pepper, and nutmeg. ❧ Drizzle with the remaining oil and serve hot.

- 12 oz/350 g fresh cranberry, red kidney, or white beans, shelled
- 4 sage leaves
- 1/2 cup/75 g diced bacon
- 1 small leek, cleaned and sliced (white part only)
- 1 stalk celery, cleaned and sliced
- 1 medium carrot, diced
- 7 oz/200 g young Swiss chard/silverbeet, coarsely chopped
- 1/2 tsp red pepper flakes
- 1 clove garlic, finely chopped
- 1 cup/225 g pearl barley
- 3 cups/750 ml boiling *Beef Stock* (see page 140)
- 6 tbsp extra-virgin olive oil
- salt and freshly ground white or black pepper to taste
- dash of nutmeg

SPELT & BEAN SOUP

S auté the onion, garlic, carrot, celery, and leek in a saucepan in half the oil until soft. Add the bacon and sauté until golden. ❧ Add the spelt and cook, stirring for 5 minutes. ❧ In a food processor, chop two-thirds of the cannellini beans until smooth. ❧ Add the puréed beans and enough of their cooking water to make a dense soup. ❧ Cook over low heat, adding extra bean water as necessary, until the spelt is tender, about 45 minutes. ❧ Add the rest of the beans and cook for 5 more minutes. ❧ Let the soup rest for 10 minutes, drizzle with the remaining oil, and serve.

Serves: 6

Preparation: 20'+ time to soak

Cooking: 1¼ h

Level of difficulty: 1

- 1 onion, chopped
- 2 cloves garlic, 1 stalk celery, 1 leek, all finely chopped
- 4–6 tbsp extra-virgin olive oil
- ½ cup/75 g diced bacon
- 11 oz/300 g spelt, soaked in salted water overnight
- 11 oz/300 g dried cannellini beans, pre-soaked and boiled in salted water with sage (reserve the cooking water)
- salt and freshly ground black pepper to taste

FAVA BEAN PURÉE

Serves: 4

Preparation: 40' +
12 h to soak beans

Cooking: 2 h

Level of difficulty: 2

- **11 oz/300g dried fava beans/ broad beans**
- **1 celery stalk, chopped**
- **1 large potato, chopped**
- **2 medium onions, chopped**
- **salt to taste**
- **6 tbsp extra-virgin olive oil**
- **1 lb/500 g boiled chicory (or spinach)**
- **red pepper flakes, to taste**

Soak the fava beans overnight. Drain and rinse well. ❧ Place the fava beans in a large saucepan with the celery, potato, and onions. Cover with water and simmer over low heat for 2 hours. Season with salt and add half the olive oil. ❧ Chop in a food processor until smooth. Heat 1 tablespoon of oil in a saucepan and add the fava bean purée. Cook for 5 minutes. ❧ Ladle into individual soup bowls and top with the chicory. Sprinkle with the red pepper flakes and drizzle with the remaining oil. ❧ Serve hot.

CHICKEN STOCK & PARMESAN CROUTONS

P reheat the oven to 300°F/150°C/gas 2. ❧ Place the eggs, butter, Parmesan, salt, and nutmeg in a large bowl. Mix well with a fork, then gradually stir the flour into the mixture, making sure that no lumps form. ❧ Pour into a lightly

These Parmesan croutons can be served with most light cream of vegetable soups.

buttered 8-in (23-cm) square pan. ❧ Bake for 1 hour, or until golden brown. ❧ Leave to cool in the pan, then cut into small cubes. ❧ Pour the boiling stock into a tureen and sprinkle with the cubes. ❧ Serve immediately.

118

Serves: 4

Preparation: 10'

Cooking: 1 h

Level of difficulty: 1

- **4 eggs**
- **4 tbsp melted butter**
- **1 cup/150 g freshly grated Parmesan cheese**
- **1 cup/150 g all-purpose/plain flour**
- **salt to taste**
- **dash of nutmeg**
- **6 cups/1.5 liters boiling *Chicken Stock* (see page 140)**

FRENCH ONION SOUP

P lace the onions, oil, celery, and carrot (if using) in a deep, heavy-bottomed saucepan or earthenware pot. Cover and sauté over low heat, stirring frequently. ❧ After 20 minutes season with salt and pepper. ❧ Continue cooking, stirring and adding stock gradually, for another 20 minutes. ❧ Pour in the remaining stock. ❧ Place the toast in a tureen or individual soup bowls and pour the soup over the top. Sprinkle with the Parmesan and serve.

Serves: 4

Preparation: 15'

Cooking: 40'

Level of difficulty: 1

- **3 lb/1.5 kg onions, cut in thin slices**
- **4 tbsp extra-virgin olive oil**
- **1 stalk celery, finely chopped**
- **1 small carrot, finely chopped**
- **salt and freshly ground black pepper to taste**
- **4 cups/1 liter boiling *Beef Stock* (see page 140)**
- **4 slices firm-textured bread, toasted**
- **6 tbsp freshly grated Parmesan cheese**

PORCINI MUSHROOM SOUP

Serves: 4

Preparation: 40'

Cooking: 35–40'

Level of difficulty: 2

- 1 oz/30 g dried porcini mushrooms
- 1 cup/250 ml tepid water
- 1 tbsp finely chopped parsley
- 1 clove garlic, finely chopped
- 5 tbsp extra-virgin olive oil
- 1¼ lb/625 g porcini (or white) mushrooms, thinly sliced
- ½ cup/125 ml dry white wine
- 4 cups/1 liter boiling *Beef Stock* (see page 140)
- 1 tbsp all-purpose/ plain flour
- salt and freshly ground black or white pepper to taste
- 4 slices firm-textured bread, toasted

Soak the dried porcini mushrooms in the tepid water for 30 minutes. Drain and chop finely. ❧ Strain the water in which they were soaked and set aside. ❧ Sauté the parsley and garlic in 4 tablespoons of oil in a heavy-bottomed saucepan over medium heat for 1–2 minutes. ❧ Add the dried mushrooms, and after a couple of minutes, the fresh mushrooms. Sauté for 4–5 minutes. ❧ Pour in the wine, and after a couple of minutes, begin gradually adding the stock and mushroom water. ❧ Simmer for 25 minutes. ❧ Heat the remaining oil in a small saucepan over low heat. Add the flour and brown slightly, stirring carefully. ❧ Remove the skillet from the heat and add 3–4 tablespoons of the mushroom liquid, mixing well so that no lumps form. ❧ Pour this mixture into the soup. Cook 2–3 more minutes, stirring continuously. ❧ Arrange the bread in individual soup bowls, or in a tureen, and pour the soup over the top. ❧ Serve hot.

WINTER MINESTRONE

Place the carrot, turnip, zucchini, potato, leek, celery, and bacon in a large saucepan. ❧ Add the stock and when it returns to a boil, add the barley. Cover the pot and simmer for $1\frac{1}{2}$ hours, stirring occasionally. ❧ Season with salt and pepper and drizzle with the oil.

Serves: 4
Preparation: 30'
Cooking: $1\frac{1}{2}$ h
Level of difficulty: 1

- 1 carrot, 1 medium turnip, 1 zucchini /courgette, 1 large potato, all cleaned and diced
- 1 leek (white part only), 2 small celery hearts, cleaned and sliced
- 1 medium onion, and 1 oz/30 g spinach, cleaned and coarsely chopped
- 1 tbsp finely chopped parsley
- $\frac{1}{2}$ cup/75 g diced bacon
- 6 cups/1.5 liters boiling *Beef Stock* (see page 140)
- 1 cup/225 g pearl barley
- salt and freshly ground black pepper to taste
- 4 tbsp extra-virgin olive oil

CREAM OF SQUASH

Serves: 4

Preparation: 30'

Cooking: 30'

Level of difficulty: 1

- 2 lb/1 kg yellow squash (hubbard or pumpkin) peeled and cut in pieces
- 11 oz/300 g carrots, sliced
- 11 oz/300 g leeks, cleaned and sliced (white part only)
- 3 stalks celery sliced
- 2 cloves garlic
- 4 cups/1 liter boiling *Beef Stock* (see page 140)
- ¹/₂ cup/125 ml light/single cream
- salt and freshly ground white pepper to taste
- 8 tbsp freshly grated Parmesan cheese
- croutons or squares of toasted bread

Place the squash, carrots, leeks, celery, and garlic in a large saucepan and add the stock. Cover and simmer for 25 minutes, stirring occasionally. ❧ Chop in a blender or food processor to obtain a smooth, fairly dense purée. ❧ Set over medium heat for 1–2 minutes. ❧ Stir in the cream and season with salt and pepper. ❧ Let stand for a minute, sprinkle with the Parmesan, then serve.

VEGETABLE & BREAD SOUP

P lace the tomatoes in a large saucepan with the beans, garlic, and sage. Cover with cold water. If using fresh beans, add salt to taste at this point. ❧ Bring slowly to a boil, cover and simmer for about 25 minutes for fresh beans or about 1 hour for dried beans. The beans should be tender. If using dried beans, add salt when they are almost cooked. ❧ Discard the garlic and sage and chop half the beans in a food processor. ❧ Put the parsley, thyme, onion, leek, carrots, Swiss chard, cabbage, tomatoes and other vegetables in a large saucepan with the oil over medium heat and sauté for 5 minutes, stirring constantly. ❧ Add the puréed beans and the whole beans, followed by about two-thirds of the stock. Season with salt. Cover and simmer gently for about 1½ hours, adding more stock if the soup becomes too thick. ❧ Heat a medium saucepan and add a ladle or two of the soup and a slice of bread. Keep adding layers of soup and bread until finished. Drizzle with oil and sprinkle with pepper. Cover and leave to stand for 2–3 hours. ❧ Return to heat and bring slowly to a boil. Simmer very gently for 20 minutes without stirring. Alternatively, reheat the soup in the oven at 400°F/200°C/gas 6 for about 10 minutes. ❧ This soup is equally good served hot or at room temperature, depending on the season.

Serves: 6–8

Preparation: 45' + 12 h to soak; 2–3 h to stand

Cooking: 2–3 h

Level of difficulty: 2

- 3 cherry tomatoes
- 1 lb/500 g fresh cannellini beans or 1¼ cups/280 g dried white beans
- 2 cloves garlic
- 6 leaves fresh sage
- 2 tbsp finely chopped parsley
- 1 sprig fresh thyme
- 1 onion, thinly sliced
- 1 leek, thinly sliced
- 2 carrots, diced
- 8 oz/250 g Swiss chard/silverbeet, shredded
- ½ small Savoy cabbage, shredded
- 8 oz/250 g canned tomatoes
- 1 lb/500 g vegetables (new potatoes, French beans, zucchini/ courgettes, peas)
- 6 tbsp extra-virgin olive oil
- salt and freshly ground black pepper to taste
- 4 cups/1 liter *Beef Stock* (see page 140)
- 11 oz/300 g firm textured bread, sliced

SPINACH & RICE SOUP

Wash the spinach leaves under cold running water and, without draining, place in a large saucepan. Cover tightly and cook over medium heat for 2–3 minutes. ❧ Remove from heat and, when cool enough to handle, squeeze out as much moisture as possible. Chop coarsely. ❧ Melt the butter in the same saucepan, then add the spinach and salt. Cook over medium heat for 3 minutes, stirring constantly. Set aside. ❧ Bring the stock to a boil in a large saucepan. Add the rice and cook for 13–15 minutes. ❧ Add the spinach. ❧ Beat the egg lightly in a bowl with salt and pepper. Add the Parmesan, then pour the mixture into the hot soup while beating with a balloon whisk. Turn off the heat. ❧ Let stand for 30 seconds before serving.

Serves: 4

Preparation: 10'

Cooking: 20–25'

Level of difficulty: 1

- **12 oz/350 g net weight, washed, trimmed fresh spinach leaves**
- **2 tbsp butter**
- **salt to taste**
- **4 cups/1 liter Beef Stock (see page 140)**
- **1 cup/225 g short-grain rice**
- **1 egg**
- **freshly ground white pepper to taste**
- **6 tbsp freshly grated Parmesan cheese**

BREAD & CHEESE SOUP

Serves: 4

Preparation: 15'

Cooking: 15'

Level of difficulty: 1

- **8 thick slices of coarse-textured white bread**
- **2 cloves garlic, peeled**
- **7 oz/200 g thinly sliced Gruyère cheese**
- **salt and freshly ground black pepper to taste**
- **5 cups/1.25 liters boiling *Beef Stock* (see page 140)**

Preheat the oven to 400°F/200°C/gas 6. ♣ Toast the bread in the oven. Leave the oven on. ♣ When the slices are crisp, rub them all over with the garlic. ♣ Arrange the toast in the bottom of a deep earthenware pot or casserole in layers, alternating with the Gruyère slices. Season with salt and pepper. ♣ Slowly pour in sufficient stock to completely cover the toast. ♣ Bake in the oven for 15 minutes. The toast should absorb all the stock during cooking ♣ Serve at once.

Variation
- Substitute the Gruyère with the same amount of freshly grated Parmesan cheese

RICE & PEA SOUP

Melt half the butter with the oil in a medium saucepan. Add the onion and sauté over medium heat until soft and translucent. ❧ Add the parsley and garlic and sauté for 2–3 more minutes. ❧ Add the peas and a few tablespoons of stock, cover and cook over low heat for 8–10 minutes. ❧ Stir in the remaining stock and the rice and cook for 13–15 minutes. ❧ Taste to see if the rice is tender. Season with salt and pepper. ❧ Add the remaining butter and finish cooking. This will take 2–3 more minutes, depending on the rice. ❧ Add the Parmesan, mix well, and serve.

Serves: 4

Preparation: 10'

Cooking: 30'

Level of difficulty: 1

- **3 tbsp butter**
- **3 tbsp extra-virgin olive oil**
- **1 small onion, finely chopped**
- **1 clove garlic**
- **1 tbsp finely chopped parsley**
- **2^1/$_2$ cups/350 g shelled baby peas**
- **4 cups/1 liter boiling *Beef Stock* (see page 140)**
- **1 cup/225 g short-grain rice**
- **salt and freshly ground white pepper to taste**
- **6 tbsp freshly grated Parmesan cheese**

DUMPLING SOUP

Combine the milk (reserving $^1/_2$ cup/125 ml) with the bread in a large bowl and let stand for at least 30 minutes, mixing once or twice. The bread should become soft but not too wet. If necessary, add the remaining milk. ❧ Squeeze out the excess milk by hand and put the bread back in the bowl, discarding the milk first. ❧ Gradually add the eggs, sausage meat, bacon, Parma ham, onion, half the parsley, and 3 tablespoons of flour, stirring continuously until the mixture is firm. If needed, add a little more flour. ❧ In the meantime, bring 3 cups (750 ml) of water to a boil with 2 tablespoons of salt in a fairly deep saucepan. ❧ Shape the bread mixture into balls about 2 in (5 cm) in diameter and dust with flour. ❧ When they are all ready, drop the dumplings into the pot of boiling water. Turn the heat up to high until the water begins to boil, then lower the heat slightly and cook for 15 minutes. ❧ Remove from the water with a slotted spoon. ❧ Drain, transfer to a tureen, and ladle in the boiling stock. Garnish with the parsley and serve hot.

Serves: 4

Preparation: 45'

Cooking: 15'

Level of difficulty: 2

- **1$^1/_4$ cups/310 ml milk**
- **8 oz/250 g firm-textured stale bread, crusts removed, cut in pieces**
- **2 eggs**
- **3 oz/90 g fresh pork sausage meat**
- **$^1/_2$ cup/75 g finely chopped bacon**
- **$^1/_2$ cup/75 g finely chopped Parma ham**
- **1 tbsp onion, finely chopped**
- **2 tbsp finely chopped parsley**
- **$^1/_2$ cup/75 g all-purpose/plain flour**
- **salt to taste**
- **4 cups/1 liter boiling *Beef Stock* (see page 140)**

BREAD SOUP WITH TOMATO

Preheat the oven to 325°F/160°C/gas 3. Place the bread in the oven for 10 minutes to dry it out, but without toasting. In the meantime, plunge the tomatoes into boiling water for 1 minute and then into cold. Slip off their skins and cut them in half horizontally. Squeeze gently to remove the seeds and chop the flesh into small pieces. Pour 6 tablespoons of the oil into a heavy-bottomed pan or earthenware pot and add the garlic and bay leaves. As soon as the oil is hot, add the bread and cook over medium-low heat for 3–4 minutes, stirring frequently. Season with salt and pepper. Stir in the tomatoes and, using a ladle, add the water. Cook for 15 minutes, stirring occasionally. If the soup becomes too thick, add a little more water (remember, however, that this soup should be very thick). Drizzle the remaining oil over the top and serve hot.

Serves: 4

Preparation: 15'

Cooking: 20–25'

Level of difficulty: 1

- **8 oz/250 g densely textured home-style bread, coarsely chopped**
- **8 tbsp extra-virgin olive oil**
- **2 cloves garlic, finely chopped**
- **1–2 bay leaves**
- **salt and freshly ground black pepper to taste**
- **1 lb/500 g firm ripe tomatoes**
- **1¼ cups/310 ml water**

POTATO & RICE SOUP

Put the bacon, onion, and rosemary in a pot and sauté over low heat for 2–3 minutes, stirring frequently. ❧ Add the potatoes and the stock. As soon as it begins to boil, add the rice, stir once or twice and cook for 15 minutes, or until the rice is tender. ❧ Season with salt. ❧ Sprinkle with the parsley and cheese just before serving.

Serves: 4

Preparation: 20'

Cooking: 20–25'

Level of difficulty: 1

- 4 tbsp finely chopped lean bacon
- 1 small onion, finely chopped
- 1 tbsp finely chopped rosemary leaves
- 4 medium potatoes, peeled and sliced
- 1 cup/225 g short-grain rice
- 5 cups/1.25 liters boiling *Beef Stock* (see page 140)
- salt to taste
- 2 tbsp coarsely chopped parsley
- 6 tbsp freshly grated Parmesan cheese

BASIC STOCK WITH PASTA

Makes:	about 2 quarts/2 liters
Preparation:	10'
Cooking:	1–3 h
Level of difficulty:	1

Place all the ingredients in a large saucepan and bring to a boil. ❧ Simmer for 1 hour for Vegetable Stock and 2–3 hours for Beef or Chicken Stock. ❧ Mash the vegetables into the Vegetable Stock, but remove them and the meat and bones from the Beef and Chicken Stock. ❧ To serve with pasta, allow about 1 cup (250 ml) of stock 2–3 tablespoons of small pasta per person. Add the pasta to the stock and cook until it is *al dente*. ❧ Serve hot with freshly grated Parmesan cheese. ❧ Make large quantities of stock and freeze until needed.

BEEF STOCK

- 1 potato, 2 carrots, 1 onion, 2 tomatoes, 1 stalk celery, bunch of parsley
- 2 lb/1 kg lean boiling beef
- 2 lb/1 kg marrow bones
- salt to taste
- 3 quarts/3 liters cold water

CHICKEN STOCK

- 1 potato, 2 carrots, 1 onion, 2 tomatoes, 1 stalk celery, bunch of parsley
- 1 boiling chicken, about 4 lb/2 kg
- salt to taste
- 3 quarts/3 liters cold water

VEGETABLE STOCK

- 1 potato, 2 carrots, 1 onion, 2 zucchini/courgettes, 1 tomato, 2 stalks celery, 2 leeks, bunch of parsley
- salt to taste
- 3 quarts/3 liters cold water

Serves: 4

Preparation: 15'

Cooking: 20'

Level of difficulty: 1

- 3 tbsp butter
- 2 cloves garlic, finely chopped
- 1 onion, chopped
- $^1/_2$ cup/75 g bacon, diced
- 1 small cabbage, cut into strips
- 6 cups/1.5 liters boiling *Vegetable Stock* (see page 140)
- salt and freshly ground black pepper to taste
- 4 slices firm-textured bread, toasted
- 6 oz/180 g sharp Cheddar cheese, thinly sliced

CABBAGE & CHEESE SOUP

Melt the butter in a large, heavy-bottomed saucepan and sauté the garlic, onion, and bacon until golden. Add the cabbage, cover and cook for 5 minutes. ❧ Pour in the stock and cook for 15 minutes. Season with salt and pepper. ❧ Place a slice of bread in the bottom of each soup bowl and cover with the cheese. Ladle the hot soup over the bread and cheese and serve.

PASTA

Homemade Pasta

Mixing plain pasta dough

For 4 servings you will need 3 cups (450 g) of all-purpose/plain flour and 3 eggs. Place the flour in a mound on a work surface and make a well in the center. Break the eggs into the well one by one and use a fork to gradually incorporate the flour. Work the mixture with your hands until it is smooth, moist,

and firm. To test for the correct consistency, press a finger into the dough. If it comes out clean, the dough is ready to knead. If it is too moist, add more flour. If it is too dry, add a little milk. Roll the dough into a ball.

Kneading
On a clean, lightly floured work surface, push down and forward on the ball of pasta dough with the heel of your palm. Fold the slightly extended

piece of dough in half, give it a quarter-turn, and repeat. Continue for 8–10 minutes, or until the dough is smooth. Place the ball of dough on a plate and cover with a bowl. Let rest for at least 15–20 minutes.

Rolling dough by hand
Place the ball of dough on a clean work surface and flatten it a little with your hand. Place the rolling pin on the center of the ball and, applying light but

firm pressure, roll the dough away from you. Give the ball a quarter-turn and repeat. When the dough is about 1/4 in (6 mm) thick, curl the far edge over the pin while holding the edge closest to you with your hand. Gently stretch the pasta as you roll it all onto the pin. Unroll, give the dough a quarter-

turn, and repeat. Continue rolling and stretching the dough until it is transparent.

Rolling dough with a pasta machine

Divide the dough into several pieces and flatten slightly. Set the machine with its rollers at their widest, and run each piece through. Repeat, reducing the rollers' width by one notch each time, until all the pasta has passed at thinnest roller setting.

Cutting dough

For ribbon pasta, fold the dough into a loose, flat roll. Cut into 1/8-in (3-mm) slices for *tagliolini*, 1/4-in (6-mm) slices for *fettuccine*, 1/3-in (8-mm) slices for

tagliatelle, or 3/4-in (2-cm) slices for *pappardelle*.

Stuffed pasta

For stuffed pasta the dough needs to be moist, so try to work quickly and keep the dough you are not using covered.

For *agnolotti*, *tortelli*, and square-shaped *ravioli*: cut the rolled pasta into strips about 4 in

(10 cm) wide. Put teaspoonfuls of the filling at intervals of 2 in (5 cm) down the middle. Moisten the edges of the pasta, fold them over and seal. Use a wheel cutter to cut between the stuffing. Run it along the sealed edges to give a fluted edge.

For half-moon shaped *ravioli*: use a glass to cut the rolled pasta into disks. Place 1 teaspoonful of the filling at the center, moisten the edges of the pasta and fold it over. Pinch the edges to seal.

For *tortellini*: as above but use 1/2 teaspoonfuls of filling and twist the half moon

shape around your index finger until the edges meet. Pinch together to seal.

For *cappelletti*: cut the rolled pasta into strips 2 in (5 cm) wide. Cut each strip into 2-in (5-cm) squares. Place 1/2 teaspoonfuls of filling in the center of each. Fold the square diagonally in half to form a triangle. Moisten the edges and seal them. Pick up the triangle by one corner, take the other corner and wrap it around your index finger. Pinch the edges to seal.

145

SPAGHETTI WITH SIMPLE TOMATO SAUCE

S auté the garlic in the oil in a large skillet (frying pan) over medium heat until light gold. ❧ Add the basil and tomatoes. Season with salt and pepper, and simmer for 15–20 minutes, or until the oil begins to separate from the tomatoes. ❧ Cook the pasta in a large saucepan of salted, boiling water until *al dente*. ❧ Drain well and transfer to a heated serving dish. Toss well with the sauce and serve at once.

This sauce is delicious with plain, spinach, and whole wheat pasta of all shapes and sizes.

Serves: 6
Preparation: 15'
Cooking: 20'
Level of difficulty: 2

Variations

• Sauté 1 small onion, 1 carrot, 1 stalk celery, and 1 tablespoon parsley, all finely chopped, with the garlic.

• Add ¹/₂ teaspoon red pepper flakes with the tomatoes.

• Crumble 4 anchovy fillets into the sauce with the tomatoes.

• Add 2 tablespoons of small salted capers 5 minutes before the sauce is cooked.

- **4 cloves garlic, finely chopped**
- **6 tbsp extra-virgin olive oil**
- **10 fresh basil leaves, torn**
- **1¹/₂ lb/750 g tomatoes, (fresh or canned), peeled and chopped**
- **salt and freshly ground black pepper to taste**
- **1 lb/500 g spaghetti (or other dried pasta)**

SPAGHETTINI WITH GARLIC, OIL, & CHILE

Serves: 4

Preparation: 3'

Cooking: 10'

Level of difficulty: 1

- **1 lb/500 g spaghettini (thin spaghetti)**
- **4 cloves garlic, finely chopped**
- **2 tbsp finely chopped parsley**
- **1 dried red chile, crumbled**
- **¹/₂ cup/125 ml extra-virgin olive oil**
- **salt to taste**

Cook the spaghettini in a large saucepan of salted, boiling water until *al dente*. ❧ While the pasta is cooking, sauté the garlic, parsley, and chile in the oil in a small skillet (frying pan) over medium heat until the garlic begins to change color. ❧ Remove from heat and season with salt. ❧ Drain the pasta (not too thoroughly) and place in a heated serving dish. ❧ Pour the sauce over the top and toss well. Serve hot.

SPAGHETTI WITH LEMON & CHILE PEPPER

Grate the zest of one lemon and cut the fruit into small pieces. Squeeze the juice from the other lemon. ❧ Sauté the garlic in the oil in a heavy-bottomed pan until it begins to color. Add the cream, salt, and lemon zest and pieces and cook over medium heat for 4–5 minutes. ❧ Add the lemon juice and cook for 2–3 minutes more. ❧ Meanwhile cook the pasta in a large pan of salted, boiling water until *al dente*. ❧ Drain and transfer to the pan. Add the chile pepper and Parmesan, toss well, and serve.

Serves: 4

Preparation: 20'

Cooking: 20'

Level of difficulty: 1

- **2 lemons**
- **1 clove garlic, finely chopped**
- **1 cup/250 ml heavy/double cream**
- **salt to taste**
- **1 lb/500 g spaghetti**
- **3 oz/90 g freshly grated Parmesan cheese**
- **1 spicy green or red chile pepper, sliced**

BOWTIE PASTA IN SUMMER SAUCE

Serves: 4

Preparation: 12–15'

Cooking: 15'

Level of difficulty: 1

- 1 clove garlic, cut in half
- 1 tsp red pepper flakes
- 2 tbsp extra-virgin olive oil
- 2 lb/1 kg cherry tomatoes, cut in half
- salt and freshly ground black pepper to taste
- 1 tbsp capers
- 6 basil leaves, torn
- 1 lb/500 g bowtie pasta
- 4 oz/125 g Mozzarella cheese, diced

Sauté the garlic and red pepper flakes in the oil in a large skillet (frying pan) for 2–3 minutes. ❧ Add the tomatoes and season with salt and pepper. Cover and cook over low heat for 5 minutes. ❧ Add the capers and basil and cook for 5 minutes more. ❧ Meanwhile cook the pasta in a large pan of salted, boiling water until *al dente*. ❧ Drain and toss with the sauce and Mozzarella. ❧ Let the pasta sit for a few minutes before serving.

PASTA WITH RICOTTA & EGGPLANT

Serves: 4

Preparation: 15' + 1 h to disgorge

Cooking: 35'

Level of difficulty: 2

- **3 medium eggplants/ aubergines**
- **1–2 tbsp coarse sea salt**
- **5 oz/150 g salted Ricotta cheese or semi-hard Pecorino cheese**
- **1¹/₂ lb/750 g fresh or canned tomatoes, peeled and chopped**
- **1 clove garlic, finely chopped**
- **salt and freshly ground black pepper to taste**

- **6 tbsp extra-virgin olive oil**
- **1 lb/500 g spaghetti**
- **2 cups/500 ml oil, for frying**
- **8 fresh basil leaves, torn**

Cut the eggplants in ¹/₂-in (1-cm) slices lengthwise. Place in layers in a colander and sprinkle each layer with salt. Let stand for 1 hour, then rinse thoroughly and dry on paper towels. ♣ Use a fork to break the salted Ricotta into fairly small, crumbly pieces (or chop the Pecorino into small pieces with a knife). ♣ Place the tomatoes in a large, heavy-bottomed saucepan with the garlic and olive oil and simmer for 30 minutes, stirring occasionally. Season with salt and pepper. ♣ Sieve the thick tomato sauce and return to the pan. Keep hot over very low heat. ♣ Heat the frying oil in a large skillet (frying pan) and fry the eggplant in batches until browned on both sides. Drain on paper towels. ♣ Meanwhile cook the pasta in a large pan of salted, boiling water until *al dente*. ♣ Transfer to a serving bowl. Add the tomato sauce and stir in half the cheese and the basil. ♣ Serve immediately, topping each portion with eggplant slices and the remaining Ricotta or Pecorino cheese.

This recipe comes from Sicily where eggplants thrive in summer and are used in may dishes.

153

SPAGHETTI WITH SPICY OLIVE SAUCE

Serves: 4

Preparation: 10'

Cooking: 25'

Level of difficulty: 1

- 8 oz/250 g pitted black olives
- 2 tbsp extra-virgin olive oil
- 2 cloves garlic, peeled and whole
- $^1/_2$ tsp red pepper flakes
- 4 anchovy fillets (optional)
- 2 tbsp capers
- 1 lb/500 g ripe tomatoes, peeled and diced
- salt and freshly ground black pepper to taste
- 1 lb/500 g *spaghetti*

Chop about three-quarters of the olives coarsely with a large knife. ♣ Heat the oil in a skillet (frying pan) and sauté the garlic with the red pepper flakes. Discard the garlic when it has turned pale gold. Add the anchovies, if using, crushing them with a fork so that they dissolve in the oil. ♣ Add the chopped olives and capers, then the tomatoes. Season with salt and pepper (the anchovies and olives are both quite salty, so be sure to taste the sauce before seasoning). Cook over medium-low heat for 15 minutes, or until reduced. ♣ Meanwhile cook the pasta in a large pan of salted, boiling water until *al dente*. ♣ Drain well and transfer to a heated serving dish. Pour the sauce over the top, sprinkle with the whole olives, toss well, and serve.

This fiery dish is called "puttanesca" in Italian after "puttana," a not very polite word for a woman who is employed in the oldest profession in the world!

SPAGHETTI WITH OLIVES & TOMATOES

Place the tomatoes in a heavy-bottomed saucepan. Add the garlic and simmer over low heat for 20 minutes. ✧ Add the oil, olives, oregano, and red pepper flakes, and cook for 5 minutes more. Season with salt. ✧ Meanwhile, cook the pasta in a large pan of salted, boiling water until *al dente*. ✧ Drain and place on a heated serving dish. Toss with the tomato mixture and serve.

156

Like most spicy pasta dishes, this one is best without Parmesan cheese sprinkled on top.

Serves: 4
Preparation: 10'
Cooking: 25'
Level of difficulty: 1

- 1 lb/500 g fresh or canned tomatoes, peeled and chopped
- 2 cloves garlic, finely chopped
- 4 tbsp extra-virgin olive oil
- 1½ cups/180 g black olives, pitted and coarsely chopped
- 2 tsp oregano
- ½ tsp red pepper flakes
- salt to taste
- 1 lb/500 g spaghetti

SPAGHETTI WITH TOMATO & CRUMB SAUCE

Serves: 4

Preparation: 10'

Cooking: 20–25'

Level of difficulty: 1

- 2 cloves garlic, lightly crushed
- 4 tbsp extra-virgin olive oil
- 10 anchovy fillets
- 1 tbsp finely chopped parsley
- 1 lb/500 g fresh or canned tomatoes, peeled and chopped
- 1 lb/500 g spaghetti
- salt
- 8 tbsp fine toasted bread crumbs

Sauté the garlic in the oil in a large, heavy-bottomed saucepan until it begins to color, then remove and discard. ❧ Add the anchovies, crushing them with a fork so that they dissolve in the flavored oil. ❧ Add the parsley and tomatoes. Simmer over low heat for 15–20 minutes. ❧ Meanwhile, cook the pasta in a large pan of salted, boiling water until *al dente*. ❧ Drain, add to the sauce, and toss briefly. ❧ Transfer to a heated serving dish. Sprinkle with the toasted bread crumbs and serve.

This simple dish is traditionally served during Lent in Italy.

SWEET AND SOUR BUCATINI

B oil the cauliflower in plenty of salted water until it is just tender. Drain, reserving the water. Divide the cauliflower into small florets. ✿ Bring the water back to a boil and add the pasta. ✿ Meanwhile, sauté the onion for 1–2 minutes in the oil in a large, heavy-bottomed saucepan. Add the anchovies, raisins, pine nuts, and saffron. Stir for 2–3 minutes, then add the cauliflower and cook over very low heat, stirring occasionally. ✿ When the pasta is cooked *al dente*, drain and add to the cauliflower mixture. ✿ Combine carefully, then transfer to a heated serving dish and sprinkle generously with pepper and Pecorino, if using. ✿ Serve hot.

The surprising mix of flavors in this dish is typical of traditional Sicilian cooking.

Serves: 4

Preparation: 15'

Cooking: 40'

Level of difficulty: 1

* 1 small cauliflower
* salt
* 1 lb/500 g bucatini pasta
* 1 medium onion, thinly sliced
* 6 tbsp extra-virgin olive oil
* 4 anchovy fillets
* 2 tbsp small seedless white raisins/sultanas
* 2 tbsp pine nuts
* ¼ tsp saffron, dissolved in 3 tbsp hot water
* freshly ground black pepper to taste
* 6 tbsp freshly grated Pecorino cheese (optional)

Variation
• For a hearty winter dish, preheat the oven to 450°F/230°C/gas 7. Transfer the pasta and cauliflower mixture to a heated ovenproof dish and sprinkle with the Pecorino cheese. Bake for 10 minutes, or until the cheese topping has turned golden brown.

TAGLIATELLE WITH ARTICHOKE SAUCE

Serves: 4

Preparation: 15'

Cooking: 30'

Level of difficulty: 1

- **8 very fresh baby artichokes (or 16 defrosted frozen artichoke hearts)**
- **1 lemon**
- **4 tbsp finely chopped onion**
- **5 tbsp extra-virgin olive oil**
- **salt and freshly ground black pepper to taste**
- **$^1/_2$ cup/125 ml water**
- **1 lb/500 g tagliatelle (ribbon noodles)**
- **3–4 very fresh eggs**
- **8 tbsp freshly grated Pecorino cheese**

Strip the tough outer leaves off the artichokes and cut off the top third of the leaves. Remove any fuzzy choke and peel the stalk. Rub all the cut surfaces with lemon juice to prevent discoloration. Cut lengthwise into thin slices. ❧ Sauté the onion in the oil in a skillet (frying pan) until translucent. ❧ Add the artichokes and season with salt and pepper. Stir over medium heat for 2–3 minutes. Add the water, cover, and cook for about 20 minutes, or until the artichokes are very tender. ❧ Meanwhile, cook the pasta in a large pan of salted, boiling water until *al dente*. ❧ Break the eggs into a deep, heated serving dish, beat with a fork, and add about 5 tablespoons of the cheese. ❧ Drain the pasta well. Toss first with the egg mixture, then with the artichokes. ❧ Sprinkle with the remaining cheese and serve.

The addition of eggs to the artichoke mixture gives the sauce a rich and creamy texture.

HOT & SPICY SPAGHETTI

Sauté the bacon in the oil for 2–3 minutes in a large skillet (frying pan). Add the red pepper flakes and onion, if using, and sauté for 2–3 minutes more. ❧ Pour in the wine and cook for 2–3 minutes until it has evaporated. Season with salt and pepper. ❧ Add the tomatoes and cook over medium heat for about 15 minutes, or until they have reduced. ❧ Meanwhile, cook the pasta in a large pan of salted, boiling water until *al dente*. ❧ Drain well and transfer to a heated serving dish. ❧ Pour the sauce over the top and sprinkle with the cheese. Toss well and serve.

This recipe comes from Amatrice, a lovely town in the hills of central Italy.

162

Serves: 4

Preparation: 10'

Cooking: 25'

Level of difficulty: 1

- ³/₄ cup/125 g diced bacon
- 2 tbsp extra-virgin olive oil
- ¹/₂ tsp red pepper flakes
- 1 onion, finely chopped (optional)
- 4 tbsp dry white wine
- salt and freshly ground black pepper to taste
- 1 lb/500 g ripe tomatoes, peeled and diced
- 1 lb/500 g bucatini
- 4 tbsp freshly grated Pecorino cheese

SPAGHETTI
WITH EGG & BACON

Serves: 4

Preparation: 10'

Cooking: 15'

Level of difficulty: 1

- ³/₄ **cup/125 g diced smoked bacon**
- **1 clove garlic, lightly crushed but still whole**
- **1 tbsp extra-virgin olive oil**
- **1 lb/500 g spaghetti**
- **5 eggs**
- **4 tbsp cream**
- **8 tbsp each of freshly grated Parmesan and Pecorino cheese**
- **salt and freshly ground black pepper to taste**

Sauté the bacon and garlic in the oil in a large skillet (frying pan). Discard the garlic when it has turned pale gold. ❧ Cook the pasta in a large pan of salted, boiling water until *al dente*. ❧ While the *spaghetti* is cooking, beat the eggs with the cream, Parmesan, Pecorino, salt, and pepper in a large bowl. ❧ Drain the pasta very thoroughly and transfer to the bowl with the egg mixture. Add the bacon and oil and toss vigorously over low heat for 2 minutes. ❧ Serve hot.

This tasty combination is a classic Roman dish. 163

TRENETTE
WITH PESTO

Combine the basil, pine nuts, garlic, olive oil, and salt in a food processor and process until smooth. Place the mixture in a large serving bowl and stir in the cheeses. ❧ Cook the pasta in a large pan of salted, boiling water until *al dente*. ❧ Drain well and transfer to a heated serving dish. Add 2 tablespoons of the water used to cook the pasta and the butter. ❧ Toss vigorously with the Pesto and serve hot.

Variation
• For a richer sauce, add 1 tbsp fresh Ricotta cheese just before serving.

Serves: 4

Preparation: 10'

Cooking: 15'

Level of difficulty: 1

• **2 cups/400 g fresh basil leaves**
• **2 tbsp pine nuts**
• **1 clove garlic**
• **¹/₂ cup/125 ml extra-virgin olive oil**
• **salt to taste**
• **2 tbsp freshly grated Parmesan cheese**
• **2 tbsp grated Pecorino cheese**
• **1 lb/500 g trenette pasta (or spaghetti)**
• **1 tbsp butter**

FUSILLI SALAD WITH TOMATO, GARLIC, & MOZZARELLA CHEESE

Serves: 4

Preparation: 10' + time to cool pasta

Cooking: 10–12'

Level of difficulty: 1

- salt and freshly ground black pepper to taste
- 4 tbsp extra-virgin olive oil
- 4 large ripe tomatoes
- 2 cloves garlic, finely chopped
- 2 tbsp finely chopped parsley
- 12 oz/375 g Mozzarella cheese
- 6 fresh basil leaves
- 1 lb/500 g fusilli, plain, whole wheat or colored

If short of time, cool the cooked pasta under cold running water. Dry well in a clean tea towel. This dish can be prepared up to a day before serving. Keep chilled in the refrigerator.

Cook the fusilli in a large pan of salted, boiling water until *al dente*. Drain well. Transfer to a large salad bowl and toss vigorously with half the oil. Set aside to cool. ❧ Cut the tomatoes into bite-size pieces and add to the pasta. Combine the garlic and parsley with the remainder of the oil and a sprinkling of salt, and add to the salad bowl. Leave to cool completely. ❧ Just before serving, dice the Mozzarella into small cubes on a cutting board. Slant the board slightly so that the extra liquid runs off. Sprinkle over the top of the salad with the torn basil leaves and freshly ground black pepper. ❧ Toss gently and serve.

BAKED TOMATOES WITH PASTA FILLING

Rinse the tomatoes and dry well. Cut the top off each tomato (with its stalk) and set aside. Hollow out the insides of the bottom parts with a teaspoon. Put the pulp in a bowl. ❧ Place a basil leaf in the bottom of each hollow shell. ❧ Preheat the oven to 350°F/180°C/gas 4. ❧ Cook the pasta in a medium pot of salted, boiling water for half the time indicated on the package. Drain well. ❧ Combine the pasta with the tomato pulp. Add the parsley and 2 tablespoons of the oil. Season with salt and pepper. ❧ Stuff the hollow tomatoes with the mixture. ❧ Grease an ovenproof dish with the remaining oil and carefully place the tomatoes on it. Cover each tomato with its top. ❧ Bake for about 40–45 minutes, or until the tomatoes are tender and the pasta fully cooked. ❧ Serve hot or at room temperature.

Serves: 4
Preparation: 20'
Cooking: 45–50'
Level of difficulty: 1

Choose firm, ripe tomatoes for this dish. Serve at room temperature in the summertime as an entrée.

- **8 medium tomatoes**
- **8 basil leaves**
- **2 tbsp finely chopped parsley**
- **3 tbsp extra-virgin olive oil**
- **salt and freshly ground black pepper to taste**
- **8 tbsp ditaloni rigati or other small, tubular pasta**

SPAGHETTI WITH CHERRY TOMATOES

Wash and dry the tomatoes. Cut them in half, and place in a bowl with the garlic, red pepper flakes, oregano, and basil. 🍃 Heat the oil in a large skillet (frying pan) over high heat and add the tomato mixture. Cook for 5–6 minutes, stirring often with a wooden spoon. Season with salt and pepper and remove from heat. Do not overcook the tomatoes: they should still be firm and retain their skins. 🍃 Meanwhile, cook the pasta in a large pan of salted, boiling water for 8–10 minutes. 🍃 Drain the spaghetti and add to the tomato mixture in the skillet. Cook for about 5 minutes more over high heat, tossing constantly, so that the tomato sauce is absorbed by the pasta as it finishes cooking. 🍃 Serve hot.

Serves: 4

Preparation: 15'

Cooking: 15'

Level of difficulty: 1

- 2½ lb/1.25 kg cherry tomatoes
- 2 cloves garlic, peeled but whole
- ½ tsp crushed red pepper flakes
- dash of oregano
- 4 fresh basil leaves, torn
- 6 tbsp extra-virgin olive oil
- salt and freshly ground black pepper to taste
- 1 lb/500 g spaghetti

PENNE WITH RICOTTA CHEESE

Serves: 4

Preparation: 5'

Cooking: 10'

Level of difficulty: 1

- ³/₄ **cup/180 ml full cream milk**
- **8 oz/250 g very fresh Ricotta cheese**
- **1 tbsp sugar**
- **1 tsp ground cinnamon**
- **salt and freshly ground white pepper to taste**
- **1 lb/500 g penne**

Warm the milk and place in a bowl with the Ricotta, sugar, and cinnamon. Season with salt and pepper. Mix with a fork to obtain a smooth creamy sauce. ❧ Cook the pasta in a large pan of salted, boiling water until *al dente*. ❧ Drain well and place in a heated serving bowl. ❧ Toss well with the sauce and serve.

SPAGHETTI WITH SEAFOOD SAUCE

S crub the beards off the mussels and soak them with the clams in a bowl of cold water for 1 hour. ❧ Chop the squid into bite-sized chunks. ❧ Do not peel the shrimp. ❧ Put 3 tablespoons of the oil in a large skillet (frying pan), add the mussels and clams, and cook over medium heat until they open. Discard any that have not opened. ❧ Extract the mollusks from their shells. Leave just a few in their shells to make the finished dish look more attractive. ❧ Heat 2 tablespoons of the remaining oil in a large skillet and sauté the garlic, parsley, and red pepper flakes for 2 minutes over medium heat. ❧ Add the squid. Season with salt and pepper, cook briefly, then add the wine. ❧ Cook for 20 minutes, then add the shrimp tails. ❧ After 5 minutes, add the clams and mussels. Mix well and cook for 2 minutes more. Turn off the heat, cover, and set aside. ❧ Meanwhile, cook the pasta in a large pan of salted, boiling water until *al dente*. ❧ Drain, and add to the pan with the seafood sauce. Toss for 1–2 minutes over high heat. ❧ Place in a heated serving dish and serve.

Serves: 4

Preparation: 25' + 1 h to soak

Cooking: 30'

Level of difficulty: 2

- **11 oz/300 g each mussels and clams, in shell**
- **1 lb/500 g squid, cleaned (see page 89)**
- **10 oz/300 g shrimp tails**
- **6 tbsp extra-virgin olive oil**
- **2 cloves garlic, finely chopped**
- **3 tbsp finely chopped parsley**
- **1 tsp red pepper flakes**
- **¹/₂ cup/125 ml dry white wine**
- **salt and freshly ground black pepper to taste**
- **1 lb/500 g spaghetti**

SPAGHETTI WITH CLAMS

Serves: 4

Preparation: 10' + 1 h
to soak

Cooking: 30'

Level of difficulty: 1

- 1 1/2 lb/750 g clams, in shell
- 6 tbsp extra-virgin olive oil
- 6 tbsp dry white wine
- 3 cloves garlic, finely chopped
- 1/2 tsp red pepper flakes
- 6 ripe tomatoes, peeled and chopped
- salt and freshly ground black pepper to taste
- 2 tbsp finely chopped parsley
- 1 lb/500 g spaghetti

Soak the clams in cold water for 1 hour. ❧ Heat 2 tablespoons of the oil in a large skillet (frying pan) with the clams and wine. Cook until all the clams are open. Remove the clams, discarding any that have not opened, and set aside. Strain the cooking liquid into a bowl and set aside. ❧ In the same pan, sauté the garlic and red pepper flakes in the remaining oil until the garlic is pale gold. ❧ Add the tomatoes and cook for 5 minutes. ❧ Pour in the clam liquid. Season with salt and pepper. Cook for 15 more minutes. ❧ Add the clams and parsley, and cook for 2–3 minutes. ❧ Meanwhile, cook the pasta in a large pan of salted, boiling water until al dente. ❧ Drain and place in the skillet with the sauce. Toss for 1–2 minutes over high heat and serve.

PASTA WITH SARDINES

B ring the water to a boil in a very large saucepan and add the salt and fennel. Simmer for 15 minutes, then drain, reserving the water to cook the pasta. ❧ Squeeze the fennel to remove excess moisture and chop coarsely. ❧

This sweet pasta dish comes from Sicily. Like many Sicilian dishes, it shows Middle Eastern influences. Remove any scales from the sardines and gently pull off their heads (the viscera will come away with the heads). Use kitchen scissors to cut down their bellies and lay them out flat. ❧ Preheat the oven to 425°F/220°C/gas 7. ❧ Sauté the onion in the oil, then add the anchovies, crushing them with a fork so that they dissolve in the oil. ❧ Add the sardines, raisins, pine nuts, and almonds, and season with salt and pepper. ❧ Cook over medium heat for 10 minutes before adding the fennel and saffron. Stir gently to avoid breaking up the fish. Reduce the heat, cover, and simmer for 10 more minutes. ❧ Bring the fennel-flavored water to a boil, add the pasta, and cook until *al dente*. Drain and mix carefully with the sardines and sauce. ❧ Transfer to an oiled ovenproof dish and sprinkle the bread crumbs over the top. ❧ Bake for 10 minutes, or until the bread crumbs are browned. ❧ Serve hot.

Serves: 4

Preparation: 30'

Cooking: 50'

Level of difficulty: 3

- 3 quarts/3 liters water
- 1 tbsp salt
- 7 oz/200 g wild fennel
- 12 oz/350 g fresh or defrosted frozen sardines
- 1 medium onion, finely chopped
- 6 tbsp extra-virgin olive oil
- 2–3 salted anchovies (rinsed and boned) or 4–6 anchovy fillets
- 2 tbsp small, seedless white raisins/sultanas
- 3 tbsp pine nuts
- $1/4$ cup/45 g toasted almonds, chopped
- freshly ground black pepper to taste
- $1/4$ tsp saffron, dissolved in 2 tbsp hot water
- 1 lb/500 g bucatini
- $1/2$ cup/75 g dry bread crumbs

SPAGHETTI WITH TUNA FISH & TOMATO

Sauté the garlic and parsley in the oil in a large skillet (frying pan) over medium heat for 3–4 minutes. ❧ Add the tomatoes, season with salt and pepper, and cook for 15 minutes, or until the sauce reduces. ❧ Meanwhile, cook the pasta in a large pan of salted, boiling water until *al dente*. ❧ Mix the tuna into the tomato sauce, stir well, and remove from heat. ❧ Drain the pasta and transfer to a heated serving dish. Add the tomato and tuna sauce and toss vigorously for 1–2 minutes. ❧ Serve hot.

This sauce is easy to prepare and very tasty. It goes well with spaghetti and other long pasta shapes.

Serves: 4
Preparation: 10'
Cooking: 15'
Level of difficulty: 1

- **2 cloves garlic, finely chopped**
- **2 tbsp finely chopped parsley**
- **4 tbsp extra-virgin olive oil**
- **6 large ripe tomatoes, peeled and diced**
- **salt and freshly ground black pepper to taste**
- **1 lb/500 g spaghetti**
- **8 oz/250 g tuna fish, packed in oil, drained, and flaked**

PASTA WITH BACON, MUSHROOMS, & PEAS

Serves: 6

Preparation: 15'

Cooking: 30–40'

Level of difficulty: 1

- **1 onion, sliced**
- **2 tbsp finely chopped parsley**
- **3 tbsp extra-virgin olive oil**
- **$^1/_2$ cup/75 g diced fatty bacon**
- **3 cups/400 g fresh or frozen peas**
- **1 cup/250 ml *Beef Stock* (see page 140)**
- **6 tbsp butter**
- **11 oz/300 g mushrooms**
- **1 lb/500 g bowtie pasta**
- **1 cup/150 g freshly grated Parmesan cheese**
- **salt and freshly ground black pepper**

Sauté the onion and parsley in the oil in a large skillet (frying pan). ❧ Add the bacon and sauté until lightly browned and crisp. Add the peas. ❧ Cook for a few minutes while stirring, then pour in the stock and simmer over low heat for 20 minutes. ❧ Season with salt and pepper and remove from heat. ❧ Heat half the butter in a separate skillet with a dash of salt. Slice the mushrooms and add to the skillet. Cook until tender (this can take up to 20 minutes). ❧ Meanwhile, cook the pasta in a large pan of salted, boiling water until *al dente*. ❧ Drain well and add to the skillet with the bacon. Add the mushrooms and remaining butter and toss well. ❧ Sprinkle with Parmesan and serve.

RIGATONI WITH FISH SAUCE

Place the fish and rosemary in a large saucepan. Cover with cold water and bring to a boil. Cook for 15 minutes over medium-low heat. Take the fish out, remove the skin and bones, and crumble the cooked meat. Strain and reserve the liquid and discard the rosemary leaves. ❧ Sauté the onion and garlic in a large skillet (frying pan) with the oil until light gold. Add the fish and 3 cups (750 ml) of the stock in which it was cooked. Season with salt and pepper and simmer over low heat for about 30–35 minutes. ❧ Meanwhile, cook the pasta in a large pan of salted, boiling water until *al dente*. ❧ Drain well and transfer to the skillet with the fish sauce. Add the parsley and toss well. ❧ Serve hot.

Many types of fish will work in this sauce.
Ask your fish vendor for ones that are suitable.

Serves: 4
Preparation: 15'
Cooking: 50'
Level of difficulty: 2

- 1¹/₂ lb/750 g assorted fresh fish, such as hake, sea bass, sea bream, and red snapper, cleaned and gutted
- 2 tbsp fresh rosemary leaves
- 1 onion, finely chopped
- 1 clove garlic, finely chopped
- 6 tbsp extra-virgin olive oil
- salt and freshly ground black pepper to taste
- 1 lb/500 g rigatoni pasta
- 2 tbsp finely chopped parsley

FETTUCCINE WITH MUSHROOM SAUCE

Serves: 4

Preparation: 10' + 20'

Cooking: 30'

Level of difficulty: 1

- 14 oz/450 g coarsely chopped fresh porcini mushrooms (or 13 oz/400 g fresh white mushrooms and 1 oz/30 g dried porcini)
- 2 cloves garlic, finely chopped
- sprig of fresh rosemary, finely chopped
- 1 tbsp butter
- 4 tbsp extra-virgin olive oil
- salt and freshly ground black pepper to taste
- 1 lb/500 g fresh or dried fettuccine pasta (or potato gnocchi)

If using dried porcini, soak them in 1 cup (250 ml) of warm water for about 20 minutes. Drain and squeeze out the excess water. Chop coarsely. ❧ Sauté the garlic and rosemary in a large skillet (frying pan) with the butter and oil over medium heat for 4–5 minutes. ❧ Add the mushrooms and season with salt and pepper. Cover and cook over medium-low heat for about 20–25 minutes, or until the mushrooms are very tender. ❧ Meanwhile, cook the pasta in a large pan of salted, boiling water until *al dente*. ❧ Drain and place on a heated serving dish. Cover with the sauce and toss. Serve hot.

The dried porcini have such a strong taste they will flavor your dish almost as well as the fresh ones.

TORTELLINI WITH MEAT SAUCE

Serves: 4

Preparation: 10'

Cooking: 1 h

Level of difficulty: 1

- 1 onion, finely chopped
- 1 carrot, finely chopped
- 1 stalk celery, finely chopped
- 2 tbsp butter
- 8 oz/250 g ground lean pork
- 8 oz/250 g ground lean beef
- 2 chicken livers, coarsely chopped
- 1 cup/250 ml dry red wine
- 14 oz/400 g canned tomatoes
- salt and freshly ground black pepper to taste
- 1 lb/500 g tortellini, homemade (see page 106) or store-bought

Sauté the onion, carrot, and celery in the butter in a large heavy-bottomed saucepan for 5–7 minutes. ❧ Add the pork, beef, and chicken livers, moisten with the wine and cook until it has evaporated. ❧ Stir in the tomatoes, salt, and pepper. ❧ Cover and leave to simmer gently for at least 1 hour. ❧ Meanwhile, cook the pasta in a large pan of salted, boiling water until *al dente*. ❧ Drain well and transfer to a heated serving dish. Spoon the sauce over the top and toss gently. ❧ Serve hot.

GARGANELLI WITH MEAT SAUCE & PEAS

Sauté the bacon, onion, carrot, and celery in the butter in a large skillet (frying pan) over medium-low heat for 10 minutes. ❧ Stir in the pork and beef and sauté for 5 minutes. ❧ Pour in half the wine and a third of the stock. Simmer until the liquid has reduced, then add the tomatoes. Saeson with salt and pepper. ❧ Gradually stir in the remaining wine and stock as the sauce cooks. ❧ Add the peas 15 minutes before the sauce is ready. ❧ Meanwhile, cook the pasta in a large pan of salted, boiling water until *al dente*. ❧ Drain well and add to the skillet. Toss well and serve.

Garganelli is a specialty of Emilia-Romagna in central Italy. Substitute with penne, if preferred.

Serves: 4
Preparation: 15'
Cooking: 2 h
Level of difficulty: 2

- 4 tbsp diced bacon
- 1 small onion, 1 small carrot, 1 stalk celery, all finely chopped
- 4 tbsp butter
- 4 oz/125 g lean ground pork
- 8 oz/250 g ground beef
- 1 cup/250 ml dry red wine
- 1¼ cups/310 ml *Beef Stock* (see page 140)
- 14 oz/400 g canned tomatoes
- salt and freshly ground black pepper to taste
- 5 oz/150 g peas
- 1 lb/500 g garganelli (or penne)

TAGLIATELLE WITH PARMA HAM & PEAS

Serves: 4

Preparation: 10'

Cooking: 20'

Level of difficulty: 1

- **2 cups/300 g fresh or frozen peas**
- **salt to taste**
- **4 tbsp butter**
- **1 small onion, finely chopped**
- **¹/₂ cup/75 g Parma ham, chopped**
- **salt and freshly ground black pepper to taste**
- **1 lb/500 g homemade (see pages 144–5) or store-bought tagliatelle**
- **6 tbsp freshly grated Parmesan cheese**

Cook the peas in a small saucepan of salted, boiling water until just cooked. Drain and set aside. ❧ Sauté the onion and Parma ham in the butter in a large skillet (frying pan) for 5 minutes. ❧ Add the peas and season with salt and pepper. Cook for 5 minutes. ❧ Meanwhile, cook the pasta in a large pan of salted, boiling water until *al dente*. ❧ Drain well and transfer to a heated serving dish. Spoon the sauce over the top, sprinkle with the Parmesan and serve.

The sweet flavor of the peas is set off by the salty Parma ham and mellowed by the egg-based pasta.

189

TAGLIATELLE WITH SHRIMP & WHITE WINE

Preheat the oven to 400°F/200°C/gas 6. ❧ Cook the shrimp in 4 cups (1 liter) of boiling water for 10 minutes. Remove with a slotted spoon. Use a pair of sharply pointed scissors to cut down the center of their backs. Pull the sides of the shell apart

Try adding a few shucked clams with the shrimp, or cup 6 oz/180 g poached, filleted fish.

and take out the flesh, keeping it as intact as possible, and set aside. ❧ Return the shells and heads to the stock and continue boiling until it has reduced by two-thirds. ❧ In a skillet (frying pan), heat the garlic and onion in the oil and 4 tablespoons of butter. ❧ Add the reserved shrimp flesh. Sprinkle with the wine and cook until it has evaporated. Season with salt. Remove from heat. ❧ Melt the remaining butter in a small saucepan. Stir in the flour and keep stirring to prevent lumps forming as you add first the hot milk and then the strained hot stock. Continue cooking and stirring for up to 10 minutes, when the sauce should be thick and glossy. ❧ Meanwhile, cook the pasta in a large pan of salted, boiling water until *al dente*. ❧ Drain and add to the skillet. Pour in the sauce and stir gently while cooking over low heat. Transfer to a heated serving dish. Sprinkle with the Parmesan and parsley, and bake for 10–15 minutes, or until a golden crust has formed on top. ❧ Serve hot.

Serves: 6
Preparation: 40'
Cooking: 40'
Level of difficulty: 3

- 1¼ lb/625 g shrimp
- 1 clove garlic, finely chopped
- 1 small onion, finely chopped
- 3 tbsp extra-virgin olive oil
- 6 tbsp butter
- ½ cup/125 ml dry white wine
- salt to taste
- 3 tbsp all-purpose/ plain flour
- 1 cup/250 ml hot milk
- 1 lb/500 g homemade (see pages 144–5) or store-bought tagliatelle
- 1 cup/150 g freshly grated Parmesan cheese
- 2 tbsp finely chopped parsley

WHOLE-WHEAT SPAGHETTI WITH ONIONS

Prepare the spaghetti and spread them out on a floured board or work surface to dry for about 30 minutes. ❧ Rinse the anchovies thoroughly, remove the bones, and

These homemade spaghetti take a while to make but are well worth the effort.

chop the flesh coarsely. ❧ Heat the oil in a large skillet (frying pan) and add the onions. Cook gently until tender, adding a spoonful or two of water, if necessary, to prevent them from browning. ❧ Add the anchovies, then turn up the heat and use a fork or wooden spoon to break them up so that they dissolve in the oil. Season generously with salt and pepper and turn off the heat. ❧ Cook the spaghetti in a large pan of salted, boiling water for 5–7 minutes. Drain and stir into the onion, oil, and anchovy mixture. Sprinkle with the parsley and serve.

Serves: 4–6

Preparation: 45'+ 30 to rest

Cooking: 20'

Level of difficulty: 2

- **1 quantity whole-wheat spaghetti (see page 194)**
- **7 oz/200 g salted anchovies (or sardines)**
- **4 tbsp extra-virgin olive oil**
- **3 large white onions, finely sliced**
- **2 tbsp finely chopped parsley**
- **salt and freshly ground black pepper to taste**

ANGEL HAIR PASTA WITH OIL & LEMON SAUCE

Serves: 4

Preparation: 3'

Cooking: 5'

Level of difficulty: 1

- 1 medium onion, finely chopped
- 1 cup/250 ml extra-virgin olive oil
- 1 lb/500 g angel hair pasta
- juice of 3 lemons
- salt and freshly ground black pepper to taste
- 6 tbsp freshly grated Parmesan cheese

Sauté the onion in the oil in a large skillet (frying pan) until translucent. ❧ Cook the pasta in a large pan of salted, boiling water until *al dente*. ❧ Drain well and transfer to the pan with the onion. Toss briefly over medium heat and transfer to a heated serving dish. ❧ Add the lemon juice, salt, pepper, and Parmesan. Toss well and serve hot.

WHOLE-WHEAT SPAGHETTI WITH DUCK SAUCE

P lace the flour and salt in a mound on a pastry slab or in a large mixing bowl. Make a well in the center and break the eggs into it. Stir *These fat, whole wheat spaghetti* *are a specialty of northeastern Italy.* with a fork, gradually incorporating the flour and adding the water a little at a time, as needed; the dough should be smooth and elastic. Place in a bowl, cover with a damp cloth, and let stand for 30 minutes. ♣ Make the thick spaghetti using an electric or hand-cranked pasta machine, then spread them out on a floured board to dry for 30 minutes. ♣ Wash and dry the duck. Place in a large saucepan, then add enough water to cover, a dash of salt, and the onion, celery, and carrot. Bring to a boil and simmer for 1 hour. ♣ While the duck is cooking, chop the liver and heart coarsely and sauté in the oil and butter over high heat. When lightly browned, add the sage, salt, and a generous grinding of pepper. ♣ Remove the cooked duck from the saucepan and strain and reserve the stock. Remove and discard the skin and break the meat into small pieces. ♣ Place the stock in a large pan and bring to a boil. Add the spaghetti carefully and cook for 5–7 minutes. ♣ Drain the pasta and place in a heated serving dish. Add the duck meat, liver mixture, and Parmesan, and toss gently.

194

Serves: 6

Preparation: 30' + 30' to rest

Cooking: 1 h

Level of difficulty: 3

PASTA

• 3 cups/450 g whole-wheat flour
• 1 tsp salt
• 4 eggs
• 1/2 cup/125 ml cold water

SAUCE

• 1 duck, with liver and heart, weighing about 3 lb/1.5 kg
• 1 onion, 1 stalk celery, 1 carrot
• 4 tbsp extra-virgin olive oil
• 5 tbsp butter
• 2–3 fresh sage leaves, torn
• salt and freshly ground black pepper to taste
• 6 tbsp freshly grated Parmesan cheese

MUSHROOM LASAGNE

Preheat the oven to 400°F/200°C/gas 6. ♣ Cook the pasta in a large pan of salted, boiling water until *al dente*. ♣ Drain the pasta and lay the pieces out on a clean cloth, making sure that they do not overlap. ♣ Sauté the carrots, celery, and shallots in the oil in a large skillet (frying pan) over medium heat for 5–6 minutes. ♣ Add the meat and cook, stirring often, for 10 minutes. ♣ Add the tomatoes and cook for 20 minutes. ♣ Stir in the mushrooms and cook for 20 minutes more. ♣ Remove from heat. Stir in the Parma ham and season with the salt and pepper. ♣ Spoon a layer of meat into an ovenproof dish. Cover with a layer of pasta. ♣ Cover with a layer of Fontina and sprinkle with the Parmesan. Repeat until the dish is full. Finish with a cheese layer. ♣ Bake for 25–30 minutes, or until golden brown. ♣ Serve hot.

Serves: 4

Preparation: 30'

Cooking: 1¼ h

Level of difficulty: 2

- **12 oz/350 g lasagne pasta**
- **1 carrot, finely chopped**
- **2 stalks celery, finely chopped**
- **2 shallots, finely chopped**
- **4 tbsp extra-virgin olive oil**
- **8 oz/250 g ground beef**
- **14 oz/400 g chopped tomatoes**
- **1 lb/500 g mushrooms, finely chopped**
- **¹/₂ cup/75 g finely chopped Parma ham**
- **salt and freshly ground black pepper to taste**
- **7 oz/200 g sliced Fontina cheese**
- **1 cup/150 g freshly grated Parmesan cheese**

POTATO DUMPLINGS

Boil the potatoes without peeling until tender, then slip off their skins. Mash or put through a potato ricer and place in a large bowl. ❧ Beat the egg whites in a large bowl until stiff. Gently fold in the yolks, flour, salt, pepper, nutmeg, and, finally, the potatoes. Mix gently but thoroughly. ❧ Bring a large saucepan of salted water to the boil and drop rounded spoonfuls of the potato mixture into the boiling water. When the dumplings bob up to the surface, they are done. Scoop out with a slotted spoon and transfer to a heated serving dish. Sprinkle with the Parmesan. ❧ Melt the butter and sage together in a small saucepan until the butter is pale golden brown. ❧ Drizzle the flavored butter all over the dumplings and serve.

These large potato dumplings come from Northern Italy. Serve with a glass of good red wine.

Serves: 4

Preparation: 25'

Cooking: 2'

Level of difficulty: 2

- 1¹/₂ lb/750 g white, floury potatoes
- 3 eggs, separated
- 1 cup/150 g all-purpose/plain flour
- salt and freshly ground white pepper to taste
- freshly grated nutmeg
- 4 tbsp freshly grated Parmesan cheese
- 4 tbsp butter
- 5–6 fresh sage leaves

AUSTRIAN GNOCCHI

Serves: 4

Preparation: 25' + 30' to rest

Cooking: 2–3'

Level of difficulty: 2

- 2 tbsp extra-virgin olive oil
- 5 oz/150 g mushrooms, finely chopped
- 6 tbsp butter, melted
- 3 eggs
- 2 tbsp corn starch/cornflour
- 1 tbsp finely chopped parsley
- salt and freshly ground black pepper to taste
- 7 oz/200 g bread crumbs
- 1 quantity *Basic Tomato Sauce* (see page 932)

Sauté the mushrooms in the oil in a large skillet (frying pan) over medium heat until tender. Set aside to cool. ❧ Beat the butter and eggs in a medium bowl until pale in color. Add the corn starch, parsley, and mushrooms and season with salt and pepper. ❧ Stir in enough bread crumbs to form a firm dough. ❧ Set aside to rest for 30 minutes. ❧ Shape the mixture into walnut-sized gnocchi (balls). ❧ Cook the gnocchi in batches in a large saucepan of salted, boiling water for 2–3 minutes, or until the bob up to the surface. ❧ Scoop out with a slotted spoon and serve hot with the Basic Tomato Sauce.

RICE & RISOTTO

Risotto

Delicious risotto is another Italian dish that has become popular all over the world. Try to use imported Italian rice — Arborio is one of the best and is widely available abroad. *Vialone nano* is also good. When preparing risotto always add the liquids very gradually, stirring all the time. The gradual release of the starch in the rice during cooking is what makes a good creamy risotto and this can only be achieved by patient cooking and stirring.

MILANESE RISOTTO

Serves:	4
Preparation:	10'
Cooking:	25'
Level of difficulty:	2

+ **4 tbsp butter**
+ **2 tbsp finely chopped ox-bone marrow**
+ **1 small onion, finely chopped**
+ **2 cups/450 g Italian Arborio rice**
+ **1/2 cup/125 ml white wine**
+ **2 quarts/2 liters *Beef Stock* (see page 140)**
+ **6 tbsp freshly grated Parmesan cheese**
+ **1/2 tsp powdered saffron**
+ **salt to taste**

Melt 2 tablespoons of butter and the bone marrow in a large, heavy-bottomed saucepan. ❧ Add the onion and sauté over medium heat until soft and translucent. ❧ Increase the heat to medium-high and add the rice. Cook for 2–3 minutes, stirring constantly. ❧ Stir in the wine, and this has been absorbed, begin stirring in the stock, 1/2 cup (125 ml) at a time. Cook and stir until each addition has been absorbed, until the rice is tender, about 15–18 minutes. Add half the Parmesan and the saffron 1 minute before the rice is ready. Season with salt. ❧ Add the remaining butter just before serving and mix well. ❧ Serve with the remaining Parmesan passed separately.

MILANESE RISOTTO—THE DAY AFTER

In Milan, this was once the classic dish to order after an evening at the theater. It is prepared with leftover Milanese Risotto, so make a double quantity and serve this the next day.

Serves: 4

Preparation: 5'

Cooking: 10'

Level of difficulty: 2

- 1 quantity Milanese Risotto
- 4 tbsp butter
- 4 tbsp freshly grated Parmesan cheese

Melt a quarter of the butter in each of two 12 in (30 cm) skillets (frying pans). ❧ Divide the rice in two and flatten each portion to make 2 round cakes about 1-in (2.5-cm) thick. ❧ Cook them in the skillets over high heat for 5 minutes, until a crisp crust forms. ❧ Turn them (using a plate) and slip them back into the skillets in which you have melted the remaining butter. ❧ When both sides are crisp and golden brown, sprinkle with the Parmesan and cut each one in half. ❧ Serve hot.

ASPARAGUS RISOTTO

R inse the asparagus and trim the tough parts off the stalks. Cut the green tips into 2–3 pieces. ❧ Melt 3 tablespoons of butter in a deep skillet (frying pan). Add the onion and sauté for 1 minute; then add the asparagus and sauté for 5 minutes. ❧ Increase the heat to medium-high and add the rice. Cook for 2 minutes, stirring constantly. ❧ Stir in the wine and when this has been absorbed, begin stirring in the stock, ¹/₂ cup (125 ml) at a time. Cook and stir until each addition has been absorbed, until the rice is tender, about 15–18 minutes. ❧ Add the remaining butter and the Parmesan. Mix well. Season with salt and pepper. ❧ Serve hot.

Always use very fresh, tender young asparagus spears for this risotto.

Serves: 4

Preparation: 15'

Cooking: 25'

Level of difficulty: 2

- 1³/₄ lb/800 g **asparagus**
- 4 tbsp **butter**
- 1 small **onion**, finely chopped
- 2 cups/450 g **Italian Arborio rice**
- ¹/₂ cup/125 ml dry **white wine**
- 3 cups/750 ml *Beef Stock* (see page 140)
- 4 tbsp freshly grated **Parmesan cheese**
- **salt** and freshly ground **white pepper** to taste

BASIL & PARSLEY RISOTTO

Serves: 4

Preparation: 10'

Cooking: 25'

Level of difficulty: 1

- 2 tbsp finely chopped ox-bone marrow
- 2 tbsp butter
- 3 tbsp extra-virgin olive oil
- 2 cloves garlic, finely chopped
- 2 cups/450 g Italian Arborio rice
- 3 cups/750 ml *Beef Stock* (see page 140)
- 4 tbsp finely chopped basil,
- 4 tbsp finely chopped parsley,
- salt and freshly ground white pepper to taste
- 6 tbsp freshly grated Pecorino cheese

Dissolve the marrow in a deep skillet (frying pan) over low heat. ❧ Add the butter, oil, and garlic, and sauté for 1 minute. ❧ Increase the heat to medium-high and add the rice. Cook for 2 minutes, stirring constantly. ❧ Begin stirring in the stock, $^1/_2$ cup (125 ml) at a time. Cook and stir until each addition has been absorbed, until the rice is tender, about 15–18 minutes. ❧ A few minutes before the rice is ready, add the basil and parsley. ❧ Season with salt and pepper. Stir in the Pecorino and serve hot.

This fragrant recipe comes all the way from the Italian Riviera, near the French border.

RISOTTO WITH FENNEL

C lean the fennel bulbs and cut vertically into slices about $1/8$ in (3 mm) thick. ❧ Melt half the butter with the oil in a deep skillet (frying pan). Add the onion, celery, and fennel and sauté for 5–7 minutes. ❧ Increase the heat to medium-high and add the rice. Cook for 2 minutes, stirring constantly. ❧ Begin stirring in the stock, $1/2$ cup (125 ml) at a time. Cook and stir until each addition has been absorbed, until the rice is tender, about 15–18 minutes. ❧ Add the remaining butter and the Parmesan and mix well. ❧ Season with salt and pepper and serve hot.

Be sure to discard all the tough outer leaves from the fennel when making this delicately flavored risotto.

Serves: 4

Preparation: 15'

Cooking: 25'

Level of difficulty: 1

- • **4 medium fennel bulbs, cleaned**
- • **4 tbsp butter**
- • **2–3 tbsp extra-virgin olive oil**
- • **1 small onion, finely chopped**
- • **1 small stalk celery, finely chopped**
- • **2 cups/450 g Italian Arborio rice**
- • **3 cups/750 ml *Beef Stock* (see page 140)**
- • **4 tbsp freshly grated Parmesan cheese**
- • **salt and freshly ground white pepper to taste**

ORANGE RISOTTO

Peel the squash and remove the seeds and fibrous matter. Slice thinly. ❧ Heat half the butter with the oil in a deep skillet (frying pan). Add the squash, cover tightly, and cook over low heat until almost tender, about 15–20 minutes. ❧ Increase the heat to medium-high and add the rice. Cook for 2 minutes, stirring constantly. ❧ Stir in the wine and when this has been absorbed, begin stirring in the stock, $1/2$ cup (125 ml) at a time. Cook and stir until each addition has been absorbed, until the rice is tender, about 15–18 minutes. ❧ Season with salt and pepper. Remove from heat and stir in the remaining butter. Sprinkle with the Parmesan and serve hot.

Variation
• For added flavor, add a little grated nutmeg or a dash of cinnamon with the butter at the end.

Serves: 6
Preparation: 10'
Cooking: 40'
Level of difficulty: 1

- **2 lb/1 kg orange-fleshed squash or pumpkin**
- **7 tbsp butter**
- **4 tbsp extra-virgin olive oil**
- **2 cups/450 g Italian Arborio rice**
- **$1/2$ cup/125 ml dry white wine**
- **salt and freshly ground black pepper to taste**
- **3 cups/750 ml *Beef Stock* (see page 140)**
- **1 cup/150 g freshly grated Parmesan cheese**

RICE WITH PEAS & ARTICHOKES

Serves: 4

Preparation: 10'

Cooking: 25–30'

Level of difficulty: 1

- 4–5 baby artichokes or 12–16 defrosted frozen artichoke hearts
- 1 lemon
- 1 medium onion, thinly sliced
- 4 tbsp extra-virgin olive oil
- 1–2 cloves garlic, finely chopped
- 2 salted anchovies (rinsed and boned) or 4 anchovy fillets
- 1 cup/150 g peas, fresh or frozen
- salt and freshly ground black pepper to taste
- about 4 tbsp water
- 2 cups/450 g Italian Arborio rice
- about 4 tbsp boiling water
- 1/2 cup/60 g freshly grated Pecorino cheese

Strip the tough outer leaves off the artichokes and cut off the top third of the leaves. Remove any fuzzy choke and peel the remaining stalk, rubbing all the cut surfaces with lemon juice to prevent discoloration. Cut into quarters lengthwise. ✿ If using defrosted artichoke hearts, cut them in halves or quarters. ✿ Sauté the onion in the oil. Add the garlic, cook for 1 minute and then add the anchovies, crushing them with a fork so that they dissolve in the oil. ✿ Add the artichokes and peas. Season with salt and pepper and moisten with the first measure of water. Cover and cook until it has evaporated. ✿ Add the rice and stir for 1 minute, then add the boiling water and continue to cook, stirring frequently, and adding more water as necessary. ✿ When the rice is cooked *al dente*, serve at once, sprinkled with the cheese.

ARTICHOKE RISOTTO

Serves: 4

Preparation: 20'

Cooking: 30'

Level of difficulty: 2

- 6–8 artichokes, trimmed and sliced
- juice of 1 lemon
- 3 tbsp butter
- 1/2 small onion, finely chopped
- 2 cups/450 g Italian Arborio rice
- 3 cups/750 ml Beef Stock (see page 140)
- salt and freshly ground black pepper to taste
- 2 tbsp finely chopped parsley
- 4 tbsp freshly grated Parmesan cheese

S trip the tough outer leaves off the artichokes and cut off the top third of the leaves. Remove any fuzzy choke and peel the remaining stalk, rubbing all the cut surfaces with lemon juice to prevent discoloration. Cut into quarters lengthwise. ❧ Melt the butter in a deep skillet (frying pan). Add the onion and sauté for a few minutes. ❧ Drain the artichoke slices and add to the onion. Sauté for 5 minutes. ❧ Increase the heat to medium-high and add the rice. Cook for 2 minutes, stirring constantly. ❧ Begin stirring in the stock, 1/2 cup (125 ml) at a time. Cook and stir until each addition has been absorbed, until the rice is tender, about 15–18 minutes. ❧ Season with salt and pepper. Stir in the parsley and Parmesan, mix well, and serve.

SPINACH RISOTTO

Sauté the onion, celery, and leek in 2 tablespoons of butter in a deep skillet (frying pan) for 3–4 minutes over low heat. ❧ Add the spinach, stir well, and sauté for 2 minutes. ❧ Increase the heat to medium-high and add the rice. Cook for 2 minutes, stirring constantly. ❧ Begin stirring in the stock, ½ cup (125 ml) at a time. Cook and stir until each addition has been absorbed, until the rice is tender, about 15–18 minutes. ❧ Season with salt, pepper, and nutmeg, if liked. ❧ Add the remaining butter and Parmesan, mix well, and serve hot.

Variations

• If fresh spinach is not available, use 6 oz/180 g frozen spinach instead.

• Replace one-third of the Parmesan with 1 tablespoon of soft, fresh Ricotta cheese.

• Just before serving, add 2–3 tablespoons of cream to the risotto, in addition to, or instead of, the remaining butter.

Serves: 4

Preparation: 20'

Cooking: 25'

Level of difficulty: 2

- ♦ 1 small onion, finely chopped
- ♦ 1 celery stalk, cleaned and chopped
- ♦ 1 leek, cleaned and sliced (white part only)
- ♦ 3 tbsp butter
- ♦ 8 oz/250 g spinach, cleaned, cooked, squeezed dry, and finely chopped
- ♦ 2 cups/450 g Italian Arborio rice
- ♦ 5 cups/1.25 liters Beef Stock (see page 140)
- ♦ salt and freshly ground white pepper to taste
- ♦ dash of nutmeg (optional)
- ♦ 4 tbsp freshly grated Parmesan cheese

MUSHROOM RISOTTO

Serves: 4

Preparation: 30'

Cooking: 25–30'

Level of difficulty: 2

- 2 oz/60 g dried porcini mushrooms
- 1 cup/250 ml tepid water
- 4 tbsp extra-virgin olive oil
- 1 small onion, finely chopped
- ½ cup/125 ml dry white wine
- 2 cups/450 g Italian Arborio rice
- 4 cups/1 liter *Vegetable Stock* (see page 140)
- 2 tbsp finely chopped parsley
- salt to taste

Soak the mushrooms in the water for 30 minutes. Drain, reserving the water, and chop the mushrooms coarsely. ❧ Strain the mushroom water and set aside. ❧ Heat the oil in a deep skillet (frying pan). Add the onion and sauté over low heat until soft and translucent. ❧ Add the mushrooms and sauté for 2–3 minutes. ❧ Increase the heat to medium-high and add the rice. Cook for 2 minutes, stirring constantly. ❧ Stir in the wine and when this has been absorbed, add the mushroom water and stir until it has been absorbed. Begin stirring in the stock, ½ cup (125 ml) at a time. Cook and stir until each addition has been absorbed, until the rice is tender, about 15–18 minutes. ❧ Stir in the parsley just before the rice is cooked. ❧ Season with salt and serve hot.

Variation

• Add 2–3 tablespoons of freshly grated Parmesan cheese just before serving.

PEA RISOTTO

S hell the peas. Set aside and rinse the pods well. Boil the pods for 20–30 minutes in salted water. Drain and push through a fine sieve. ❧ Stir the pea pod puree into the stock in a large saucepan and keep hot. ❧ Sauté the bacon and onion in 4

This classic Venetian risotto should always be made with fresh spring peas.

tablespoons of butter in a deep skillet (frying pan). ❧ Increase the heat to medium-high and add the rice. Cook for 2 minutes, stirring constantly. ❧ Stir in the wine and when this has been absorbed, add the peas and cook for 3 minutes. Begin stirring in the stock, $^1/_2$ cup (125 ml) at a time. Cook and stir until each addition has been absorbed, until the rice is tender, about 15–18 minutes. ❧ Stir in the remaining butter and the Parmesan. Season to taste, sprinkle with the parsley, and serve hot.

Serves: 6

Preparation: 30'

Cooking: 50'

Level of difficulty: 1

- 2$^1/_3$ lb/1.3 kg peas in the pod
- 2 cups/500 ml *Beef or Chicken Stock* (see page 140)
- 6 tbsp butter
- 4 tbsp diced bacon
- 1 onion, finely chopped
- 2$^1/_4$ cups/500 g rice
- $^1/_2$ cup/125 ml dry white wine
- 1 cup/125 g freshly grated Parmesan cheese
- salt and freshly ground black pepper to taste
- 2 tbsp finely chopped parsley

HAZELNUT & MUSHROOM RISOTTO

Serves: 4

Preparation: 30'

Cooking: 30'

Level of difficulty: 1

- 6 oz/180 g whole hazelnuts
- 1 onion, chopped
- 1 clove garlic, chopped
- 1 fresh red chile, chopped
- 2 tbsp extra-virgin olive oil
- 1½ cups/300 g brown rice
- salt and freshly ground black pepper to taste
- 1 tsp lemon juice
- 4 cups/1 liter **Vegetable Stock** (see page 140)
- 2 oz/60 g white mushrooms, chopped

Preheat the oven to 350°F/180°C/gas 4 and toast the hazelnuts on a baking sheet for 15–20 minutes. ❧ Tip onto a clean cloth and rub off the skins. ❧ Chop the nuts coarsely and set aside. ❧ Sauté the onion, garlic, and chile in the oil in a deep skillet (frying pan) for about 5 minutes until soft. ❧ Increase the heat to medium-high and add the rice. Cook for 2 minutes, stirring constantly. ❧ Season with salt and pepper to taste and stir in the lemon juice. ❧ Begin stirring in the stock, ½ cup (125 ml) at a time. After about 10 minutes, add the mushrooms. Keep adding stock and cook and stir until each addition has been absorbed, until the rice is tender, about 15–18 minutes. ❧ Scatter with the nuts. Cover and set aside for 3–4 minutes before serving.

RISOTTO WITH MOZZARELLA

Sauté the onion in the butter in a deep skillet (frying pan) over medium heat for 3–4 minutes until soft and translucent. ❧ Increase the heat to medium-high and add the rice. Cook for 2 minutes, stirring constantly. ❧ Stir in the wine and when this has been absorbed, begin stirring in the stock, ½ cup (125 ml) at a time. ❧ After about 10 minutes, add half the cream, stir well and then add the other half. ❧ After 2–3 minutes add the Mozzarella. Keep adding stock and cook and stir until the rice is tender, about 15–18 minutes. ❧ Season with salt and pepper. ❧ Sprinkle with the Parmesan and serve hot.

Because of its delicate flavor, this recipe requires very fresh Mozzarella if it is to be a success.

Serves: 4
Preparation: 5'
Cooking: 20–25'
Level of difficulty: 1

- 1 small onion, finely chopped
- 2 tbsp butter
- 2 cups/450 g Italian Arborio rice
- ½ cup/125 ml dry white wine
- 3 cups/750 ml *Beef Stock* (see page 140)
- ⅔ cup/150 ml light/single cream
- 8 oz/250 g Mozzarella cheese, diced
- salt and freshly ground white pepper to taste
- 8 tbsp freshly grated Parmesan cheese

LEMON RISOTTO

Serves: 4

Preparation: 10'

Cooking: 25'

Level of difficulty: 1

- ¹/₂ **small onion, finely chopped**
- **4 tbsp extra-virgin olive oil**
- **2 cups/450 g Italian Arborio rice**
- ¹/₂ **cup/125 ml dry white wine**
- **3 cups/750 ml** *Beef Stock* **(see page 140)**
- **grated zest and juice of 1 large lemon**
- **salt and freshly ground white pepper to taste**
- **1 tbsp finely chopped parsley**

S auté the onion in the oil for 3–4 minutes over medium-low heat in a deep skillet (frying pan) until soft and translucent. ❦ Increase the heat to medium-high and add the rice. Cook for 2 minutes, stirring constantly. ❦ Stir in the wine and when this has been absorbed, begin stirring in the stock, ¹/₂ cup (125 ml) at a time. After about 10 minutes add the lemon zest. Add more stock and cook and stir until each addition has been absorbed, until the rice is tender, about 15–18 minutes. ❦ Season with salt and pepper. Stir in the lemon juice and parsley, and serve.

The flavor of this risotto does not go well with wine. Serve with cold, sparkling mineral water with wedges of lemon.

223

GORGONZOLA RISOTTO

Sauté the onion in the butter in a deep skillet (frying pan) over medium heat until soft and translucent. ☙ Increase the heat to medium-high and add the rice. Cook for 2 minutes, stirring constantly. ☙ Stir in the wine and when this has been absorbed, begin stirring in the stock, ¹/₂ cup (125 ml) at a time. Cook and stir until each addition has been absorbed, until the rice is tender, about 15–18 minutes. ☙ Add the Gorgonzola and mix well. Season with salt and pepper. Sprinkle with the Parmesan and serve.

Use a fresh, creamy Gorgonzola rather than a sharp blue cheese type for this recipe.

Variation
• Replace the Gorgonzola with the same quantity of well-ripened Taleggio; in this case, add half a finely chopped garlic clove and a dash of nutmeg to the onion before adding the rice.

Serves: 4

Preparation: 10'

Cooking: 25'

Level of difficulty: 1

- ¹/₂ **small onion, finely chopped**
- **2 tbsp butter**
- **2 cups/450 g Italian Arborio rice**
- **1 cup/250 ml dry white wine**
- **3 cups/750 ml *Beef Stock* (see page 140)**
- **8 oz/250 g Gorgonzola cheese, chopped**
- **salt and freshly ground black pepper to taste**
- **4 tbsp freshly grated Parmesan cheese**

ORIENTAL PORK RISOTTO

Serves: 4

Preparation: 15'

Cooking: 30–40'

Level of difficulty: 1

Cook the chops until tender in half the oil. Remove and keep warm. ❧ Drain the peaches and add 2–3 tablespoons of the syrup (reserving the rest) to the pan where the chops were cooked. ❧ Add the peaches and ginger. Cut the meat off the chops in small strips, add to the pan and leave on very low heat. ❧ Sauté the onion, bell pepper, cumin, and garlic in the remaining oil in a deep skillet (frying pan) for 4–5 minutes. ❧ Raise the heat slightly, add the rice and stir for 2 minutes. ❧ Pour in about half the reserved peach juice and stir for 2–3 minutes. ❧ Begin stirring in the stock, 1/2 cup (125 ml) at a time. Cook and stir until each addition has been absorbed, until the rice is tender, about 15–18 minutes. ❧ Remove from heat and season with salt and pepper. ❧ Transfer the risotto to a serving dish. ❧ Spoon the pork mixture over the top, garnish with the tomatoes, and serve.

- 4 lean pork chops
- 4 tbsp extra-virgin olive oil
- 14 oz/450 g canned peaches, chopped
- 2 tbsp stem ginger, finely chopped
- 1 medium onion, chopped
- 1 yellow bell pepper/capsicum, chopped
- 1 teaspoon cumin
- 1 clove garlic, finely chopped
- 2 cups/450 g short-grain rice
- 3 cups/750 ml *Beef Stock* (see page 140)
- salt and freshly ground black pepper to taste
- 10 cherry tomatoes, cut in half

Serves: 4

Preparation: 15'

Cooking: 25–30'

Level of difficulty: 1

- 1 onion, finely sliced
- 1 apple, peeled, cored, and diced
- 2 sticks celery, finely sliced
- 1 clove garlic, finely chopped
- 2 tsp medium curry powder
- 3 tbsp extra-virgin olive oil
- 2 cups/450 g Italian Arborio rice
- ⅔ cup/150 ml apple juice
- 3 cups/750 ml *Beef Stock* (see page 140)
- salt and freshly ground black pepper to taste
- 6 hard-boiled eggs, shelled and cut into 8, lengthwise
- 1 tbsp fresh cilantro /coriander, chopped

CURRIED EGG RISOTTO

In a large, heavy-bottomed pan saute the onion, apple, celery, garlic, and curry powder in the oil for about 5 minutes until the vegetables are soft. ❧ Increase the heat to medium-high and add the rice. Cook for 2 minutes, stirring constantly. ❧ Add the juice and stir for a further 2–3 minutes. ❧ Begin stirring in the stock, ½ cup (125 ml) at a time. Cook and stir until each addition has been absorbed, until the rice is tender, about 15–18 minutes. ❧ Remove from heat and season with salt and pepper. ❧ Transfer to a serving dish and arrange the eggs on top. ❧ Leave to stand in a warm place for 3–4 minutes. Garnish with the cilantro and serve.

RISOTTO
WITH BEANS

P lace the beans in a pot with the stock and half the salt pork. Cover and simmer over low heat for 50 minutes. ❧ Place the bacon and remaining salt pork in a deep skillet (frying pan) over low heat. When the fat has melted a little, add the onion and sauté for 5 minutes. ❧ Increase the heat to medium-high and add the rice. Cook for 2 minutes, stirring constantly. ❧ Stir in the wine and when this has been absorbed, begin stirring in the beans and their stock, 1/2 cup (125 ml) at a time. Cook and stir until each addition has been absorbed, until the rice is tender, about 15–18 minutes. ❧ Season with salt and pepper. ❧ Serve hot.

This is a hearty winter dish from northern Italy. Serve with plenty of pepper rather than grated cheese.

Serves: 4

Preparation: 30'

Cooking: 1 1/4 h

Level of difficulty: 2

- **2 1/2 cups/250 g fresh cranberry (or red kidney) beans, shelled**
- **3 cups/750 ml *Vegetable Stock* (see page 140)**
- **1/2 cup/125 g finely chopped salt pork/lard**
- **4 tbsp finely chopped bacon**
- **1 small onion, finely chopped**
- **2 cups/450 g Italian Arborio rice**
- **1 cup/250 ml robust red wine**
- **salt and freshly ground white or black pepper to taste**

Variation
• If using dry beans, soak in cold water for 10–12 hours, then cook slowly with the salt pork for 1–2 hours.

CREAMY LENTIL RISOTTO

S auté the onion and garlic in the butter and oil in a deep skillet (frying pan) over medium heat until soft and translucent. ❧ Increase the heat to medium-high and add the rice. Cook for 2 minutes, stirring constantly. ❧ Begin stirring in the stock, ¹/₂ cup (125 ml) at a time. After about 10 minutes add the drained lentils. Add more stock and cook and stir until each addition has been absorbed, until the rice is tender, about 15–18 minutes. ❧ Add the cheese and season with salt and pepper. Mix well and serve hot.

Variation
• Add 1 tablespoon of tomato paste with the lentils.

Serves: 4
Preparation: 10'
Cooking: 20–25'
Level of difficulty: 1

- **1 small onion, finely chopped**
- **1 clove garlic, finely chopped**
- **2 tbsp butter**
- **3 tbsp extra-virgin olive oil**
- **2 cups/450 g Italian Arborio rice**
- **3 cups/750 ml *Beef Stock* (see page 140)**
- **14 oz/400 g canned lentils**
- **4 tbsp freshly grated Pecorino cheese**
- **salt and freshly ground white or black pepper to taste**

RISOTTO WITH JOHN DORY

Eviscerate (gut) and clean the fish. ❧ Place the fish in a large saucepan with the carrot, celery, and onion. Add sufficient cold water to cover. Heat the water slowly and simmer for 30 minutes. Strain the stock, reserving the onion. ❧ Sauté the parsley and garlic for 4–5 minutes in half the butter and half the olive oil in a deep skillet (frying pan). ❧ Increase the heat to medium-high and add the rice. Cook for 2 minutes, stirring constantly. ❧ Begin stirring in the fish stock, $^1/_2$ cup (125 ml) at a time. Cook and stir until each addition has been absorbed, until the rice is tender, about 15–18 minutes. ❧ Sauce: Finely chop the reserved onion and sauté in the remaining butter and oil. ❧ Add the tomatoes and $^3/_4$ cup (180 ml) of the fish stock. Simmer over low heat for 10 minutes. ❧ Season with salt, drizzle over the risotto, and serve.

Serve the fish with the risotto as a meal in itself, or reserve and serve later as the main course.

Serves: 4–6

Preparation: 1 h

Cooking: 1 h

Level of difficulty: 2

- 1 large John Dory/ St. Peter's fish, weighing about 2 lb/1 kg
- 1 carrot
- 1 stalk celery
- 1 large onion, peeled
- 1 cup/20 g parsley, finely chopped
- 1 clove garlic, finely chopped
- 6 tbsp butter
- 6 tbsp extra-virgin olive oil
- 2 cups/450 g Italian Arborio rice
- 1 cup/250 ml canned tomatoes

FISH RISOTTO

Serves: 6

Preparation: 30'

Cooking: 40'

Level of difficulty: 1

- 1 sea bass, about 1³/₄ lb/800 g
- 10 black peppercorns
- 1 garlic clove, peeled and whole
- 1 bay leaf
- 1 shallot, finely chopped
- 4 tbsp extra-virgin olive oil
- 6 tbsp butter
- 2 cups/450 g Italian Arborio rice
- ¹/₂ cup/125 ml dry white wine
- 1 cup/100 g freshly grated Parmesan cheese
- salt to taste

Eviscerate (gut) and clean the fish. ❧ Place in a large saucepan with the peppercorns and enough cold water to cover. Bring slowly to a boil and simmer for 10 minutes. ❧ Drain the fish and remove its head, bones, and skin. Break up the flesh into small pieces. ❧ Return the head, bones, and skin to the saucepan. Add the garlic and bay leaf and boil until the liquid has reduced considerably. ❧ Sauté the shallot in the oil and half the butter in a deep skillet (frying pan). Add the pieces of fish and the rice. ❧ Pour in a little of the strained fish stock and continue cooking and adding stock until the rice is almost done. ❧ Add the wine, let it evaporate, then remove from the heat. ❧ Stir in the remaining butter and sprinkle with Parmesan. Serve hot.

233

BLACK RISOTTO WITH INK SQUID

To clean the ink squid, detach the head from the body by grasping the two parts with your hands and tugging sharply. The insides and two sacs will come out attached to the head. Carefully separate the ink sacs from the squid (discarding the yellow ones). Set the dark ones aside in a cup with 2–3 tablespoons of cold water. Discard the eyes and the beak at the base of the tentacles. Open the body at the side with kitchen scissors and extract the bone. Rinse the body and head well and cut into $1^1/4$-in (3-cm) strips. ❧ Heat the onion, garlic, parsley, and squid in the oil in a deep skillet (frying pan). Cover and cook for 15 minutes over low heat, stirring frequently. ❧ Add the tomato paste, wine, and $1/2$ cup (125 ml) boiling water, and cook over low heat for 20–40 minutes. Test the squid with a fork after 20 minutes; if it is tender, go on to the next stage. If squid is cooked for too long it becomes tough. ❧ Cut the ink sacs with scissors and collect the ink in a bowl, diluting with 2 cups (500 ml) of cold water. ❧ Pour the black liquid into the saucepan, raise the heat slightly, and bring to a boil. ❧ Cook for 5 minutes then add the rice. ❧ Continue cooking, stirring continuously, and adding more boiling water as required until the rice is cooked. ❧ Season with salt and pepper and serve hot.

Serves: 4

Preparation: 25'

Cooking: $1^1/2$ h

Level of difficulty: 2

- **2 fresh ink squid, weighing about $1^1/2$ lb/750 g**
- **1 small onion, finely chopped**
- **1 clove garlic, finely chopped**
- **1 tbsp finely chopped parsley**
- **6 tbsp extra-virgin olive oil**
- **1 tbsp tomato paste**
- **$1/2$ cup/125 ml dry white wine**
- **2 cups/450 g Italian Arborio rice**
- **salt and freshly ground white pepper to taste**

If possible, get your fish vendor to clean the squid. Make sure the ink sacs are set aside without being broken.

RISOTTO WITH WINE AND SMOKED SALMON

Sauté the onion, leek, and garlic in the oil for 4–5 minutes in a deep skillet (frying pan). Increase the heat to medium-high and add the rice. Cook for 2 minutes, stirring constantly. Add the wine and stir for 3–4 minutes. Begin stirring in the stock, ½ cup (125 ml) at a time. Cook and stir until each addition has been absorbed, until the rice is tender, about 15–18 minutes. Remove from heat and season with salt and pepper. Stir the salmon and Parmesan into the risotto. Cover the pan and let stand for 3–4 minutes before serving.

Serves: 4

Preparation: 10'

Cooking: 25'

Level of difficulty: 1

- 1 onion and 1 leek, medium-sized, finely sliced
- 2 cloves garlic, finely chopped
- 2 tbsp extra-virgin olive oil
- 2 cups/450 g Italian Arborio rice
- 1 cup/250 ml dry white wine
- 3 cups/750 ml *Vegetable Stock* (see page 140)
- salt and freshly ground black pepper to taste
- 5 oz/150 g smoked salmon slices, diced
- 8 tbsp freshly grated Parmesan cheese

RICE PATTIES

Serves: 4

Preparation: 15'

Cooking: 20'

Level of difficulty: 1

- 1¼ cups/250 g rice
- 2 cups/500 ml milk
- 1 cup/250 ml water
- ½ cup/125 g ham, finely chopped
- 4 tbsp grated Parmesan cheese
- 1 tbsp finely chopped parsley
- 4 tbsp fresh bread crumbs
- 1 egg, beaten
- salt and freshly ground black pepper to taste
- 2 tbsp flour, 1 beaten egg, and ½ cup/ 200 g dry bread crumbs
- 8 tbsp olive oil, for frying
- 1 quantity Basic Tomato Sauce (see page 932)

Place the rice, milk, and water in a large saucepan, bring to a boil and simmer for about 15 minutes, or until the rice is tender. Stir occasionally to stop the rice sticking to the bottom of the pan. ❧ Drain off any milk residue and transfer to a large bowl with the ham, cheese, parsley, and fresh bread crumbs. Stir in one egg and seasonings. ❧ Combine well and form into small patties. ❧ Dredge in the flour, dip in the beaten egg, and roll in the bread crumbs. ❧ Heat the oil in a heavy-bottomed pan and fry the patties on both sides until golden brown. ❧ Drain on kitchen paper and place in an ovenproof serving dish. ❧ Heat the Basic Tomato Sauce and pour over the patties. ❧ Serve hot.

Use any leftover cooked meat instead of the ham. These patties are also good cold.

RISOTTO WITH PANCETTA & PARMA HAM

Melt the butter in a deep skillet (frying pan), add the onion and sauté for 1 minute. Add the pancetta and sauté over low heat until the onion is soft. ❧ Increase the heat to medium-high and add the rice. Cook for 2 minutes, stirring constantly. ❧ Stir in the wine and when this has been absorbed, begin stirring in the stock, ¹/₂ cup (125 ml) at a time. Cook and stir until each addition has been absorbed, until the rice is tender, about 15–18 minutes. ❧ Just before the rice is cooked, add the nutmeg, salt, pepper, Parma ham, cream, and Parmesan, mixing carefully to combine the ingredients well. ❧ Serve hot.

Variation
• Replace the Parmesan with the same amount of Emmental, Scamorza, or another similar type of cheese, in flakes or shavings.

Serves: 4

Preparation: 15'

Cooking: 25–30'

Level of difficulty: 2

• 3 tbsp butter
• 1 small onion, finely chopped
• 4 tbsp diced pancetta
• 2 cups/450 g Italian Arborio rice
• ¹/₂ cup/125 ml dry white wine
• 3 cups/750 ml *Beef Stock* (see page 140)
• dash of nutmeg
• salt and freshly ground white pepper to taste
• ¹/₂ cup/75 g diced Parma ham
• 6 tbsp cream
• 4 tbsp freshly grated Parmesan cheese

CHICKEN RISOTTO

Serves: 6

Preparation: 20'

Cooking: 1 h

Level of difficulty: 1

- **1 chicken, weighing about 2¹⁄₂ lb/1.25 kg, cut in 6 pieces**
- **2 quarts/2 liters *Chicken Stock* (see page 140)**
- **2 onions**
- **2 carrots**
- **2 stalks celery**
- **4 tbsp extra-virgin olive oil**
- **6 tbsp butter**
- **2 cups/450 g Italian Arborio rice**
- **¹⁄₂ cup/125 ml dry white wine**
- **1 cup/200 g freshly grated Parmesan cheese**
- **salt and freshly ground black pepper to taste**

R inse and dry the chicken. ❧ Bring the stock to a boil with 1 onion, 1 carrot, and 1 stalk of celery. ❧ Simmer while you chop the remaining vegetables finely, then sauté gently in the oil and half the butter in a deep skillet (frying pan). ❧ Add the chicken and brown lightly. Continue cooking, moistening with some of the hot chicken stock at intervals, until the chicken is nearly done. ❧ Add the rice and stir. ❧ Stir in the wine and when this has been absorbed, begin stirring in the stock, ¹⁄₂ cup (125 ml) at a time. Cook and stir until each addition has been absorbed, until the rice is tender, about 15–18 minutes. ❧ Stir in the remaining butter and season with salt and pepper. Sprinkle with Parmesan and serve hot.

Another version entails taking the chicken flesh off the bone and cutting it into small pieces before cooking.

RICE⚡STUFFED TOMATOES

Preheat the oven to 400°F/200°C/gas 6. 🐾 Rinse the tomatoes and dry well. Cut the top off each tomato (with its stalk) and set aside. Scoop out the pulp with a teaspoon and place in a bowl. Place the tomato shells upside down on a chopping board to drain for 5 minutes. 🐾 Combine the rice, tomato pulp, garlic, parsley, 2 tablespoons of the oil, and salt. Sprinkle the tomato shells lightly with salt and fill with the rice mixture. Cover with the tomato tops and place in an ovenproof dish. 🐾 Drizzle with the water and the remaining oil. 🐾 Bake in a preheated oven at for about 30 minutes, or until the rice is tender.

Serve hot or at room temperature as an appetizer, a light lunch, or a main course.

Variation
• Add a few coarsely chopped olives and capers to the rice mixture.

Serves: 4

Preparation: 15'

Cooking: 30'

Level of difficulty: 2

• **8 medium ripe tomatoes**
• **³/₄ cup/150 g cooked short-grain rice**
• **2 cloves garlic, finely chopped**
• **1 tbsp finely chopped parsley**
• **5 tbsp extra-virgin olive oil**
• **salt to taste**
• **3 tbsp water**

BROWN RICE WITH UNCOOKED TOMATO SAUCE

Serves: 4

Preparation: 25'

Cooking: 45'

Level of difficulty: 1

- 2 cups/450 g brown rice
- 1 lb/500 g firm, ripe tomatoes
- 5 tbsp extra-virgin olive oil
- 1 small red salad onion, thinly sliced
- 1 clove garlic, finely chopped
- generous dash of oregano or sweet marjoram
- 8 fresh basil leaves, torn
- salt and freshly ground black pepper to taste

Cook the rice in 2 quarts/2 liters of boiling, salted water, stirring once or twice. It will be cooked in about 45 minutes. ❧ Wash the tomatoes and cut them in half. Leave

The nutty taste of the brown rice works very well with the fresh tang of the raw tomatoes.

upside down in a colander to drain for about 20 minutes. ❧ Chop the tomatoes coarsely and transfer to a bowl. ❧ Add 3 tablespoons of the oil, the onion, garlic, oregano or marjoram, basil, salt, and pepper. Mix well. ❧ When the rice is done, drain thoroughly, and transfer to a large bowl (a wooden bowl is very attractive with the brown tones of the rice). ❧ Pour the remaining oil over the rice and toss vigorously. ❧ Add the tomato and herb mixture, toss carefully, and serve.

Variations

• Add a handful each of diced Mozzarella cheese and large black olives to the salad before serving.

• Crumble 2 anchovy fillets into the tomato sauce with the herbs.

• Add 1 tablespoon of small salted capers to the tomato sauce.

RICE WITH FOUR CHEESES

Serves: 4

Preparation: 15'

Cooking: 30–35'

Level of difficulty: 1

P reheat the oven to 375°F/190°C/gas 5. ❧ Cook the rice in a large pan of salted, boiling water for 10–12 minutes, or until just tender. Drain briefly (it should still be moist) and place in a bowl. ❧ Mix the rice with half the butter, three-quarters of the Parmesan, a dash of nutmeg (if liked), salt, and white pepper. ❧ Melt 1 tablespoon of the butter in a deep skillet (frying pan). Add the rice and cook, stirring continuously, for 3–4 minutes over medium heat. ❧ Transfer one-third of the rice to a greased, deep ovenproof dish. Sprinkle this first rice layer with half each of the Fontina, Gruyère, and Provolone cheeses. Cover with half the remaining rice and sprinkle with the remaining cheeses. ❧ Top with a final layer of rice and sprinkle with the remaining Parmesan. Melt the remaining butter and drizzle over the rice. ❧ Bake for 15–20 minutes.

This recipe comes from Piedmont, in northern Italy, where Tagliatelle is also be prepared in this way.

- **2 cups/450 g Italian Arborio rice**
- **6 tbsp butter, cut up**
- **$1/2$ cup/75 g Parmesan cheese, grated**
- **freshly grated nutmeg (optional)**
- **salt and freshly grated white pepper to taste**
- **$1/2$ cup/75 g Fontina cheese, grated**
- **$1/2$ cup/75 g Gruyère cheese, grated**
- **$1/2$ cup/75 g Provolone cheese, grated**

Serves: 4

Preparation: 15'

Cooking: 25'

Level of difficulty: 1

- **1 quantity *Pesto* (see page 164)**
- **salt and freshly ground black pepper to taste**
- **2 cups/400 g short-grain rice**
- **2 cups/400 g fresh or frozen peas**
- **4 tbsp butter**
- **1/2 cup/75 g diced bacon**
- **1 large onion, finely chopped**
- **1 tbsp each finely chopped parsley and thyme**
- **8 tbsp freshly grated Parmesan cheese**

RICE WITH PEAS & PESTO

P repare the Pesto. ❧ Bring a large pot of salted water to the boil and add the rice and peas. Cook for 12–15 minutes, or until the rice is tender. ❧ Heat half the butter in a large skillet (frying pan) and sauté the bacon and onion over medium heat for 5 minutes, or until the onion is soft. ❧ Lower the heat and add the parsley and thyme. Cook for 2–3 more minutes. ❧ Drain the rice and peas and add to the skillet together with 2 tablespoons of the cooking water. Stir until well mixed. ❧ Stir in the remaining butter, the Pesto, Parmesan, and pepper. Serve hot.

BREAD

Making Bread at Home

The art of bread-making stretches back into the mists of time to when our ancestors first learned to harvest wild cereals and to pound them into flour. Despite this antiquity, or perhaps because of it, there is a lot of satisfaction to be had from the simple act of combining yeast and flour to make a "living" dough and in kneading it, knowing that the warmth of our hands helps it to rise and grow. The wonderful aroma of freshly baked bread filling our kitchens and the delight of family and friends when we offer them slices of crusty fresh bread are also powerful rewards for this ancient art.

Yeast
Yeast for making bread is available in two forms: active dry and fresh (compressed). Active dry yeast is sold in packages weighing $1/4$ oz (7.5 g) each.

Flour
Wheat flour is the most suitable flour for bread making because it develops an elastic protein called gluten that gives bread its structure. Almost all the recipes in this chapter can be made using all-purpose (plain) flour. Where other flour is required, it has been indicated in the recipes.

Preparing the yeast
You will need a small bowl, a wooden spoon, warm water, and a little sugar. Exact quantities are given in each recipe.

2

1 Put the yeast in a small bowl. If using fresh yeast, crumble it with your fingertips.

2 Add the sugar and 6 tablespoons of warm water (or other liquid.) Stir until the yeast has dissolved.

3 Set the mixture aside for about 10 minutes. It will look creamy when ready. Stir again before proceeding to make the dough.

3

1

Preparing the dough

Use a bowl, flour, salt, the yeast mixture, a wooden spoon, and the remaining water. Some recipes use slightly different ingredients.

1 Place the flour in a mixing bowl and sprinkle with the

salt. Make a hollow in the center and pour in the yeast mixture, the remaining water, and any other ingredients listed in the recipe. Use a wooden spoon to stir the mixture. Stir until the flour has almost all been absorbed.

2 The dough will be a rough and shaggy ball in the bottom of the bowl. Sprinkle a work surface, preferably made of wood, with a little flour. Note that the flour used to prepare the work surface

is not included in the quantities given in the recipes. You will need about ¹/₂ cup (75 g) extra for this. Transfer the dough to the work surface. Curl your fingers around it and press it together to form a compact ball.

3 Press down on the dough with your knuckles to spread it a little. Take the far end of the dough, fold it a short distance toward you, then push it away again with the heel of your palm. Flexing your wrist, fold it toward you again, give it a quarter turn, then push it away. Repeat these motions, gently and with the lightest possible touch, for about 8–10 minutes. When the dough is firm and no longer sticks to your hands or the work surface, lift it up and bang it down hard against the work surface a couple of times. This will develop the gluten. When ready, the dough should be smooth and elastic. It should show definite air bubbles beneath the surface and should spring back if you flatten it with your palm.

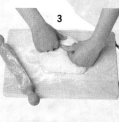

4 Place the kneaded dough in a large clean bowl and cover with a cloth. Most of the breads in this book have two rising times. The dough should double in volume during rising. To test whether it has risen sufficiently, poke your finger gently into the dough;

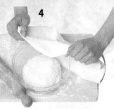

if the impression remains, then the dough is ready. The rising times given in each recipe are approximate; remember that yeast is a living ingredient and is affected by air temperature and humidity, among other things. Some days it will take longer to rise than others.

WHITE BREAD

Makes: about 2 lb/
1 kg of bread

Preparation: 30'

Rising time: 2 h

Cooking: 25–40'

Level of difficulty: 2

* 1 oz/30 g fresh
  yeast or 2 ($^1/_4$ oz)
  packages active
  dry yeast
* 1 tsp sugar
* about 1$^1/_3$ cups/
  350 ml lukewarm
  water
* 5 cups/750 g all-
  purpose/plain flour
* 1–2 tsp salt

Use the first 3 ingredients to prepare the yeast as explained on page 250. ❧ Place the flour in a large bowl with the yeast mixture, salt, and remaining water, and prepare the dough as shown on page 251. ❧ When the rising time has elapsed (about 1$^1/_2$ hours), use a spatula to transfer the dough to a lightly floured work surface. Knead for several minutes. ❧ Place the dough on an oiled baking sheet and shape it into an oval or elongated loaf. ❧ Sprinkle the surface with flour and, using a serrated knife, make 5 or 6 diagonal slashes about $^1/_2$ in (1 cm) deep along the top of the loaf. ❧ For a large, ring-shaped loaf about 12 in (30 cm) in diameter, gently flatten the dough and make a hole in the middle with your fingers. Carefully enlarge the hole, shaping the dough into a ring. ❧ To make rolls, divide the dough into 8–10 equal portions and shape them into long rolls. Remember that the volume of the dough will double during rising, so position the rolls at least 1$^1/_2$ in (4 cm) apart. ❧ Cover with a cloth and set aside to rise for about 30 minutes. ❧ Preheat the oven to 450°F/230°C/gas 7. ❧ Bake the large loaves for about 40 minutes, the ring-shaped loaf for about 30 minutes, and the rolls for about 25 minutes.

RYE BREAD

Use the first 3 ingredients to prepare the yeast as explained on page 250. ❧ Combine both flours in a large bowl with the fennel seeds, salt, yeast mixture, oil (or lard), and the remaining water, and prepare the dough as shown on page 251. ❧ When the rising time has elapsed (about 2 hours), use a spatula to transfer the dough to a lightly floured work surface and knead for 2–3 minutes. The dough should be quite soft. ❧ Divide into 4–6 equal portions and shape into round loaves. Transfer to two oiled baking sheets. Cover with a cloth and set aside to rise for about 1 hour. ❧ Preheat the oven to 400°F/200°C/ gas 6. ❧ Bake for 30 minutes, or until well browned and hollow-sounding when tapped on the bottom.

Makes: about 2 lb/ 1 kg of bread

Preparation: 30'

Rising time: 3 h

Cooking: 30'

Level of difficulty: 2

- 1 oz/30 g fresh yeast or 2 (¹/₄ oz) packages active dry yeast
- 1 tsp sugar
- about 1¹/₄ cups/ 300 ml lukewarm water
- 3 cups/450 g rye flour
- 1¹/₃ cups/200 g all-purpose/plain flour
- 1 tbsp fennel seeds
- 2 tsp salt
- 2 tbsp extra-virgin olive oil or lard, at room temperature

WALNUT & ROSEMARY BREAD

Makes: about 2 lb/
1 kg of bread

Preparation: 25'

Rising time: 2 h

Cooking: 45'

Level of difficulty: 2

- 1 oz/30 g fresh yeast or 2 (¹/₄ oz) packages active dry yeast
- 1 tsp sugar
- about 1¹/₂ cups/ 325 ml lukewarm water
- 2 cups/300 g all-purpose/plain flour
- 3 cups/450 g whole-wheat flour
- 1 tbsp fresh chopped or 1 tsp dried rosemary
- 1–2 tsp salt
- 2 tbsp extra-virgin olive oil
- 1 clove garlic, finely chopped
- 2 oz/60 g walnuts, coarsely chopped
- ¹/₂ tsp freshly ground black pepper

Use the first 3 ingredients to prepare the yeast as explained on page 250. ☙ Combine both flours with the rosemary and salt in a large bowl. ☙ Stir half the oil into the yeast mixture then gradually stir it into the flours. Prepare the dough as shown on page 251. ☙ Meanwhile, sauté the garlic in the remaining oil in a small skillet (frying pan) over medium heat. Stir in the walnuts and pepper. Remove from heat and set aside to cool. ☙ When the rising time has elapsed (about 1¹/₂ hours), use a spatula to transfer the dough to a lightly floured work surface. ☙ Roll the dough into a 12-in (30-cm) disk. Spread the walnut mixture over the top then fold the dough over it. Knead for 3 minutes to distribute the walnuts evenly. ☙ Shape the dough into ball and place on an oiled baking sheet. Cover with a cloth and set aside to rise for about 30 minutes. It should almost double in bulk. ☙ Preheat the oven to 375°F/190°C/gas 5. ☙ Bake for about 45 minutes, or until the bread is golden brown and hollow-sounding when tapped on the bottom.

This nourishing bread makes a healthy after-school snack for hungry children.

MEDITERRANEAN CORN BREAD

Use the first 3 ingredients to prepare the yeast as explained on page 250, using 6 tablespoons of the milk instead of water. ❧ Combine both flours in a large bowl with the salt, egg, yeast mixture, and remaining milk, and prepare the dough as shown on page 251. ❧ When the rising time has elapsed (about 1 hour), transfer the dough to a lightly floured work surface and knead for 2–3 minutes. ❧ Divide the dough in half and shape into two round loaves. Sprinkle with flour and transfer to an oiled baking sheet. ❧ Cover with a cloth and set aside to rise for 30 minutes. ❧ Preheat the oven to 400°F/200°C/gas 6. ❧ Bake for about 30 minutes, or until golden brown and hollow sounding when tapped on the bottom.

Makes: about 1¹/₂ lb/ 750 g bread
Preparation: 30'
Rising time: 1¹/₂ h
Cooking: 30'
Level of difficulty: 2

- 1¹/₂ oz/45 g fresh yeast or 3 (¹/₄ oz) packages active dry yeast
- 1 tsp sugar
- about 1 cup/250 ml warm milk
- 2 cups/300 g all-purpose/plain flour
- 2 cups/300 g finely ground cornmeal
- 2 tsp salt
- 1 egg, lightly beaten

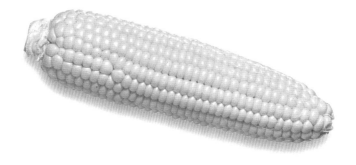

IRISH SODA BREAD

Preheat the oven to 400°F/200°C/gas 6. ❧ Place both flours, baking soda, cream of tartar, and salt in a large bowl (tipping in the bran from the whole-wheat flour that won't go through the sifter). ❧ Make a well in the center and pour in enough of the milk to obtain a soft but not sloppy dough. ❧ Knead lightly on a floured surface for 2–3 minutes, then form into an oval or round loaf. ❧ Place on a baking sheet. Bake for 15 minutes, then drop the oven temperature to 350°F/180°C/gas 4 and bake for 15 more minutes, or until lightly browned and hollow-sounding when tapped on the bottom. ❧ Tip out onto a rack and wrap in a clean cloth until ready to serve.

Makes: 1 small loaf
Preparation: 15'
Cooking: 30'
Level of difficulty: 1

- **1 1/3 cups/200 g all-purpose/plain white flour**
- **1 cup/150 g whole-wheat flour**
- **1/2 tsp baking soda**
- **1/2 tsp cream of tartar**
- **1/2 tsp salt**
- **about 1 cup/250 ml lukewarm milk**

WHEATGERM BREAD

*Makes: about 2 lb/
   1 kg bread*

Preparation: 20'

Rising time: 1¹/₂ h

Cooking: 30'

Level of difficulty: 2

- **1 oz/30 g fresh yeast or 2 (¹/₄ oz) packages active dry yeast**
- **1 tsp sugar**
- **about 1¹/₂ cups/ 325 ml warm water**
- **2 tbsp butter**
- **4 cups/600 g whole-wheat flour**
- **6 oz/180 g wheatgerm**
- **1–2 tsp salt**
- **2 tsp malt extract**
- **1 egg, beaten**

U se the first 3 ingredients to prepare the yeast as explained on page 250. ✿ Place the flour, wheatgerm, salt, and malt extract in a large bowl and cut in the butter. ✿ Make a well in the center and stir in the yeast mixture and enough of the remaining water to form a soft dough. Prepare the dough as shown on page 251. ✿ When the rising time has elapsed (about 1 hour), transfer the dough to a lightly floured work surface and knead for 2–3 minutes. ✿ Place the dough in two greased 1 lb (500 g) loaf pans. Let rise for about 30 minutes, or until the dough rises just above the tops of the pans. ✿ Preheat the oven to 450°F/230°C/gas 7. ✿ Brush the loaves with the egg and bake for about 30 minutes, or until golden brown and hollow-sounding when tapped on the bottom.

PARMESAN BREAD

Makes: about 1½ lb/
750 g bread

Preparation: 40'

Rising time: 2 h

Cooking: 30'

Level of difficulty: 2

- 1 oz/30 g fresh
  yeast or 2 (¼ oz)
  packages active
  dry yeast
- 2 tsp sugar
- about 1½ cups/
  325 ml warm water
- 3 cups/450 g all-
  purpose/plain flour
- 2½ oz/75 g nonfat
  dry milk
- 5 oz/150 g freshly
  grated Parmesan
  cheese
- 1 tsp salt
- 1 tsp ground
  cayenne pepper
- 1 egg, beaten
- 3 tbsp extra-virgin
  olive oil
- 1 tbsp spicy
  ketchup
- 1 egg white, lightly
  beaten

Use the first 3 ingredients to prepare the yeast as explained on page 250. ❧ Place the flour, dry milk, all but 2 tablespoons of the cheese, salt, and pepper in a large bowl. Add the egg, 1 tablespoon of the oil, the ketchup, yeast mixture, and enough of the water to obtain a firm, kneadable dough. Knead as shown on page 251. Place the dough in a large bowl oiled with the remaining oil. Turn the dough in the bowl so that it is well-coated. Let rise. ❧ When the rising time has elapsed (about 1½ hours), transfer the dough to a lightly floured work surface and knead for 2–3 minutes. ❧ Divide the dough in half to form 2 balls and place them on an oiled baking sheet. Cover with a cloth and leave to rise for about 30 minutes, or until the dough doubles in bulk. Preheat the oven to 350°F/180°C/gas 4. ❧ Brush the loaves with the egg white, sprinkle with the remaining cheese, and bake for about 30 minutes, or until golden brown and hollow-sounding when tapped on the bottom.

BREADSTICKS

U se the first 3 ingredients to prepare the yeast as explained on page 250. ❧ Combine the flour in a bowl with the salt, yeast mixture, and remaining water, and prepare the dough as shown on page 251. ❧ When the rising time has elapsed (about 1 hour), transfer the dough to a lightly floured work surface and knead for 2–3 minutes. ❧ Divide the dough into portions about the size of an egg, and shape into sticks about the thickness of your little finger. ❧ Sprinkle with flour and transfer to three oiled baking sheets, keeping them a finger's width apart. ❧ Cover with a cloth and let rise for 1 hour. ❧ Preheat the oven to 450°F/ 230°C/gas 7. ❧ Bake for 5 minutes, or until golden brown. ❧ Leave to cool before removing from the sheets.

Makes: about 1 lb/ 500 g breadsticks

Preparation: 30'

Rising time: 2 h

Cooking: 5'

Level of difficulty: 2

• ³/₄ oz/25 g fresh yeast or 1¹/₂ (¹/₄ oz) packages active dry yeast

• 1 tsp sugar

• about 1 cup/250 ml lukewarm water

• 3 cups/450 g all-purpose/plain flour

• 1 tsp salt

Variations

• Use whole-wheat flour instead of white, or a mixture of the two.

• Add 2–3 tablespoons of extra-virgin olive oil to the dough. Reduce the amount of water proportionally. The breadsticks will be even tastier and crisper. Increase the amount of compressed yeast in the recipe to 1 oz (30 g) or 2 (¹/₄ oz) packages of active dry yeast.

• Replace the water with milk partially or totally.

SWEET RAISIN BREAD

U se the first 3 ingredients to prepare the yeast as explained on page 250. ❧ Soak the raisins in a bowl of warm water for 10 minutes. Drain, dry well, and sprinkle lightly with flour. ❧ Put the flour, raisins, lemon zest, and sugar in a large bowl. Stir in the yeast mixture and butter. ❧ Combine the remaining water with the milk and stir enough of the mixture into the flour to obtain a firm dough. Knead the dough as shown on page 251. ❧ When the rising time has elapsed (1 hour), transfer to a lightly floured work surface and knead for 2–3 minutes. ❧ Shape into two loaves and place on an oiled baking sheet. Leave to rise for 45 minutes. ❧ Bake in a preheated oven at 400°F/ 200°C/gas 6 for 30 minutes, and hollow-sounding when tapped on the bottom.

Makes:	about 2 lb/ 1 kg bread
Preparation:	30'
Rising time:	1³/₄ h
Cooking:	5'
Level of difficulty:	2

- 1 oz/30 g fresh yeast or 2 (¹/₄ oz) packages active dry yeast
- 1¹/₂ oz/45 g sugar
- about ¹/₂ cup/125 ml warm water
- 5 oz/150 g seedless raisins
- 5 cups/750 g all-purpose/plain flour
- grated zest of 1 lemon
- 4 tbsp butter, melted
- ¹/₂ cup/125 ml milk

HERB ROLLS

Makes: 24 rolls

Preparation: 20'

Rising time: 1¹⁄₄ h

Cooking: 20'

Level of difficulty: 2

- 1 oz/30 g fresh yeast or 2 (¹⁄₄ oz) packages active dry yeast
- 1 tbsp sugar
- about 1¹⁄₄ cups/ 300 ml warm water
- 2 tbsp dried herbs (mixed tarragon, chervil, sage, marjoram, thyme, parsley, and basil)
- 1 tsp dried lavender flowers
- 4 tbsp extra-virgin olive oil
- 5 cups/750 g all-purpose/plain flour
- 1 tbsp salt
- ¹⁄₂ cup/125 ml muscat dessert wine

U se the first 3 ingredients to prepare the yeast as explained on page 250. ❧ In a large bowl, combine half the flour with the salt and herbs. Make a well in the center and pour in the yeast mixture, remaining water, wine, and half the oil. Mix well, then add enough of the remaining flour to obtain a medium dough. ❧ Knead as shown on page 251. ❧ Place in a bowl greased with the remaining oil, turning until well-coated. Set aside. ❧ When the rising time has elapsed (about 1 hour), transfer the dough to a floured surface and divide into 24 pieces. ❧ Roll each piece into a ball and place about 2 in (5 cm) apart on oiled baking sheets. Pinch the ends of the rolls to elongate slightly. ❧ Cover with a cloth and let rise for 15 minutes. ❧ Preheat the oven to 400°F/ 200°C/gas 6. ❧ Slash the top of each roll with a sharp knife and bake for about 20 minutes, or until golden brown and hollow-sounding when tapped on the bottom.

NAAN

Use the first 3 ingredients to prepare the yeast as explained on page 250. ❧ Place the flour, baking powder, and salt in a large bowl. Make a well in the center and add the yeast mixture, remaining milk, yogurt, egg, and ghee. Mix until smooth. ❧ Knead the dough as shown on page 251 and set aside to rise. ❧ When the rising time has elapsed (about 1½ hours), transfer to a lightly floured work surface and knead for 2–3 minutes. ❧ Roll the dough out into oval shapes about 10 in (25 cm) in diameter. Sprinkle with the onion seeds and place on oiled baking sheets. Preheat the oven to 400°F/ 200°C/gas 6. ❧ Bake for 10–12 minutes, or until puffed and light golden brown.

Naan, a type of Indian bread, is traditionally cooked in a tandoor, or clay oven.

Makes: about 1½ lb/ 750 g bread

Preparation: 20'

Rising time: 1½ h

Cooking: 10–12'

Level of difficulty: 2

- ³/₄ oz/25 g fresh yeast or 1½ (¼ oz) packages active dry yeast
- 2 tsp sugar
- about 1 cup/250 ml warm milk
- 3⅓ cups/500 g all-purpose/plain flour
- 1 tsp baking powder
- ³/₄ tsp salt
- ²/₃ cup/150 ml plain yogurt
- 1 egg, lightly beaten
- 2 tbsp ghee, melted
- 2 tbsp onion seeds

SESAME SEED BREAD

Use the first 3 ingredients to prepare the yeast as explained on page 250. ❧ Place both flours, the salt and half the sesame seeds in a large bowl. Mix carefully. ❧ Add the yeast mixture and remaining water and prepare the dough as shown on page 251. ❧ When the rising time has elapsed (about 1 hour), transfer the dough to a lightly floured work surface and knead for 2–3 minutes. ❧ Divide the dough into two equal portions to make soft loaves, or in 8–10 equal portions for crusty rolls. ❧ Arrange the loaves or rolls on one or two oiled baking sheets, keeping them well spaced (their volume will double as they rise). ❧ Lightly beat the egg white with 1 teaspoon of water and brush the surface of the loaves or rolls with the mixture. Sprinkle with the remaining sesame seeds. ❧ Cover with a cloth and set aside to rise for 1 hour. ❧ Preheat the oven to 400°F/200°C/gas 6. ❧ Bake in a for 35–40 minutes for loaves and 30 minutes for rolls.

Makes: about 2 lb/ 1 kg of bread

Preparation: 30'

Rising time: 2 h

Cooking: 30–40'

Level of difficulty: 2

- 1 oz (30 g) fresh yeast or 2 (¹/₄ oz) packages active dry yeast
- 1 tsp sugar
- about 1¹/₄ cups/ 300 ml lukewarm water
- 3 cups/450 g unbleached white flour
- 2 cups/300 g whole-wheat flour
- 6 tbsp sesame seeds
- 1–2 tsp salt
- 1 egg white

CUMIN BREAD

U se the first 3 ingredients to prepare the yeast as explained on page 250. ❧ In a large bowl, combine the flour with the salt, half the cumin seeds, the yeast mixture, and remaining water, and prepare the dough as shown on page 251. ❧ When the rising time has elapsed (about 1 hour), transfer to a lightly floured work surface and knead for 2–3 minutes. ❧ Divide the dough into two loaves and place on an oiled baking sheet. Sprinkle with the remaining cumin and leave to rise for 30 minutes. ❧ Preheat the oven to 400°F/200°C/gas 6. ❧ Bake for 20 minutes. ❧ Brush the top with the egg white and the oil and cook for 20 more minutes, or until golden brown and hollow-sounding when tapped on the bottom.

Makes: about 2¹/₂ lb/ 1.2 kg of bread

Preparation: 20'

Rising time: 1¹/₂ h

Cooking: 40'

Level of difficulty: 2

- 1¹/₂ oz/45 g compressed yeast or 3 (¹/₄ oz) packages active dry yeast
- 1 tbsp sugar
- about 2 cups/500 ml warm water
- 6²/₃ cups/1 kg all-purpose/plain flour
- salt
- 4 tsp cumin seeds
- 2 tbsp extra-virgin olive oil, beaten with 1 egg white

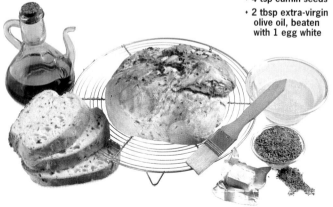

HONEY WHOLE-
WHEAT BREAD

Makes: about 2¹/₄ lb/
1.2 kg of bread

Preparation: 20'

Rising time: 1¹/₂ h

Cooking: 45'

Level of difficulty: 2

- 1¹/₂ oz/45 g
  compressed yeast
  or 3 (¹/₄ oz)
  packages active
  dry yeast
- 1 tsp sugar
- about 2 cups/500
  ml warm water
- 6²/₃ cups/1 kg
  whole-wheat flour
- 2 tsp salt
- 6 tbsp honey
- 6 tbsp butter

Use the first 3 ingredients to prepare the yeast as explained on page 250. ❧ In a large bowl, combine the flour with the salt, honey, 4 tablespoons of butter, the yeast mixture, and enough of the remaining water to make a smooth dough. Knead the dough as shown on page 251. ❧ When the rising time has elapsed (about 1 hour), transfer the dough to a lightly floured work surface and knead for 2–3 minutes. ❧ Divide the dough between 2 oiled (5 x 12-in/13 x 30-cm) loaf pans. Let rise for 30 minutes. ❧ Preheat the oven to 375°F/190°C/gas 5. ❧ Bake for 45 minutes, or until golden brown and hollow-sounding when tapped on the bottom. ❧ Melt the remaining butter and brush the tops of the hot loaves.

OREGANO BREAD

Use the first 3 ingredients to prepare the yeast as explained on page 250. ❧ Place the flour in a large bowl with the oregano, yeast mixture, salt, and remaining water, and prepare the dough as shown on page 251. ❧ When the rising time has elapsed (about 1½ hours), use a spatula to transfer the dough to a lightly floured work surface. Knead for several minutes. ❧ Divide the dough into 4–6 equal portions and shape each into a loaf about 14 in (35 cm) long. ❧ Place the loaves on two oiled baking sheets. Pull the ends of each loaf round and join them to make circular loaves, or leave them straight, as preferred. ❧ Use a serrated knife to make a ½-in (1-cm) deep slash along the top of each loaf. ❧ Cover with a cloth and set aside to rise for 30 minutes.❧ Preheat the oven to 400°F/200°C/gas 6. ❧ Bake for about 30 minutes, or until golden brown and hollow-sounding when tapped on the bottom.

Makes about 2 lb/ 1 kg of bread

Preparation: 30'

Rising time: 1½ h

Cooking: 30'

Level of difficulty: 2

- 1 oz (30 g) fresh yeast or 2 (¼ oz) packages active dry yeast
- 1 tsp sugar
- about 1¼ cups/ 300 ml lukewarm water
- 5 cups/750 g all-purpose/plain flour
- 1 tbsp finely chopped fresh oregano
- 2 tsp salt
- 6 tbsp extra-virgin olive oil

SPICY TOMATO BREAD

U se the first 2 ingredients to prepare the yeast as explained on page 250. ❧ Add enough water to the tomatoes to make 2 cups (500 ml). ❧ In a large bowl, combine Place the flour, butter, salt, sugar, red pepper flakes, half the cumin, the corn meal, and yeast mixture in a large bowl. Add as much of the tomato mixture to obtain a smooth dough. Knead as shown on page 251. ❧ When the rising time has elapsed (about 1½ hours), transfer the dough to a lightly floured work surface. Knead for 2 minutes, then divide in half. ❧ Sauté the onion and chillies in the oil until soft, then knead them into the dough. ❧ Shape into 2 loaves and let rise for 30 minutes. ❧ Preheat the oven to 375°F/190°C/ gas 5. ❧ Brush with the egg wash, and sprinkle with the remaining cumin. ❧ Bake for 30 minutes, or until golden brown and hollow-sounding when tapped on the bottom.

Makes about 2 lb/ 1 kg of bread

Preparation: 30'

Rising time: 2 h

Cooking: 30'

Level of difficulty: 2

- 1 oz/30 g fresh yeast or 1 (¼ oz) packages active dry yeast
- 4 tbsp lukewarm water
- 1 (15 oz/400 g) can tomatoes, chopped
- 4 tbsp butter, melted
- 1–2 tsp salt
- 6 tbsp brown sugar
- 2 tbsp red pepper flakes
- 2 tbsp whole cumin seeds
- 3 oz/90 g corn meal
- 4 cups/600 g all-purpose/plain flour
- 1 medium onion, finely chopped
- 2 chilies
- 1 tbsp extra-virgin olive oil
- 1 egg, beaten with 1 tbsp water and dash of salt

ROMAGNA-STYLE FLATBREAD

Makes: about 10 flatbreads

Preparation: 25' + 30' to rest

Cooking: 15'

Level of difficulty: 2

- 3¹/₃ cups/500 g all-purpose/plain flour
- 1 tsp baking soda
- 1 tsp salt
- 4 tbsp melted lard
- about ¹/₂ cup/125 ml warm water

lace the flour, baking soda, and salt on a clean work surface. ❧ Shape into a mound and make a well in the center. Pour in the lard and a little of the lukewarm water. Gradually mix in the flour, adding enough of the water to make a firm dough. ❧ Knead the dough for 2–3 minutes, or until smooth. ❧ Place in a bowl and cover with a cloth. Set aside for 30 minutes. ❧ Roll the dough into a very thin sheet. ❧ Cut out disks about 8 in (20 cm) in diameter. ❧ Cook on a griddle or dry-fry in a very hot cast iron skillet (frying pan), turning once. ❧ Serve very hot, with slices of Parma ham, salami, and soft fresh cheeses.

ROSEMARY & RAISIN ROLLS

Makes: 6–8 rolls

Preparation: 30'

Rising time: 1½ h

Cooking: 20'

Level of difficulty: 2

- **2 tbsp fresh rosemary leaves**
- **5 tbsp extra-virgin olive oil**
- **½ oz/15 g fresh yeast or 1 (¼ oz) package active dry yeast**
- **2 tsp sugar**
- **about ⅔ cup/150 ml warm water**
- **2⅔ cups/350 g all-purpose/plain flour**
- **1–2 tsp salt**
- **3 oz/90 g raisins**

Combine 1½ tablespoons of rosemary with 4 tablespoons of oil in a small pan and cook over low heat for about 10 minutes. Remove from heat, discard the rosemary, and set the oil aside to cool. ❧ Use the yeast, sugar, and warm water to prepare the yeast mixture as explained on page 250. ❧ Place the flour in a large bowl with the salt, rosemary oil, yeast mixture, sugar, and remaining water, and prepare the dough as shown on page 251. ❧ Rinse the raisins, drain, and pat dry with paper towels. ❧ When the rising time has elapsed (about 1 hour), transfer the dough to a lightly floured work surface and knead for 2–3 minutes. Incorporate the raisins and remaining rosemary into the dough as you knead. ❧ Divide the dough in 6–8 equal portions, drizzle with the remaining oil, and shape into oval rolls. ❧ Place on an oiled baking sheet, keeping them well spaced (their volume will double as they rise). Use a serrated knife to cut a cross into the surface of each roll. ❧ Cover with a cloth and let rise for 30 minutes. ❧ Preheat the oven to 400°F/200°C/gas 6. ❧ Bake for 20 minutes, or until golden brown.

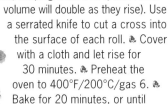

QUICK CHEESE & BEER BREAD

Place the flour, sugar, and cheese in a large bowl. Stir well, then pour in the beer. Mix until smooth. ❧ Grease a 9 x 5 in (23 x 13 cm) loaf pan and sprinkle with bread crumbs. Place the dough in the pan. ❧ Preheat the oven to 350°F/180°C/gas 4. ❧ Bake for 45 minutes. ❧ Remove from the oven and brush with the butter. ❧ Bake for 10 more minutes, or until golden brown.

Makes: 1 small loaf

Preparation: 10'

Cooking: 55'

Level of difficulty: 1

- **2²/₃ cups/350 g all-purpose/plain flour**
- **2 tsp baking powder**
- **2 tbsp sugar**
- **8 oz/200 g Cheddar or Emmental cheese, grated**
- **1¹/₄ cups/375 ml beer**
- **2 tbsp fine dry bread crumbs**
- **2 tbsp butter, melted**

WHOLE=WHEAT CHAPATIS

Makes: 10 chapatis

Preparation: 20'

Cooking: 50'

Level of difficulty: 2

- **2²/₃ cups/350 g chapati flour (or whole wheat flour)**
- **1 tsp salt**
- **lukewarm water, to mix**
- **2 tbsp vegetable oil, to oil hands for kneading**
- **4 tbsp ghee or butter, to brush when cooked**

Place the flour and salt in a large bowl. Make a well in the center and gradually stir in enough water to obtain a smooth dough. ❧ Oil your hands well and knead the dough for about 3 minutes. ❧ Divide the dough into 10 equal portions. Working quickly, shape each portion into a ball, then flatten it with your hands. Set aside on a floured work surface. ❧ Roll out to about 7 in (18 cm) in diameter. ❧ Heat a heavy griddle and cook the chapatis on each side, pressing the edges down gently. ❧ When both sides are cooked, brush one side lightly with ghee or butter. Serve hot.

FRUIT BREAD

Makes: 3 loaves

Preparation: 30'

Rising time: 2¹/₂ h

Cooking: 45'

Level of difficulty: 2

- 1 lb/500 g dried figs
- 1 lb/500 g dried prunes
- 1 lb/500 g dates
- 2 oz/60 g raisins
- 2 oz/60 g dried currants
- 1 tbsp chopped candied lemon
- 1 tbsp chopped candied lemon and orange peel
- 2 oz/60 g chopped blanched almonds
- 1 oz (30 g) fresh yeast or 2 (¹/₄ oz) packages active dry yeast
- 3¹/₃ cups/500 g flour
- ¹/₄ tsp ground cloves
- ¹/₄ tsp ground cinnamon
- ¹/₂ tsp salt
- 2 tbsp milk
- 3 tbsp slivered almonds

Soak figs and prunes in warm water for 1 hour. ❧ Place in a large saucepan with the dates and water and simmer over low heat for 15 minutes. ❧ Scoop out the fruit with a slotted spoon, and chop coarsely. Place in a bowl with the Raisins, currants, candied lemon and orange peel, and almonds. ❧ Reduce the liquid in the pan to ³/₄ cup (200 ml). ❧ Cool to lukewarm, then add yeast and stir until well blended. ❧ Place half the flour in a large bowl and stir in the yeast mixture. Let rise for 1 hour. ❧ Stir the spices, salt, fruit mixture, and enough of the remaining flour into the yeast mixture and flour to obtain a stiff dough. Knead as shown on page 251. ❧ When the second rising time has elapsed (about 1 hour), shape into oval loaves. Brush the milk and sprinkle with split almonds. ❧ Let rise again for 30 minutes. ❧ Preheat the oven to 400°F/200°C/gas 6. ❧ Bake for about 50 minutes, or until golden brown and hollow-sounding when tapped on the bottom.

This healthy bread is very nourishing. It will keep in an airtight container for up to 5 days.

FOCACCIA

BASIC FOCACCIA

Use the first 3 ingredients to prepare the yeast as explained on page 250. ❧ Place the flour in a large bowl with the fine salt, yeast mixture, half the oil, and the remaining water, and prepare the dough as shown on page

This is the basic focaccia recipe. Serve hot, warm or cold; focacce are always delicious. 251. ❧ Preheat the oven to 450°F/ 230°C/gas 7. ❧ When the rising time has elapsed (about 1¹⁄₂ hours), transfer the dough to a lightly floured work surface and knead for 2–3 minutes. ❧ Place the dough on an oiled baking sheet and, using your hands, spread it into a disk about 12 in (30 cm) in diameter. Dimple the surface with your fingertips, drizzle with the remaining oil, and sprinkle with the coarse salt. ❧ Bake for about 20 minutes, or until pale golden brown.

Makes: one (12-in/ 30-cm) focaccia

Preparation: 20'

Rising time: 1¹⁄₂ h

Cooking: 20'

Level of difficulty: 1

- ¹⁄₂ oz/15 g fresh yeast or 1 (¹⁄₄ oz) package active dry yeast
- 1 tsp sugar
- ³⁄₄ cup/200 ml warm water
- 2¹⁄₃ cups/350 g all-purpose/plain flour
- 1 tsp fine salt
- 6 tbsp extra-virgin olive oil
- 1 tsp coarse salt

ROSEMARY FOCACCIA

Prepare the focaccia as described in the recipe above. ❧ Incorporate the rosemary into the dough as you knead after the second rising. ❧ Alternatively, instead of chopping the rosemary leaves, sprinkle them whole over the surface of the dough before drizzling with the oil.

- 1 quantity *Basic Focaccia Dough* (see recipe above)
- 1 tbsp finely chopped fresh rosemary leaves

ONION FOCACCIA

P repare the dough. ❧ Preheat the oven to 450°F/230°C/gas 7. ❧ Cook the onion in a pot of salted, boiling water for 3–4 minutes. Drain well and cut into fairly thick slices. ❧ Spread the onion over the surface of the focaccia before sprinkling with the salt and drizzling with the oil. ❧ Bake for about 20 minutes, or until pale golden brown. ❧ Serve hot or at room temperature.

Makes: one (12-in/ 30-cm) focaccia

Preparation: 20'

Rising time: 1¹/₂ h

Cooking: 20'

Level of difficulty: 1

- **1 quantity *Basic Focaccia Dough* (see page 286)**
- **1 large white onion**

FOCACCIA WITH BLACK OLIVES

Makes: one (12-in/ 30-cm) focaccia

Preparation: 20'

Rising time: 1½ h

Cooking: 20'

Level of difficulty: 1

- 1 quantity *Basic Focaccia Dough* (see page 286)
- 2 cups/200 g pitted and coarsely chopped black olives

Prepare the dough. ❧ Preheat the oven to 450°F/230°C/gas 7. ❧ Incorporate half the olives into the dough as you knead after rising and sprinkle the rest over the top. ❧ Bake for about 20 minutes, or until pale golden brown. ❧ Serve hot or at room temperature.

SAGE FOCACCIA

Prepare the dough. ❧ Preheat the oven to 450°F/230°C/gas 7. ❧ Incorporate the sage into the dough as you knead after rising. ❧ Alternatively, sauté the sage in 1 tablespoon of extra-virgin olive oil over medium heat for 1 minute. In this case, reduce the amount of oil added to the flour by 1 tablespoon. ❧ Bake for about 20 minutes, or until pale golden brown. ❧ Serve hot or at room temperature.

Makes: one (12-in/
30-cm) focaccia

Preparation: 20'

Rising time: 1½ h

Cooking: 20'

Level of difficulty: 1

- **1 quantity *Basic Focaccia Dough* (see page 286)**
- **1 heaped tbsp coarsely chopped fresh sage leaves**

FOCACCIA WITH GREEN OLIVES

Prepare the dough. ❧ Preheat the oven to 450°F/230°C/gas 7. ❧ When the focaccia is ready, arrange the olives face down on the dough. Press them down with your fingers to make them sink into the dough a little. ❧ Bake for about 20 minutes, or until pale golden brown. ❧ Serve hot or at room temperature.

Makes: one (12-in/
30-cm) focaccia

Preparation: 20'

Rising time: 1½ h

Cooking: 20'

Level of difficulty: 1

- **1 quantity *Basic Focaccia Dough* (see page 286)**
- **1 cup/100 g pitted green olives, cut in half**

CHEESE FOCACCIA

Makes: one (12-in/
   30-cm) focaccia

Preparation: 20'

Rising time: 1½ h

Cooking: 20'

Level of difficulty: 1

Prepare the dough. ❧ Preheat the oven to 450°F/230°C/gas 7. ❧ When the focaccia is ready, arrange the slices of cheese on top. ❧ Bake for about 20 minutes, or until pale golden brown. ❧ Serve hot or at room temperature.

* 1 quantity *Basic Focaccia Dough* (see page 286)
* 7 oz/200 g Fontina cheese (or other cooking cheese, such as Cheddar or Emmental), cut in thin slices

WHOLE=WHEAT FOCACCIA

U se the first 3 ingredients to prepare the yeast as explained on page 250. ❧ Place both flours in a large bowl with the salt, yeast mixture, 3 tablespoons of the oil, and the remaining water. Prepare the dough as shown on page 251. ❧ Preheat the oven to 450°F/230°C/gas 7. ❧ When the rising time has elapsed (about 1½ hours), transfer the dough to a lightly floured work surface and knead for 2–3 minutes. ❧ Place the dough on an oiled baking sheet and, using your hands, spread it into a disk about 12 in (30 cm) in diameter. Sprinkle with the olives and chillies, pressing lightly into the dough with your fingertips. Drizzle with the remaining oil. ❧ Bake for 25 minutes, or until pale golden brown. ❧ Serve hot.

The slightly nutty flavor of the whole=wheat flour goes beautifully with the olives and chilies.

Makes: one (12-in/ 30-cm) focaccia

Preparation: 30'

Rising time: 1½ h

Cooking: 25'

Level of difficulty: 1

- 1 oz/30 g fresh yeast or 2 (¼ oz) packages active dry yeast
- 1 tsp sugar
- about 1 cup/250 ml warm water
- 1 cup/150 g all-purpose/plain flour
- 1²/₃ cups/250 g whole-wheat flour
- 1–2 tsp salt
- 5 tbsp extra-virgin olive oil
- 1 cup/100 g pitted black olives, thinly sliced
- 1–2 fresh green chilies, thinly sliced

FOCACCIA FILLED
WITH CREAMY CHEESE

*Makes: one (10 x 15-in/
25 x 38-cm) focaccia*

Preparation: 30'

Rising time: 1¹/₂ h

Cooking: 20'

Level of difficulty: 2

- **³/₄ oz/25 g fresh yeast or 1¹/₂ (¹/₄ oz) packages active dry yeast**
- **1 tsp sugar**
- **about 1 cup/250 ml warm water**
- **3 cups/450 g all-purpose/plain flour**
- **1 tsp salt**
- **6 tbsp extra-virgin olive oil**
- **11 oz/300 g fresh, creamy cheese, such as Philadelphia Light, Robiola or Crescenza**

Use the first 3 ingredients to prepare the yeast as explained on page 250. ♣ Place the flour in a large bowl with the salt, yeast mixture, 2 tablespoons of the oil, and the remaining water. Prepare the dough as shown on page 251. ♣ Preheat the oven to 450°F/230°C/gas 7. ♣ When the rising time has elapsed (about 1¹/₂ hours), transfer the dough to a lightly floured work surface and knead for 2–3 minutes. ♣ Divide the dough into two equal portions and roll them out to into rectangles large enough to line an oiled 10 x 15-in (25 x 38-cm) jelly-roll pan. ♣ Place one piece of dough in the pan and spread with the cheese, leaving a 1-in/2-cm border around the edge. ♣ Cover with the other piece of dough and press the edges down to make a crust around the edges. Prick the surface with a fork and brush with the remaining oil. ♣ Bake for 20 minutes, or until pale golden brown. ♣ Serve hot or at room temperature.

This wonderful focaccia is made in northwest, near the city of Genoa, on the Italian Riviera.

FOCACCIA WITH SUMMER VEGETABLES

U se the first 3 ingredients to prepare the yeast as explained on page 250. ❧ Place the flour in a large bowl with the sugar, yeast mixture, 2 tablespoons of the oil, the remaining water, and the wine. Prepare the dough as shown on page 251.❧

Vary the vegetables according to the season for a year round focaccia.

Preheat the oven to 400°F/200°C/gas 6. ❧ When the rising time has elapsed (about 1½ hours), transfer the dough to a lightly floured work surface and knead for 2–3 minutes. ❧ Place the dough in an oiled 10 x 15-in (25 x 38-cm) jelly-roll pan and spread evenly. Prick well with a fork. ❧ Sprinkle with the bell peppers, onions, tomatoes, salt, pepper, and parsley. Drizzle with the remaining oil. ❧ Bake for 30–35 minutes, or until the vegetables are cooked.

Makes: one (10 x 15-in/ 25 x 38-cm) focaccia

Preparation: 30'

Rising time: 1½ h

Cooking: 30–35'

Level of difficulty: 2

- **1 oz/30 g fresh yeast or 2 (¼ oz) packages active dry yeast**
- **1 tsp sugar**
- **about ⅔ cup/150 ml warm water**
- **3⅓ cups/500 g all-purpose/plain flour**
- **1 tsp salt**
- **½ cup/125 ml extra-virgin olive oil**
- **2 tbsp white wine**
- **1 lb/500 g green bell peppers/ capsicums, sliced**
- **1 lb/500 g finely chopped onion**
- **1 lb/500 g tomatoes, chopped**
- **salt and freshly ground black pepper to taste**
- **3 tbsp finely chopped parsley**

FOCACCIA
WITH ZUCCHINI

Makes: one (10 x 15-in/
25 x 38-cm) focaccia

Preparation: 20'

Rising time: 1½ h

Cooking: 25'

Level of difficulty: 2

- 1 oz/30 g fresh
  yeast or 2 (¼ oz)
  packages active
  dry yeast
- 1 tsp sugar
- about ¾ cup/200 ml/
  warm water
- 3⅓ cups/500 g all-
  purpose/plain flour
- 1 tsp salt
- ½ cup/125 ml
  extra-virgin olive
  oil
- 1½ lb/750 g
  zucchini/
  courgettes, thinly
  sliced

Use the first 3 ingredients to prepare the yeast as explained on page 250. ❧ Place the flour in a large bowl with the sugar, salt, yeast mixture, 2 tablespoons of the the oil, and the remaining water. Prepare the dough as shown on page 251. ❧ Preheat the oven to 450°F/230°C/gas 7. ❧ When the rising time has elapsed (about 1½ hours), transfer the dough to a lightly floured work surface and knead for 2–3 minutes. ❧ Place the dough in an oiled 10 x 15-in (25 x 38-cm) jelly-roll pan and spread evenly. Prick well with a fork. ❧ Sprinkle with the zucchini and drizzle with the remaining oil. ❧ Bake for 25–30 minutes, or until the zucchini are tender.

EMPANADA WITH PORK

Makes: one (14-in/ 35-cm) focaccia

Preparation: 30' + 30' to chill

Cooking: 30'

Level of difficulty: 2

Place the flour in a large bowl and make a well in the center. Add the wine, 4 tablespoons of oil, butter, salt, sugar, and the water. Mix well to obtain a smooth, elastic dough. ❧ Refrigerate for 30 minutes. ❧ Preheat the oven to 350°F/180°C/gas 4. ❧ In a large skillet (frying pan), sauté the pork in the remaining oil for 3–4 minutes. Remove the pork and set aside. ❧ Sauté the onion and garlic in the skillet for 2–3 minutes. Add the ham and bell peppers and sauté over high heat for 5 minutes more. ❧ Return the pork to the skillet, and add the tomato sauce, salt, pepper, and red pepper flakes. ❧ Divide the dough into two equal portions and roll them out on a lightly floured work surface. Use one portion to line an oiled 14-in (30-cm) pizza pan. ❧ Spread with the pork filling and cover with the second piece of dough. Seal the edges by pinching them together. ❧ Brush with the egg yolk and bake for 30 minutes, or until golden brown.

- 3¹⁄₃ cups/500 g all-purpose/plain flour
- 1 tbsp white wine
- 5 tbsp extra-virgin olive oil
- 1 tbsp butter, melted
- salt and freshly ground black pepper to taste
- 1 tsp sugar
- ¹⁄₂ cup/125 ml warm water
- 1 lb/500 g pork loin, cut in strips
- 2 large onions, finely chopped
- 2 cloves garlic, finely chopped
- 4 oz/125 g ham, diced
- 2 green bell peppers/ capsicums, finely chopped
- 2 tbsp tomato sauce
- 1 tsp red pepper flakes
- 1 egg yolk

Makes: one (14-in/
35-cm) focaccia

Preparation: 30' + 30'
to chill

Cooking: 30'

Level of difficulty: 2

• 3¹/₃ cups/500 g all-
purpose/plain flour
• 1 tbsp white wine
• 5 tbsp extra-virgin
olive oil
• 1 tbsp butter,
melted
• salt and freshly
ground black
pepper to taste
• 1 tsp sugar
• ¹/₂ cup/125 ml
warm water
• 1 lb/500 g clams, in
their shells
• 2 red onions, cut in
thin rings
• 2 cloves garlic,
finely chopped
• 1 green bell pepper/
capsicum, finely
chopped
• 2 tbsp finely
chopped parsley
• 1 egg yolk

EMPANADA
WITH CLAMS

Prepare the dough as explained on page
300. ♣ Preheat the oven to 350°F/150°C/
gas 4. ♣ In a large skillet (frying pan), sauté
the clams over medium-high heat until they are all
open. Discard any that have not opened. Take all
the mollusks out of their shells, discarding the
shells. ♣ Sauté the onion and garlic in the
remaining oil for 2–3 minutes. Add the bell
peppers and parsley and sauté over high heat for
5 minutes. Return the clams to the pan and
remove from heat. ♣ Divide the dough into two
equal portions and roll them out on a lightly
floured work surface. Use one portion to line an
oiled 14-in (30-cm) pizza pan. ♣ Spread with the
clam filling and cover with the second piece of
dough. Seal the edges by pinching them together.
♣ Brush with the egg yolk and bake for 30
minutes, or until golden brown.

FOCACCIA WITH RED ONIONS

Makes: one (12-in/
30-cm) focaccia

Preparation: 30'

Rising time: 2 h

Cooking: 30'

Level of difficulty: 1

• ²/₃ oz/20 g fresh
  yeast or 2 (¹/₄ oz)
  packages active dry
  yeast
• 1 tsp sugar
• about 1 cup/
  250 ml warm water
• 3 cups/450 g all-
  purpose/plain flour
• 1–2 tsp salt
• 1 lb/500 g red
  onions
• 2 tbsp butter

U se the first 3 ingredients to prepare the yeast as explained on page 250. ❧ Place the flour in a large bowl with the salt, yeast mixture, and remaining water, and prepare the dough as shown on page 251. The dough should be rather soft; if it is difficult to knead, leave it in the bowl and mix for several minutes with a wooden spoon. ❧ While the dough is rising, peel and slice the onions. Cook over medium-low heat with the butter and 1–2 tablespoons of water for about 30 minutes. Remove from heat and let cool. ❧ When the rising time has elapsed (about 1¹/₂ hours), transfer the dough to a lightly floured work surface and knead for 2–3 minutes. ❧ Shape into a thin loaf about 3 ft (1 m) long. ❧ Transfer to an oiled baking sheet, and shape it into a ring, joining the two ends together, and leaving a large hole in the middle. ❧ Cover with a cloth and let rise for about 30 minutes. ❧ Preheat the oven to 400°F/200°C/gas 6. ❧ When the second rising time has elapsed, flatten the dough a little with your hands and spread the onions on top. Sprinkle with salt. ❧ Bake for about 30 minutes. ❧ Serve hot.

This recipe is a specialty of Como, a town on one of the beautiful northern Italian lakes.

303

TOMATO & GARLIC FOCACCIA

Use the first 3 ingredients to prepare the yeast as explained on page 250. ❧ Place the flour in a large bowl with the salt, yeast mixture, 2 tablespoons of the oil, and the remaining water, and prepare the dough as shown on page 251. ❧ Place the tomatoes in boiling water for 1 minute, then peel. Chop each tomato into 4–6 segments. ❧ Preheat the oven to 450°F/230°C/gas 7. ❧ When the rising time has elapsed (about 1½ hours), transfer the dough to a lightly floured work surface and knead for 1 minute. ❧ Place the dough in an oiled 10 x 15-in (25 x 38-cm) jelly-roll pan and spread evenly. ❧ Dimple the surface with your fingertips and fill the dimples with pieces of garlic and tomato. ❧ Drizzle with the remaining oil and sprinkle with the oregano and pepper. ❧ Bake for 20–25 minutes, or until pale golden brown. ❧ Serve hot or at room temperature.

Another delicious Italian focaccia. This one comes from Apulia, the "heel" on the Italian "boot."

Makes: one (10 x 15-in/ 25 x 38-cm) focaccia

Preparation: 30'

Rising time: 1½ h

Cooking: 20–25'

Level of difficulty: 1

- ¾ oz/25 g fresh yeast or 1½ (¼ oz) packages active dry yeast
- 1 tsp sugar
- about ⅔ cup/150 ml lukewarm water
- 3 cups/450 g all-purpose/plain flour
- 1 tsp salt
- 5 tbsp extra-virgin olive oil
- 6 small ripe tomatoes
- 3 cloves garlic, each sliced into in 4 pieces
- 2 tsp dried oregano
- freshly ground black pepper to taste

GORGONZOLA & CREAM FOCACCIA

U se the first 3 ingredients to prepare the yeast as explained on page 250. ✿ Place the flour in a large bowl with the salt, yeast mixture, oil, and the remaining water, and prepare the dough as shown on page 251. ✿ Preheat the oven to 450°F/ 230°C/gas 7. ✿ When the rising time has elapsed (about 1¹⁄₂ hours), transfer the dough to a lightly floured work surface and knead for 1 minute. ✿ Place the dough in an oiled 10 x 15-in (25 x 38-cm) jelly-roll pan and spread evenly. ✿ Mash the cheese in a bowl. Add the cream and thyme and mix until smooth. ✿ Spread the cheese mixture over the dough. ✿ Bake for 20 minutes, or until golden brown.

This focaccia is best served straight from the oven.
It can become heavy if allowed to cool.

306

Makes: one (10 x 15-in/
    25 x 38-cm) focaccia

Preparation: 15'

Rising time: 1¹⁄₂ h

Cooking: 20'

Level of difficulty: 1

• 1 oz/30 g fresh yeast or 2 (¹⁄₄ oz) packages active dry yeast
• 1 tsp sugar
• 1 cup/250 ml lukewarm water
• 3¹⁄₃ cups/500 g all-purpose/ plain flour
• 2 tsp salt
• 4 tbsp extra-virgin olive oil
• 4 tbsp heavy/ double cream
• 8 oz/250 g Gorgonzola cheese
    • 1 tbsp finely chopped fresh thyme

FOCACCIA
WITH POTATOES

Makes: one (12-in/
30-cm) focaccia

Preparation: 20'

Rising time: 1½ h

Cooking: 20–25'

Level of difficulty: 1

- ½ oz/15 g fresh yeast or 1 (¼ oz) package active dry yeast
- 1 tsp sugar
- 6 tbsp warm water
- 8 oz/250 g boiled potatoes, still warm
- 2 cups/300 g all-purpose/plain flour
- 1–2 tsp fine salt
- 3–4 tbsp extra-virgin olive oil
- 1 level tsp coarse sea salt

Use the first 3 ingredients to prepare the yeast as explained on page 250. ❧ Mash the boiled potatoes while still hot. ❧ Combine the potatoes in a large bowl with the flour, salt, yeast mixture and 1 tablespoon of the oil, and prepare the dough as shown on page 251.

This soft, delicious focaccia is always a great success. It will keep for at least 3 days.

The dough will be too soft to knead by hand; leave it in the bowl and mix vigorously with a wooden spoon for 2–3 minutes. Set aside to rise. ❧ Preheat the oven to 400°F/200°C/gas 6. ❧ When the rising time has elapsed (about 1 hour), mix again for 1 minute. ❧ Transfer to an oiled 12-in (30-cm) pizza pan. Spread the dough with your hands. Cover with a cloth and set aside to rise for 30 minutes. ❧ Sprinkle with the semi-coarse salt. Dimple the surface with your fingertips and drizzle with the remaining oil. ❧ Bake for 20–25 minutes, or until pale golden brown. ❧ Serve hot or warm.

TOMATO & ROCKET FOCACCIA

Prepare the dough. ✿ Preheat the oven to 450°F/230°C/gas 7. ✿ When the rising time has elapsed (about 1¹/₂ hours), transfer the dough to a lightly floured work surface and knead for 2–3 minutes. ✿ Place the dough in an oiled 10 x 15-in (25 x 38-cm) jelly-roll pan and spread evenly. ✿ Cover with the slices of tomato and sprinkle with the oregano. ✿ Drizzle with the remaining oil and sprinkle with the coarse salt. ✿ Bake for about 20 minutes, or until pale golden brown. ✿ When cooked, arrange the rocket over the top and serve hot. If liked, drizzle with a little extra olive oil.

The freshness of the tomatoes and rocket tastes wonderful with the warm focaccia.

Makes: one (10 x 15-in/ 25 x 38-cm) focaccia

Preparation: 20'

Rising time: 1¹/₂ h

Cooking: 20'

Level of difficulty: 1

- **1¹/₂ quantities Basic Focaccia Dough (see page 286)**
- 1 lb/500 g ripe tomatoes, sliced
- 1 tbsp oregano
- 2 bunches arugula/ rocket, washed and dried well

MOZZARELLA & TOMATO FOCACCIA

Prepare the dough. Preheat the oven to 450°F/230°C/gas 7. When the rising time has elapsed (about 1½ hours), transfer the dough to a lightly floured work surface and knead for 2–3 minutes. Place the dough in an oiled

Another summer favorite. Be sure to use very fresh Mozzarella cheese (not the type for pizza).

10 x 15-in (25 x 38-cm) jelly-roll pan and spread evenly. Drizzle with the remaining oil and sprinkle with the coarse salt. Bake for 20–25 minutes, or until pale golden brown. When cooked, slice the focaccia open down the middle. Cover half with the tomatoes, Mozzarella, and basil. Season with salt and pepper. Cover with the other half, then cut into 4 or 6 sandwiches.

Makes: one (10 x 15-in/ 25 x 38-cm) focaccia

Preparation: 20'

Rising time: 1½ h

Cooking: 20–25'

Level of difficulty: 1

- **1½ quantities** *Basic Focaccia Dough* **(see page 286)**
- **1 lb/500 g ripe tomatoes, sliced**
- **14 oz/400 g fresh Mozzarella cheese, sliced**
- **10 leaves fresh basil**
- **salt and freshly ground black pepper to taste**

PECAN & APRICOT FOCACCIA

Makes: one (10-in/25-cm) focaccia

Preparation: 20'

Rising: 1¹/₂ h

Cooking: 20'

Level of difficulty: 1

- • ²/₃ oz/20 g fresh yeast or 1 (¹/₄ oz) packages active dry yeast
- • 1 tbsp sugar
- • ²/₃ cup/150 ml lukewarm water
- • 2¹/₃ cups/350 g all-purpose/plain flour
- • ¹/₄ tsp salt
- • 4 tbsp extra-virgin olive oil
- • 2¹/₂ oz/75 g soft dried apricots, finely chopped
- • 1 oz/30 g pecans, coarsely chopped

Use the first 3 ingredients to prepare the yeast as explained on page 250. ❧ Place the flour in a large bowl with the yeast mixture, 3 tablespoons of the oil, and the remaining water, and prepare the dough as shown on page 251. ❧ After 45 minutes knead again for 2–3 minutes and set aside to rise for another 45 minutes. ❧ Preheat the oven to 400°F/200°C/gas 6. ❧ Mix in the apricots and pecans and knead for 2–3 minutes to incorporate them into the dough. ❧ Place on an oiled baking sheet and shape into a disk about10-in (25-cm) in diameter. ❧ Bake for 20 minutes, or until pale golden brown.

Serve this slightly sweet, delicious focaccia to the family at brunch on Sunday mornings.

FRUITY FOCACCIA

Use the first 3 ingredients to prepare the yeast as explained on page 250. ❧ Place the flours and cinnamon in a large bowl with the yeast mixture, 3 tablespoons of the oil, salt, and the remaining water, and prepare the dough as shown on page 251. ❧ After 45 minutes knead again for 2–3 minutes and set aside to rise for another 45 minutes. ❧ Mix in the dried fruit and knead for 2–3 minutes to incorporate them into the dough. ❧ Preheat the oven to 400°F/200°C/gas 6. ❧ Place on an oiled baking sheet and shape into a disk about 12-in (30-cm) in diameter. ❧ Bake for 25 minutes, or until golden brown.

This nourishing focaccia is good for winter breakfasts or after school snacks.

Makes: one (12-in/ 30-cm) focaccia

Preparation: 20'

Rising time: 1 1/2 h

Cooking: 25'

Level of difficulty: 1

- ✦ 2/3 oz/20 g fresh yeast or 1 (1/4 oz) packages active dry yeast
- ✦ 1 tbsp brown sugar
- ✦ 2/3 cup/150 ml lukewarm water
- ✦ 1 1/3 cups/200 g all-purpose/plain flour
- ✦ 1 cup/150 g whole wheat flour
- ✦ 1 tsp ground cinnamon
- ✦ 4 tbsp extra-virgin olive oil
- ✦ 1/4 tsp salt
- ✦ 4 oz/125 g mixed dried fruits

GARBANZO BEAN FOCACCIA

Combine the water and salt in a bowl and sift in the flour. ❧ Add 2 tablespoons of the oil and stir thoroughly with a fork. Let rest at room temperature for 4–6 hours. ❧ Preheat the oven to 375°F/190°C/gas 5. ❧ Add the basil and olives to the mixture. (It will be quite thin). ❧ Grease a 12 in (30 cm) pizza pan with the remaining oil. ❧ Pour the batter into the pan and sprinkle with the salt and pepper. ❧ Bake for about 40 minutes, or until the edges are browned. ❧ Remove from the oven and cut into wedges. ❧ Serve warm.

Makes: one (12-in/ 30-cm) focaccia

Preparation: 10' + 4–6 h

Cooking: 40'

Level of difficulty: 1

- 2 cups/500 ml water
- 1 tsp salt
- 2 cups/300 g garbanzo bean/ chick pea flour
- 3 tbsp extra-virgin olive oil
- 1 tbsp basil leaves, chopped
- 8 black olives, chopped
- coarse salt and freshly ground black pepper to taste

SESAME & CHEESE FOCACCIA ROLLS

U se the first 3 ingredients to prepare the yeast as explained on page 250. ❧ Place both flours and the salt in a large bowl with the yeast mixture, 3 tablespoons of the oil, and the remaining water, and prepare the dough as shown on page

Serve these rolls with a piping hot bowl of vegetable soup for lunch.

251. ❧ After 45 minutes add the sesame seeds and knead again for 2–3 minutes. Let rise for another 45 minutes. ❧ Preheat the oven to 400°F/200°C/gas 6. ❧ Roll out the dough on a floured surface in a rectangular shape to about ²/₃-in (1.5-cm) thick. ❧ Cut into 12 pieces and place on an oiled baking sheet. ❧ Brush with the remaining oil and sprinkle with the Parmesan, patting it in with your fingertips. ❧ Bake for 12–15 minutes, or until golden brown. ❧ Serve hot or warm.

Makes 12 rolls	
Preparation: 25'	
Rising: 1¹/₂ h	
Cooking: 12–15'	
Level of difficulty: 1	

- ²/₃ oz/20 g fresh yeast or 1 (¹/₄ oz) packages active dry yeast
- 1 tbsp brown sugar
- ²/₃ cup/150 ml lukewarm water
- 2 cups/300 g all-purpose/plain flour
- 1 cup/150 g whole-wheat flour
- 1 tsp salt
- 4 tbsp extra-virgin olive oil
- 2 tbsp sesame seeds
- 2 tbsp freshly grated Parmesan cheese

WALNUT & GINGER FOCACCIA ROLLS

U se the first 3 ingredients to prepare the yeast as explained on page 250. ❧ Place the flour and salt in a large bowl with the yeast mixture, 3 tablespoons of the oil, and the remaining water, and prepare the dough as shown on page 251. ❧

Bake a batch of these sweet rolls to delight visitors for morning coffee.

After 45 minutes mix in the walnuts and ginger and knead for 2–3 minutes. Let rise for another 45 minutes. ❧ Preheat the oven to 400°F/200°C/gas 6. ❧ Roll the dough out on a floured surface to about $^3/_4$-in (2-cm) thick. ❧ Cut into 12 pieces and place on an oiled baking sheet. ❧ Brush with the remaining oil, and sprinkle with the demerara sugar, pressing it into the surface with your fingertips. ❧ Bake for 12–15 minutes, or until golden brown. ❧ Serve hot or at room temperature.

Makes 12 rolls

Preparation: 25'

Rising: 1$^1/_2$ h

Cooking: 12–15'

Level of difficulty: 1

- $^2/_3$ oz/20 g fresh yeast or 1 ($^1/_4$ oz) packages active dry yeast
- 1 tbsp sugar
- $^2/_3$ cup/150 ml lukewarm water
- 3$^1/_4$ cups/350 g all-purpose/plain flour
- $^1/_2$ tsp salt
- 4 tbsp extra-virgin olive oil
- 1 oz/30 g walnuts, shelled and coarsely chopped
- 1 tbsp candied ginger, finely chopped
- 1 tbsp demerara sugar

PIZZA & CALZONE

Making Pizza at Home

Making pizza at home is fun and simple. It also fits in well with busy schedules since the dough can be prepared ahead of time, and many toppings only take a few minutes to prepare. Most children love to eat pizza; they will also enjoy helping to knead the dough and sprinkling it with cheese and herbs for the toppings.

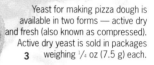

1

Yeast for making pizza dough is available in two forms — active dry and fresh (also known as compressed). Active dry yeast is sold in packages weighing ¼ oz (7.5 g) each.

3

Preparing the dough

This recipe will make about 12 oz (350 g) of dough. This is enough to make one round or oblong pizza, sufficient for 1 or 2 people.

- ½ oz/15 g fresh yeast or 1 (¼ oz) package active dry yeast
- ⅔ cup/150 ml warm water
- 2 cups/300 g all-purpose/ plain flour
- 1 tsp salt

1 Put the yeast in a small bowl. Add half the warm water and stir with a fork until the yeast has dissolved. Set aside for 10 minutes.

2 Place the flour and salt in a medium bowl. Pour in the yeast mixture, remaining water, and any other ingredients listed in the recipe. Stir well until the flour has been absorbed.

3 Shape the dough into a compact ball and place on a lightly floured work surface. Press down with your knuckles to spread it a little. Take the far end of the dough, fold it a short distance toward you, then push it away again with the heel of your palm. Flexing your wrist, fold it toward you again, give it a quarter turn, then push it away. Repeat until the dough is well-kneaded (about 5 minutes).

4 Place the dough in a large clean bowl and cover with a cloth. Let rise for about 1 hour, or until doubled in bulk. To test whether it has risen sufficiently, poke your finger gently into the dough; if the impression remains, then it is ready.

2

Shaping the pizza

1 When the rising time has elapsed, knead the dough for 1 minute on a lightly floured work surface. If making more than one pizza, divide the dough into the number of pizzas you wish to make. Roll each piece of dough into a ball and flatten a little with your hands. Roll the dough out into a disk about 12 in (30 cm) in diameter. Place on an oiled baking sheet. To finish, use your fingertips to make a rim around the edge of the pizza so that the topping won't drip out during cooking.

2 To shape the pizza by hand, place the dough in an oiled 12"-in (30-cm) pizza pan and push it outward with the palms of your hands and fingertips to cover the bottom of the pan.

3 When the pizza dough has been shaped and is in the pizza pan or on the baking sheet, set it aside for 10 minutes before adding the topping. This will give the dough time to regain some volume and will make the crust lighter and more appetizing.

4–5 To make calzones, proceed as for pizza, rolling the dough into a 12-in (30-cm) disk. Place the topping on one half of the disk only, leaving a 1-in (2.5-cm) border around the edge. Fold the other half over the filling and press the edges together with your fingertips to seal.

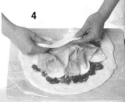

TOMATO, CAPER & ANCHOVY PIZZA

Makes: one (12 in/ 30 cm) pizza

Preparation: 30'

Rising time: 1 h

Cooking: 15–20'

Level of difficulty: 2

BASE

• 1 quantity *Pizza Dough* (see page 324)

TOPPING

• 8 oz/250 g drained and chopped canned tomatoes

• 8 oz/250 g Mozzarella cheese, thinly sliced

• 6 anchovy fillets, crumbled or whole

• 1 tbsp capers

• 3 tbsp extra-virgin olive oil

• 1 heaped tsp oregano

Prepare the dough as explained on page 324. Preheat the oven to 450°F/230°C/gas 7. When the rising time has elapsed, knead the dough for 1 minute on a lightly floured work surface. Shape the pizza as explained on page 325 and transfer to an oiled pizza pan. Spread the tomatoes evenly over the top, then add the Mozzarella, anchovies, and capers. Drizzle with 1 tablespoon of oil. Bake for about 12 minutes. Take the pizza out of the oven and sprinkle with the oregano. Return to the oven to finish cooking. When cooked, drizzle with the remaining oil and serve hot.

FRESH TOMATO & GARLIC PIZZA

Makes: one (12 in/
30 cm) pizza

Preparation: 30'

Rising time: 1 h

Cooking: 20–25'

Level of difficulty: 1

BASE

• 1 quantity *Pizza Dough* (see page 324)

TOPPING

• 12 oz/350 g ripe tomatoes
• 2 cloves garlic, thinly sliced
• 1 tsp oregano
• salt and freshly ground black pepper to taste
• 3 tbsp extra-virgin olive oil

Prepare the dough as explained on page 324. ☙ Preheat the oven to 450°F/230°C/gas 7. ☙ Plunge the tomatoes in boiling water for 1 minute, then remove and peel. Cut in half and gently squeeze out as many seeds as possible. Slice in half again and place in a colander to drain for 10 minutes. *Add 8 oz/250 g thinly sliced Mozzarella cheese, if liked.* ☙ When the rising time has elapsed, knead the dough for 1 minute on a lightly floured work surface. ☙ Shape the pizza as explained on page 325 and transfer to an oiled baking sheet. ☙ Spread the tomatoes and garlic evenly over the top. Sprinkle with the oregano, salt, and pepper and drizzle with 1 tablespoon of the oil. ☙ Bake for 20–25 minutes, or until the edges are golden brown. ☙ When cooked, drizzle with the remaining oil and serve hot.

DEEP-CRUST PIZZA

Prepare the dough as explained on page 324. 🖙 Preheat the oven to 450°F/230°C/gas 7. 🖙 When the rising time has elapsed, knead for 1 minute on a lightly floured work surface. 🖙 Shape the pizza as explained on page 325 and transfer to an oiled baking sheet. 🖙 Spread with the tomatoes, and sprinkle with the basil, olives, onion, Parmesan, and oregano. Finish with the anchovies, if using, and drizzle with 1 tablespoon of oil. 🖙 Bake for 30 minutes, or until the edges are golden brown. 🖙 Drizzle with the remaining oil and serve hot.

Makes: one (12 in/ 30 cm) pizza

Preparation: 30'

Rising time: 2 h

Cooking: 30'

Level of difficulty: 1

BASE

• 1¹/₂ **quantities** *Pizza Dough* **(see page 324)**

TOPPING

• **12 oz/350 g drained and chopped canned tomatoes**

• **6 leaves fresh basil, torn**

• **3 oz/90 g black olives**

• **1 small onion, thinly sliced**

• **2 oz/60 g freshly grated Parmesan cheese**

• **1 tsp oregano**

• **6 anchovy fillets, crumbled (optional)**

• **3 tbsp extra-virgin olive oil**

PIZZA MARGHERITA

Makes: one (12 in/
    30 cm) pizza

Preparation: 30'

Rising time: 1 h

Cooking: 15–20'

Level of difficulty: 1

BASE
- 1 quantity *Pizza Dough* (see page 324)

TOPPING
- 8 oz/250 g drained and chopped canned tomatoes
- 8 oz/250 g Mozzarella cheese, thinly sliced
- salt to taste
- 2 tbsp freshly grated Parmesan cheese
- 3 tbsp extra-virgin olive oil
- 9 leaves fresh basil, torn

Prepare the dough as explained on page 324. ❧ Preheat the oven to 450°F/230°C/gas 7. ❧ When the rising time has elapsed, knead the dough for 1 minute on a lightly floured work surface. ❧ Shape the pizza as explained on page 325 and transfer to an oiled baking sheet. ❧ Spread with the tomatoes, cover with the Mozzarella, and sprinkle with salt and Parmesan. Drizzle with 1 tablespoon of oil. ❧ Bake for 15–20 minutes, or until the edges are golden brown. ❧ Sprinkle with the basil leaves, drizzle with the remaining oil, and serve hot.

FOUR⚡SEASONS PIZZA

Makes: one (12 in/ 30 cm) pizza

Preparation: 15' + 1 h to soak mussels

Rising time: 1 h

Cooking: 15–20'

Level of difficulty: 1

BASE

• 1 quantity *Pizza Dough* (see page 324)

TOPPING

• 12 oz/350 g mussels, in shell
• 5 oz/150 g white mushrooms
• 3 tbsp extra-virgin olive oil
• dash of salt
• 7 oz/200 g drained and chopped canned tomatoes
• 3 oz/90 g artichokes in oil, drained and halved
• 3 oz/90 g pitted black olives
• 2 anchovy fillets, chopped
• 1 clove garlic, thinly sliced

Prepare the dough as explained on page 324. ❧ Soak the mussels in a large bowl of water for 1 hour. Scrub off their beards and rinse well in cold water. ❧ Preheat the oven to 450°F/ 230°C/gas 7. ❧ Clean the mushrooms and slice. Sauté in 1 tablespoon of oil over high heat for 3–4 minutes. Season with salt and set aside. ❧ Place the mussels in a large sauté pan over high heat, shaking the pan frequently. When open, discard the shells of all but 4 mussels. Strain the liquid they have produced and set aside with the mussels in a bowl. ❧ When the rising time has elapsed, knead the dough for 1 minute on a lightly floured work surface. ❧ Shape the pizza as explained on page 325 and transfer to an oiled baking sheet. ❧ Spread the tomatoes on top and sprinkle with salt. ❧ Imagine the pizza divided into 4 equal parts: garnish one quarter with the mushrooms, one with the artichokes, one with the olives and anchovies, and one with the garlic. ❧ Bake for 15–20 minutes, or until the edges are golden brown. ❧ Arrange the mussels on the part garnished with tomato and garlic. Drizzle the pizza with the remaining oil and serve hot.

PIZZA WITH MIXED TOPPING

P repare the dough as explained on page 324. ❧ Preheat the oven to 450°F/230°C/ gas 7. ❧ When the rising time has elapsed, knead the dough for 1 minute on a lightly floured work surface. ❧ Shape the pizza as explained on page 325 and transfer to an oiled 10 x 15-in (25 x 38-cm) jelly-roll pan. ❧ Spread the tomatoes evenly over the top, then add the ham, anchovies, Mozzarella, artichokes, mushrooms, olives, and garlic. Sprinkle with oregano and drizzle with 1 tablespoon of the oil. ❧ Bake for 15–20 minutes, or until the edges are golden brown. ❧ Drizzle with the remaining oil and serve hot.

Makes: one (10 x 15-in/ 25 x 38-cm) pizza

Preparation: 30'

Rising time: 1 h

Cooking: 15–20'

Level of difficulty: 1

BASE

- 1½ **quantities Pizza Dough (see page 324)**

TOPPING

- 8 oz/250 g drained and chopped canned tomatoes
- 2 oz/60 g ham, cut in strips
- 6 anchovy fillets
- 4 oz/125 g Mozzarella cheese, diced
- 2 oz/60 g artichokes in oil, cut in half
- 2 oz/60 g button mushrooms in oil, cut in half
- 2 oz/60 g pitted green olives, in thin rings
- 2 cloves garlic, sliced
- 1 tsp oregano
- 3 tbsp extra-virgin olive oil

PROSCIUTTO & ARUGULA PIZZA

Makes: one (12 in/
30 cm) pizza

Preparation: 30'

Rising time: 1 h

Cooking: 14–18'

Level of difficulty: 1

BASE

• 1 quantity *Pizza Dough* (see page 324)

TOPPING

• 2 tbsp extra-virgin olive oil
• salt to taste
• 5 oz/150 g Mozzarella cheese, sliced
• 3 oz/90 g Parma ham, thinly sliced
• 1 bunch arugula/ rocket, washed, dried, and coarsely chopped

Prepare the dough as explained on page 324. ❧ Preheat the oven to 450°F/230°C/gas 7. ❧ When the rising time has elapsed, knead the dough for 1 minute on a lightly floured work surface. ❧ Shape the pizza as explained on page 325 and transfer to an oiled baking sheet. ❧ Brush the surface with 1 tablespoon of oil and sprinkle with a little salt. ❧ Bake for 7–9 minutes. ❧ Take the pizza out of the oven and sprinkle with the Mozzarella. Return to the oven and cook for 7–9 minutes more. ❧ Garnish with the Parma ham and arugula, drizzle with the remaining oil, and serve hot.

If liked, add two thinly sliced ripe tomatoes to the pizza on top of the ham and salad greens.

EGGPLANT PIZZA

Prepare the dough as explained on page 324. ❧ Preheat the oven to 450°F/230°C/gas 7. ❧ Chop the eggplant into ½-in (1-cm) thick slices and brush lightly with half the oil. ❧ Cook for 5 minutes in a hot grill pan, turning frequently until the flesh is cooked. Sprinkle with salt, garlic, and parsley. Set aside. ❧ When the rising time has elapsed, knead the dough on a lightly floured work surface for 1 minute. ❧ Shape the pizza as explained on page 325 and transfer to an oiled oiled 10 x 15-in (25 x 38-cm) jelly-roll pan. ❧ Spread the tomatoes over the top and sprinkle with the Mozzarella. Drizzle with 1 tablespoon of oil. ❧ Bake for 10–15 minutes, or until the edges are golden brown. ❧ Take the pizza out of the oven and cover with the slices of eggplant, then cook for 5 more minutes. ❧ Sprinkle with the basil, drizzle with the remaining oil, and serve hot.

Makes: one (10 x 15-in/ 25 x 38-cm) pizza

Preparation: 40'

Rising time: 1 h

Cooking: 15–20'

Level of difficulty: 1

BASE

- **1½ quantities Pizza Dough (see page 324)**

TOPPING

- **1 eggplant/ aubergine, about 12 oz/350 g**
- **4 tbsp extra-virgin olive oil**
- **salt to taste**
- **2 cloves garlic, finely chopped**
- **2 tbsp finely chopped parsley**
- **8 oz/250 g drained and chopped canned tomatoes**
- **6 oz/180 g Mozzarella cheese, diced**
- **8 leaves fresh basil, torn**

PIZZA WITH CHICORY TOPPING

Makes: one (12 in/ 30 cm) pizza

Preparation: 26'

Rising time: 1 h

Cooking: 25'

Level of difficulty: 1

BASE

- 1 quantity *Pizza Dough* (see page 324)

TOPPING

- 5 tbsp extra-virgin olive oil
- 4 firm, ripe tomatoes, peeled and chopped
- 1 head chicory/ curly endive
- 8 oz/250 g semi-hard, tasty cheese, cubed
- 4 anchovy fillets, coarsely chopped (optional)
- 12 capers

P repare the dough as explained on page 324. ♠ Preheat the oven to 450°F/230°C/gas 7. ♠ When the rising time has elapsed, knead the dough for 1 minute on a lightly floured work surface. ♠ Shape the pizza as explained on page 325 and transfer to an oiled 12-in (30-cm) pizza pan. Press the surface of the dough with your fingertips to make dimples. ♠ Drizzle with 2 tablespoons of oil and sprinkle with the tomato. ♠ Bake for 15 minutes. ♠ While the pizza is cooking, rinse the chicory thoroughly. Discard the tough outer leaves, drain well, and chop coarsely. ♠ Take the pizza out of the oven, spread with the chicory, cheese, anchovy, and capers. Drizzle with the remaining oil. ♠ Return to the oven for 10 minutes, or until the chicory is wilted but still be crunchy.

MUSHROOM PIZZA

Makes: one (12 in/ 30 cm) pizza

Preparation: 30'

Rising time: 1 h

Cooking: 15–20'

Level of difficulty: 1

BASE

- 1 quantity *Pizza Dough* (see page 324)

TOPPING

- 8 oz/250 g mushrooms
- 3 tbsp extra-virgin olive oil
- 1 tbsp finely chopped parsley
- 1 clove garlic, finely chopped
- salt and freshly ground black pepper to taste

Prepare the dough as explained on page 324. ❧ Preheat the oven to 450°F/230°C/gas 7. ❧ Clean the mushrooms and rinse carefully under cold running water. Pat dry and slice thinly. ❧ Sauté the mushrooms with 1 tablespoon of oil in a skillet (frying pan) over very high heat for 2–3 minutes. Drain off any excess liquid and add the parsley and garlic. Set aside. ❧ When the rising time has elapsed, knead the dough for 1 minute on a lightly floured work surface. ❧ Shape the pizza as explained on page 325 and transfer to an oiled baking sheet. ❧ Spread the mushrooms over the top and sprinkle with salt and pepper. Drizzle with the remaining oil. ❧ Bake for 15–20 minutes, or until the edges are golden brown. ❧ Serve hot.

ARTICHOKE PIZZA

Prepare the dough as explained on page 324. 🌿 Preheat the oven to 450°F/230°C/gas 7. 🌿 Trim the artichoke stems, discard the tough outer leaves, and trim the tops. Cut in half and remove any fuzzy choke. Place in a bowl of cold water with the lemon juice for 10 minutes. 🌿 Drain the artichokes, pat dry with paper towels, and slice thinly. 🌿 Transfer to a skillet (frying pan) with 1 tablespoon of oil and sauté over medium heat for 3 minutes. Season with salt. 🌿 When the rising time has elapsed, knead the dough for 1 minute on a lightly floured work surface. 🌿 Shape the pizza as explained on page 325 and transfer to an oiled baking sheet. 🌿 Brush the pizza with half a tablespoon of oil and spread with the slices of artichoke. Season with salt and pepper and arrange the Fontina on top. Drizzle with 1 tablespoon of oil. 🌿 Bake for 15–20 minutes, or until the edges are golden brown. 🌿 Drizzle with the remaining oil and serve hot.

Makes: one (12 in/ 30 cm) pizza

Preparation: 30'

Rising time: 1 h

Cooking: 15–20'

Level of difficulty: 1

BASE

- **1 quantity *Pizza Dough* (see page 324)**

TOPPING

- **4 artichokes**
- **juice of 1 lemon**
- **4 tbsp extra-virgin olive oil**
- **salt and freshly ground black pepper to taste**
- **4 oz/125 g Fontina cheese, very thinly sliced**

PIZZA WITH BELL PEPPERS

Makes: one (10 x 15-in/ 25 x 38-cm) pizza

Preparation: 20'

Rising time: 1 h

Cooking: 25–30'

Level of difficulty: 1

BASE

- 1½ quantities *Pizza Dough* (see page 324)

TOPPING

- 1 small onion, sliced
- 3 tbsp extra-virgin olive oil
- 12 oz/350 g bell peppers/ capsicums, cut in strips
- 8 oz/250 g canned tomatoes, (not drained)
- 1 tbsp capers
- salt to taste
- 6 leaves fresh basil, torn
- 4 tbsp freshly grated Pecorino or Parmesan cheese

Prepare the dough as explained on page 324. Preheat the oven to 450°F/230°C/gas 7. Sauté the onion in a skillet (frying pan) with 2 tablespoons of oil for 3 minutes over medium heat. Add the bell peppers and, after 1–2 minutes, the tomatoes and capers. Season with salt and sauté for 10 minutes. Add the basil leaves and remove from heat. When the rising time has elapsed, knead the dough for 1 minute on a lightly floured work surface. Shape the pizza as explained on page 325 and transfer to an an oiled 10 x 15-in (25 x 38-cm) jelly-roll pan. Spread the bell pepper mixture evenly over the pizza, sprinkle with the cheese, and drizzle with the remaining oil. Bake for 15–20 minutes, or until the edges are golden brown. Serve hot.

OLIVE, ONION & ANCHOVY PIZZA

Prepare the dough as explained on page 324, adding 2 tablespoons of oil to the flour mixture. ❧ Preheat the oven to 450°F/230°C/gas 7. ❧ Sauté the onions in the second measure of oil for 15 minutes, or until they are soft and lightly browned. Season with salt and pepper and set aside to cool. ❧ When the rising time has elapsed, knead the dough for 1 minute on a lightly floured work surface. ❧ Shape the pizza as explained on page 325 and transfer to an oiled baking sheet. ❧ Spread the onions over the pizza and sprinkle with the olives, anchovies, garlic, and oregano. Bake for 20–25 minutes, or until the edges are golden brown. Serve hot.

Makes: one (12 in/ 30 cm) pizza
Preparation: 20'
Rising time: 1 h
Cooking: 35–40'
Level of difficulty: 1

BASE

- 1 quantity *Pizza Dough* (see page 324)
- 2 tbsp extra-virgin olive oil

TOPPING

- 11 oz/300 g red onions, thinly sliced
- 2 tbsp extra-virgin olive oil
- salt and freshly ground black pepper to taste
- 3 oz/90 g black olives
- 12 anchovy fillets, crumbled
- 3 cloves garlic, finely chopped (optional)
- 1 tsp oregano

FRESH ANCHOVY PIZZA

Makes: one (12 in/
30 cm) pizza

Preparation: 30'

Rising time: 1 h

Cooking: 15–20'

Level of difficulty: 2

BASE

- 1 quantity *Pizza Dough* (see page 324)

TOPPING

- 12 oz/350 g fresh anchovies
- 3 tbsp extra-virgin olive oil
- 3 cloves garlic, thinly sliced
- 1 tsp oregano
- salt and freshly ground black pepper to taste

Prepare the dough as explained on page 324. ♣ Preheat the oven to 450°F/230°C/gas 7. ♣ To clean the anchovies, remove the heads, slit the bodies open, and discard the bones, then separate the two halves. If liked, leave them joined at the tail. Rinse well and pat dry with paper towels. ♣ When the rising time has elapsed, knead the dough for 1 minute on a lightly floured work surface. ♣ Shape the pizza as explained on page 325 and transfer to an oiled baking sheet. ♣ Brush the dough with a little oil and arrange the anchovies on top. Sprinkle with the garlic, oregano, and a little salt and pepper. Drizzle with 1 tablespoon of oil. ♣ Bake for 15–20 minutes, or until the edges are golden brown. ♣ Drizzle with the remaining oil and serve hot.

This pizza is the ultimate treat for anchovy lovers!

351

HAM & CHEESE PIZZA

P repare the dough as explained on page 324. ♣ Preheat the oven to 450°F/230°C/gas 7. ♣ When the rising time has elapsed, knead the dough for 1 minute on a lightly floured work surface. ♣ Shape the pizza as explained on page 325 and transfer to an oiled baking sheet. ♣ Brush the dough with a little oil and arrange the ham on top. Sprinkle with the Mozzarella and the red pepper flakes, if using. Drizzle with 1 tablespoon of oil. ♣ Bake for 15–20 minutes, or until the edges are golden brown. ♣ Drizzle with the remaining oil, and serve hot.

Makes: one (12 in/ 30 cm) pizza

Preparation: 20'

Rising time: 1 h

Cooking: 15–20'

Level of difficulty: 1

BASE

• 1 quantity *Pizza Dough* (see page 324)

TOPPING

• 2 tbsp extra-virgin olive oil

• 4 oz/125 g sliced ham, each slice torn in 2–3 pieces

• 6 oz/180 g Mozzarella cheese, diced

• 1 tsp red pepper flakes (optional)

PEAR, WALNUT, & GORGONZOLA PIZZA

Makes: one (10 x 15-in/
25 x 38-cm) pizza

Preparation: 20'

Rising time: 1 h

Cooking: 15–20'

Level of difficulty: 1

BASE

• 1 quantity whole-
  wheat *Pizza Dough*
  (see page 324)
• 4 oz/125 g grated
  Parmesan cheese

TOPPING

• 5 oz/150 g
  Gorgonzola
  cheese, crumbled
• 5 oz/150 g
  Mozzarella cheese,
  diced
• 2 oz/60 g dried
  pears, chopped
• 1 tsp finely
  chopped fresh
  rosemary needles
• 1 large red onion,
  thinly sliced
• 2 oz/60 g walnuts,
  chopped
• salt and freshly
  ground black
  pepper to taste
• 6 tbsp extra virgin
  olive oil

Prepare the whole-wheat pizza dough following the instructions for plain pizza dough as explained on page 324. ❧ Preheat the oven to 450°F/230°C/gas 7. ❧ When the rising time has elapsed, knead the dough on a lightly floured work surface, working the Parmesan cheese into it. ❧ Shape the pizza as explained on page 325 and transfer to an oiled 10 x 15-in (25 x 38-cm) jelly-roll pan. ❧ Sprinkle the cheeses over the pizza, followed by the pears, rosemary, onion, and walnuts. Season lightly with salt and pepper and drizzle with half the oil. ❧ Bake for 20–25 minutes, or until the edges are golden brown. ❧ Drizzle with the remaining oil, and serve hot.

LILLIPUT PIZZAS

Prepare the dough as explained on page 324. ❧ Preheat the oven to 450°F/230°C/gas 7. ❧ Tomato Topping: Plunge the tomatoes into boiling water for 1 minute and then into cold. Slip off the skins and chop the flesh. Place in a bowl and add the salt, pepper, garlic, if using, and capers. ❧ When the rising time has elapsed, knead the dough for 1 minute on a lightly floured work surface, then divide into 16 equal portions. ❧ Stretch the dough into small disks, about 2 in (5 cm) in diameter. ❧ Place the pizzas on two lightly oiled baking sheets. Spread some of the topping and Mozzarella on half of the small pizzas and drizzle with a little oil. ❧ Bake for 10–15 minutes, or until the edges are golden brown. ❧ Cheese Topping: Chop the Gorgonzola and place in a heavy-bottomed pan over very low heat. When it has warmed through and melted a little, spread on the remaining pizzas. ❧ Sprinkle with Mozzarella and pepper and place a piece of sage leaf on each one. ❧ Drizzle with the oil and bake for 10–15 minutes, or until the edges are golden brown.

These scrumptious little pizzas make ideal snacks for hungry children. Vary the toppings.

Makes: 16 small pizzas

Preparation: 40'

Rising time: 1 h

Cooking time: 10–15'

Level of difficulty: 1

BASE

- **2 quantities *Pizza Dough* (see page 324)**

TOMATO TOPPING

- **4–6 ripe tomatoes**
- **salt and freshly ground black pepper to taste**
- **2 cloves garlic, thinly sliced**
- **1 tbsp capers**
- **4 tbsp extra-virgin olive oil**
- **4 oz/125 g Mozzarella, diced**

CHEESE TOPPING

- **8 oz/250 g Gorgonzola cheese**
- **freshly ground black pepper to taste**
- **4 oz/125 g Mozzarella, diced**
- **6 sage leaves, torn**
- **2 tbsp extra-virgin olive oil**

PIZZA IN A HURRY

Makes: 4 "pizzas"

Preparation: 10'

Cooking: 8–10'

Level of difficulty: 1

• **4 large, thick slices bread**

• **4 tbsp extra-virgin olive oil**

• **8 oz/250 g drained and chopped canned tomatoes**

• **7 oz/200 g Mozzarella cheese, sliced**

• **4 anchovy fillets (optional)**

• **1 tbsp capers**

• **1 tsp oregano**

Preheat the oven to 450°F/230°C/gas 7. ❧ Brush both sides of the slices of bread with half the oil. ❧ Spread the tomato on top, followed by the Mozzarella, anchovies, if using, capers, and oregano. ❧ Drizzle with the remaining oil and place on a baking sheet. ❧ Bake for 8–10 minutes, or until the Mozzarella melts and turns light gold. ❧ Serve hot.

FRIED PIZZAS

Prepare the dough as explained on page 324. When the rising time has elapsed, knead the dough briefly on a lightly floured work surface, then divide into 6 equal portions. ❧ Roll or stretch the dough into 9 in (23 cm) disks. ❧ Cover half of each disk with slices of Mozzarella and tomato, leaving a 1-in (2.5-cm) border around the edge. Sprinkle with anchovies, parsley, salt, and pepper. Fold the other half of the dough over the top, pressing down carefully on the edges to seal. ❧ Heat the oil to very hot in a large skillet (frying pan) and fry the pizzas two at a time until golden brown. ❧ Serve hot.

Makes: 4 fried pizzas
Preparation: 25'
Rising time: 1 h
Cooking: 20–25'
Level of difficulty: 1

BASE
- 3 quantities *Pizza Dough* (see page 324)

FILLING
- 14 oz/450 g Mozzarella, sliced
- 6 tomatoes, sliced
- 8 anchovy fillets, chopped
- 2 tbsp finely chopped parsley
- salt and freshly ground black pepper to taste
- 2 cups/500 ml oil, for frying

PIZZA WITH RICOTTA STUFFING

Makes: 4 calzone

Preparation: 25'

Rising time: 1 h

Cooking: 20'

Level of difficulty: 2

BASE

* 3 quantities *Pizza Dough* (see page 324)

FILLING

* 1¼ lb/625 g Ricotta cheese
* about 2½ cups/ 350 g fresh, spicy Italian sausage meat
* 3 tbsp extra-virgin olive oil
* salt and freshly ground black pepper to taste

Prepare the dough as explained on page 324. Preheat the oven to 450°F/230°C/gas 7. When the rising time has elapsed, knead the dough briefly on a lightly floured work surface, then divide into 4 equal portions. Stretch the dough into disks, about 9 in (23 cm) in diameter, as explained on page 325. Spread a quarter of the Ricotta over one half of each rectangle, leaving a 1-in (2.5-cm) border around the edge. Place a quarter of the sausage meat on top of the Ricotta and sprinkle with salt, pepper, and oil. Fold the other half of the dough over the top, pressing down carefully on the edges to seal. Bake for 20 minutes, or until puffed and golden brown. Serve hot.

SPICY SALAMI & CHEESE CALZONE

Prepare the dough as explained on page 324. ✿ Preheat the oven to 450°F/230°C/gas 7. ✿ Mix the Ricotta, Parmesan, and eggs in a bowl. Add the Mozzarella, salami, and salt. Mix well and set aside. ✿ When the rising time has elapsed, knead the dough briefly on a lightly floured work surface, then divide into 4 equal portions. ✿ Stretch the dough into disks, about 9 in (23 cm) in diameter, as explained on page 325. ✿ Spread the filling on one half of each calzone, leaving a 1-in (2.5-cm) border around the edge. Fold the other half of the dough over the top, pressing down carefully on the edges to seal. Brush the calzone with the oil and tomatoes, and arrange on lightly oiled baking sheets. ✿ Bake for 20–25 minutes. The calzone will be puffed and golden brown when cooked. ✿ Serve hot.

Makes: 4 calzone

Preparation: 35'

Rising time: 1 h

Cooking: 20–25'

Level of difficulty: 1

BASE
- 3 quantities *Pizza Dough* (see page 324)

FILLING
- 8 oz/250 g soft Ricotta cheese
- 6 tbsp freshly grated Parmesan cheese
- 2 eggs
- 8 oz/250 g Mozzarella cheese, diced
- 4 oz/125 g spicy salami, cubed
- salt to taste
- 2 tbsp extra-virgin olive oil
- 4 tbsp peeled and chopped tomatoes

SWISS CHARD CALZONE

Makes: 4 calzone

Preparation: 40'

Rising time: 1 h

Cooking time: 20–25'

Level of difficulty: 1

BASE

- 3 quantities *Pizza Dough* (see page 324)

FILLING

- 1 1/2 lb/750 g fresh Swiss chard/silver beet
- 4 tbsp extra-virgin olive oil
- 2 cloves garlic, sliced
- 1 tsp red pepper flakes (optional)
- dash of salt
- 7 oz/200 g black olives, pitted

Prepare the dough as explained on page 324. ❧ Preheat the oven to 450°F/230°C/gas 7. ❧ Clean the Swiss chard, rinse thoroughly, drain well, and cut into strips. Place in a heavy-bottomed saucepan with 2–3 tablespoons of oil, the garlic, red pepper flakes, if using, and salt to taste. Cook over medium-low heat, initially with the lid on, for 10 minutes, stirring from time to time. The Swiss chard should be tender but not watery. Add the olives and cook for 2–4 minutes more. Set aside to cool. ❧ When the rising time has elapsed, knead the dough for 1 minute on a lightly floured work surface, then divide into 4 equal portions. ❧ Stretch the dough into disks, about 9 in (23 cm) in diameter, as explained on page 325. ❧ Spread the filling on one half of each calzone, leaving a 1-in (2.5-cm) border around the edge. Fold the other half of the dough over the top, pressing down carefully on the edges to seal. ❧ Brush the calzone with the remaining oil, and arrange them on two lightly oiled baking sheets. ❧ Bake for 20–25 minutes, or until puffed and golden brown. ❧ Serve hot.

ONION SUPREME CALZONE

Prepare the dough as explained on page 324. ❧ Preheat the oven to 450°F/230°C/ gas 7. ❧ Cook the onions with 2–3 tablespoons of oil in a large sauté pan for 5 minutes. Add the tomatoes, olives, anchovies, capers, basil, and salt. Mix and cook over medium heat for 5 minutes more. Remove from heat. ❧ When the mixture is cool, add the Pecorino. ❧ When the rising time has elapsed, knead the dough on a lightly floured work surface, then divide into 4 equal portions. ❧ Stretch the dough into disks about 9 in (23 cm) in diameter, as explained on page 325. ❧ Spread the filling on one half of each calzone, leaving a 1-in (2.5-cm) border around the edge. Fold the other half of the dough over the top, pressing down firmly on the edges to seal. ❧ Brush the calzone with the remaining oil, and arrange them on two lightly oiled baking sheets. ❧ Bake for 20–25 minutes, or until puffed and golden brown. ❧ Serve hot.

Makes: 4 calzone
Preparation: 35'
Rising time: 1 h
Cooking: 30–35'
Level of difficulty: 2

BASE
- 3 quantities *Pizza Dough* (see page 324)

FILLING
- 1¼ lb/600 g onions, sliced
- 4 tbsp extra-virgin olive oil
- 8 oz/250 g canned, drained, and chopped tomatoes
- 7 oz/200 g black olives, pitted and halved
- 8 anchovy fillets, crumbled
- 2 tbsp capers
- 8 leaves fresh basil, torn
- salt to taste
- 4 oz/125 g Pecorino cheese, diced

SAVORY
PIES

Pastry

PLAIN PASTRY

For: one (9 in/23 cm) pan

Preparation: 10' +50'

Level of difficulty: 2

• 1¹/₂ cups/225 g all-purpose/plain
  flour
• 1 egg yolk
• dash of salt
• ¹/₂ cup/125 g butter, softened
• ¹/₂ cup/125 ml water, ice cold

Place the flour in a medium bowl and add
the egg yolk, salt, and butter. Mix with a
wooden spoon, gradually working in the
flour and adding water as you go along. ♣
Transfer to a clean work surface and
knead quickly until the dough is soft but
stays together in one piece without
sticking to the work surface. ♣ Form the
dough into a ball, wrap in plastic wrap and
refrigerate for 40–50 minutes. ♣ Follow
the instructions in each recipe for baking.

SPECIAL PASTRY

For: one (9 in/23 cm) pan

Preparation: 15' + 30'

Level of difficulty: 3

• 1¹/₂ cups/225 g all-purpose/plain
  flour
• 1 tsp salt
• 4 tbsp butter
• 6 tbsp cold water

Place the flour and salt in a medium
bowl. Make a hollow in the center and

fill with the butter and water. Mix the
ingredients with a fork, mashing the
butter as you work. ♣ When the
ingredients are roughly mixed, transfer
to a lightly floured work surface and
knead until the dough is soft, smooth,
and elastic. ♣ Flatten the dough with a
rolling pin and shape it into a
rectangle. Fold the shorter sides of the
rectangle inward, one over the other.
Roll the dough into another rectangle,
working in the opposite direction to the
folds. Fold the shorter sides of the
rectangle inward again. Repeat the two
steps once more. ♣ Roll the dough into
a rectangle or circle, depending on the
pan or pie plate you are using. The
dough should be about ¹/₄-in (5-mm)
thick. ♣ Line the base and sides of the
pan or pie plate, cover with plastic
wrap, and refrigerate for at least 30
minutes.

RICOTTA PASTRY

For: one (9 in/23 cm) pan

Preparation: 10 '+ 50'

Level of difficulty: 2

• 1¹/₂ cups/225 g all-purpose/plain
  flour
• dash of salt
• ¹/₂ cup/125 g butter, softened
• 4 oz/125 g soft Ricotta cheese

Follow the Plain Pastry method. Add the
Ricotta when the flour and butter are
almost mixed.

PUFF PASTRY

Puff pastry is time-consuming to make, but not especially difficult. For a light, flaky pastry, be sure to use high-gluten (strong or bread) flour, which retains more air while the dough is being made, then releases it during cooking. Puff pastry freezes well, so make it in large quantities and freeze in single portions.

Preparation: 30' + 1 h

Level of difficulty: 2

• 3^1/$_3$ **cups/500 g all-purpose/plain flour**
• ^{1}/$_2$ **tsp salt**
• 1 **cup/250 ml water**
• 2 **cups/500 g butter, softened**
• 1 **egg white**
• ^{1}/$_2$ **tsp sugar**

Place 3 cups (450 g) sifted flour on a clean work surface. Make a well in the center. ♣ Dissolve the sugar and salt in the water and gradually work in enough of the water to make a smooth dough. Wrap in plastic wrap and refrigerate for 30 minutes. ♣ Place the remaining flour on a clean work surface and combine the butter with the egg white. When smooth and well mixed, shape into a rectangle, wrap in plastic wrap and refrigerate for 30 minutes. ♣ Using a well-floured rolling pin, roll the dough out into a large square shape. ♣ Place the flour-and-butter mixture in the center of the pastry and fold the edges over it. ♣ Roll into a rectangular shape about 1 in (2.5 cm) thick. Wrap the dough carefully in plastic wrap and refrigerate for 20 minutes. ♣ Roll the dough out into a rectangle about ^{1}/$_2$-in (1 cm) thick. Flatten it, using gentle strokes of the rolling pin. Continue rolling, making sure that the rolling pin always moves in the same direction, from the center to the edges. Never roll twice in exactly the same place. Fold the dough over on itself to form a slab consisting of three equal folds, then roll it out in the other direction and fold into three again. ♣ Refrigerate the dough again for 20 minutes. ♣ Repeat the folding, turning and chilling 4 times. ♣ After the last time, the dough can be used in the recipes that follow or frozen for later use.

LEEK PIE

Prepare the pastry. ᔍ Thinly slice the leeks, using the white part and only the start of the green. ᔍ Sauté the leeks in a large skillet (frying pan) in the first measure of butter over medium-low heat for 15–20 minutes, stirring frequently. Season with salt and pepper and set aside to cool. ᔍ Preheat the oven to 350°F/180°C/gas 4. ᔍ Melt the second measure of butter in a small saucepan. Add the flour and cook over low heat for 2 minutes, stirring constantly. Add the milk, a little at a time, stirring constantly. In 4–5 minutes you will obtain a smooth creamy sauce; it should be rather dense, so do not use too much milk. ᔍ Beat the egg white until stiff and combine with the leeks, creamy sauce, cheese, salt, and pepper. Mix well. ᔍ Remove the pastry base from the refrigerator and discard the plastic wrap. ᔍ Pour the leek mixture into the pastry base and sprinkle with the Parmesan. Bake in a preheated oven at for 40 minutes. ᔍ Serve hot.

Makes: one (12-in/ 30-cm) pie

Preparation: 25' + 30' to rest dough

Cooking: 1 h

Level of difficulty: 2

- 1 quantity *Special Pastry* (see page 370)

FILLING
- 2 lb/1 kg leeks, cleaned
- 3 tbsp butter
- salt and freshly ground black pepper to taste
- 2 tbsp butter
- 1 tbsp all-purpose/ plain flour
- 1 cup/250 ml hot milk
- 1 egg white
- 4 tbsp freshly grated Gruyère (or similar) cheese
- 2 tbsp freshly grated Parmesan cheese

BROCCOLI & LEEK PIE

Prepare the pastry. ❧ Preheat the oven to 350°F/180°C/gas 4. ❧ Cut the root and the green tops off the leeks and chop the white parts into thin wheels. ❧ Sauté the leeks in a skillet (frying pan) with the oil, then cover and cook for 15 minutes. Remove from the heat and set aside. ❧ Sauté the bacon in the same skillet until crispy and brown. Set aside. ❧ Divide the broccoli into small florets with stems and cook in a pot of boiling, salted water for 7–10 minutes. Drain and set aside. ❧ Roll out the pastry dough and line a 12-in (30-cm) greased quiche dish. Prick well with a fork. Cover with a sheet of aluminum foil, higher than the sides, and fill with pie weights. ❧ Bake for 15 minutes. Remove the foil and pie weights and bake for 5 minutes more. ❧ Beat the eggs in a bowl and add the milk, cream, Parmesan, salt, and pepper. Beat with a whisk until frothy. ❧ Put the leeks and broccoli in the baked pastry shell, and sprinkle the bacon, eggs, and cheese over the top. ❧ Bake for 35 minutes, turning from time to time to make sure it cooks evenly. After 35 minutes check if the cream is cooked by sticking a toothpick into it; if it comes out coated in cream, cook for 5–10 minutes more. ❧ Serve hot.

Makes: one (12-in/ 30-cm) pie

Preparation: 1 h +1 h

Cooking: 1 1/2 h

Level of difficulty: 2

- 1 quantity *Plain Pastry* (see recipe, p. 370)

- 2 medium leeks
- 1 1/2 tbsp extra-virgin olive oil
- 1/2 cup/75 g diced bacon
- 1 lb/500 g broccoli
- butter for greasing
- salt and freshly ground black pepper to taste
- 3 eggs + 2 yolks
- 1 1/2 cups/375 ml milk
- 1 cup/250 ml cream
- 1 cup/150 g freshly grated Parmesan cheese

ASPARAGUS PIE

Makes: one (12-in/ 30-cm) pie

Preparation: 40' + 30'

Cooking: 35–40'

Level of difficulty: 2

- 1 quantity *Plain Pastry* (see recipe, p. 370)

- 3 lb/1.5 kg fresh asparagus
- 3 tbsp butter
- 4 eggs
- ¹/₂ cup/75 g freshly grated Parmesan cheese
- 1 cup/250 g soft Ricotta cheese
- 3 tbsp oil
- salt and freshly ground black pepper to taste

A sparagus Pie is prepared in the same way as the *Onion Pie* on page 384. ❧ Steam the asparagus, drain and discard all but the green tips. Divide the tips into 2–3 strips and sauté for a few minutes in the butter. ❧ Mix with the egg, cheese, oil, salt, and pepper and follow the method and cooking instructions for *Onion Pie*. ❧ In the same way it is possible to use French beans (about 1³/₄ lb/800 g), boiled and sautéed briefly in butter, or the same amount of mushrooms sautéed for 7–8 minutes over high heat with 4 tablespoons of extra-virgin olive oil, 2 cloves of finely chopped garlic, and 2 tablespoons of finely chopped parsley.

SPINACH PIE

P repare the pastry. ⚘ Preheat the oven to 350°F/180°C/ gas 4. ⚘ Mix the spinach and Ricotta in a bowl. Add the Parmesan, eggs, cream, salt, pepper, and nutmeg, if using. Mix well. ⚘ Roll the pastry out and use it to line a 12-in (30-cm) pie plate. ⚘ Spread evenly with the filling and sprinkle with the bread crumbs. ⚘ Sprinkle with the butter and bake for about 40 minutes, or until nicely browned. ⚘ Serve hot or at room temperature.

Makes: one (12-in/ 30-cm) pie

Preparation: 10' + 1 h

Cooking: 40'

Level of difficulty: 2

- ◆ 1 quantity *Plain Pastry* (see recipe, p. 370)

FILLING

- ◆ 1¹/₂ lb/750 g spinach, cooked, squeezed dry and chopped
- ◆ 1 cup/250 g Ricotta cheese
- ◆ 5 tbsp freshly grated Parmesan cheese
- ◆ 2 eggs, beaten
- ◆ ²/₃ cup/150 ml cream
- ◆ salt and freshly ground black pepper to taste
- ◆ dash of nutmeg (optional)
- ◆ 2 tbsp dry bread crumbs
- ◆ 2 tbsp butter, chopped

MUSHROOM PIE

Makes: one (10-in/
25-cm) pie

Preparation: 20' + 30'
to chill dough

Cooking time: 40'

Level of difficulty: 2

- 1½ quantities
  **Special Pastry (see
  recipe, p. 370)**

- 8 oz/250 g spinach
- 2 cloves garlic,
  finely chopped
- 4 tbsp extra-virgin
  olive oil
- 4 potatoes, boiled
- 3 oz/90 g butter
- salt and freshly
  ground black
  pepper to taste
- 12 oz/350 g
  mixed
  mushrooms
- ½ cup/125 ml
  cream
- 6 tbsp
  vegetable
  stock
- 5 oz/150 g
  ham, chopped
- 4 tbsp freshly
  grated Parmesan
  cheese

Prepare the pastry. ❧ Preheat the oven to 350°F/180°C/ gas 4. ❧ Sauté the spinach and 1 clove garlic in the oil until the spinach is tender. Chop finely when cool. ❧ Mash the potatoes with half the butter. Stir in the spinach mixture and season with salt and pepper. ❧ Cook the mushrooms in a saucepan filled with boiling water for 2 minutes. Drain well. ❧ Melt the remaining butter in a large skillet (frying pan) over medium heat. Stir in the mushrooms, remaining garlic, cream, and stock. Season with salt and pepper. Cook until the sauce has reduced. ❧ Roll out half the pastry and use it to line a 10-inch (25-cm) pan. ❧ Place the ham, potato mixture, and mushroom sauce in the crust. Sprinkle with the Parmesan. Roll out the remaining pastry to form a top. Pinch the pastry to seal. ❧ Bake for 40 minutes, or until golden brown.

FRIED VEGETABLE PIES

Makes: 6–8 small pies

Preparation: 30'

Cooking: 20'

Level of difficulty: 1

FILLING
- 1½ lb/750 g spinach, or Swiss chard, or spinach beet
- 1 small onion, finely chopped
- 3 tbsp butter
- salt and freshly ground black pepper to taste

DOUGH
- 1½ cups/225 g all-purpose/plain flour
- 3 eggs
- ⅓ cup/90 ml milk

- 2 cups/500 ml oil, for frying

Wash the greens thoroughly and cook in a little boiling, salted water for 5–7 minutes. Drain, then squeeze out the excess moisture and chop coarsely. ❧ Sauté the onion gently in the butter until soft. Add the spinach and sauté briefly. Season with salt and pepper. ❧ Sift the flour and a dash of salt into a mixing bowl. Make a well in the center. Break the eggs into it and stir with a fork, gradually incorporating the flour and adding enough milk, a little at a time, to form a soft dough that leaves the sides of the bowl clean. ❧ Knead the dough until smooth and elastic. ❧ Using a well-floured rolling pin and board, roll the dough out into a thin sheet and cut out disks of 4 in (10 cm) in diameter. ❧ Spread a little of the spinach filling over half of each disk (stopping well short of the edge). Fold the uncovered half over the top, to make semi-circular pies. ❧ Press down on the curved edges with the tines (prongs) of a fork to seal. ❧ Fry the pies until golden brown on both sides in plenty of very hot lard or oil. ❧ Drain the pies on paper towels and serve while still very hot.

GREEN PIE

Wash the chard or spinach leaves well, but do not dry; cook for a few minutes with a little water left clinging to the leaves. Remove from the heat, squeeze out as much moisture as possible, and chop very coarsely. ꧁ Sauté the bacon, parsley, garlic, and scallions in the butter in a large skillet (frying pan) until the onion is translucent. ꧁ Set 1 tablespoon of this mixture aside. Leave the rest in the skillet and add the chopped chard or spinach, Parmesan, salt, and pepper. Stir well. ꧁ Sift the flour and a dash of salt into a large bowl. Make a well in the center and pour the melted lard into it. Gradually stir in the flour, adding a little warm water at intervals, to form a soft and elastic dough. ꧁ Knead the dough until smooth and elastic. ꧁ Divide it into two parts, one slightly larger than the other, and roll out into two thin disks. Use the larger one to line a deep, greased 10-in (25-cm) springform pan. It should overlap the edges a little. ꧁ Fill with the filling mixture and smooth until level. Cover with the other disk, pinching the edges to seal them. ꧁ Spread the reserved 1 tablespoon of fried mixture over the surface of the dough. Bake for 30 minutes, or until golden brown. ꧁ Serve warm rather than hot.

Makes: one (10-in/ 25-cm) pie

Preparation: 30'

Cooking: 35'

Level of difficulty: 1

- 2$\frac{1}{2}$ lb/1.2 kg Swiss chard, or spinach beet, or spinach leaves
- 5 oz/150 g bacon, finely chopped
- 2 tbsp parsley, finely chopped
- 1 clove garlic, finely chopped
- 6 scallions/spring onions, finely chopped
- 2 tbsp butter
- $\frac{3}{4}$ cup/100 g Parmesan cheese, freshly grated
- salt and freshly ground black pepper to taste
- 2$\frac{1}{3}$ cups/350 g all-purpose/plain flour
- dash of salt
- 4 tbsp lard, melted
- warm water for the dough

VEGETABLE PIE

Makes: one (12-in/
30-cm) pie

Preparation: 20' + time
to make pastry

Cooking: 1 h

Level of difficulty: 1

- 1 quantity *Special Pastry* (see page 370)

- 2 red bell peppers/ capsicums
- 4 zucchini/ courgettes
- 4 large carrots
- salt and freshly ground black pepper to taste
- 3 tbsp extra-virgin olive oil
- 2 tbsp butter
- $^1/_2$ cup/125 g white wine
- 2 cups/200 g dried beans

Prepare the pastry. ❧ Preheat the oven to 375°F/190°C/gas 5. ❧ Cut the bell peppers in thin strips, the zucchini in wheels, and the carrots in ribbons. ❧ Sauté the bell peppers in the oil with a dash of salt in a skillet (frying pan) over high heat for 10 minutes, stirring frequently. Take the bell peppers out and set aside. ❧ Use the same oil to sauté the zucchini with a pinch of salt for 7–8 minutes. Remove from the skillet and set aside. ❧ Use a paper towel to eliminate the oil in the skillet. Put the butter, carrots, wine, and a pinch of salt in it and cook until the liquid has evaporated and the carrots are soft. Set the carrots aside. ❧ Take the pie pan out of the refrigerator and remove the plastic wrap. Prick well with a fork. ❧ Cover with a sheet of aluminum foil, weigh it down with pie weights, and bake for 35 minutes. ❧ Remove the foil and weights and bake for 10 minutes more. ❧ Garnish with the vegetables and serve.

ONION PIE

repare the pastry. ☙ Sauté the onions in the butter in a medium saucepan over low heat for 25–30 minutes, stirring frequently. When cooked, the onions should be soft and golden brown. ☙ Preheat the oven to 350°F/180°C/gas 4. ☙ Beat the egg in a medium bowl, and add the milk and flour, mixing well so that no lumps form. Season with salt and pepper. ☙ Roll out the pastry and use it to line a 12-in (30-cm) springform pan. ☙ Cover the pastry with a sheet of foil, pressing it down carefully so that it adheres to the pastry. ☙ Bake for 15 minutes. ☙ Take the springform pan out of the oven and, using the palm of a gloved hand, carefully press the base down so that it contracts a little. ☙ Discard the foil and return the pie to the oven for 5 minutes more. ☙ Take the base out again, spread with the onion mixture and pour the egg and milk mixture over the top. ☙ Bake for 20 minutes, or until golden brown. ☙ Serve hot.

Makes: one (12-in/ 30-cm) pie

Preparation: 40' + time to make pastry

Cooking: 1¼ h

Level of difficulty: 2

BASE

• 1 quantity *Plain Pastry* (see page 370)

FILLING

• 2 lb/1 kg onions, sliced
• 3 oz/90 g butter
• 1 egg
• ¾ cup/200 ml milk
• 1 tbsp all-purpose/ plain flour
• salt and freshly ground black pepper to taste

SALMON QUICHE

Preheat the oven to 325°F/170°C/gas 3. ❧
Place the flour, baking powder, cheese,
onions, salt, and pepper into a large bowl. ❧
In a separate bowl, beat the eggs, milk, and butter
together. ❧ Pour the milk and egg mixture into the
flour and beat until
smooth. ❧ Fold the
salmon gently into the mixture so that it stays in
small chunks. ❧ Transfer to a greased 10-in (25-
cm) pie plate or quiche dish. ❧ Bake for 25–30
minutes, or until cooked through and browned on
the top. ❧ Serve hot or at room temperature.

*This quiche is very quickly made and is delicious
served with a salad and some fresh, crusty bread.*

*Makes: one (10-in/
25-cm) pie*

Preparation: 15'

Cooking: 25–30'

Level of difficulty: 1

- **¹/₂ cup/60 g all-
  purpose/plain flour**
- **¹/₂ tsp baking
  powder**
- **1¹/₄ cups/150 g
  Cheddar cheese,
  grated**
- **2 small onions,
  chopped**
- **salt and freshly
  ground black
  pepper to taste**
- **3 eggs, beaten**
- **1 cup/250 ml milk**
- **2 tbsp butter,
  melted**
- **8 oz/250 g canned
  salmon**

TOMATO QUICHE

Makes: one (12-in/ 30-cm) pie

Preparation: 20' + 30 to chill dough

Cooking time: 35'

Level of difficulty: 2

- 1½ cups/225 g all-purpose/plain flour
- 1 tsp salt
- ½ cup/125 g butter, cubed
- ⅔ cup/150 ml ice cold water
- 1 scallion/spring onion, chopped
- 1 tbsp extra-virgin olive oil
- 6 tbsp light/single cream
- 3 eggs
- ½ cup/60 g grated Emmental cheese
- dash of oregano
- 14 oz/450 g ripe tomatoes
- salt to taste

Sift the flour and salt into a bowl. Add the butter and, working quickly, rub it into the flour with your fingertips. When the mixture resembles fine bread crumbs, add the ice water, and shape the dough into a ball. ❧ Wrap the pastry in a plastic wrap and refrigerate for 30 minutes. ❧ Preheat the oven to 350°F/180°C/gas 4. ❧ Sauté the scallion in the oil until soft. ❧ Beat the cream with the eggs, cheese, oregano, and scallion. ❧ Thinly slice the tomatoes, season lightly with salt, and set aside for a moment to drain. ❧ Grease a 12-in (30-cm) springform pan. ❧ Roll out the pastry to about ¼-in (6-mm) thick and use it to line the base and 1-in (2.5-cm) up the sides of the pan. ❧ Prick well with a fork and fill with the cream and egg mixture. Arrange the tomato slices on top so they sink into the liquid. ❧ Bake for about 35 minutes, or until pale golden brown. ❧ Serve at room temperature.

POTATO PIE

Makes: one (9-in/
23-cm) pie

Preparation: 45'

Cooking: 45' + 30'

Level of difficulty: 1

FILLING
* 2 lb/1 kg potatoes
* 1 onion, finely
  chopped
* 1 tbsp butter
* 4 tbsp pork
  fat/lard, finely
  chopped
* 2 tbsp cooking
  juices from roast
  meat or poultry
* 1 cup/150 g freshly
  grated Parmesan
  cheese
* 4 tbsp milk
* salt to taste

DOUGH
* 1½ cups/225 g all-
  purpose/plain flour
* ½ tsp salt
* 2 tbsp extra-virgin
  olive oil
* 4–6 tbsp war water
* butter for greasing
* 2 tbsp fine, dry
  bread crumbs

Boil the potatoes until tender. Mash while still hot. ❧ Preheat the oven to 350°F/180°C/gas 4. ❧ Sauté the onion in the butter and pork fat over low heat in a large skillet (frying pan) until translucent. ❧ Add the roast meat juices and turn off the heat. ❧ Stir in the potatoes, Parmesan, milk, and salt. ❧ Place the flour and salt in a medium bowl. Make a well in the center and add 1 tablespoon of the olive oil and a little warm water. Gradually mix in the flour, adding enough water to obtain a firm dough. ❧ Knead the dough until smooth and elastic. ❧ Working with a well-floured rolling pin and pastry board, roll out the dough into a thin sheet. Cut out two disks, one larger than the other. ❧ Use the larger one to line the base and sides of an oiled 9-in (23-cm) springform pan. ❧ Fill with the potato mixture, then cover with the remaining disk of pastry and seal the edges. Brush with the remaining oil and prick several times with a fork. ❧ Bake for 45 minutes, or until the pastry is pale golden brown. ❧ Serve hot.

This hearty pie is good in winter. Serve with a green or mixed salad.

391

TOMATO & MOZZARELLA PIE

Prepare the pastry. ❧ Preheat the oven to 350°F/180°C/gas 5. ❧ Beat the eggs and yolks in a large bowl, stir in the milk and cream, then the Parmesan, oregano, and basil. Season with the salt and pepper. ❧ Take the pie pan out of the refrigerator and remove the plastic wrap. Prick well with a fork. ❧ Bake for 5 minutes. Remove and fill with the tomato and Mozzarella. Pour the egg and cream mixture over the top and sprinkle with the sausage. Return to the oven for 15 minutes, or until the topping is lightly colored. ❧ Serve at room temperature.

Makes: one (12-in/ 30-cm) pie

Preparation: 45'

Cooking: 45' + 30'

Level of difficulty: 3

BASE
- 1 quantity *Special Pastry* (see page 370)

TOPPING
- 2 eggs + 2 yolks
- 1 cup/250 ml milk
- 1 cup/250 ml cream
- $^1/_2$ cup/60 g freshly grated Parmesan cheese
- 10 leaves basil, torn
- dash of dried oregano
- 4 oz/125 g Mozzarella cheese, diced
- 2 large ripe tomatoes, thinly sliced
- 4 oz/125 g spicy sausage, skinned and crumbled

POTATO, BACON, & CHEESE PIE

Makes: one (12-in/ 30-cm) pie

Preparation: 45'

Cooking: 20'

Level of difficulty: 2

- **8 large potatoes, thinly sliced**
- **salt and freshly ground black pepper to taste**
- **8–10 rashers thinly sliced bacon**
- **8 oz/250 g Cheddar cheese, sliced**

Preheat the oven to 400°F/200°C/gas 6. Steam the potatoes for 5 minutes, or until half-cooked. Season with salt and pepper. Place a layer of bacon in an oiled 12-in (30-cm) baking dish. Cover with a layer of potatoes and a layer of cheese. Repeat until all the ingredients are in the dish, finishing with a layer of cheese. Bake for 20–25 minutes, or until the potatoes are fully cooked and the cheese is melted. Serve hot.

NEAPOLITAN FILLED BREAD

Crumble the yeast into a bowl and add the sugar. Mix with the milk (or water) and set aside for 5 minutes. ❧ Place the flour and salt in a medium bowl and make a hollow in the center. Fill with the yeast mixture, butter, and eggs. Mix with a wooden spoon until the flour absorbs the other ingredients. ❧ Transfer to a lightly floured work surface. ❧ Knead until smooth and elastic, about 5 minutes. ❧ Place in a bowl, cover with a cloth, and let rise in a warm, sheltered place for 2 hours. ❧ Cut the tomatoes in half, and remove the seeds. ❧ Sauté the tomatoes in the oil over high heat for 3–4 minutes. Shake the skillet (frying pan) from time to time to move and turn the tomatoes, rather than stirring them. ❧ Butter and flour a 9 in (23 cm) springform pan. ❧ When the rising time has elapsed, transfer the dough to a lightly floured work surface and tap lightly with your fingers so that it contracts a little. ❧ Break off about a third of the dough and set aside. ❧ Place the rest in the springform pan and spread by hand to line the base and sides. ❧ Cover with half the Mozzarella, followed by the tomatoes. Sprinkle with salt and pepper, sprinkle with the basil, and cover with the Parma ham and remaining Mozzarella. ❧ Sprinkle with the Parmesan and, if liked, more pepper. ❧ Roll the remaining dough into a disk as large as the springform pan. Brush the edges of the dough with half the beaten egg. Cover the filling with the sheet

Makes: one (9-in/ 23-cm) pie	
Preparation: 45'	
Rising time: 3 h	
Cooking: 25–30'	
Level of difficulty: 3	

DOUGH

- ⅔ oz/20 g fresh yeast or 1 (¼ oz) package active dry yeast
- 2 tsp sugar
- 3–4 tbsp warm milk (or water)
- 2½ cups/225 g all-purpose/plain flour
- 1 tsp salt
- ⅔ cup/150 g butter, at room temperature, in thin slices
- 4 eggs, lightly beaten

FILLING

- 14 oz/450 g ripe tomatoes, peeled
- 2 tbsp extra-virgin olive oil
- 2 tbsp butter
- 11 oz/300 g Mozzarella cheese, sliced

- salt and freshly ground black pepper to taste
- 8–10 leaves fresh basil, torn
- 5 oz/150 g Parma ham, sliced and cut in strips
- 4 tbsp freshly grated Parmesan cheese
- 1 egg, beaten

and seal the edges of the two sheets by pressing them together lightly with your fingers. ❧ Let rise for 1 hour. ❧ Preheat the oven to 400°F/200°C/gas 6. ❧ Brush the surface with the remaining egg and bake for 25–30 minutes, or until golden brown. ❧ Serve hot.

RICE & PUMPKIN PIE

P reheat the oven to 350°F/180°C/gas 4. ♣
Bring the water, milk, and a dash of salt to a
boil. Add the rice. Cook for 10 minutes then
drain. ♣ Peel the pumpkin. Remove the seeds and
grate the raw flesh finely onto a clean cloth.

The rice and pumpkin combine beautifully with the Ricotta in a creamy, almost sweet filling.

Gather up the cloth and twist it round tightly, squeezing some of the moisture out
of the pumpkin. ♣ Mix the grated pumpkin with
the rice, then add the Parmesan, Ricotta, egg,
butter, salt, and pepper. ♣ Place the flour and salt
in a large bowl and make a well in the center.
Pour in 2 tablespoons of oil and enough water to
make a firm dough. ♣ Transfer to a lightly floured
work surface and knead until smooth and elastic.
♣ Divide into 2 portions, one slightly larger than
the other. Roll the pastry out very thin and use the
larger sheet to line an oiled 10 in (25 cm)
springform pan. ♣ Fill with the rice and pumpkin
mixture and cover with the other disk of pastry,
pinching the edges together to seal. Brush the
surface with the remaining oil and prick several
times with a fork. ♣ Bake for about 45 minutes,
or until the pastry is golden brown. ♣ Serve hot or
at room temperature.

Makes: one (12-in/
30-cm) pie

Preparation: 45'

Cooking: 45'

Level of difficulty: 2

FILLING
- 2 cups/500 ml water
- 1³/₄ cups/450 ml milk
- salt and freshly ground black pepper to taste
- 1³/₄ cups/300 g short-grain rice
- piece of squash, weighing about 1 lb/500 g
- 6 tbsp freshly grated Parmesan cheese
- ¹/₂ cup/125 g fresh Ricotta cheese
- 1 egg
- 1¹/₂ tbsp butter

DOUGH
- 1¹/₂ cups/225 g all-purpose/plain flour
- ¹/₂ tsp salt
- 4 tbsp extra-virgin olive oil
- 4–6 tbsp warm water

LEEK & FONTAL COUNTRY PIE

Prepare the pastry. ❧ Preheat the oven to 375°F/190°C/gas 5. ❧ Sauté the leeks in the oil in a large skillet (frying pan) until soft. Season with salt and pepper. ❧ In a large bowl, beat the 2 whole eggs then add the cheese and parsley. Stir in the leeks. ❧ On a floured work surface, roll out two-thirds of the pie dough with a rolling pin. Use it to line an oiled 12 in (30 cm) pie pan. Fill with the leek and egg mixture. ❧ Roll out the remaining dough and cut into strips. Place them in a spoke pattern on top of the filling. ❧ Brush with an egg wash made from the remaining egg yolk mixed with a little water. ❧ Bake for 30 minutes, then lower the temperature and bake for 15 minutes more. ❧ Serve hot or warm.

Makes: one (12-in/ 30-cm) pie

Preparation: 20'

Cooking: 45'

Level of difficulty: 2

- ◆ **1 quantity Plain Pastry (see page 370)**

FILLING

- ◆ **2 lb/1 kg leeks, thinly sliced**
- ◆ **2 tbsp extra-virgin olive oil**
- ◆ **salt and freshly ground black pepper to taste**
- ◆ **2 eggs + 1 extra egg yolk**
- ◆ **11 oz/300 g tasty Cheddar cheese, diced**
- ◆ **2 tbsp finely chopped parsley**

HAM & WALNUT POTATO GRATIN

Makes: one (9-in/ 23-cm) pie

Preparation: 20'

Cooking: 1 h

Level of difficulty: 1

- 2 lb/1 kg potatoes
- 1 quantity Béchamel sauce (see page 950)
- 4 tbsp freshly grated Parmesan cheese
- 2 tbsp butter
- salt and freshly ground black pepper to taste
- 7 oz/200 g ham
- 7 oz/200 g shelled walnuts, (5 oz/150 g coarsely chopped and 2 oz/50 g halved)
- 7 oz/200 g Mozzarella cheese
- 2 tbsp bread crumbs

Cook the potatoes in their skins in salted, boiling water for 25 minutes, or until tender. Drain and set aside to cool. ❧ Preheat the oven to 350°F/180°C/gas 4. ❧ Prepare a thick Béchamel sauce and stir in the Parmesan. ❧ Peel the potatoes and cut in ½-in (1-cm) slices. Butter a deep 9-in (23-cm) dish and cover the bottom with a layer of potatoes. Fill in the gaps so that the bottom is sealed. ❧ Cover with a layer of Béchamel and sprinkle with the ham and chopped walnuts. Continue with another layer of potatoes and cover with the Mozzarella and a little Béchamel sauce. Make a top layer of potatoes and cover with the remaining Béchamel. Sprinkle with the bread crumbs and dot with the remaining butter. ❧ Bake for about 25 minutes, or until golden brown. ❧ Garnish with remaining walnut halves and serve hot.

399

CHEESE FLATBREAD

Makes: one (10-in/
25-cm) pie

Preparation: 40'

Rising time: 4 h

Cooking: 40'

Level of difficulty: 1

- • ²/₃ oz/20 g fresh
  yeast or 1 (¹/₄
  oz) package active
  dry yeast
- • 4 tbsp warm water
- • 1 tsp sugar
- • 3 eggs + 1 yolk,
  beaten
- • 6 tbsp extra-virgin
  olive oil
- • 2 cups/300 g all-
  purpose/plain flour
- • 2 tsp salt
- • 8 oz/250 g
  Pecorino Romano
  cheese, freshly
  grated
- • ¹/₂ tsp white pepper

Mix the yeast with the water, add the sugar and set aside for 10 minutes. ❧ Beat the eggs with the oil in a medium bowl. ❧ Place the flour and salt in another medium and make a hollow in the center. Stir in the yeast and egg mixtures until the flour absorbs all the ingredients. The dough will be soft and sticky. ❧ Mix for 6–8 minutes with a wooden spoon. Cover with a cloth and let rise in a warm, sheltered place for 2 hours. ❧ When the rising time has elapsed, add the cheese and pepper and mix again for 3–4 minutes. ❧ Oil and flour a 10 in (25 cm) springform pan or quiche dish. Fill with the dough and leave to rise for 2 hours. ❧ Preheat the oven to 375°F/ 190°C/gas 5. ❧ Bake for 40 minutes, or until golden brown. ❧ Serve hot.

A specialty from central Italy, traditionally served piping hot with a platter of ham and salami.

SAFFRON CHEESE PIE

Prepare the pastry. ❧ Preheat the oven to 350°F/180°C/gas 4. ❧ Place the Ricotta in a large bowl and mash with a fork. Add the Gruyère, butter, saffron and, one at a time, the egg yolks, mixing well. ❧ Beat the egg whites until stiff and fold into the mixture. ❧ Roll out the dough and line an oiled 12-in (30-cm) pie pan. ❧ Fill with the cheese mixture. ❧ Bake for 45 minutes, or until the pastry edges are golden brown. ❧ Serve hot or at room temperature.

Makes: one (12-in/ 30-cm) pie

Preparation: 20' + 1 h to chill

Cooking: 45'

Level of difficulty: 2

BASE

* 1 quantity *Plain Pastry* (see page 370)

FILLING

* 14 oz/450 g Ricotta cheese
* 5 oz/150 g Gruyère cheese, grated
* 6 tbsp butter
* generous dash of saffron
* 6 eggs, separated

CHEESE, CREAM, & BACON PIE

Makes: one (12-in/
30-cm) pie

Preparation: 15' + 30'

Cooking: 30–35'

Level of difficulty: 2

BASE

• 1 quantity *Ricotta Pastry* (see page 370)

FILLING

• 3 eggs, lightly beaten
• 1 cup/125 g freshly grated Emmental cheese
• ²/₃ cup/150 ml cream
• salt and freshly ground black pepper to taste
• ¹/₂ cup/75 g bacon, coarsely chopped

Prepare the pastry. ♠ Preheat the oven to 350°F/180°C/gas 4. ♠ Place the eggs in a bowl with the Emmental, cream, salt, and pepper. ♠ Remove the pastry base from the refrigerator and discard the plastic wrap. Sprinkle the bacon over the base, then pour the egg, cheese, and cream mixture over the top. ♠ Bake for 30–35 minutes, or until golden brown. ♠ Serve hot.

BACON & EGG PIE

Prepare the pastry. ❧ Preheat the oven to 400°F/200°C/gas 6. ❧ Cut the bacon into small pieces and sauté in a skillet (frying pan) for a 3–5 minutes. ❧ Roll out two-thirds of the pastry and use it to line a 10-in (25-cm) quiche dish. ❧ Place about half the bacon pieces on the pastry and break the eggs over the top. Stab each yolk with a knife so that they "run" a little. ❧ Arrange the remaining bacon on top. ❧ Roll out the rest of the pastry and make decorative leaves or a crimped edging, if desired. ❧ Bake for 30–40 minutes, or until the pastry is golden brown. ❧ Serve hot or at room temperature.

Most children love a Bacon & Egg Pie and it is also a very useful addition to a picnic.

Makes: one (10-in/ 25-cm) pie

Preparation: 10' + 2 h

Cooking time: 30–40'

Level of difficulty: 1

- 12 oz/350 g **Puff Pastry**, homemade (see page 371) or store-bought

- 5–6 rashers lean bacon
- 5–6 eggs
- salt and freshly ground black pepper to taste

BLUE CHEESE SAVORIES

Makes: about 12 savories

Preparation: 15' + 2 h

Cooking time: 15'

Level of difficulty: 2

- 12 oz/350 g *Puff Pastry*, homemade (see page 371) or store-bought
- 8 oz/250 g blue cheese
- 5 oz/150 g cream cheese
- freshly ground black pepper to taste
- 1 egg, beaten

Prepare the pastry. ❧ Preheat the oven to 400°F/200°C/gas 6. ❧ In a bowl, crumble the blue cheese, combine with the cream cheese, and season with pepper. ❧ Roll the dough out into a thin sheet. Cut 3 in (8 cm) disks, rerolling the offcuts until all the pastry is used. ❧ Place half the disks on a baking sheet. ❧ Moisten the pastry edges with some of the egg. ❧ Divide the cheese mixture between the disks and cover with the remaining pastry disks. ❧ Ensure that the edges are sealed by pinching them together with your fingers. ❧ Make a small slit in each top to allow steam to escape and brush with egg. ❧ Bake for 15 minutes, or until the pastry is golden brown. ❧ Serve hot or at room temperature.

MACARONI PIE

Makes: one (9-in/
23-cm) pie

Preparation: 1 h + 30'

Cooking: 1¹/₄ h

Level of difficulty: 3

S ift the flour into a large bowl and stir in the salt and sugar. Rub the butter into the flour, work quickly using the tips of your fingers. The mixture will look like very fine bread crumbs. ♣ Mix the egg yolks in with a fork, then work briefly by hand, just enough to bind the mixture. ♣ Shape the dough into a ball. Wrap in plastic wrap (cling film) and refrigerate for 30 minutes. ♣ Meat sauce: Melt the butter in a heavy-bottomed skillet (frying pan). Sauté the bacon for 3–5 minutes. Add the veal and chicken livers and sauté until golden brown, stirring all the time. ♣ Pour in the wine and cook until it has evaporated. ♣ Add the sieved tomatoes and season with the cinnamon, nutmeg, salt, and pepper. ♣ Simmer for 40 minutes over low heat. ♣ Prepare the Béchamel Sauce. ♣ Preheat the oven to 350°F/180°C/gas 4. ♣ Grease a 9-in (23-cm) springform pan with the remaining butter and sprinkle with the bread crumbs. ♣ Roll out two-thirds of the pastry dough into a disk large enough to line the bottom and sides of the springform pan. Line the pan. ♣ Cook the macaroni in a large pot of boiling, salted water for half the time indicated on the package. ♣ Drain and mix with half the meat sauce. ♣ Spoon a layer of macaroni over the pastry. Cover with a layer of the remaining meat sauce, followed by a layer of Béchamel sauce. Sprinkle with a little Parmesan. ♣ Repeat the process until

Dough

- 2 cups/300 g all-purpose/plain flour
- dash of salt
- 4 tbsp sugar
- ²/₃ cup/150 g butter, chopped
- 3 egg yolks

Meat sauce

- 4 tbsp butter
- 4 tbsp bacon, finely chopped
- 8 oz/250 g finely diced veal
- 7 oz/200 g trimmed, diced chicken livers
- ¹/₂ cup/125 ml dry red wine
- 11 oz/300 g canned tomatoes
- dash of ground cinnamon
- dash of freshly grated nutmeg
- salt and freshly ground black pepper to taste

- 1 quantity Béchamel Sauce (see page 950)

- 1 tbsp butter
- ¹/₂ cup/60 g fine dry bread crumbs

- **14 oz/450 g** *macaroni*
- **1 cup/150 g freshly grated Parmesan cheese**

you have used up all the ingredients. ✿ Roll out the remaining pastry into a disk to form a lid for the pie. Pinch the edges to seal tightly. ✿ Bake in a preheated oven for 35 minutes, or until golden brown. ✿ Remove from the oven and leave to stand for 10 minutes before serving.

SWEET & SOUR CALAMARI PIE

Crumble the yeast into a small bowl, add the sugar and half the water, stirring until the yeast dissolves. Let stand for 10 minutes in a warm place. ❧ Place the flour and salt in a medium bowl. Make a well in the center and pour in the yeast mixture, oil, and most of the remaining water. ❧ Stir with a wooden spoon until the flour has been absorbed. Add a little more warm water if necessary. ❧ Place the dough on a floured work surface and knead until smooth and elastic. ❧ Shape into a ball and place in a large bowl. Cover with a clean cloth and let rise in a warm, sheltered place for 1 hour, or until the dough has doubled in bulk. ❧ Preheat the oven to 400°F/200°C/gas 6. ❧ Knead the dough briefly on a lightly floured surface just before using. ❧ Heat the oil in a large skillet (frying pan) and sauté the garlic for 2–3 minutes. Remove the garlic and add the calamari. Cook over medium heat, stirring frequently for 15 minutes. ❧ Stir in the other ingredients and cook for 5 minutes. Season with salt and pepper. ❧ Divide the dough into two portions, one almost twice as large as the other. Roll the larger piece out to a thickness of about ⅛ in (3 mm). Use it to line the bottom and sides of a springform pan. Leave enough dough to slightly overlap the edges. ❧ Fill the dough-lined springform pan with the calamari mixture. ❧ Roll out the smaller piece of dough to the same thickness as the first and use it to cover the springform pan. Fold the

Serves: 4

Preparation: 30'

Rising time: 1 h

Cooking: 1 h

Level of difficulty: 1

DOUGH

- ⅔ oz/20 g fresh yeast or 1 (¼ oz) package active dry yeast
- 1 tsp sugar
- ¾ cup/200 ml lukewarm water
- 2⅓ cups/350 g all-purpose/plain flour
- 1–2 tsp salt
- 2 tbsp extra-virgin olive oil

FILLING

- 4 tbsp extra-virgin olive oil
- 1 clove garlic, crushed but whole
- 13 oz/400 g calamari (cleaned weight – ask your fish vendor to prepare it), coarsely chopped
- 4 ripe tomatoes, peeled and diced
- 1¾ cups/200 g pitted black olives

- **4 tbsp golden raisins/sultanas**
- **4 tbsp pine nuts**
- **4 tbsp capers**
- **salt and freshly ground black pepper to taste**

overlapping dough over the top to seal. ⚜ Bake for 30 minutes, or until the pastry is pale golden brown. ⚜ Serve hot or at room temperature.

EGGS

Eggs

Nutritious and versatile, eggs contain vitamins, minerals, fats, and complete protein. The yolk contains most of the protein, and all the fats, vitamins, and minerals, while the white is made up of water and some protein. Eggs can be boiled, poached, fried, scrambled, or made into omelets and served as a meal in themselves, but they are also important ingredients in a huge range of other dishes, from savory entrées and snacks and high energy breakfasts, to desserts, cookies, and cakes. In the kitchen, eggs can be used to bind ingredients together (think of meatballs or croquettes), or to help other ingredients, such as bread crumbs, stick. They can be brushed onto breads or cakes to provide glazing. They are efficient rising agents, for example in cakes and desserts like meringue that call for stiffly beaten egg whites, and can also be used to thicken sauces.

Health issues and concerns

Despite their nutritional value, versatility, and delicious taste, eggs have had their reputations tarnished in recent years on a number of counts concerning health. Several years ago their consumption was discouraged even for healthy people because of their high cholesterol content. Recently this position has been reevaluated and health authorities (including the American Heart Foundation) now consider up to 4 eggs a week safe.

The second concern regards the consumption of raw or lightly cooked eggs, although this has been a much greater issue in North America than in Europe. A tiny minority of eggs are infected with a bacteria called *Salmonella enteritidis*, which can cause serious illness and even death in people whose immune systems are already weakened. The risk is very small but can be eliminated altogether by making sure any egg eaten has first been heated to 160°F (54°C).

Crabmeat omelet

- 2 oz/60 g all-purpose/plain flour
- 14 oz/450 g crabmeat, diced
- 1/2 cup/125 ml extra-virgin olive oil
- 8 eggs
- salt and freshly ground black pepper to taste

Lightly flour the crab meat. ♣ Heat half the oil in a medium skillet (frying pan) and fry the crabmeat for 4–5 minutes. ♣ Beat the eggs with the salt and pepper in a medium bowl, then add the prepared crabmeat and mix well. ♣ Heat the remaining oil in the skillet used to fry the crabmeat, and pour in the egg mixture. Cook for 4–5 minutes. Turn the omelet carefully and cook for 4 minutes more. It should be firm and lightly browned on both sides. ♣ Turn out onto a heated serving dish and serve hot.

Egg size and weight

Chicken eggs are the most commonly used eggs in most cuisines (the following weights and categories apply to them) and are usually graded according to shell color and size. Size classifications a are applied to a dozen eggs as follows:

Egg size	min. weight
Jumbo	30 oz
Extralarge	27 oz
Large	24 oz
Medium	21 oz
Small	18 oz
Peewee	15 oz

The size sensitive recipes in this book are all based on the use of large (2 oz/60 g eggs).

SCOTCH EGGS

Serves: 2–4

Preparation: 15'

Cooking: 8–10'

Level of difficulty: 1

- 8 oz/250 g sausage meat
- 1 tbsp finely chopped parsley
- 1 tsp chopped chives
- 1 tbsp tomato paste
- salt and freshly ground black pepper to taste
- 4 hard-boiled eggs, shelled
- 1 cup/150 g all-purpose/plain flour, seasoned with salt and pepper
- 1 small egg, beaten
- 1/2 cup/60 g fine dry bread crumbs
- 2 cups/500 ml oil, for frying

P lace the sausage meat in a large bowl with the parsley, chives, and tomato paste and mix well. ❧ Season with salt and pepper. ❧ Roll the hard-boiled eggs in the seasoned flour. ❧ Divide the sausage meat mixture into four. ❧ On a floured board, flatten each portion out into a piece big enough to wrap around the eggs. Place one egg on a piece of sausage meat and carefully enclose it, overlapping at the seams. Smooth the seams, forming a neat ball and making sure that no egg is showing. ❧ Repeat with the other eggs. ❧ Carefully dip the eggs in the beaten egg and roll them in the bread crumbs. ❧ Heat the oil in a deep skillet (frying pan) until very hot. Test the oil by dropping a small piece of bread into it. When hot enough, the bread will turn brown instantly. ❧ Fry the eggs in the oil for 8–10 minutes, or until golden brown all over. ❧ Drain on paper towels and serve hot or at room temperature.

CURRIED EGGS

Melt the butter in a medium heavy-bottomed saucepan and add the onion. ♣ Cook for 3–4 minutes over medium heat until soft. ♣ Add the apple and cook for 3–4 minutes more. ♣ Add the flour, curry powder, and cumin and stir for 2–3 minutes. ♣

Serve with rice and a green salad for a healthy and complete lunch or supper.

Slowly add the stock, stirring constantly, to ensure a smooth texture. ♣ Simmer for a few minutes and then add the eggs. ♣ Sprinkle with the parsley and serve.

Serves: 4

Preparation: 15'

Cooking: 15'

Level of difficulty: 1

- **4 tbsp butter**
- **1 large onion, finely chopped**
- **1 cooking apple, peeled and diced**
- **1 oz/30 g all-purpose/plain flour**
- **1–2 tbsp curry powder**
- **1 tsp cumin seeds, crushed**
- **2^1/$_2$ cups/625 ml hot *Chicken Stock* (see page 140)**
- **6 eggs, hard-boiled, shelled and cut in half**
- **1 tbsp finely chopped parsley**

PLAIN OMELET

I n a small bowl, beat the eggs, water, salt, and pepper briskly with a fork. ❧ Drop the butter into a small omelet pan and place over high heat. ❧ When the butter is foaming, pour the eggs into the pan. ❧ Start lifting the edges of the mixture around the pan with the fork to allow the runny, uncooked egg to get underneath. ❧ Continue to do this until the omelet is set — it will only take a minute or two. ❧ Slip the fork under one side and fold the omelette in half and slide it all out onto a warmed plate. ❧ Garnish with the parsley and serve immediately.

This simple offering is perfect at any time of the day. Serve with a salad for a nutritious lunch.

- **2 eggs**
- **1 tbsp cold water**
- **salt and freshly ground black pepper to taste**
- **1 tbsp butter**
- **sprig of parsley to garnish**

Serves: 4

Preparation: 10–15'

Cooking: 15–20'

Level of difficulty: 1

- **2 tbsp butter, melted**
- **3 oz/90 g ham, finely chopped**
- **2 tomatoes, peeled and sliced**
- **6 eggs**
- **¹/₂ cup/125 ml cream or milk**
- **salt and freshly ground black pepper to taste**
- **2 tbsp mixed fresh herbs, finely chopped (chives, cilantro/coriander, parsley, oregano, basil, or other)**

BAKED HERB OMELET

Preheat the oven to 400°F/200°C/gas 6. ❧ Grease a medium ovenproof dish with the butter. ❧ Place the ham and tomatoes in the bottom and bake for 4–5 minutes. ❧ Break the eggs into a bowl, add the cream or milk, salt, pepper, and herbs and beat lightly. ❧

Serve this dish as is for breakfast, or with a green salad as a light lunch.

Take the dish out of the oven and carefully pour the egg mixture over the ham and tomatoes. ❧ Bake for 15–20 minutes until set. ❧ Serve straight from the oven with hot, buttered triangles of toast.

SPICY BROCCOLI OMELET

Clean the broccoli. Dice the stalk into bite-sized pieces and break the head into small florets. Cook in salted, boiling water until tender but still crunchy, about 5–7 minutes. Drain well and set aside. ❧ Combine the eggs, soy sauce, chilies, peanuts, and parsley in a bowl with the broccoli. ❧ Heat the oil in a large skillet (frying pan) and sauté the garlic and scallions until soft. ❧ Pour in the egg mixture and stir well. Cover and cook over medium-low heat until the bottom of the omelet is lightly browned. ❧ Brown the top of the omelet under the broiler (grill) and serve hot or at room temperature.

422

Serves: 4

Preparation: 10'

Cooking time: 25'

Level of difficulty: 1

- 11 oz/300 g broccoli
- 5 eggs
- 3 tsp light soy sauce
- 2 medium red chilies, finely chopped
- 2 oz/60 g finely chopped roasted peanuts
- 4 tbsp finely chopped parsley
- 2 tbsp extra-virgin olive oil
- 2 cloves garlic, finely chopped
- 6 scallions/spring onions, finely chopped

SCRAMBLED EGGS, MEXICAN STYLE

Heat the oil in a large skillet (frying pan). ❧ Beat the eggs until frothy, then add the chilies, onion, cilantro, and salt. ❧ Pour the mixture into the hot oil and cook until the eggs are softly scrambled, stirring them with a fork so they cook evenly. ❧ To serve, spoon the beans onto a deep platter and top with the scrambled eggs.

Serves: 8

Preparation: 10'

Cooking: 10'

Level of difficulty: 1

- 1/2 cup/125 ml extra-virgin olive oil
- 18 large eggs
- 2 green chilies, finely chopped
- 1 white onion, finely chopped
- 6 tbsp finely chopped cilantro/coriander
- dash of salt
- 3 cups/600 g cooked black beans

ARTICHOKE OMELET

Serves: 4

Preparation: 10' + 15' to soak

Cooking: 15'

Level of difficulty: 2

- 8 baby globe artichokes, or 16 frozen artichoke hearts, thawed
- juice of 1 lemon
- 2 oz/60 g all-purpose/plain flour
- 1/2 cup/125 ml extra-virgin olive oil
- 5 large fresh eggs
- salt and freshly ground black pepper to taste

I f using fresh artichokes, trim the tops and remove the tough outer leaves. Cut the stalk at the base leaving 3/4 in (2 cm) attached. Wash, cut in quarters, and place in a bowl of cold water with the lemon juice for 15 minutes. ❧ Drain well and pat dry. ❧ Coat the artichoke pieces or thawed hearts with flour, shaking off any excess. ❧ Heat all but 2 tablespoons of the oil in a large skillet (frying pan) over high heat. ❧ Fry the artichokes for about 8 minutes, or until lightly browned. Drain on paper towels. ❧ Discard the oil used for frying and replace with the remaining oil. Put the artichokes in the skillet and return to medium-high heat. ❧ Beat the eggs lightly with the salt and pepper and pour over the artichokes. Cook for 4–5 minutes. ❧ Turn the omelet carefully and cook for 4 minutes more. When firm and lightly browned on both sides, turn out onto a heated serving dish and serve hot.

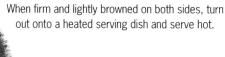

SWISS CHARD FRITTATA

Cook the Swiss chard in a little salted, boiling water for 8–10 minutes, or until tender. Drain well, squeeze out excess moisture, and chop coarsely. ❧ Break the eggs into a bowl, beat briefly with a fork and season with salt and pepper. Stir in the cheese followed by the Parma ham and Swiss chard. ❧ Heat the oil in a large skillet (frying pan) over medium heat. Pour in the egg mixture and cook for about 5 minutes, or until the eggs have set and the underside is lightly browned. ❧ To turn the frittata, place a large plate over the skillet, turn it upside down and then slide the egg mixture back into the skillet, browned side up. Cook for 3–4 minutes more. ❧ Turn the cooked frittata out onto a heated serving dish and serve at once.

Serves: 2–4

Preparation: 5'

Cooking: 20'

Level of difficulty: 1

- **1 lb/500 g trimmed tender young Swiss chard, well-washed**
- **6 large fresh eggs**
- **salt and freshly ground black pepper to taste**
- **¹/₂ cup/60 g freshly grated Parmesan cheese**
- **2 oz/60 g finely chopped Parma ham**
- **4 tbsp extra-virgin olive oil**

ASPARAGUS & EGG LUNCH DISH

Cook the asparagus in salted, boiling water for 10 minutes, or until tender. Drain, reserving the cooking water. ❧ Preheat the oven to 300°F/150°C/gas 2. ❧ Sauté the bacon lightly and set aside. ❧ Melt the butter in a small saucepan and add the flour and mustard powder. Stir for a few minutes over medium heat. ❧ Make the milk up to 2 cups/500 ml with the reserved asparagus water and slowly add to the saucepan, stirring steadily. ❧ Season with salt and pepper. Stir in half the cheese and cook for 2–3 minutes. ❧ Arrange the asparagus in an ovenproof dish. ❧ Cut the hard-boiled eggs into quarters and place on the asparagus. ❧ Sprinkle with the bacon and pour the sauce over the top. ❧ Mix the remaining cheese with the bread crumbs and sprinkle over the surface. ❧ Bake for 25–30 minutes, or until the topping is browned.

Serves: 4

Preparation: 10'

Cooking: 30–35'

Level of difficulty: 1

- 1 bunch asparagus, trimmed
- 2 rashers bacon, cut into small pieces
- 2 tbsp butter
- 4 tbsp all-purpose/ plain flour
- $^1/_2$ tsp mustard powder
- $^2/_3$ cup/180 ml milk, warmed
- 4 oz/125 g Cheddar cheese, grated
- salt and freshly ground black pepper to taste
- 6 hard-boiled eggs, shelled
- 2 tbsp dry bread crumbs

SPICY EGG & CHEESE SOUFFLÉ

Serves: 4

Preparation: 10'

Cooking: 30–40'

Level of difficulty: 1

- **4 eggs, separated**
- **1¼ cups/310 ml milk, warmed**
- **1 tbsp butter, melted**
- **1 tsp mustard**
- **3 oz/90 g fresh bread crumbs**
- **4 oz/125 g Cheddar or Emmental cheese, grated**
- **salt and freshly ground black pepper to taste**

Preheat the oven to 350°F/180°C/gas 4. ❧ Lightly beat the egg yolks in a large bowl. ❧ Add the milk, butter, and mustard to the eggs and mix well. ❧ Stir in the bread crumbs and cheese and season with the salt and pepper. ❧ Beat the egg whites until stiff with a dash of salt and fold them into the mixture. ❧ Pour into a buttered soufflé dish and bake for 30–40 minutes, or until well risen, brown on top, and set in the middle. ❧ Serve at once.

CHEESE SOUFFLÉ

Serves: 4

Preparation: 10'

Cooking: 30'

Level of difficulty: 2

- 3 tbsp butter
- 4 tbsp all-purpose/ plain flour
- 1 cup/250 ml milk
- ½ tsp salt
- freshly ground black pepper to taste
- dash cayenne pepper (optional)
- 1 pinch grated nutmeg (optional)
- 4 large egg yolks
- 5 egg whites
- ¼ tsp cream of tartar
- 4 oz/125 g Emmental or Cheddar cheese, grated

Preheat the oven to 400°F/200°C/gas 6. ❧ Melt the butter in a heavy-bottomed saucepan over low heat. Stir in the flour and cook for 2 minutes. Do not allow the mixture to brown. ❧ Remove from heat. When the mixture has stopped bubbling, pour in the milk and stir with a whisk. ❧ Whisk in the salt, peppers, and nutmeg, if using. ❧ Return to medium-high heat and bring to a boil. Cook for 1 minute, beating constantly with the whisk. The sauce should be very thick. Remove from heat. ❧ Use the whisk to beat the egg yolks into the hot sauce one at a time. ❧ Beat the egg whites with a dash of salt and cream of tartar until stiff peaks form. ❧ Fold the egg whites into the sauce, followed by the cheese. Reserve 2 tablespoons of cheese. ❧ Grease the inside of a soufflé mold with 1 tablespoon of butter and sprinkle with 1 tablespoon of grated cheese. ❧ Spoon the mixture into the mold. Sprinkle the remaining cheese on top. ❧ Place on the middle rack of the oven and lower heat immediately to 375°F/190°C/gas 5. Cook for 25–30 minutes, or until puffed and golden brown. ❧ Serve hot straight from the oven.

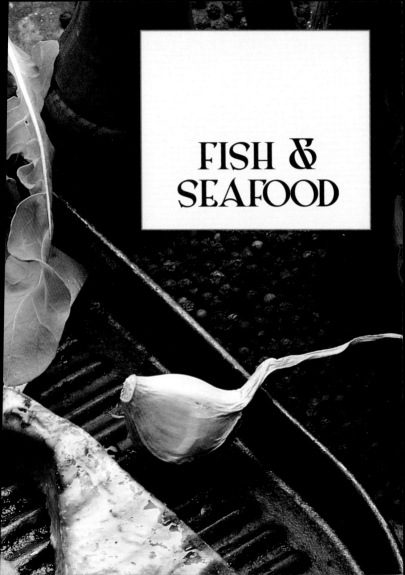

FISH & SEAFOOD

SPICY PRAWN COCONUT CURRY

Place the prawns, crumbled chilies, salt, pepper, turmeric, ginger, and garlic in a bowl and set aside for 10 minutes. ❧ Heat the oil in a large skillet (frying pan) and sauté the cumin and mustard seeds until aromatic. ❧ Add the onion and sauté until transparent. ❧ Add the prawn mixture and sauté for 5 minutes. ❧ Stir in the coconut milk, cucumber, sliced green chilies, and lime juice and sauté for 4–5 more minutes. ❧ Serve hot.

Serves: 6

Preparation: 20'

Cooking: 10'

Level of difficulty: 1

- **1¹⁄₂ lb/750 g deveined king prawns**
- **2–4 crumbled dried chilies**
- **salt and freshly ground black pepper to taste**
- **1 tsp turmeric**
- **1 tbsp finely chopped ginger root**
- **4 cloves garlic, finely chopped**
- **4 tbsp extra-virgin olive oil**
- **1 tsp cumin seeds**
- **1 tsp mustard seeds**
- **1 onion, sliced**
- **1 cup/250 ml coconut milk**
- **12 oz/350 g cucumber, peeled and cubed**
- **2 green chilies, sliced**
- **1 tbsp lime juice**

CLAMS WITH WHITE WINE

Serves: 6

Preparation: 20' + 1 h
to soak clams

Cooking: 10–15'

Level of difficulty: 1

- 4 lb/2 kg fresh clams, in shell
- ½ cup/125 ml extra-virgin olive oil
- 2 medium onions, finely chopped
- 1 cup/250 ml dry white wine
- 4 tbsp boiling water
- salt and freshly ground black pepper to taste
- 2 tbsp finely chopped parsley
- 1 clove garlic, finely chopped (optional)

Soak the clams in cold water for 1 hour, then rinse thoroughly in cold running water. ❧ Heat the oil in a large skillet (frying pan) and sauté the onions until light gold. ❧ Add the clams, followed by the wine and then the water. Season with salt and pepper. Cover tightly and simmer over low heat for 10–15 minutes. ❧ By this time the clams should have opened. Discard any that have not opened. ❧ Sprinkle with parsley and garlic, if using, and serve.

PLAICE ROLLS WITH PEAS

Wash the plaice under cold running water and dry with paper towels. Cut each fillet in half lengthwise. ❧ Heat the oil in a large skillet (frying pan) and sauté the onion, garlic, basil, and bay leaves. After about 5 minutes, add the tomatoes and season with salt and pepper. Cover and cook for 5 minutes. ❧ Add the peas to the skillet and cook for 15 minutes. ❧ While the peas are cooking, roll up the plaice fillets, securing them with wooden cocktail sticks. Sprinkle with flour. ❧ Melt the butter in a skillet with the sage. Add the rolled-up plaice fillets and brown gently for 5 minutes. ❧ Remove from heat and transfer to the pan with the peas. Add a little water if necessary. Season with salt and pepper. Cover the skillet and cook over low heat for 10 minutes. Serve hot.

Serves: 4

Preparation: 15'

Cooking: 40'

Level of difficulty: 2

- 4 plaice or flounder fillets, about 8 oz/ 250 g each
- 4 tbsp extra-virgin olive oil
- 1 onion, finely chopped
- 2 cloves garlic, finely chopped
- 6 basil leaves, torn
- 2 bay leaves
- 4 large tomatoes, peeled and finely chopped
- salt and freshly ground black pepper to taste
- 1 lb/500 g fresh or frozen peas
- 4 tbsp all-purpose/ plain flour
- 2 tbsp butter
- 4 sage leaves, chopped

SPICY CALAMARI WITH PARSLEY

Serves: 6

Preparation: 10'

Cooking: 20'

Level of difficulty: 1

- **2 cloves garlic and 1 bunch parsley, finely chopped**
- **1–2 tsp red pepper flakes**
- **4 tbsp extra-virgin olive oil**
- **8 calamari, cleaned**
- **$^1/_2$ cup/125 ml dry white wine**
- **8 slices firm-textured bread, toasted**

I n a large skillet (frying pan), sauté the garlic, parsley, and red pepper flakes in the oil for 2 minutes. ❧ Add the calamari and cook over high heat for 8 minutes. ❧ Pour in the wine and cook until the calamari are tender. ❧ Stir in the parsley and mix well. ❧ Put the toast in a serving dish and spoon the calamari and their sauce over the top. Serve hot or warm.

MUSSELS
IN PEPPER SAUCE

Serves: 6

Preparation: 10' + 1 h to soak mussels

Cooking: 10'

Level of difficulty: 1

- 1½ lb/750 g mussels, in shell
- 4 tbsp parsley, finely chopped
- 2 cloves garlic, finely chopped
- 2 tbsp extra-virgin olive oil
- dash of salt
- 2 tsp freshly ground black pepper
- 6 slices firm-textured bread, toasted and rubbed with garlic

Soak the mussels in a large bowl of water for at least 1 hour to purge them of sand. Pull off their beards, scrub, and rinse well in abundant cold water. ❧ Sauté the parsley and garlic in a skillet (frying pan) with the oil for 4–5 minutes. Season with salt. ❧ Add the mussels and cook over medium heat until they are all open. Discard any that haven't opened. ❧ Add the pepper and cook for 2 minutes more, stirring all the time. ❧ Prepare the toast and place a slice in each serving dish. Cover with mussels and spoon some of the sauce from the skillet over each portion. ❧ Serve hot.

This fiery dish makes a perfect appetizer when followed by oven-roasted fish.

ORANGE-FLAVORED SHRIMP COCKTAIL

Rinse the shrimp tails in a colander under cold running water. ❧ Fill a large pan with 2 quarts (2 liters) salted water and bring to a boil. ❧ Plunge the shrimp tails into the water and drain after 2 minutes. Let cool to lukewarm. ❧ In a serving bowl, mix together the mayonnaise, ketchup, and Tabasco. ❧ Rinse the orange and grate the zest into fine julienne strips with a grater. ❧ Squeeze the juice of half the orange and add it to the cocktail sauce. If the orange is not particularly juicy, squeeze the juice from the whole fruit until you have obtained $1/2$ cup (125 ml). ❧ Mix the peeled shrimp tails into the sauce. ❧ Rinse the lettuce leaves and dry in a salad spinner. ❧ Arrange a lettuce leaf in each of 6 ramekins. Do not worry if the leaves overlap the side of the ramekins, this makes the presentation more attractive. ❧ Divide the shrimp cocktail equally between the ramekins and garnish with a few strips of orange zest. Refrigerate for 5 minutes, then serve immediately.

Serves: 6
Preparation: 35'
Cooking: 2'
Level of difficulty: 2.

- 1 lb/500 g fresh shrimp/prawn tails
- 1 cup/250 ml mayonnaise
- 6 tbsp g ketchup
- 4 drops Tabasco
- 1 orange
- 6 large lettuce leaves

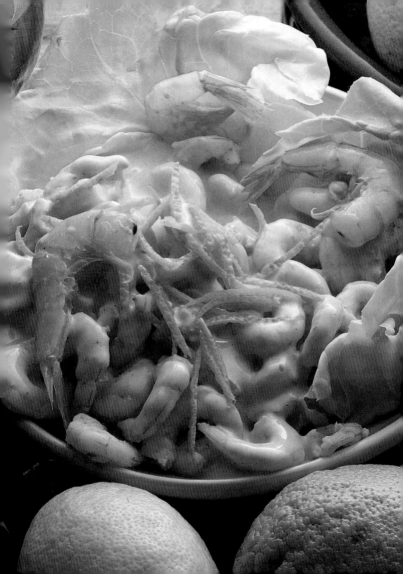

MUSSELS IN WHITE WINE

Serves: 6

Preparation: 30'

Cooking: 10'

Level of difficulty: 1

- **2 lb/1 kg fresh mussels**
- **4 tbsp extra-virgin olive oil**
- **2 cloves garlic**
- **1/2 cup/125 ml dry white wine**
- **salt and freshly ground black pepper to taste**
- **juice of 1 lemon**

Soak the mussels in a large bowl of cold water for 1 hour. Scrub the mussels thoroughly, removing all beards and barnacles, then rinse them in several changes of water ❧ Heat the oil in a large skillet (frying pan) and sauté the garlic for 1 minute. Add the mussels and increase the heat. ❧ Season with salt and a generous grinding of pepper and moisten with the wine. ❧ Cover and cook until all the mussels have opened, 6–10 minutes. Discard any that have not opened. ❧ Turn off the heat, pour away some of the liquid, if it is excessive, and drizzle with the lemon juice. ❧ Mix well and serve immediately.

DEEP-FRIED SEAFOOD SANDWICHES

Remove the crusts from the bread and cut each slice into 2 triangles. ❧ Wash the shrimp under cold running water and remove the shells. Place in a blender or food processor together with the sole fillet, 1 egg, the white wine, soy sauce, if using, and cornstarch and blend until smooth. Spread the mixture on the bread triangles. Beat the other egg in a small bowl and brush the surface of the open sandwiches with it, using a pastry brush. ❧ Heat the oil in a deep pan until very hot. Deep-fry the triangles a few at a time, turning them gently until golden all over, about 3 minutes each side. ❧ Drain well on paper towels and serve hot.

Serves: 4

Preparation: 20'

Cooking: 6–8'

Level of difficulty: 2

- 12 slices firm-textured bread
- 7 oz/200 g shrimp
- 11 oz/300 g sole filets
- 2 eggs
- 1 tbsp dry white
- 1 tbsp soy sauce
- 1/2 tsp salt
- 1 tbsp corn starch/cornflour
- 2 cups/500 ml oil, for frying

ROASTED SEA BASS

Preheat the oven to 400°C/200°F/gas 6. ❧ Make an opening along the belly of the fish. ❧ Rinse carefully under cold running water and pat dry with paper towels. ❧ Mix the rosemary, parsley, and garlic in a small bowl. Season with salt and pepper. ❧ Stuff the fish with the herb mixture. ❧ Arrange the lemon slices along the opening in the fish. Season with salt and pepper. ❧ Place the fish in a sheet of aluminum foil and transfer to a baking dish. Drizzle with the olive oil and fold the paper over the fish. ❧ Bake for 25 minutes, or until the fish is tender. ❧ Serve hot.

Serves: 4

Preparation: 15'

Cooking: 25'

Level of difficulty: 1

- **1 fresh sea bass, weighing about 2 lb/1 kg**
- **1 tbsp finely chopped rosemary**
- **1 tbsp finely chopped parsley**
- **2 cloves garlic, lightly crushed**
- **$^1/_2$ lemon, thinly sliced**
- **salt and freshly ground black pepper to taste**
- **4 tbsp extra-virgin olive oil**

SWORDFISH STEAKS WITH ARUGULA & BASIL SAUCE

Wash and dry the swordfish steaks, but do not remove the skin. Put them on a plate and sprinkle with salt and pepper. Drizzle with the oil, coating on both sides, and set aside. ❧ Heat a grill pan and, when hot, put the fish in it (an electric grill pan will also do, or a barbecue). Cook the swordfish for 15 minutes, turning twice. ❧ Put the garlic, parsley, basil, arugula, and remaining oil in a pitcher. Season with salt and pepper and drizzle with the lemon juice. Beat with a fork until thoroughly blended. ❧ When the steaks are done, place on a heated serving dish and spoon the sauce over the top. ❧ Serve hot.

Serves: 4

Preparation: 20'

Cooking: 15'

Level of difficulty: 1

- **4 swordfish steaks, cut $^1/_2$ in/1 cm thick**
- **salt and freshly ground black pepper to taste**
- **4 tbsp extra-virgin olive oil**
- **2 cloves garlic, lightly crushed**
- **1 tbsp chopped parsley**
- **7 basil leaves, chopped**
- **1 bunch arugula/ rocket, chopped**
- **juice of 1 lemon**

ANCHOVIES WITH MINT

Place the flour in a large dish and dredge the anchovies in it. ❧ Heat the frying oil to very hot in a large skillet (frying pan) and fry the anchovies in batches until golden brown. Drain well on paper towels. Season lightly with salt. ❧ Remove the skillet from heat and carefully pour off the oil. ❧ Heat the olive oil in the same skillet and sauté the garlic for 2 minutes. Pour in the vinegar and cook for 5 minutes more. Add the mint and remove from heat. ❧ Place the anchovies in a large serving dish and pour the vinegar and mint liquid over the top. Refrigerate for at least 3 hours before serving.

Serves: 4

Preparation: 20' + 3 h to chill

Cooking: 20'

Level of difficulty: 1

- 1 cup/150 g all-purpose/plain flour
- 2 lb/1 kg fresh small anchovies, heads removed
- 2 cups/500 ml oil, for frying
- salt to taste
- 2 tbsp extra-virgin olive oil
- 2 cloves garlic, finely chopped
- ½ cup/125 ml white wine vinegar
- 2 tbsp coarsely chopped mint

BAKED PLAICE WITH CAPERS

Serves: 6

Preparation: 20'

Cooking: 35'

Level of difficulty: 1

- 1¼ lb/650 g plaice or flounder filets
- 4 tbsp extra-virgin olive oil
- salt and freshly ground white pepper to taste
- 2 tbsp capers
- 16 cherry tomatoes, cut in half

Preheat the oven to 350°F/180°C/gas 4. ☙ Rinse the fillets under cold running water and dry with paper towels. ☙ Grease a large ovenproof dish with half the oil. ☙ Place the fillets in the dish and sprinkle with salt, pepper, capers, and the cherry tomatoes. Drizzle with the remaining oil. ☙ Bake for 15 minutes, or until the fish is very tender. ☙ Serve hot.

455

MIXED DEEP-FRIED FISH

Cut the calamari bodies into rings and leave the tentacles whole. ❧ Do not shell the shrimp. ❧ Sprinkle the flour in a large dish and dredge all the fish in it, shaking off the excess. Place the floured fish on a large sheet of aluminum foil laid on a work surface or in a tray or platter. ❧ Heat the oil in a deep skillet (frying pan) to very hot. Deep-fry the fish in batches until golden brown all over. Drain well and pat dry with paper towels. ❧ Season with salt lightly and transfer to a serving plate. Decorate with the wedges of lemon. ❧ Serve hot.

Serves: 4

Preparation: 20'

Cooking: 20–25'

Level of difficulty: 2

- 14 oz/450 g calamari, cleaned
- 14 oz/450 g shrimp
- 11 oz/300 g strips of filleted sole
- 2 cups/300 g all-purpose/plain flour
- 1 quart/1 liter oil, for frying
- salt to taste
- 1 lemon, cut into wedges

BAKED COCKLES

Serves: 4

Preparation: 20'

Cooking: 20'

Level of difficulty: 1

- 2 lb/1 kg cockles
- 1 cup/125 g fine dry bread crumbs
- juice of 1 lemon
- salt to taste

Preheat the oven to 425°F/220°C/gas 7. ❧ Place the cockles in a large skillet (frying pan) over high heat and cook for 10 minutes. ❧ Remove the shells from the pan as they open, placing them on a serving plate. Take the mollusks out of the shells and chop finely. As you remove the mollusks check that they are not full of sand. If they are, rinse carefully before chopping. ❧ Discard half the shells and arrange those you have reserved in a large ovenproof pan and put the chopped mollusks inside. ❧ Sprinkle with the bread crumbs, drizzle with lemon juice, season with salt, and put in a preheated oven at for 10 minutes. ❧ Serve hot with a side dish of Sweet and Sour Baby Onions, if liked (see page 651).

FRIED TUNA BALLS

lace the Ricotta in a large bowl and mash well with a fork. ❧ Mash the tuna, breaking it into flakes. Add to the bowl with the chopped parsley, Parmesan, salt, and egg and mix until evenly blended. ❧ Scoop up spoonfuls of the mixture with a tablespoon and shape into balls about the size of golf balls. Dredge the balls in the flour. ❧ Heat the oil in a large skillet (frying pan) until very hot and fry the balls in batches of 6–8 for about 5 minutes each, turning constantly, until golden brown all over. ❧ Remove from the skillet with a slotted spoon and drain on paper towels. ❧ Garnish with the sprigs of parsley, sprinkle with extra salt, if liked, and serve hot.

Serves: 4

Preparation: 15'

Cooking: 15'

Level of difficulty: 2

- **12 oz/350 g fresh Ricotta cheese**
- **10 oz/300 g canned tuna, drained**
- **2 tbsp finely chopped parsley + sprigs to garnish**
- **6 tbsp freshly grated Parmesan cheese**
- **salt to taste**
- **1 egg**
- **$^1/_2$ cup/75 g all-purpose/plain flour**
- **2 cups/500 ml oil, for frying**

STOCKFISH CREAM

Serves: 6

Preparation: 10' + 20'
to stand

Cooking: 10'

Level of difficulty: 3

• 2 lb/1 kg pre-
  soaked stockfish
• 1 cup/250 ml
  extra-virgin olive
  oil
• salt and freshly
  ground black
  pepper to taste
• 2 cloves garlic,
  finely chopped
• 2 tbsp finely
  chopped parsley

Put the stockfish in a large saucepan with enough cold water to cover and place over medium heat. When it comes to a boil, turn off the heat. ❧ Let stand in the water for 20 minutes and drain. Remove the skin and bones, taking care to remove the small ones as well. ❧ Break up into small pieces and transfer to a large bowl. Beat vigorously with a whisk while gradually adding the oil in a steady trickle. ❧ Keep beating in the same direction and adding oil until the fish will absorb no more. The mixture should be light and fluffy like a mousse. Add a little salt, if needed, and season generously with pepper. Stir in the garlic and parsley. ❧ Serve at room temperature.

OCTOPUS SALAD

Fill a deep pan with water and add the tomato, celery, carrot, onion, the bunch of parsley, vinegar, salt and octopus. ♣ Partially cover the pan and bring to a boil over medium heat. Reduce the heat once the water has boiled and simmer for 50–55 minutes. If you notice that the tentacles are breaking up, turn off the heat immediately: this means the octopus is done. ♣ Let the octopus to cool in its cooking liquid. This will make it more tender. Drain and rinse under cold running water. ♣ Cut out the eyes with a small knife then push out and remove the beak (the mouth parts). Rub the skin away from the body and remove the tentacles. Cut the body into pieces and chop the tentacles. Place in a serving dish. ♣ Mix the oil, chopped parsley, garlic, red pepper flakes, lemon juice, salt, and pepper in a small bowl. ♣ Pour over the octopus and allow to stand for a couple of hours for the flavors to combine.

Serves: 4

Preparation: 30' + 3 h

Cooking: 1 h

Level of difficulty: 2

- 1 tomato
- 1 onion
- 1 carrot
- 1 stalk celery
- 1 bunch parsley + 3 tbsp finely chopped parsley
- 1 cup/250 ml white wine vinegar
- 1 tsp salt
- 1 large octopus, weighing about 2 lb/1 kg, cleaned
- $^1/_2$ cup/125 ml extra-virgin olive oil
- 1 clove garlic, chopped
- 1 tsp red pepper flakes
- juice of $^1/_2$ lemon
- salt and freshly ground black pepper to taste

SALMON BURGERS

R inse the salmon under cold running water. Pat dry with paper towels. Skin with a sharp knife, carefully bone, and chop. ❧ Dice the boiled potatoes. ❧ Put the drained crabmeat in a large bowl, chop coarsely, and add the salmon, potatoes, egg, and salt, mixing well with a fork. ❧ Using your hands, shape the mixture into medium-sized balls, then flatten to form burgers. ❧ Place the flour on a plate and dredge the salmon burgers. ❧ Heat the oil in a large skillet (frying pan) until very hot. Add the burgers and cook for 5 minutes, or until nicely browned, on each side. Drain on paper towels. ❧ Serve hot.

Serves: 4;
Preparation: 20'
Cooking: 20'
Level of difficulty: 2

- **8 oz/250 g salmon fillet**
- **8 oz/250 g boiled potatoes**
- **8 oz/250 g canned crabmeat**
- **1 egg**
- **salt to taste**
- **½ cup/75 g all-purpose/plain flour**
- **1 cup/250 ml oil, for frying**

SICILIAN ANCHOVIES

Preheat the oven to 350°F/180°C/gas 4. Clean the anchovies, gently pulling off their heads, then slit them down their bellies so that they can be opened out flat. Remove their backbones, and pat dry with paper towels. Use half the oil to grease an ovenproof dish in which the anchovies will fit snugly when arranged in two layers. Place half the anchovies in the dish, tails toward the center, fanned out like the spokes of a wheel. Season with salt and pepper. Arrange the lemon slices on top. Sprinkle with half the olives and pine nuts and drizzle with half the remaining oil. Cover with a second layer of anchovies and the remaining olives and pine nuts. Drizzle with the wine and sprinkle with the bread crumbs. Drizzle with the remaining oil and bake for 15 minutes. Remove from the oven, drizzle with orange juice, and return to the oven for 15 minutes. Serve hot or at room temperature

| Serves 4–5 |
| Preparation: 30' |
| Cooking: 30' |
| Level of difficulty: 1 |

- 1 1/2 lb/750 g fresh anchovies
- 4 tbsp extra-virgin olive oil
- salt and freshly ground black pepper to taste
- 1 lemon, thinly sliced
- 12 green olives, pitted and coarsely chopped
- 3 tbsp pine nuts
- 6 tbsp dry white wine
- 4 tbsp fine dry bread crumbs
- juice of 1 orange

SHARK STEAKS WITH SAVORY TOPPING

Serves 4

Preparation: 10'

Cooking: 30'

Level of difficulty: 1

- **4 shark steaks, cut ³/₄ in/2 cm thick**
- **salt and freshly ground black pepper to taste**
- **3 tbsp all-purpose/plain flour**
- **6 tbsp extra-virgin olive oil**
- **1 onion, thinly sliced**
- **1–2 cloves garlic, crushed**
- **1 large fresh tomato, chopped**
- **2 tbsp pine nuts**
- **2 tbsp golden raisins/sultanas**
- **1 tbsp coarsely chopped parsley**

Season the shark steaks with salt and pepper and coat them lightly with flour. ❧ Heat the oil in a large skillet (frying pan) until very hot. Add the steaks and fry over a medium-high heat, browning well on both sides. ❧ Remove from the skillet and, in the same oil, sauté the onion and the garlic until soft and translucent. Add the tomato and cook for 10 minutes over low heat, then add the pine nuts, raisins, and parsley. ❧ Stir well, then return the steaks to the pan. Cover and simmer over low heat for 10–15 minutes, turning once. ❧ Remove from heat and set aside to cool for 2–3 hours. This will allow the fish so to absorb the flavors of the sauce. ❧ Serve at room temperature.

POULTRY

SWEET & SOUR CHICKEN SALAD

Serves: 6–8

Preparation: 30'

Cooking: 1 h

Level of difficulty: 2

- 1 oven-ready chicken, weighing about 4 lb/2 kg
- 1 small onion
- 1 clove garlic
- 1 stalk celery, 1 carrot, chopped
- 15 black peppercorns
- 1 tsp salt
- 4–5 cloves
- 4–5 coriander seeds
- 1 cinnamon stick
- 1 tsp cumin seeds
- dash of nutmeg
- 11 oz/300 g salad greens
- 7 oz/200 g cooked green beans
- 3 tbsp balsamic vinegar
- 4 tbsp extra-virgin olive oil
- 4 tbsp golden raisins/sultanas
- piece of candied lemon peel, cut into small strips

Rinse the chicken well inside and out and dry with paper towels. ❧ Use a mortar and pestle to grind the cloves, coriander seeds, cinnamon, and cumin. ❧ Mix these spices with the nutmeg, onion, garlic, celery, carrot, peppercorns, and salt in a small bowl and stuff the cavity with the mixture. ❧ Boil the chicken, breast uppermost, very gently in a large pan of simmering water for about 1 hour, or until very tender. Let cool. ❧ Arrange the salad greens and green beans on a platter and place the chicken on top. ❧ Prepare a dressing by beating the balsamic vinegar and oil with the raisins and lemon peel. ❧ Drizzle over the salad and serve.

CHICKEN IN A SPICED PEANUT SAUCE

Preheat the oven to 350°F/180°C/gas 4. ❧ Sauté the onion, garlic, and green pepper in 1 tablespoon of the oil in a deep skillet (frying pan) over medium heat until soft and translucent. ❧ Remove the vegetables from the skillet and set aside. ❧ Add the remaining oil to the same skillet and fry the chicken pieces until golden brown all over. ❧ Return the vegetables to the skillet. ❧ Place the peanut butter, chicken stock, tumeric, coriander, cumin, red pepper flakes, salt, and pepper in a small saucepan over low heat. Cook and stir until well mixed, about 5 minutes. ❧ Place the chicken in an ovenproof dish and spoon the sauce over the top. Bake for about 30 minutes, or until the chicken is very tender.

This sauce can also be used for chicken kebabs.

472

Serves: 4

Preparation: 25'

Cooking: 45'

Level of difficulty: 1

- 1 medium onion, chopped
- 1 clove garlic, finely chopped
- 1 green bell pepper/capsicum, chopped
- 4 tbsp extra-virgin olive oil
- 2 lb/1 kg boneless chicken pieces
- 5 oz/150 g peanut butter
- 2 cups/500 ml Chicken Stock (see page 140)
- 1 tsp turmeric
- 1 tsp coriander
- 1 tsp cumin
- 1 tsp red pepper flakes
- salt and freshly ground black pepper to taste

CHICKEN MARYLAND

Preheat the oven to 350°F/180°C/ gas 4. ❧ Season the flour with salt and pepper. Roll the chicken in the flour. ❧ Dip each piece of chicken into the beaten egg mixture, then coat with bread crumbs. ❧ If preparing ahead of time, the

Fried bananas and corn fritters make good accompaniments for Chicken Maryland.

pieces can be left in the refrigerator until cooking. ❧ Place the coated chicken pieces on a rack over a baking dish. ❧ Bake for 50–60 minutes, until the chicken is tender and golden brown. ❧ Serve hot or at room temperature.

474

Serves: 4

Preparation: 15'

Cooking: 50–60'

Level of difficulty: 1

- 2 lb/1 kg chicken pieces
- ¹/₂ cup/75 g all-purpose/plain flour
- salt and freshly ground black pepper to taste
- 1 egg, beaten with 2 tbsp water
- 3 cups/180 g fine dry bread crumbs

CHICKEN
IN A HURRY

Serves: 4

Preparation: 20–25'

Cooking: 1 h

Level of difficulty: 1

- **2 lb/1 kg chicken pieces**
- **12 oz/350 g canned apricots**
- **½ cup/125 ml dry white wine or water**
- **1 package powdered onion or mushroom soup**
- **salt and freshly ground black pepper to taste**

Preheat the oven to 375°F/190°C/ gas 5. Place the chicken pieces in a casserole. Arrange the apricots over the chicken and pour the juice and wine over the top. Sprinkle with the soup powder, salt, and pepper. Let stand for about 15 minutes.

This tasty casserole can be prepared beforehand and popped into the oven as you dash in the door!

475

Bake for about 1 hour, or until the chicken is very tender. Check occasionally and add more wine or water if necessary. Serve hot.

FIJIAN COCONUT CREAM CHICKEN

Preheat the oven to 350°F/180°C/ gas 4. ❧ Season the flour with salt and pepper. Roll the chicken pieces in the flour. ❧ Heat the oil in a skillet (frying pan) and sauté the chicken on both sides until golden brown. Transfer to a large casserole. ❧ Combine the cornstarch, coconut cream, onion, salt, pepper, and red pepper flakes, if using, in a small saucepan. Mix well, place over medium heat and bring almost to a boil, stirring continuously. Simmer, but do not boil, for about 3 minutes. ❧ Pour over the chicken and bake for 20–30 minutes, or until tender. ❧ Serve hot with rice, polenta, or couscous.

Imagine yourself on a beautiful Fijian island as you eat this unusually-flavored chicken dish.

Serves: 4

Preparation: 15'

Cooking: 30'

Level of difficulty: 1

- **4 chicken breasts**
- **¹/₂ cup/75 g all-purpose/plain flour**
- **salt and freshly ground black pepper to taste**
- **2 tbsp extra-virgin olive oil**
- **1 tbsp cornstarch/ cornflour**
- **1¹/₂ cups/400 ml coconut cream, tinned**
- **1 medium onion, finely chopped**
- **1 tsp red pepper flakes (optional)**

ROAST STUFFED CAPON

Preheat the oven to 400°F/200°C/ gas 6. ❧ Use a very sharp knife to bone the capon partially. Start with an incision down its backbone, gradually cutting the flesh away from the bones, taking great care not to puncture the skin. Carefully cut out and remove most of the breast meat and set aside, leaving only a thin layer attached to the skin. ❧ In a large bowl, mix the veal, pork, mortadella, hard-boiled eggs, Parmesan, Marsala, nutmeg, salt, and pepper. ❧ Cut the breast meat into short, thin strips. ❧ Stuff the boned capon with one-third of the mixture, spreading it inside the boned bird as evenly as possible. Cover with a layer of one-third each of the strips of chicken breast, ham, and Parma ham. Repeat this layering process twice. ❧ Sew the cut edges of the capon skin with kitchen thread, as neatly as possible, aiming to restore the capon almost to its original shape. Tie the legs and wings closely to the stuffed body with kitchen string and place in a large roasting pan. ❧ Season with salt and pepper, then drizzle with the oil and dot the surface with the butter. ❧ Bake for about 2 hours, or until tender, basting often. ❧ Leave to cool for 1 hour. Slice off the legs and wings. Cut the stuffed section into slices and arrange on a platter, sprinkled with the cooking juices.

Serves: 6–8

Preparation: 1 h

Cooking: 2 h + 1 h

Level of difficulty: 3

- 1 oven-ready capon, weighing about 4 lb/2 kg
- 1 cup/250 g ground lean veal
- 1 cup/250 g ground lean pork
- ³/₄ cup/180 g diced mortadella
- 4 hard-boiled eggs, finely chopped
- 1 cup/150 g freshly grated Parmesan cheese
- 6 tbsp dry Marsala wine
- dash of freshly grated nutmeg
- salt and freshly ground black pepper to taste
- 5 oz/150 g lean ham
- 5 oz/150 g Parma ham
- 6 tbsp extra-virgin olive oil
- 4 tbsp butter

CHICKEN GALANTINE

Serves: 8

Preparation: 40' + 12 h

Cooking time: 1½ h

Level of difficulty: 3

- 1 lb/500 g lean ground beef
- 6 oz/180 g lean ground pork
- 6 oz/180 g ground turkey breast
- 6 oz/180 g ground suckling veal
- 4 oz/125 g ground mortadella
- ½ cup/60 g shelled pistachios
- 1 egg
- 1 oz/30 g black truffle, finely sliced (optional)
- salt and freshly ground black pepper to taste
- 1 chicken, boned, weighing about 4 lb/2 kg
- 1 onion, cut in half
- 1 carrot, cut in 3
- 1 stalk celery, cut in 3
- 2 sprigs parsley
- 7–8 peppercorns
- 1 chicken stock cube
- 2 gelatin cubes
- juice of ½ lemon

Combine the beef, pork, turkey, veal, and mortadella in a large bowl. Mix well and add the pistachios, egg, and truffle, if using. Sprinkle with salt and pepper and mix thoroughly. ♣ Stuff the boned chicken with the mixture and sew up the neck and stomach cavities with a trussing needle and string. ♣ Use your hands to give it a rectangular shape. Wrap in a piece of cheesecloth (muslin) and tie with kitchen string. ♣ Place a large saucepan of salted water over medium heat. Add the onion, carrot, celery, parsley, peppercorns, and stock cube. ♣ When the water is boiling, carefully add the stuffed chicken and simmer over low heat for1½ hours. ♣ Remove from the heat and drain the stock. ♣ Remove the cheesecloth and place the chicken between two trays, with a weight on top. ♣ When cool, transfer to the refrigerator, with the weight still on top, and leave for at least 12 hours. ♣ In the meantime prepare the gelatin, following the directions on the packet. Be sure to add the lemon juice while the gelatin is still liquid. ♣ Serve the galantine thinly sliced on a serving dish, topped with the diced gelatin.

This delicate dish can be prepared well in advance and will keep for up to a week in the refrigerator.

481

CHICKEN WITH BELL PEPPERS & BLACK OLIVES

Serves: 6
Preparation: 20' + 1 h to purge
Cooking: 45'
Level of difficulty: 2

Cut the eggplant in thick slices, sprinkle with salt, and place in a colander for 1 hour. Rinse well and cut into cubes. ❧ Heat half the oil in a large skillet (frying pan) over medium heat and sauté the garlic and onion until translucent. ❧ Add the bell peppers, eggplant, zucchini, tomatoes, and olives. Season with salt and pepper. Stir and cook for about 20 minutes, adding a little water if the skillet becomes too dry. ❧ In the meantime, combine the chicken, bread, Parmesan, egg, parsley, and a little salt in a bowl and mix thoroughly. ❧ Form the mixture into small round balls, then coat with flour. ❧ Put the remaining oil in a large skillet over medium heat and brown the balls thoroughly all over. ❧ Add the vegetable mixture, sprinkle with salt and pepper to taste, and cook for 15 minutes more, stirring carefully. If the dish dries out too much, add stock as needed. ❧ Transfer to a heated serving dish, sprinkle with torn basil, if liked, and serve hot.

- 1 eggplant/aubergine
- salt and freshly ground black pepper to taste
- 8 tbsp extra-virgin olive oil
- 1 clove garlic
- 1 onion, sliced
- 2 bell peppers/capsicums, diced
- 1 zucchini/courgette, diced
- 10 cherry tomatoes, halved
- 1/2 cup/50 g black olives
- 1 1/4 lb/600 g ground chicken breast
- 2 tbsp bread, soaked in milk and squeezed
- 4 tbsp freshly grated Parmesan cheese
- 1 egg
- 1 tbsp finely chopped parsley
- 1/2 cup/75 g all-purpose/plain flour
- 1/2 cup/125 ml Beef Stock (see page 140)

CHICKEN & LENTIL PATTIES

Fill a large saucepan with water and bring to a boil. ❧ Add the lentils and cook for 30 minutes, or until soft. ❧ Drain and transfer to a bowl with the remaining ingredients (except the oil), and mix well. ❧ Shape into 8 patties. ❧ Heat the oil in a large skillet (frying pan) to very hot and fry the patties for 8–10 minutes, or until golden brown on both sides. ❧ Drain on paper towels and serve hot.

Serve with a spicy sauce or homemade pickles.

484

Serves: 4

Preparation: 15'

Cooking: 30' + 20'

Level of difficulty: 1

- ♦ ³/₄ cup/100 g red lentils
- ♦ 12 oz/350 g ground cooked chicken
- ♦ 1 cup/60 g bread crumbs
- ♦ 1 tbsp lemon juice
- ♦ 1 tsp fresh oregano, chopped
- ♦ salt and freshly ground black pepper to taste
- ♦ 2 cups/500 ml oil, for frying

BRAISED CHICKEN
WITH MUSHROOMS

Serves: 6

Preparation: 20'

Cooking: 40'

Level of difficulty: 1

• 1 oven-ready
  chicken, weighing
  about 4 lb/2 kg, cut
  in 6–8 pieces
• 1 small onion, finely
  chopped
• 1 stalk celery, finely
  chopped
• 1 small carrot, finely
  chopped
• ¹/₂ cup/125 g butter
• 3 tbsp extra-virgin
  olive oil
• 1 cup/150 g all-
  purpose/plain flour
• 1 cup/250 ml dry
  white wine
• 3 cloves
• dash of cinnamon
• 1 lb/500 g canned
  tomatoes
• 1 lb/500 g
  mushrooms, thinly
  sliced
• salt and
  freshly
  ground
  black
  pepper

Rinse and dry the chicken. ❧ Sauté the onion, celery, and carrot briefly in a large skillet (frying pan) in 4 tablespoons of butter and 2 tablespoons of oil. ❧ Lightly flour the chicken pieces and add to the skillet. Sauté over high heat, turning them so that they brown lightly all over. ❧ Add the wine and cook until it evaporates. Add the cloves, cinnamon, and tomatoes. Season with salt and pepper. ❧ Cook over medium heat for about 30 minutes, adding a little hot water if necessary. ❧ Sauté the mushrooms in the remaining oil over high heat for 8–10 minutes. ❧ Sprinkle with a little salt and stir into the chicken shortly before it is done. ❧ Add the remaining butter and stir until it melts. ❧ Serve hot.

SPRING CHICKEN COOKED IN SEA SALT

Serves: 4

Preparation: 10'

Cooking: 1¹/₂ h

Level of difficulty: 1

* 8 lb/4 kg coarse sea salt
* 3 sprigs fresh sage
* 3 sprigs fresh rosemary
* 1 oven ready chicken, weighing about 3 lb/1.5 kg
* 1 clove garlic, whole

Preheat the oven to 375°F/ 190°C/gas 5. ❧ Spread 3 lb (1.5 kg) of coarse salt on the bottom of an attractive high-sided baking dish. ❧ Tie the herbs together and insert, with the garlic, into the abdominal cavity of the chicken. ❧ Place the chicken in the baking dish and cover with the remaining salt. No parts of the chicken should be visible. ❧ Bake for 1¹/₂ hours, or until the chicken is very tender. ❧ Take out of the oven and bring to the table as is. Open the salt encrusted chicken just before serving.

> Cooking meat or fish in salt enhances its taste. A crisp, salty crust forms on the outside, while the inside stays moist.

487

CHICKEN STEW WITH TOMATO SAUCE & GREEN OLIVES

Rinse and dry the chicken. ❧ Place the chicken in a bowl and cover with 3 tablespoons of oil, the lemon juice, salt, and a generous grinding of pepper. Set aside to marinate for at least 4 hours. ❧ Sauté the onion, carrot, and celery in the remaining oil in a large skillet (frying pan) over medium-high heat until the onion is translucent. ❧ Add the chicken pieces and sauté until golden brown. ❧ Pour in the wine and cook until it evaporates, stirring frequently. ❧ Add the tomatoes and water. Cover the skillet, lower the heat to medium and continue to cook, stirring frequently. ❧ After 15 minutes add the olives. Simmer gently over low heat for 20 more minutes, or until the chicken is tender. ❧ Serve hot.

Serves: 4–6

Preparation: 15' + 4 h to marinate

Cooking: 1 h

Level of difficulty: 1

- **1 chicken, weighing about 3 lb/1.5 kg, cut in 6–8 pieces**
- **5 tbsp extra-virgin olive oil**
- **juice of 1 lemon**
- **salt and freshly ground black pepper to taste**
- **1 onion, coarsely chopped**
- **1 carrot, coarsely chopped**
- **1 stalk celery, coarsely chopped**
- **$^1/_2$ cup/125 ml white wine**
- **2 cups/500 g canned tomatoes, peeled and chopped**
- **$^1/_2$ cup/125 ml cold water**
- **$1^1/_4$ cups/150 g large green olives**

CHICKEN & BELL PEPPER STEW

Rinse and dry the chicken. ✍ Sauté the garlic in 2 tablespoons of the oil for 2–3 minutes, then add the tomatoes. Season with salt and pepper and cook over medium heat for 15 minutes, or until the sauce reduces. ✍ Clean the bell peppers, removing the seeds and core. Cut in quarters and place under the broiler (grill) until the skin blackens. Peel the blackened skin away with your fingers. Rinse the peppers and pat them dry. Cut in thin strips. ✍ Sauté the chicken in another skillet in the remaining oil. Season with salt and pepper, then pour in the wine. Cook over medium heat for 15 minutes. ✍ Add the tomato sauce and bell peppers and cook for 10 minutes. ✍ Serve hot.

Serves: 4

Preparation: 10'

Cooking: 45'

Level of difficulty: 1

- 1 chicken, weighing about 2 lb/1 kg, cut into 8 pieces
- 3 cloves garlic, finely chopped
- 8 tbsp extra-virgin olive oil
- 13 oz/400 g canned or fresh tomatoes, peeled and chopped
- salt and freshly ground black pepper to taste
- 1 lb/500 g bell peppers/capsicums, mixed green, yellow, and red
- 1 cup/ 250 ml dry white wine

SIMPLE CHICKEN SALAD

Serves: 2

Preparation: 10'

Level of difficulty: 1

- 1 whole chicken breast, poached in chicken stock
- 2 anchovy fillets
- 4–5 tbsp extra-virgin olive oil
- 1 tbsp lemon juice
- salt and freshly ground white pepper to taste
- 1 fresh white truffle (optional)

Cut the chicken breast into thin strips and place in a medium bowl. ❧ Crumble the anchovy fillets with a fork and mix with the oil, lemon juice, salt, and pepper in a small bowl until well blended. ❧ Pour over the chicken. ❧ Transfer to a serving dish and top with wafer-thin slices of fresh truffle, if liked.

When available, truffles add a touch of class to this simple but perfect salad.

491

ROAST CHICKEN WITH LEMON

Serves: 4

Preparation: 10'

Cooking: 1 h

Level of difficulty: 1

- 1 oven-ready chicken, weighing about 3 lb/1.5 kg
- 1 tbsp finely chopped fresh sage
- 1 tbsp finely chopped fresh rosemary
- 2 cloves garlic, finely chopped
- salt and freshly ground black pepper to taste
- 1 lemon
- 4 tbsp extra-virgin olive oil

Preheat the oven to 400°F/200°C/gas 6. ❧ Rinse and dry the chicken. ❧ Combine the sage, rosemary, garlic, salt, and pepper together in a bowl. Mix well, then use to season the chicken inside and out. ❧ Wash the lemon thoroughly, prick well with a fork and insert in the abdominal cavity of the chicken. This will make the meat tastier and absorb fat. ❧ Place the chicken in a roasting pan greased with the oil. Bake in a preheated oven at for about 1 hour. ❧ Turn the chicken every 15 minutes and baste with the oil and cooking juices. When cooked, the chicken should be very tender and the meat should come off the bone easily. The skin should be crisp. ❧ Transfer to a heated serving dish. ❧ Serve hot or at room temperature.

CHICKEN & CELERY SALAD

Serves: 4–6

Preparation: 15' + 30' to chill

Level of difficulty: 1

R emove the skin from the chicken and discard sinews and bones. Cut into small pieces. ❧ Wash the celery and chop coarsely. ❧ Slice the gherkins and dice the Gruyère and ham. ❧ Combine the ingredients in a deep salad bowl and season with lemon juice, salt, and pepper. ❧ Pour the mayonnaise over the chicken. Toss carefully. ❧ Refrigerate for 30 minutes before serving.

Try serving this salad on a bed of fresh, crisp lettuce, for a refreshing contrast to the creamy mayonnaise

- 1 boiled chicken, weighing about 3 lb/1.5 kg
- 1 celery heart
- 5 gherkins
- 4 oz/125 g Gruyère cheese
- 4 oz/125 g ham, in one thick slice
- juice of 1 lemon
- salt and freshly ground black pepper to taste
- 1 cup/250 ml mayonnaise

CHICKEN STEW

Serves: 4

Preparation: 10'

Cooking: 40'

Level of difficulty: 1

- 1 large onion, finely chopped
- 2 cloves garlic, finely chopped
- 4 tbsp extra-virgin olive oil
- 1 chicken, 3 lb/1.5 kg, cut into 8 pieces
- ½ cup/125 ml dry white wine
- 13 oz/400 g potatoes, coarsely chopped
- 4 medium carrots, coarsely chopped
- 2 stalks celery, coarsely chopped
- 2 tbsp finely chopped parsley
- salt and freshly ground black pepper to taste
- ⅔ cup/150 ml Chicken Stock (see page 140)

Sauté the onion and garlic in the oil in a large, deep skillet (frying pan) until pale gold. ❧ Add the chicken and brown all over. ❧ Pour in the wine and cook until it evaporates. Add the potatoes, carrots, celery, and parsley and season with salt and pepper. ❧ Pour in enough stock to moisten the dish, cover and cook over medium heat for 30–35 minutes, stirring frequently. Add more stock as required during cooking. ❧ When the chicken is cooked and the vegetables tender, remove from heat and serve.

> The potatoes take on a lovely flavor from the stock and cooking juices, making this simple stew more sustaining.

495

CHICKEN VINDALOO

Sauté the onions in the oil in large skillet (frying pan) until lightly browned. ❧ Add the ginger, garlic, turmeric, and garam masala and sauté for 5 minutes. ❧ Add the vinegar, water, salt, and chicken pieces. Cover and simmer over medium-low heat for about 25 minutes, or until the chicken is tender. ❧ Place the chicken pieces in a serving dish. Add the coconut to the sauce and stir for 2 minutes. Pour the sauce over the chicken and serve.

- **2 large onions**
- **6 tbsp extra-virgin olive oil**
- **3 fresh green chilies, sliced**
- **4 cloves garlic, sliced**
- **2 tsp turmeric**
- **1 tsp garam masala**
- **2 tbsp vinegar**
- **1 cup/250 ml water**
- **1 tsp salt**
- **3 lb/1.5 kg chicken, cut into 8–10 pieces**
- **4 tbsp shredded coconut**

Serves: 4–6

Preparation: 15' + 30'
  to marinate

Cooking: 40'

Level of difficulty: 1

- **1 chicken, weighing about 3 lb/1.5 kg, cut into 8–10 pieces**
- **2 dried chilies**
- **1½ cups/375 g plain yogurt**
- **3 tbsp extra-virgin olive oil**
- **4 onions, sliced**
- **4 tsp finely grated ginger root**
- **4 cloves garlic, finely chopped**
- **6 green chilies, sliced**
- **1 tsp cumin seeds, crushed**
- **2 tsp coriander seeds, crushed**
- **2 cups/150 g fresh chopped cilantro/ coriander**
- **fresh mint leaves**

CHICKEN WITH YOGURT

Marinate the chicken in half the yogurt mixed with the dried chilies and salt for 30 minutes. ❧ Heat the oil in a large skillet (frying pan) and sauté the onions until transparent. Add the ginger, garlic, green chilies, coriander seeds, and cumin and sauté for 5 minutes. ❧ Add the chicken and marinade to the pan and sauté for 5 minutes. ❧ Add the remaining yogurt, together with the cilantro, cover the skillet, and simmer until the chicken is cooked, about 30 minutes. ❧ Garnish with the fresh mint leaves and serve hot.

SPICY SPANISH CHICKEN

Season the chicken pieces with salt and pepper. ❧ Heat the oil in a large shallow casserole and brown the chicken all over. ❧ Add the onions and garlic and sauté until the onions are translucent. ❧ Stir in the flour, half the parsley, the ginger, saffron, cumin, sesame seeds, and chile peppers. ❧ Pour in the stock, cover, and cook over medium-low heat for about 45 minutes, or until the chicken is very tender. ❧ Serve hot.

This full-flavored dish comes from Andalusia in Spain. It shows strong Middle Eastern influence.

Serves: 4

Preparation: 10'

Cooking: 50'

Level of difficulty: 1

- 1 chicken, weighing about 3 lb/1.5 kg, cut in 8 pieces
- salt and freshly ground black pepper to taste
- 2 tbsp extra-virgin olive oil
- 1 large onion, finely chopped
- 2 cloves garlic, finely chopped
- 1 tsp flour
- 4 tbsp finely chopped parsley
- 2 tsp grated root ginger
- few strands saffron
- 1 tsp cumin seeds, bruised in a mortar
- 2 tbsp sesame seeds
- 2–3 chile peppers, sliced
- ³/₄ cup/180 ml Chicken Stock (see page 140)

TURKEY MOLE

Serves: 4

Preparation: 45'

Cooking: 1½ h

Level of difficulty: 2

* 3 lb/1.5 kg turkey (or chicken) pieces
* 1 onion, quartered
* 2 tbsp sesame seeds
* 4 tbsp blanched almonds
* 2 tbsp raisins
* 3 black peppercorns
* 1 clove
* 1–2 tsp ground cinnamon
* 2 tsp red chile paste (or more)
* ¾ cup/200 ml water
* 1 onion, chopped
* 2 cloves garlic, finely chopped
* 3 tomatoes, peeled and chopped
* ½ cup/60 g bread crumbs
* 1 tbsp sunflower oil
* 1 square/30 g semi-sweet/dark chocolate
* salt and freshly ground black pepper to taste

Place the turkey pieces in a large saucepan with the onion, cover with water, and simmer for 1 hour, or until tender. ❧ When cool, skin the meat and cut into bite-sized pieces. ❧ Place in a large casserole. ❧ Strain and reserve the stock. ❧ Preheat the oven to 350°F/180°C/gas 4. ❧ Toast the sesame seeds and almonds in a dry skillet (frying pan), tossing over medium heat until browned. ❧ Put them into a food processor with the raisins, peppercorns, cloves, cinnamon, and process until finely ground. ❧ Add the chile paste, water, chopped onion, garlic, tomatoes, and bread crumbs, and process again until smooth. ❧ Heat the oil in a large skillet and sauté this mixture for about 5 minutes, or until the onion is translucent. ❧ Place ¾ cup/180 ml of the stock in a small saucepan with the chocolate. Stir over low heat until dissolved. ❧ Add to the chile mixture, season with salt and pepper, and pour over the turkey in the casserole. ❧ Bake for 20–30 minutes and serve hot.

This is a simplified version of the famous Mexican Mole, which is one of that country's national dishes.

TRUFFLED PHEASANT

eason the cavity of the pheasant with salt and pepper and place the juniper berries inside. ❧ Wrap the slices of pancetta around the breast of the bird and secure with kitchen string. Tie the legs and wings snugly against the bird's body so that it keeps its shape as it cooks.

Serve this special dish with a simple risotto like the ones on pages 207 and 220 in this book.

❧ Heat the butter in a saucepan just large enough to contain the pheasant and brown the bird all over for 5 minutes, turning frequently. ❧ Add the onion, celery, sage, and rosemary. Pour in the wine, cover, and reduce the heat to low. Cook for 40–45 minutes, or until the pheasant is tender. ❧ Remove and keep hot. ❧ Strain the cooking liquid and return it to the saucepan. Pour in the cream and simmer for 2–3 minutes, adding salt to taste. ❧ Remove the trussing string, bacon, and juniper berries from the pheasant and carve it into 4 pieces. ❧ Add the pheasant to the sauce, turning once or twice to moisten and reheat. ❧ After a few minutes, transfer to a preheated serving dish. Spoon the sauce over the pheasant and garnish with the shavings of truffles. ❧ Serve hot.

502

Serves: 4

Preparation: 20'

Cooking: 1 h

Level of difficulty: 2

- 1 roasting pheasant
- salt and freshly ground white pepper to taste
- 4 juniper berries, lightly crushed
- 4 slices bacon
- 2 tbsp butter
- 2 tbsp coarsely chopped onion
- 1 stalk celery, coarsely chopped
- 3 fresh sage leaves
- 1 small sprig fresh rosemary
- $^2/_3$ cup/150 ml dry white wine
- 4 tbsp cream
- 1 white truffle, in wafer-thin slices

GROUND CHICKEN SATAY

Place the shallots, garlic, chilies, ginger, coriander, peppercorns, candlenuts, shrimp paste, and cloves in a food processor and chop until smooth. ❧ Heat the oil in a heavy-bottomed saucepan over medium-high heat and sauté the spicy mixture for 5 minutes. Set aside to cool. ❧ Place the chicken in a bowl with the spicy mixture, coconut, lime juice, salt, pepper, and chilies and mix well. ❧ Press the chicken mixture around 12 skewers and grill over a barbecue or under a preheated broiler (grill) for about 10 minutes, or until the chicken is well cooked. ❧ Serve hot.

Make this classic Indonesian recipe more or less spicy by varying the amount of chile peppers.

Serves: 4–6

Preparation: 25'

Cooking: 10'

Level of difficulty: 1

- **10 shallots**
- **6 cloves garlic**
- **3 red chilies, sliced**
- **1 in/2.5 cm ginger root**
- **2 tsp coriander seeds**
- **1 tsp black peppercorns**
- **3 candlenuts**
- **1 tsp dried shrimp paste**
- **2 cloves**
- **2 tbsp extra-virgin olive oil**
- **1¼ lb/600 g ground chicken**
- **1 cup/250 g freshly grated coconut**
- **2 tbsp fresh lime juice**
- **salt and freshly ground black pepper to taste**
- **2 crumbled dried chilies**

HUNTER'S CHICKEN

Rinse the chicken inside and out under cold running water. Cut into 8–12 small pieces, leaving it on the bone. Pat dry with paper towels. ♣ Sauté the onion in the oil in a large skillet (frying pan) until pale golden brown. Remove the onion from the pan and set aside. ♣ Add the bacon to the flavored oil, followed by the chicken pieces. Cook over a slightly higher heat for about 10 minutes, turning frequently. ♣ Pour in the wine and cook until it evaporates. ♣ Add the tomatoes and the reserved onion. Season with salt and pepper. ♣ Cook for about 30 minutes, stirring and turning at intervals, until the chicken is very tender. ♣ Serve hot.

Serves: 6
Preparation: 20'
Cooking: 1 h
Level of difficulty: 1

- 1 oven-ready chicken, weighing about 3 lb/1.5 kg
- 1 medium onion, thinly sliced
- $^1\!/_2$ cup/125 ml extra-virgin olive oil
- 3 oz/90 g fat bacon, finely chopped
- 1 cup/250 ml dry white wine
- 8 oz/250 g ripe tomatoes, blanched, peeled and diced
- salt and freshly ground black pepper to taste

Serves: 4

Preparation: 20'

Cooking: 1 h

Level of difficulty: 1

- 1 oven-ready chicken, weighing about 3 lb/1.5 kg
- 3 oz/90 g pancetta, finely chopped
- 2 cloves garlic, finely chopped
- 1 heaped tsp each, finely chopped fresh sage and rosemary
- 1 tbsp finely chopped parsley
- 1 level tsp fennel seeds
- 6 tbsp extra-virgin olive oil
- salt and freshly ground black pepper to taste

CHICKEN WITH FENNEL SEEDS

reheat the oven to 350°F/180°C/gas 4. ❧ Wash the chicken inside and out and dry with paper towels. ❧ Mix the bacon, garlic, sage, rosemary, parsley, fennel seeds, salt, and pepper in a small bowl and place in the cavity. Use a trussing needle and thread to sew up the opening. ❧ Pour half the olive oil into a roasting pan, place the chicken in it and drizzle with the remaining oil. Season with salt and pepper. ❧ Roast for 1 hour, or until the chicken is very tender. ❧ Serve hot.

VEAL
& BEEF

VEAL SLICES WITH PARMA HAM & SAGE

Pound the slices of meat and lightly flour. ❧ Place half a slice of Parma ham on each and top with a sage leaf. ❧ Use a cocktail stick to fix the ham and sage to the slice of veal. ❧ Melt the butter and oil in a large skillet (frying pan). Add the veal slices, with the ham facing downward. Brown over high heat, then turn and brown the other side. ❧ Season with salt and pepper. ❧ Pour in the wine and cook for 5–6 minutes more. ❧ Serve hot.

This quick and easy dish should be served hot, straight from the pan, as soon as the veal is cooked.

Serves: 4

Preparation: 15'

Cooking: 12'

Level of difficulty: 1

- 14 oz/450 g veal, preferably rump, cut in 8 slices
- 4 oz/125 g Parma ham
- 8 leaves sage
- 4 tbsp all-purpose/plain flour
- 2 tbsp butter
- 3 tbsp extra-virgin olive oil
- salt and freshly ground black pepper to taste
- $^1/_2$ cup/125 ml dry white wine

VEAL ROLL WITH CHEESE & PARMA HAM FILLING

Remove any small pieces of fat from the meat. Cover with foil and pound lightly. ❧ Season with salt and pepper, cover with slices of Parma ham and cheese, and sprinkle with Parmesan. ❧ Roll the veal up tightly (with the grain of the meat running parallel to the length of the roll, so that it will be easier to slice) and tie firmly with kitchen string. ❧ Heat the oil over medium-low heat in a heavy-bottomed saucepan just large enough to contain the roll. ❧ Brown the roll on all sides and sprinkle with salt and pepper. ❧ Pour in the milk (which should cover the roll), partially cover the saucepan, and continue cooking over medium-low heat until the milk reduces. This will take about 1 hour. Turn the meat from time to time during cooking. ❧ Transfer to a serving dish, slice and serve hot or at room temperature. If serving cold, reheat the sauce, and pour over the sliced roll.

This versatile dish can be prepared ahead of time and reheated or served at room temperature.

Serves: 6

Preparation: 20'

Cooking: 1 h

Level of difficulty: 2

- 1½ lb/750 g slice of veal, preferably rump
- salt and freshly ground black pepper to taste
- 4 oz/125 g Parma ham
- 4 oz/125 g Fontina or Cheddar cheese, sliced
- 4 oz/125 g Parmesan cheese, in flakes
- 4 tbsp extra-virgin olive oil
- 2 cups/500 ml milk

VEAL SCALOPPINE WITH SAVORY TOPPING

Remove any small pieces of fat from the scaloppine. ❧ Pound the meat lightly, dredge in the flour, and shake off any excess. ❧ Heat the oil in a large sauté pan and brown the scaloppine on both sides. ❧ Season with salt and pepper. Place the tomatoes, garlic, capers, parsley, and oregano in a small bowl and mix well. ❧ Spoon the sauce over each slice and cook for 10–12 minutes. ❧ Serve hot.

Use salad tomatoes (or halved cherry tomatoes) in summer and or a readymade tomato sauce in winter.

Variation
• For a richer dish, place a thin slice of Mozzarella cheese on each piece of meat 3–4 minutes before it is cooked.

Serves: 4

Preparation: 25'

Cooking: 15'

Level of difficulty: 1

- ◆ 1 lb/500 g small, thinly sliced veal scaloppine, cut from rump
- ◆ 1 cup/150 g all-purpose/plain flour
- ◆ 4 tbsp extra-virgin olive oil
- ◆ salt and freshly ground black pepper to taste
- ◆ 2 cloves garlic, finely chopped
- ◆ 1 tbsp capers, coarsely chopped
- ◆ 2 tbsp parsley, finely chopped
- ◆ 4–6 tomatoes, peeled and finely chopped
- ◆ 1 tsp dried oregano
- ◆ 2 tbsp finely chopped parsley

VEAL SCALOPPINE WITH PARMESAN & FRESH TOMATOES

Remove any small pieces of fat from the scaloppine. ❧ Pound the meat lightly, dredge in the flour, and shake thoroughly. ❧ Heat the oil and butter in a large skillet (frying pan) over medium heat. Add the scaloppine and season with salt and pepper. Brown on both sides. ❧ Pour in the wine and cook until it evaporates. ❧ Remove the slices of meat and set aside in a warm oven. ❧ Add the shallots to the pan and lightly brown. ❧ Add the tomatoes, salt, and pepper, and cook until the tomatoes reduce. ❧ Add the scaloppine and sprinkle with the Parmesan, parsley, and basil. ❧ Turn off the heat, cover, and let stand for a few minutes. ❧ Serve hot or at room temperature.

Serves: 4

Preparation: 25'

Cooking: 25'

Level of difficulty: 1

- 1 lb/500 g small, thinly sliced veal scaloppine, cut from rump
- $1/2$ cup/75 g all-purpose/plain flour
- 4 tbsp extra-virgin olive oil
- 2 tbsp butter
- salt and freshly ground black pepper to taste
- $1/2$ cup/125 ml dry white wine
- 2 shallots, coarsely chopped
- 10 oz/300 g tomatoes, peeled and diced
- 4 oz/125 g Parmesan cheese, flaked
- 2 tbsp each parsley and basil, finely chopped

MILANESE-STYLE STEWED VEAL SHANKS

Make 4–5 incisions around the edge of each shank to stop them curling up during cooking. ❧ Dredge the shanks in the flour and sprinkle with salt and pepper. ❧ Heat the oil in a large saucepan over medium-high heat and cook the shanks briefly on both sides. Remove and set aside. ❧ Melt the butter in the pan and add the carrot, onion, celery, and sage. ❧ When the vegetables are soft, add the meat and cook for a few minutes. ❧ Pour in the wine. When the wine has evaporated, add the stock and tomatoes, and season with salt and pepper to taste. ❧ Cover and simmer over low heat for $1\frac{1}{2}$ hours, adding extra stock if needed. ❧ When cooked, transfer to a heated serving dish and serve hot (with Milanese Risotto — see page 202), if liked.

Serves:	4–6
Preparation:	25'
Cooking:	$1\frac{1}{2}$ h
Level of difficulty:	2

- 6 veal hind shanks, cut in thick slices
- $\frac{1}{2}$ cup/75 g all-purpose/plain flour
- salt and freshly ground black pepper to taste
- 4 tbsp extra-virgin olive oil
- 3 tbsp butter
- 1 carrot, finely chopped
- 1 onion, finely chopped
- 1 stalk celery, finely chopped
- 4 sage leaves, torn
- 1 cup/250 ml dry white wine
- 1 cup/250 ml Beef Stock (see page 140)
- 8 oz/250 ml tomatoes, peeled and diced

VEAL SCALOPPINE WITH LEMON

Serves: 4

Preparation: 15'

Cooking: 12–15'

Level of difficulty: 1

- 1 lb/500 g small, thinly sliced veal scaloppine, cut from rump
- ½ cup/75 g all-purpose/plain flour
- 3 tbsp butter
- 2 tbsp extra virgin olive oil
- salt and freshly ground black pepper to taste
- ½ cup/125 ml *Beef Stock* (see page 140)
- juice of 1 lemon
- 1 tbsp parsley, finely chopped

Remove any small pieces of fat from the scaloppine. ❧ Pound the meat lightly, dredge in the flour, and shake thoroughly. ❧ Sauté the veal in the butter and oil in a large skillet (frying pan) over high heat, turning often until both sides are evenly browned. Season with salt and pepper. ❧ Lower the heat to medium and continue cooking, adding a little stock to moisten. ❧ After about 12 minutes, when the veal is cooked, turn off the heat and pour the lemon juice over the top. ❧ Sprinkle with the parsley and serve hot.

VEAL STEW
WITH PARSLEY

Remove any pieces of fat from the veal. ♣ Heat the oil in a large heavy-bottomed pan over medium heat and sauté the garlic and parsley for 2–3 minutes. ♣ Add the meat and cook in its juices until it reduces. Season with salt and pepper. ♣ Pour in the milk and stock. The meat should be almost, but not completely, covered. Reduce the heat and partially cover the pan, so that the liquid evaporates. Cook over very low heat, stirring frequently since the milk tends to stick, until the liquid reduces, forming a dense sauce, and the veal is very tender. ♣ Transfer to a heated serving dish and serve hot.

Serves: 6

Preparation: 15'

Cooking: 1 h

Level of difficulty: 1

- 2 lb/1 kg lean veal, in bite-sized pieces
- 4 tbsp extra-virgin olive oil
- 2 cloves garlic, finely chopped
- 2 tbsp parsley, finely chopped
- 1 cup/250 ml milk
- $^1/_2$ cup/125 ml *Beef Stock* (see page 140)
- salt and freshly ground black pepper to taste

HOT VEAL CARPACCIO, MEDITERRANEAN STYLE

Preheat the oven to 430°F/225°C/gas 7. ᴥ
Grease a large baking dish with the oil and
lay the slices of veal in it, without
overlapping. Season with salt, pepper, and
oregano. ᴥ Add the sun-dried tomatoes, capers,
and lard. Cover the pan with a layer of aluminum
foil. ᴥ Wash the salad greens, dry well, and
arrange on individual plates. ᴥ Place the pan in a
very hot oven for 2–3 minutes, then take the meat
out of the dish and arrange on the salad greens. ᴥ
Pour the juices in the dish over the meat and
drizzle with the vinegar. ᴥ Serve hot.

Serves: 6

Preparation: 15'

Cooking: 2'

Level of difficulty: 1

- **6 tbsp extra-virgin olive oil**
- **1¼ lb/600 g veal, finely sliced**
- **salt and freshly ground black pepper to taste**
- **dash of oregano**
- **12 sun-dried tomatoes, coarsely chopped**
- **4 tbsp capers**
- **6 thin slices lard**
- **2 bunches mixed baby salad greens**
- **3 tbsp balsamic vinegar**

VEAL & ARTICHOKE ROLLS

Serves: 6

Preparation: 15'

Cooking: 12–15'

Level of difficulty: 1

- **12 veal scaloppine, cut from the topside, about 2 oz/60 g each**
- **6 slices Mortadella, cut in half**
- **12 slices Cheddar cheese**
- **6 artichoke hearts, thinly sliced**
- **salt and freshly ground black pepper to taste**
- **1 cup/150 g all-purpose/plain flour**
- **¾ cup/200 ml extra-virgin olive oil**
- **3 cloves garlic, finely chopped**
- **sprig fresh rosemary, finely chopped**
- **¾ cup/200 ml dry white wine**
- **1 lb/500 g canned tomatoes, chopped**
- **2 tbsp finely chopped parsley**

Pound the meat lightly. ❧ Place a piece of mortadella and a slice of cheese on each piece of meat. ❧ Place the artichoke slices on the cheese. Season with salt and pepper. ❧ Roll the meat up and secure with a cocktail stick. Dredge in the flour. ❧ Sauté the rolls with the garlic and rosemary in the oil in a large skillet (frying pan) for 8–10 minutes, then pour off most of the oil. ❧ Add the wine and cook until it has evaporated. Remove the veal rolls. ❧ Add the tomatoes to the skillet, season with salt and pepper, and cook over medium heat for 15 minutes, or until reduced. Add the veal and cook for 5 minutes more, turning carefully. Sprinkle with the parsley. ❧ Serve hot.

525

INDONESIAN BEEF STEW

Place the chilies, shallots, garlic, ginger, and black pepper corns in a blender and chop until smooth. ❧ Place the ground spices, beef, coconut milk, lime juice, cinnamon, cardamom, and salt in a large heavy-bottomed saucepan. Cover, and cook over low heat for 2 hours, or until the meat is very tender. ❧ Serve hot.

This very spicy dish comes from the Indonesian island of Sumatra. Serve with rice and yogurt to absorb the heat.

Serves: 4

Preparation: 20'

Cooking: 2 h

Level of difficulty: 1

- 6 red chilies
- 10 shallots
- 8 cloves garlic, finely chopped
- 1 in/2.5 cm root ginger
- 2 tsp black pepper
- 2 lb/1 kg beef, cut in bite-size chunks
- 4 cups/1 liter coconut milk
- grated zest and juice of 3 limes
- 3 cinnamon sticks
- 4 cardamom pods, bruised
- 1 tsp salt

TUSCAN BLACK PEPPER STEW

Serves: 6

Preparation: 20'

Cooking: 3 h

Level of difficulty: 1

- 3 lb/1.5 kg muscle from veal shanks, cut in bite-sized pieces
- 4 cloves garlic, finely chopped
- 1¼ lb/625 g tomatoes, peeled and chopped
- pinch of salt
- 4 tbsp freshly ground black pepper
- 1 quart/1 liter cold water
- 1½ cups/375 ml full-bodied, dry red wine

Place the meat in a large saucepan (preferably earthenware) with the garlic, tomatoes, salt, and pepper and add just enough of the water to cover the meat. ❧ Cook over medium heat for 2 hours, adding extra water if the sauce becomes too dry. Stir from time to time. ❧ After 2 hours, pour in the wine and cook for 1 hour more, or until the meat is very tender. ❧ Serve hot.

The meat in this hot Tuscan stew should be literally "falling apart." Cook over low heat for at least 3 hours.

527

PAN ROASTED BEEF WITH MUSHROOMS

Serves: 4

Preparation: 20'

Cooking: 20–25'

Level of difficulty: 1

- **6 tbsp extra-virgin olive oil**
- **1 lb/500 g beef tenderloin**
- **salt and freshly ground black pepper to taste**
- **11 oz/300 g mixed wild mushrooms**
- **2 cloves garlic, finely chopped**
- **2 tbsp finely chopped parsley**
- **¹/₂ cup/125 ml dry white wine**

Heat 2 tablespoons of oil in a large skillet (frying pan) over high heat. Season the meat with salt and pepper and sauté for 10–15 minutes. The outside should be nicely browned, but it should still be pink in the center. Remove from the heat and set aside in a warm oven. ♠ Sauté the mushrooms, garlic, and parsley in the remaining oil in the same skillet for 8–10 minutes, or until the mushrooms are almost tender (timing will depend on the type of mushrooms you are using). ♠ Pour in the wine and cook until it has evaporated. Season with salt and pepper. ♠ Slice the beef and spoon the mushroom sauce over the top.

The original Italian recipe calls for the meat to stay pink. If preferred, cook until the center is browned too.

MEATBALLS WITH TOMATO

Serves: 4
Preparation: 15'
Cooking: 30'
Level of difficulty: 1

Sauté the onion in the oil in a large saucepan until translucent. ❧ Add the tomatoes, basil, salt, and pepper. ❧ Cook over medium heat for 10 minutes. ❧ Place the bread crumbs in a large bowl with the milk. Stir in the meat, Pecorino, eggs, parsley, and garlic. Season with salt and pepper and mix well. ❧ Shape into meatballs and add to the tomato sauce. Simmer for 15–20 minutes, turning carefully once or twice. ❧ Serve hot.

- 1 small onion, finely chopped
- 4 tbsp extra-virgin olive oil
- 1 (15 oz/400 g) can tomatoes
- 6 fresh basil leaves
- salt and freshly ground black pepper to taste
- 1 cup/100 g dry bread crumbs
- 4 tbsp milk
- 14 oz/400 g ground beef or veal
- 1 cup/200 g freshly grated Pecorino cheese
- 2 eggs, beaten
- 2 tbsp finely chopped parsley
- 2 cloves garlic, finely chopped

KOFTAS

Serves: 4–6

Preparation: 15' + 30' to rest

Cooking: 25'

Level of difficulty: 1

- 1 lb/500 g ground beef or lamb
- 1 tbsp root ginger, freshly grated
- 2 cloves garlic, finely chopped
- 4 green chilies, finely chopped
- 1 small onion, finely chopped
- 1 egg
- 1 tsp turmeric
- 4 tbsp finely chopped cilantro/ coriander
- 4 mint leaves, chopped
- 1 large potato
- salt to taste
- 1 cup/250 ml oil, for frying

Place the beef or pork, ginger, garlic, chilies, onion, egg, turmeric, cilantro, and mint in a large bowl. Stir until well mixed. ❧ Grate the potato into the bowl. Season with salt and mix again. ❧ Shape the mixture into portions the size of golf balls. Set aside on a plate to rest for about 30 minutes. ❧ Heat the oil in a deep skillet (frying pan) and fry the koftas in small batches until golden brown all over. ❧ Drain on paper towels and serve hot.

Koftas are a popular Middle Eastern dish. There is an endless variety of possible flavor combinations.

Variation
- For a lighter dish, broil (grill) the koftas, or bake them in a hot oven with 1–2 tablespoons of oil to stop them sticking to the baking dish.

GLAZED TOPSIDE WITH MUSHROOMS SAUTÉED IN GARLIC

Preheat the oven to 400°F/200°C/gas 6. ♠ Season the meat with salt and pepper. Transfer to a roasting pan and drizzle with 5 tablespoons oil. Add the whole clove garlic, sage, and rosemary. ♠ Cook for 15 minutes, or until brown all over, pour half the wine over the top and continue cooking for about 1 hour, basting from time to time. If the meat becomes too dry, add more wine or a little stock. ♠ In the meantime, wash the mushrooms under cold running water. Cut off and discard the stems. Peel the mushroom caps and cut into large strips. ♠ Heat the remaining oil in a skillet (frying pan) over medium heat and sauté the chopped garlic and parsley for 2–3 minutes. ♠ Add the mushrooms and season with salt and pepper. Stir well and cook for 5–7 minutes. ♠ Pour in the remaining wine and cook until evaporated. Add the stock and cook over medium heat for about 20–25 minutes, or until the liquid reduces, stirring often. The mushrooms should be tender. ♠ When the meat is cooked, transfer to a heated serving dish and set aside in a warm place. ♠ Discard the garlic, rosemary, and sage from the cooking juices. Place the sauce over high heat, and stir in the flour. Pour over the meat. ♠ Arrange the mushrooms around the meat and serve hot.

Serves: 6

Preparation: 25'

Cooking: 1¹/₂ h

Level of difficulty: 2

- 2¹/₂ lb/1.2 kg slice of veal or beef, preferably rump, rolled and tied with kitchen string
- salt and freshly ground black pepper to taste
- ¹/₂ cup/125 ml extra-virgin olive oil
- 3 cloves garlic (1 whole, 2 finely chopped)
- 1 tsp sage
- 1 tsp rosemary
- 1 cup/250 ml dry white wine
- 1 cup/250 ml Beef Stock (see page 140)
- 1¹/₂ lb/750 g white mushrooms
- 1 tbsp parsley, finely chopped
- 2 tbsp all-purpose/ plain flour

BOILED BEEF IN LEEK & TOMATO SAUCE

Serves: 4

Preparation: 15'

Cooking: 30

Level of difficulty: 1

- 1 lb/500 g boiled beef (neck, shoulder, short ribs, brisket, various cuts of lean beef)
- 4 tbsp extra-virgin olive oil
- 4 leeks, sliced
- 1 cup/250 ml *Beef Stock* (see page 140)
- 12 oz/350 g tomatoes, peeled and chopped
- salt and freshly ground black pepper to taste

Cut the boiled beef into bite-sized pieces. Heat the oil in a heavy-bottomed pan and sauté the leeks for a few minutes. Pour in the stock and partially cover. Cook until the liquid has almost completely reduced. Add the meat and tomatoes, season with salt and pepper, and continue cooking for about 20 minutes, or until the meat is falling apart. Transfer to a serving dish and serve hot.

This recipe provides a good way to use up the leftover beef when you have made beef stock.

537

BEEF ROLLS WITH ARTICHOKES

Remove any small pieces of fat from the beef and pound lightly. ❧ Beat the eggs in a small bowl with the parsley, garlic, and salt. ❧ Heat 2 tablespoons of oil in a small saucepan, pour in the egg mixture and cook until set. Set aside to cool. ❧ To clean the artichokes, remove the tough outer leaves and trim the tops and stalks. Wash well in cold water and lemon juice. Cut each artichoke into 6 segments. ❧ Heat 2 tablespoons of oil in a saucepan over medium heat and cook the artichokes for 5 minutes. Season with salt and pepper and set aside. ❧ To prepare the rolls, lay the slices of meat on a work surface and place a piece of mortadella on each. ❧ Cut the cooked egg into 18 pieces. Place a piece of egg and a segment of artichoke on the mortadella. ❧ Roll the meat into filled rolls and close with a cocktail stick. ❧ Dredge in the flour and place in a saucepan with the remaining oil. Sprinkle with salt and pepper, and brown on all sides. ❧ Pour in the wine and cook for 20 minutes, adding stock if the pan becomes too dry. ❧ Serve hot.

Serves: 6

Preparation: 25'

Cooking: 20'

Level of difficulty: 2

- 1¼ lb/600 g beef rump sliced extra thin (18 slices)
- 4 eggs
- 1 tbsp parsley and garlic, finely chopped
- salt and freshly ground black pepper to taste
- ½ cup/125 ml extra-virgin olive oil
- 3 globe artichokes
- juice of ½ lemon
- 5 oz/150 g mortadella slices, cut in half (18 pieces)
- 3 tbsp all-purpose/plain flour
- ½ cup/125 ml dry white wine
- ½ cup/125 ml *Beef Stock* (see page 140)

CLUB STEAKS WITH GREEN PEPPER

Mash the green peppercorns with a fork. Use your hands to press the crushed peppercorns so that they stick to both sides of the steaks. ❧ Heat the butter and oil in a heavy-bottomed pan. ❧ Season the steaks with salt and add to the pan.

These tasty steaks are quick and easy to prepare. Serve them with potato salad.

❧ Pour in the cognac and cook until it evaporates. ❧ Add the cream and cook for about 5 minutes more, turning the meat over at least once. If the sauce is too liquid, remove the steaks and set them aside in a warm oven. Turn up the heat and cook the sauce until it reduces sufficiently. ❧ Arrange the steaks on a heated serving dish and spoon the sauce over the top. ❧ Serve hot.

Serves: 4

Preparation: 10'

Cooking: 10'

Level of difficulty: 1

- 2 tbsp soft green peppercorns (in liquid)
- 4 club steaks (boneless), weighing about 12 oz/350 g each
- 2 tbsp butter
- 4 tbsp extra-virgin olive oil
- dash of salt
- $1/2$ cup/125 ml brandy
- 2 tbsp cream

BARI-STYLE BEEF ROLLS

Lay the slices of veal out flat. Sprinkle with the garlic and parsley followed by the cheese. ❧ Roll the veal up and secure with a cocktail stick. ❧ Sauté the onion and bay leaves in the oil in a large skillet (frying pan) until soft. ❧ Add the veal rolls and cook over medium heat for 5 minutes. Season with salt and pepper. ❧ Pour in the tomatoes, partly cover the skillet, and cook until the tomatoes reduce and the meat is tender (20–30 minutes). ❧ Remove the bay leaves and serve hot.

Serves: 4

Preparation: 15'

Cooking: 25–35'

Level of difficulty: 2

- **12 thin slices of veal, weighing about 1 lb/500 g total**
- **3 cloves garlic, finely chopped**
- **2 tbsp finely chopped parsley**
- **8 oz/250 g Pecorino cheese, cut in cubes**
- **1 medium onion, finely chopped**
- **2 bay leaves**
- **2 tbsp extra-virgin olive oil**
- **salt and freshly ground black pepper to taste**
- **1 (15 oz/400 g) can tomatoes**

SLICED STEAK
WITH SALAD GREENS

Serves: 4

Preparation: 10'

Cooking: 5'

Level of difficulty: 1

- 1 lb/500 g sirloin steak, boned
- 8 oz/250 g fresh salad greens, (preferably arugula/rocket)
- salt and freshly ground black pepper to taste
- 4 tbsp extra-virgin olive oil (optional)

lace the meat over a very hot grill or under a broiler (or better still, a barbecue). Cook until rare. ❧ Transfer the meat to a chopping board and cut in thin slices. ❧ Place the salad greens on a serving dish and top with the sliced steak. ❧ Season with salt and pepper, drizzle with the oil, if liked, and serve at once.

LAMB

HOT & SPICY LAMB STEW

Heat the oil in a large saucepan, preferably earthenware. Sauté the onion, carrot, celery, garlic, parsley, red pepper flakes, and bacon over medium-high heat. ❧ When the pancetta and onion are light golden brown, add the lamb and sauté for 7–8 minutes. ❧ Season with salt and pepper and add the wine. Cook until the wine has evaporated. ❧ Add the tomatoes, lower the heat to medium, and partially cover. Cook for about 1 hour, or until the lamb is tender, adding a little hot water if the sauce reduces too much. ❧ Serve hot.

Serves: 4–6
Preparation: 15'
Cooking: 1¹/₄ h
Level of difficulty: 1

- 4 tbsp extra-virgin olive oil
- 1 onion, 1 carrot, 1 stalk celery, coarsely chopped
- 2 cloves garlic, finely chopped
- 2 tbsp finely chopped parsley
- 1 tsp red pepper flakes
- ¹/₂ cup/125 g diced bacon
- 2 lb/1 kg lamb, shoulder or leg, cut in bite-sized pieces
- salt and freshly ground black pepper to taste
- ²/₃ cup/150 ml dry white wine
- 1 lb/500 g ripe tomatoes, peeled and chopped

BRAISED LAMB WITH LEMON

Preheat the oven to 350°F/180°C/gas 4. ✿ Melt the pork fat over low heat in a flameproof earthenware casserole. Add the lamb and season with salt and pepper. ✿ Moisten with some of the hot stock. Cover and cook in a preheated oven at for about 1 hour or until the meat is very tender, basting at frequent intervals with a little more hot stock. ✿ Drizzle with the lemon juice and serve hot.

The original recipe calls for kid meat. Since this is not widely available, use lamb instead.

546

Serves 4–5

Preparation: 10'

Cooking: 1 h

Level of difficulty: 1

- ¹/₂ **cup/75 g rendered pork fat or finely chopped fresh pork fat**
- **2 lb/1 kg lamb, cut into small pieces**
- **salt and freshly ground black pepper to taste**
- **1³/₄ cups/400 ml** *Beek Stock* **(see page 140)**
- **juice of 2 lemons**

ROAST LAMB WITH OLIVES

Serves 4–5

Preparation: 10'

Cooking: 1 h

Level of difficulty: 1

- 2 lb/1 kg lamb, cut into fairly small pieces
- 4 tbsp extra-virgin olive oil
- salt and freshly ground black pepper to taste
- 1¹⁄₂ cups/200 g large black olives, pitted and coarsely chopped
- 1¹⁄₄ cups/310 ml dry red wine

Preheat the oven to 350°F/180°C/gas 4. ❧ Place the lamb in a baking dish. Drizzle with the oil and season generously with salt and pepper. Sprinkle with the olives and moisten with half the wine. ❧ Cover and bake for about 1 hour, or until the meat is very tender, basting at frequent intervals with a little more wine. ❧ Serve hot.

The succulent flavors of the lambs blend beautifully with the olives and wine.

547

PAN-ROASTED LAMB

Cut the lamb into 2-in (5-cm) pieces. ❧ Heat the oil in a heavy-bottomed saucepan large enough to contain the meat. Add the 2 whole cloves of garlic and the lamb and sauté over medium-high heat until the lamb is golden brown all over. ❧ Sprinkle with 1 tablespoon of the rosemary and sage and season with salt and pepper. ❧ After about 10 minutes pour in the wine. When it has evaporated, lower the heat, partially cover the pan and continue cooking for about 40 minutes, turning from time to time. ❧ In the meantime, place the anchovies and finely chopped garlic in a bowl with the remaining rosemary and sage and the vinegar. ❧ When the lamb is cooked, raise the heat, pour the vinegar mixture over the top and cook for another 5 minutes. ❧ Serve hot.

Serves: 4

Preparation: 25'

Cooking: 1 h

Level of difficulty: 1

- 2 lb/1 kg lamb shoulder, with some loin attached
- 6 tbsp extra-virgin olive oil
- 3 cloves garlic (2 whole, 1 finely chopped)
- 2 tbsp rosemary and sage, finely chopped
- salt and freshly ground black pepper to taste
- 1 cup/250 ml dry white wine
- 4 anchovy fillets, crumbled
- ½ cup/125 ml white vinegar

BREADED LAMB CHOPS

P ound the chops lightly to spread the meat as much as possible. ❧ Sprinkle with salt, dredge in the flour, and shake to remove the excess. ❧ Dip in the egg and coat well with the bread crumbs. ❧ Heat the oil in a deep skillet (frying pan) until very hot. Fry the chops, turning them so that they are golden brown on both sides. ❧ Drain on paper towels and serve very hot.

Serves: 4

Preparation: 10'

Cooking: 5–10'

Level of difficulty: 1

- **8 lamb chops**
- **salt to taste**
- **$^1/_2$ cup/75 g all-purpose/plain flour**
- **1 egg**
- **1 cup/125 g fine dry bread crumbs**
- **2 cups/500 ml oil for frying**

LAMB & ARTICHOKE FRICASSEE

P lace the lamb in a bowl with salt, pepper, 4 tablespoons of oil, and the juice of half a lemon. Marinate for 2 hours. ♣ Remove the tough outer leaves from the artichokes and trim the stalks and tops. Slice the tender inner hearts into segments. Wash in cold water and the juice of a lemon. ♣ Heat 2 tablespoons of oil in a saucepan over medium heat. Add the garlic and artichokes, sauté for 5–6 minutes, then set aside. ♣ Drain the lamb thoroughly and sauté in a separate heavy-bottomed pan with the remaining oil. ♣ When the lamb is well browned, pour in the wine and cook until it evaporates. ♣ Transfer the lamb to the pan with the artichokes and season with salt to taste. ♣ Partially cover the pan and cook over a medium heat for 1 hour, adding stock from time to time as the sauce reduces, and stirring frequently. ♣ When the lamb is cooked, beat the egg with a little salt and the juice of half a lemon. Pour the egg mixture over the stew and turn off the heat. Toss carefully so that the egg cooks and sets. ♣ Sprinkle with the parsley and serve hot.

552

Serves: 4

Preparation: 25' + 2 h

Cooking: 1 $^1/_4$ h

Level of difficulty: 1

- 1 $^1/_4$ lb/650 g lamb (boneless leg and shoulder), cut in pieces
- salt and freshly ground black pepper to taste
- $^1/_2$ cup/125 ml extra-virgin olive oil
- juice of 1 $^1/_2$ lemons
- 3 globe artichokes
- 2 cloves garlic, finely chopped
- 1 cup/250 ml dry white wine
- 1 cup/250 ml *Beef Stock* (see page 140)
- 1 egg
- 1 tbsp parsley, finely chopped

LAMB & POTATO CASEROLE

Preheat the oven to 400°F/200°C/gas 6. ❧ Place the lamb, potatoes, tomatoes, and onion in an ovenproof casserole. ❧ Drizzle with the oil and season with salt and pepper. Sprinkle with the rosemary and oregano. ❧ Cover and roast for about 1 hour, or until the meat is very tender. Baste at frequent intervals with a little hot water. ❧ Serve hot.

554

This is a traditional Easter dish in many areas of southern Italy. Serve with a full-bodied red wine.

Serves: 4

Preparation: 15'

Cooking: 1 h

Level of difficulty: 1

- **2 lb/1 kg lamb, cut into bite-sized pieces**
- **1$\frac{1}{2}$ lb/750 g yellow, waxy potatoes, thickly sliced or in wedges**
- **4 large tomatoes, quartered or cut into 6 pieces**
- **1 medium onion, sliced**
- **4 tbsp extra-virgin olive oil**
- **salt and freshly ground black pepper to taste**
- **1 tbsp finely chopped fresh rosemary**
- **1 tsp dried oregano**

BRAISED LAMB

Serves: 4
Preparation: 15'
Cooking: 1¼ h
Level of difficulty: 1

Sauté the garlic, rosemary, and sage in the oil over medium-high heat in a large, deep skillet (frying pan).  Add the lamb and season with salt and pepper. Stir in the flour, vinegar, and water. Cover and cook over a low heat for 1 hour, adding extra water if the cooking liquid dries out too much.  Put 2 tablespoons of the cooking liquid in a small bowl and dissolve the anchovy fillets in it. Pour back into the stew and stir well.  Cook for another 2–3 minutes, then remove from the heat and serve.

- 3 cloves garlic, finely chopped
- 1 tbsp finely chopped rosemary leaves
- 4 sage leaves
- 4 tbsp extra-virgin olive oil
- 2 lb/1 kg tender young lamb shoulder, cut into bite-sized chunks, with the bone
- salt and freshly ground black pepper to taste
- 1 tbsp all-purpose/plain flour
- ½ cup/125 ml white wine vinegar
- 4 tbsp cold water
- 6 anchovy filets

Serves: 4

Preparation: 5'

Cooking: 15'

Level of difficulty: 1

- **2 lb/1 kg lamb chops**
- **2 tbsp extra-virgin olive oil**
- **salt and freshly ground black pepper to taste**

BROILED LAMB CHOPS

P lace the chops on a large plate and drizzle with the oil. Sprinkle with salt and a generous grinding of pepper. ᪣ Arrange the chops in a grill pan and place over a high heat. Turn frequently until they are well browned. If you don't have a grill pan, arrange the chops on a wire rack and place under the broiler (grill). Turn frequently until they are done. ᪣ Serve very hot.

Delight your children by serving these with mashed potatoes and Basic Tomato Sauce (see page 932).

557

PORK

ROAST SPARERIBS

reheat the oven to 350°F/180°C/gas 4. ❧
Place the spareribs in a large roasting pan.
Season with salt and pepper, sprinkle with
the rosemary, and drizzle with the oil. Use a sharp
knife to make 8 incisions in the meaty parts of the
spareribs and fill each one with garlic. ❧ Roast the
spareribs for about 45–50 minutes. The exact
cooking time will depend on how much meat is on
the spareribs ❧ Serve hot.

Serves: 6
Preparation: 10'
Cooking: 50'
Level of difficulty: 1

• **5 lb/2.5 kg
  spareribs**
• **salt and freshly
  ground black
  pepper to taste**
• **2 tbsp fresh
  rosemary leaves**
• **4 tbsp extra-virgin
  olive oil**
• **4 cloves garlic,
  peeled and cut in
  half**

PAN ROASTED PORK

T ie the meat with kitchen string so that it will keep its shape as it cooks. ❧ Choose a fireproof casserole just large enough to accommodate the meat. Pour in the oil, and vinegar, then add the garlic, rosemary, juniper berries, and meat. Marinate in the refrigerator for 24 hours, turning frequently. ❧ Pour in sufficient milk to cover the meat and cook over low heat for 1 hour. At the end of this time the milk should be completely absorbed. ❧ Turn up the heat and brown the meat all over. ❧ Serve, carving into chops, slicing between the ribs. ❧ This dish is also very good served at room temperature.

Serves: 4

Preparation: 15' + 24 h to marinate

Cooking: 1 h

Level of difficulty: 1

- 3¹/₂ lb/1.5 kg loin of pork
- 1 cup/250 ml extra-virgin olive oil
- 2 tbsp wine vinegar
- 2 cloves garlic, peeled and lightly crushed
- 1 sprig rosemary
- 6–7 juniper berries
- 4 cups/1 liter milk (or enough to cover the meat)
- salt and freshly ground black pepper to taste

PORK GOULASH

Serves: 4

Preparation: 25'

Cooking: 1³/₄ h

Level of difficulty: 1

- **2 tbsp extra-virgin olive oil**
- **4 oz/125 g bacon, diced**
- **1 lb/500 g pork, cut in cubes**
- **2 large red onions, finely chopped**
- **3 cloves garlic, finely chopped**
- **2 tbsp finely chopped parsley**
- **2 tsp red pepper flakes**
- **2 tbsp tomato concentrate**
- **salt and freshly ground black pepper to taste**
- **2 cups/500 ml Beef Stock (see page 140)**
- **2 cups/500 ml dry white wine**
- **1 tsp cumin**
- **6 potatoes, peeled and cut in bite-sized chunks**

Heat the oil in a large heavy-bottomed saucepan. Add the bacon and sauté until lightly browned. ❧ Add the pork and brown evenly all over. ❧ Add the onion, garlic, and parsley and sauté for 5 minutes. ❧ Pour in the stock and wine and bring to a boil. ❧ Add the red pepper flakes, tomato, and cumin. Season with salt and pepper. Cover the pan and simmer over medium-low heat for about 1¹/₂ hours, or until the meat is tender. ❧ Add the potatoes about 40 minutes before the meat is cooked.

PORK & POLENTA STEW

P lace the pork in a fireproof casserole with the cabbage, onion, carrot, and celery. Add a dash of salt and the water. Cover tightly and bring quickly to a boil. ❧ Reduce the heat to medium and simmer for 30 minutes. ❧ While the pork and vegetables are cooking, bring 5 cups/1.25 liters of salted water to a boil in a large saucepan. Sprinkle in the cornmeal while stirring continuously with a wooden spoon to prevent lumps from forming. Continue cooking over medium heat, stirring almost continuously for 20–25 minutes. ❧ Add the meat, vegetables, and their cooking liquid to this very soft polenta and stir well. ❧ Simmer for 20–25 more minutes, stirring almost constantly and adding a little boiling water when necessary to keep the polenta very moist and soft. ❧ Stir in the butter and Parmesan. ❧ Serve hot.

Add 2 large spicy sausages, cut in 8 pieces, for a more flavorsome dish.

Serves: 4

Preparation: 10'

Cooking: 1 h

Level of difficulty: 1

- 1 lb/500 g loin of pork, cut in bite-sized chunks
- 1 1/4 lb/625 g Savoy cabbage, cut into thin strips
- 1 small onion, thickly sliced
- 1 small carrot, sliced
- 1 stalk celery, sliced
- salt to taste
- 1/2 cup/125 ml hot water
- 1 1/2 cups/200 g coarse-grain yellow cornmeal
- 5 tbsp butter, cut up
- 4 tbsp freshly grated Parmesan cheese

ROAST SUCKLING PIG
WITH VEGETABLES

Serves: 6

Preparation: 10'

Cooking: 1¾ h

Level of difficulty: 2

* **2 onions, 2 carrots, 2 stalks celery, 2 zucchini, 3 potatoes, all diced**
* **1 leek, sliced**
* **6 tbsp extra-virgin olive oil**
* **dash of salt**
* **¹/₂ suckling pig, about 4¹/₂ lb**
* **10 black peppercorns**
* **2 bay leaves**
* **1 cup/250 ml dry white wine**
* **1 tbsp finely chopped parsley**
* **2 cloves garlic, finely chopped**

Preheat the oven to 400°F/200°C/gas 6. ❧ Sauté the vegetables in a large saucepan with 2 tablespoons of oil over high heat for 5–6 minutes. ❧ Sprinkle with salt and stir thoroughly. Remove from heat and set aside. ❧ Add the remaining oil to the same pan and brown the pork. ❧ Transfer the meat and any liquid it has produced to a roasting pan. Sprinkle with a little more salt and the peppercorns. Add the bay leaves and turn the meat in its juices. ❧ Roast for 1¹/₂ hours, basting frequently and gradually adding the wine. ❧ After about 1 hour, add the vegetables and sprinkle with the garlic and parsley. ❧ Arrange on a serving dish with the vegetables and serve hot.

STUFFED PIG'S FOOT WITH LENTILS

Serves: 4–6

Preparation: 20' +
  12 h to soak

Cooking: 3–4 h for
  the zampone, 1½ h
  for the lentils

Level of difficulty: 2

- 1 zampone (stuffed
  pig's foot) weighing
  about 2 lb/1 kg
- 1½ cups/300 g
  lentils (small brown
  or Puy type)
- ½ cup/75 g finely
  chopped pancetta
- 2 tbsp extra-virgin
  olive oil
- 1 medium onion,
  finely chopped
- 1 bay leaf
- boiling water
- 1 bouillon cube

Place the zampone in a large bowl of cold water and let soak for 12 hours. ♠ In a separate bowl, soak the lentils for 12 hours. ♠ Just before cooking the zampone, remove from the water and use a large needle to prick the skin, puncturing it at intervals along its length, making 2–3 lines of holes. Use the tip of a very sharp, pointed knife to make a small cross-cut incision on the underside of the trotter (between the three toes). Slightly loosen the string used to tie it up. ♠ Wrap the zampone in a piece of cheesecloth (muslin) and place in a large saucepan. Cover completely with cold water and simmer very gently for 3–4 hours. ♠ While the zampone is cooking, prepare the lentils: Sauté the pancetta for a few minutes in the oil, then add the onion. ♠ When the onion has softened, add the lentils and stir while cooking for a few minutes. ♠ Add sufficient boiling water to cover the lentils completely and crumble the bouillon cube into the water. ♠ Simmer gently over a low heat for 1½ hours. ♠ Unwrap the zampone, slice, and serve very hot, accompanied by the lentils.

FILET OF PORK WITH APPLE

Cut the apples in half and remove the cores. Place in a bowl, cover with the wine, and set aside to marinate for at least 2 hours (or even longer if you have the time). ❧ Preheat the oven to 400°F/200°C/gas 6. ❧ Season the pork with salt and pepper and transfer to a baking pan with the oil. ❧ Bake for 10 minutes, pour about half the wine used to marinate the apples over the pork. Turn the pork and cook for another 20 minutes. ❧ Arrange the apples around the pork in the baking pan and add more wine if the pan is dry. Cook for 30 minutes more. ❧ Slice the pork and transfer to a serving dish. Arrange the apples around the pork and serve hot with a bowl of steaming potato purée.

This dish, hearty and easy to prepare, is perfect for cold winter evenings.

570

Serves: 4
Preparation: 5' + 2 h
Cooking: 1 h
Level of difficulty: 1

- **6 Golden Delicious apples**
- **2 cups/500 ml dry white wine**
- **2 pork filets, about 1 lb/500 g**
- **salt and freshly ground black pepper to taste**
- **4 tbsp extra-virgin olive oil**

PORK LOIN WITH PRUNES

Place 10 prunes in a bowl with the cognac, diluted with enough water to cover the fruit. Set aside to marinate. ❧ After 30 minutes, drain well so that all the marinade has been removed. ❧ Preheat the oven to 350°F/180°C/gas 4. ❧ Use a sharp knife to make incisions in the pork. Fill with a little salt and pepper and the prunes. ❧ Place the rosemary on the meat and tie with kitchen string. Season with salt and pepper. ❧ Heat the butter and oil in a saucepan over medium heat. Add the pork and brown all over. ❧ Bake for 40 minutes, then pour the wine over the meat and add the remaining prunes. Continue cooking, adding stock if it dries out. ❧ Serve hot or at room temperature with the sauce (heated, if the meat is lukewarm), and prunes.

572

Serves: 6

Preparation: 20' + 30' to marinate

Cooking: 1¼ h

Level of difficulty: 1

- **20–25 dried prunes, pitted**
- **½ cup/125 ml cognac**
- **2 lb/1 kg boneless pork loin**
- **salt and freshly ground black pepper to taste**
- **4 sprigs rosemary**
- **2 tbsp butter**
- **4 tbsp extra-virgin olive oil**
- **1 cup/250 ml dry white wine**
- **1 cup/250 ml *Beef Stock* (see page 140)**

MIXED PORK STEWED IN RED WINE

Ask your butcher to chop each sparerib into 3 pieces. Cut the neck, shanks, and sausages into bite-sized pieces. ❧ Heat the oil in a saucepan over medium-high heat. Add the onion, carrot, celery, parsley, and bay leaves and sauté for 3–4 minutes. ❧ Add the pork, season with salt and pepper, and brown all over. ❧ Pour in the wine and cook until it is partially evaporated. ❧ Stir in the tomatoes. ❧ Cover and simmer gently over low heat for about 1½ hours. Add the stock gradually as the sauce dries out. Turn the meat from time to time. ❧ Serve hot.

Serves: 6
Preparation: 25'
Cooking: 1½ h
Level of difficulty: 2

- 3 lb/1.5 kg mixed cuts of pork (spareribs, boned neck, boneless shanks)
- 3 spicy pork sausages
- 6 tbsp extra-virgin olive oil
- 1 onion, 1 carrot, 1 stalk celery, coarsely chopped
- 1 clove garlic, finely chopped
- 1 tbsp parsley, finely chopped
- 2 bay leaves
- salt and freshly ground black pepper to taste
- 1 cup/250 ml robust red wine
- 12 oz/350 g canned tomatoes
- 1 cup/250 ml *Beef Stock* (see page 140)

ROAST PORK SHANKS WITH MIXED VEGETABLES

Preheat the oven to 400°F/200°C/gas 6. ❧ Remove any remaining hairs from the shanks. Rinse under cold running water and pat dry with paper towels. ❧ Roll in the flour and season with salt and pepper. ❧ Heat 4 tablespoons of the oil in a large saucepan, add the shanks, and cook over high heat until golden brown. ❧ Transfer the shanks and their cooking juices to a roasting pan. Cook for 20 minutes. Add the wine and cook for 40 minutes more, adding a little stock if the pan becomes too dry. ❧ Meanwhile, heat the remaining oil in a saucepan and sauté the vegetables over high heat for 5–7 minutes. ❧ When the shanks have been in the oven for about 1 hour, add the vegetables and their cooking juices. ❧ Return to the oven and cook for 1 hour more, basting with stock as required to stop the pan from drying out. ❧ When cooked, arrange the meat and vegetables on a heated serving dish and serve hot.

Serves: 6

Preparation: 50'

Cooking: 2 h

Level of difficulty: 2

- **3 pork shanks, weighing about 3 lb/1.5 kg**
- **4 tbsp all-purpose/ plain flour**
- **6 tbsp extra-virgin olive oil**
- **salt and freshly ground black pepper to taste**
- **1 cup/250 ml dry white wine**
- **14 oz/400 g carrots**
- **11 oz/300 g celery, chopped in large dice**
- **11 oz/300 g onions, chopped in large dice**
- **14 oz/400 g potatoes, chopped in large dice**
- **11 oz/300 g zucchini/ courgettes, chopped in large dice**
- **2 cups/500 ml *Beef Stock* (see page 140)**

CALAMARI, BACON, & BELL PEPPER KEBABS

Preheat the oven to 350°F/180°C/gas 4. ❧ Cut the calamari in rings. ❧ Cut the bacon and bell peppers into bite-size pieces. ❧ Assemble the kebabs by alternately threading the calamari, bacon, and bell peppers onto the skewers. ❧ Place the basil in a bowl with the salt, pepper, oregano, and lemon zest. Add the oil and lemon juice and mix well. ❧ Bake the kebabs in the oven, turning frequently and basting with the sauce. ❧ Drizzle with the remaining sauce and serve on a bed of fresh salad greens.

Serves: 6

Preparation: 15'

Cooking: 5'

Level of difficulty: 1

- 3 lb/750 g calamari, cleaned
- 13 oz/400 g bacon, in thick slices
- 13 oz/400 g red bell peppers/ capsicums
- 20 leaves basil, torn
- salt and freshly ground white pepper to taste
- dash of oregano
- grated zest and juice of 2 lemons
- $^1/_2$ cup/125 ml extra-virgin olive oil
- salad greens

MEDALLIONS OF HAM WITH BROCCOLI & ANCHOVIES

Serves: 6

Preparation: 20'

Cooking: 25'

Level of difficulty: 2

- **12 slices Parma ham, about 2¹/₂ oz/75 g each**
- **5 oz/150 g Mozzarella cheese, thinly sliced**
- **1 tbsp capers**
- **12 green olives, pitted and cut in half**
- **salt and freshly ground black pepper to taste**
- **6 slices bacon**
- **2 cloves garlic, finely chopped**
- **3 sage leaves, finely chopped**
- **1 sprig rosemary, finely chopped**
- **¹/₂ cup/125 ml dry white wine**
- **1¹/₂ lb/750 g broccoli, lightly boiled, in florets**
- **6 tbsp extra-virgin olive oil**
- **6 anchovy fillets**

Arrange the Mozzarella, capers, and olives on 6 slices of Parma ham. Lightly season with salt and cover with the remaining slices of Parma ham. ❧ Roll each one up in a slice of bacon and secure with a cocktail stick. ❧ Place in a skillet (frying pan) with a little water over low heat. Add the garlic, sage, rosemary, and a dash of pepper. When the bacon is lightly browned, drizzle with the wine and cook until it evaporates. ❧ In a separate pan, dissolve the anchovies in the oil and sauté the broccoli for 5 minutes. Serve the medallions hot with the broccoli.

GLAZED SPARERIBS

Place the ribs, ginger, scallions, star fruit, and first measure of soy sauce in a pot with enough water to cover. Bring to a boil and simmer for 20 minutes. ❧ Drain well and set the ribs and seasonings aside to cool. ❧ To glaze the ribs: Place a large skillet (frying pan) or wok over high heat and add the oil. Stir in the ribs to coat. ❧ Combine the sugar, stock, second measure of soy sauce, and the orange zest in a bowl and beat until the sugar is dissolved. ❧ Add to the pan and, keeping the heat on high, stir until the sauce has reduced. This will take about 7–8 minutes. ❧ Keep stirring until all the liquid has been absorbed and the ribs are evenly glazed. Be careful not to burn the meat at this stage. ❧ Place on a serving platter and set aside for 5 minutes.

Star fruit is an 8 pointed star-shaped fruit. Buy it in Asian food stores.

Serves: 4

Preparation: 20'

Cooking: 30'

Level of difficulty: 1

- 4 lb/2 kg pork ribs, cut in 2-inch/5-cm pieces
- 4 slices root ginger
- 4 scallions/spring onions, chopped
- 4 star fruit
- 6 tbsp dark soy sauce
- 2 tbsp extra-virgin olive oil
- 1 cup/200 g sugar
- 1 cup/250 ml chicken stock (homemade or stock cube)
- 4 tsp dark soy sauce
- 2 tbsp finely grated orange zest

ROAST PORK IN ORANGE SAUCE

582

Place the pork in a large bowl with 2 tablespoons of oil, mustard, garlic, half the orange zest, paprika, rosemary, thyme, salt, and pepper. Set aside to marinate for 4 hours. ❧ Preheat the oven to 400°F/200°C/gas 6. ❧ Heat the remaining oil with half the butter in an ovenproof pan and brown the pork over high heat. ❧ Drizzle with the juice of 1½ oranges and 6 tablespoons of the wine. Cover and bake for 1 hour. During cooking, baste frequently with more wine and stock mixed with the remaining orange zest and the parsley. ❧ While the pork is cooking, peel the colored part of the zest of one orange with a sharp knife. Cook in a small saucepan of boiling water for 5 minutes. Drain well. ❧ Slice the flesh of the orange thinly. Remove the seeds and brown in a small skillet (frying pan) with the remaining butter. ❧ When the meat is cooked, set aside in a warm place. ❧ Place the baking dish over low heat, add the remaining wine and stock. Use a fork to loosen the browning from the bottom of the pan. Bring to a boil, then add the cream and chile and cook over low heat until the sauce is thick and creamy. ❧ Season with salt and pepper and add the remaining orange juice and the zest cut in short strips. ❧ Slice the roast and spoon the sauce over the top.

- 2 lb/1 kg pork loin
- 3 tbsp extra-virgin olive oil
- 1 tsp mustard
- 2 cloves garlic, finely chopped
- 2 tbsp grated orange zest
- ½ tsp paprika
- 1 tsp rosemary
- 1 tsp thyme
- salt and freshly ground black pepper to taste
- 2 tbsp butter
- 3 oranges (freshly squeezed juice of 2 + the flesh and zest of 1)
- 1 cup/250 ml dry white wine
- ½ cup/125 ml *Beef Stock* (see page 140)
- 2 tbsp finely chopped parsley
- ½ cup/125 ml cream
- 2 tsp soft green peppercorns

SPARERIBS WITH HONEY & HERBS

Preheat the oven to 325°F/160°C/gas 3. ❧ Rinse the ribs under cold running water and pat dry with paper towels. ❧ Season the ribs with rosemary, oregano, thyme, salt, and pepper, and drizzle with the vinegar. ❧ Place the seasoned ribs in a roasting pan and bake for 1½ hours, or until very tender. ❧ Melt the honey over very low heat and stir in the ketchup. ❧ Brush the ribs with this mixture and return to the oven for 5 minutes before serving.

The taste of the honey blends with the vinegar and herbs to create a satisfying and sweet flavor.

584

Serves: 4–6

Preparation: 15'

Cooking: 1½ h

Level of difficulty: 1

- **5 lb/2.5 kg pork spareribs**
- **1 tbsp finely chopped fresh rosemary**
- **1 tbsp finely chopped fresh oregano**
- **1 tbsp finely chopped fresh thyme**
- **salt and freshly ground black pepper to taste**
- **½ cup/125 ml distilled white vinegar**
- **½ cup/125 g honey**
- **1 cup/250 ml ketchup**

PILOTAS

Place the pork in a large bowl and stir in the bread crumbs, eggs, parsley, garlic, pine nuts, salt, pepper, cinnamon, and nutmeg. Mix well. ❧ Heat the oil in a large skillet (frying pan) over medium-high heat and fry the meatballs until golden brown all over. ❧ Drain excess oil from the cooked pilotas on a preheated plate covered with paper towels. ❧ Serve hot with rice and a green salad.

586

Pilotas are a delicious type of meatball from Catalan cuisine. The original dish was of arabic origin.

Serves: 4

Preparation: 10'

Cooking: 25'

Level of difficulty: 1

- 1 lb/500 g ground pork
- ½ cup/60 g bread crumbs
- 2 eggs, lightly beaten
- 2 tbsp finely chopped parsley
- 3 cloves garlic, finely chopped
- 4 tbsp pine nuts
- salt and freshly ground black pepper to taste
- ½ tsp each ground cinnamon and nutmeg
- 1 cup/250 ml oil, for frying

PORK WITH STRAWBERRIES

Serves: 6

Preparation: 15'

Cooking: 10'

Level of difficulty: 1

- 7 oz/200 g torn salad greens
- 2 cups/250 g sliced fresh strawberries
- 2 stalks celery, thinly sliced
- 1 tsp finely chopped fresh chives
- 3 tbsp extra-virgin olive oil
- 1 lb/500 g pork tenderloin, thinly sliced
- 2 cloves garlic, finely chopped
- 6 tbsp honey
- 6 tbsp balsamic vinegar
- salt and freshly ground black pepper to taste
- 6 tbsp chopped walnuts, toasted

Place the salad greens, strawberries, celery, and chives in a large bowl. Toss well and set aside. ❧ Heat 1 tablespoon of oil in a large skillet (frying pan) over medium-high heat. Add half the pork and cook for 3–4 minutes, or until the pork is well cooked. Repeat with the remaining pork. Remove from the skillet and set aside in a warm place. ❧ Heat the remaining oil in the same skillet and sauté the garlic for 1 minute. ❧ Add the honey, vinegar, salt, and pepper. Cook and stir until well heated. ❧ Arrange the salad greens and strawberry mixture on a serving dish and cover with the pork. Drizzle with the sauce and top with the walnuts. ❧ Serve at once.

Use only the crunchiest salad greens and the freshest strawberries for this dish. Texture is all-important.

587

ROAST PORK
WITH APPLE CIDER

Preheat the oven to 450°F/225°C/gas 7. ❧ Use a sharp knife to make 10 incisions in the pork crackling. Insert a clove into each hole. Season well with salt and pepper. ❧ Place the pork in a roasting pan and arrange the onions and apples around it. Cover with the butter. ❧ Pour a quarter of the cider over the top. ❧ Bake for 30 minutes, or until nicely browned. ❧ Reduce the oven temperature to 400°F/200°C/gas 6 and cook for 1 hour. Baste with more cider and cooking juices at regular intervals. ❧ Drizzle the pork with the Calvados and baste with cooking juices and cook for 10 more minutes. ❧ Remove the cloves from the crackling and place the cooked pork on a heated serving dish. Set aside in a warm oven. ❧ Pour the cooking juices into a small saucepan with the cream and parsley. Cook over medium heat until thickened. ❧ Serve the roast pork with the sauce in a separate bowl.

Calvados is an apple brandy made in Calvados, in Normandy, France.

588

Serves: 4–6

Preparation: 20'

Cooking: 1½ h

Level of difficulty: 1

- **3 lb/1.5 kg pork loin, with crackling**
- **salt and freshly ground white pepper to taste**
- **10 cloves**
- **2 large onions, thinly sliced**
- **2 large Golden Delicious apples, peeled, cored, and thinly sliced**
- **2 tbsp cold butter, cut up**
- **2 cups/500 ml dry apple cider**
- **4 tbsp Calvados liqueur**
- **½ cup/125 ml cream**
- **2 tbsp finely chopped parsley**

SPICY PORK STIR≈FRY

Heat the oil in a large skillet (frying pan) or wok. ❧ Add the cumin and stir fry for 2–3 minutes. Add the onion and sauté for about 10 minutes, or until pale golden brown. ❧ Stir in the dried chilies, tomatoes, ginger, and garlic and cook for 15 minutes. Season with salt and pepper. ❧ Add the pork and fresh chilies and stir fry until the meat is tender, about 10 minutes. ❧ Drizzle the dish with the vinegar, stir well, and remove from heat. ❧ Serve hot.

Serves: 4

Preparation: 10'

Cooking: 40'

Level of difficulty: 1

- **2 tbsp extra-virgin olive oil**
- **2 tsp cumin seeds**
- **2 large onions, finely chopped**
- **2–4 dried chilies, crumbled**
- **4 large tomatoes, finely chopped**
- **1 tbsp minced ginger root**
- **4 cloves garlic, finely chopped**
- **salt and freshly ground black pepper to taste**
- **2 fresh green chilies, sliced**
- **1 lb/500 g pork, cut in bite-sized cubes**
- **1 tbsp vinegar**

SWEET & SOUR PORK

Serves: 4

Preparation: 30'

Cooking: 30'

Level of difficulty: 1

- 1 cup/200 g long-grain rice
- 4 tbsp extra-virgin olive oil
- 2 cloves garlic, finely chopped
- 12 oz/350 g lean boneless pork, cut in bite-size cubes
- 1 cup/250 g *Chicken Stock* (see page 140)
- 6 tbsp sugar
- 6 tbsp red wine vinegar
- 4 tsp cornstarch/corn flour
- 1 tbsp soy sauce
- 4 carrots, thinly sliced
- 1 each green and red bell peppers, cut into 1-in/2-cm squares
- 3 green onions, sliced
- 1 (8-oz/250 g) can pineapple chunks, drained

Preheat the oven to 375°F/190°C/gas 5. ✿ Cook the rice according to the package directions. ✿ Place half the oil and half the garlic in a skillet (frying pan) or wok, add the pork and toss to coat. ✿ Arrange the pork in a baking pan and bake for 10–12 minutes, or until tender. Set aside. ✿ Combine the stock, sugar, vinegar, cornstarch, and soy sauce in a small bowl. ✿ Heat the remaining oil in a wok over medium heat. Add the remaining garlic and stir-fry for 30 seconds. Add the carrots and stir-fry for 3 minutes. Add the peppers and onions and stir-fry for 5 minutes, or until the vegetables are crisp-tender. Set the vegetables aside. ✿ Add the sauce to the wok and stir until thick and bubbly. ✿ Stir in the vegetables and pineapple chunks. ✿ Place the rice on a heated serving plate and top with the pork and vegetables. Serve at once.

ROAST PORK WITH RED WINE

Serves: 6

Preparation: 10'

Cooking: 2 h

Level of difficulty: 1

- 5 lb/2.5 kg roasting pork, with bone
- salt and freshly ground black pepper to taste
- 1 teaspoon ground cinnamon
- $^1/_3$ cup/50 g all-purpose/plain flour
- 2 onions, coarsely chopped
- 4 bay leaves
- 4 tbsp extra-virgin olive oil
- 1 cup/250 ml robust red wine
- 1 cup/180 g raisins
- 6 oz/180 g green olives

Preheat the oven to 450°F/225°C/gas 7. ✿ Sprinkle the pork with salt, pepper, and cinnamon, then dust with the flour. ✿ Place in a roasting pan with the onions and bay leaves and drizzle with the oil. ✿ Bake for 30 minutes, drizzle with half the wine, and return to the oven. ✿ Soak the raisins in a small bowl of tepid water for 15 minutes. Drain well. ✿ After another 30 minutes, drizzle the pork with the remaining wine, and sprinkle with the raisins and olives. Return to the oven and cook for 1 more hour. ✿ Serve hot.

HOMEMADE
SAUSAGE MEAT

Grind the pork with the pork fat (or chop it coarsely with a large sharp knife). For fine grain sausages, run the pork through the grinder two or three times. ❧ Place the ground pork and fat in a large bowl and stir in the salt and pepper. ❧ Add the other seasonings as liked. Try these, then experiment to find your own preferred flavors. ❧ Shape the sausage meat into patties or croquettes and broil (grill), roast, or barbecue them.

Making sausage meat at home is fun. Children especially love squishing the meat through their fingers.

Serves: 6

Preparation: 30'

Level of difficulty: 1

Basic recipe

- 1 1/2 lb/750 g lean pork
- 8 oz/250 g pork fat
- salt and freshly ground black pepper to taste

Garlic sausages

- 2 cloves garlic, finely chopped
- 1 tbsp finely chopped fresh rosemary leaves

Fresh herb sausages

- 2 tbsp each finely chopped parsley and chives

Old spice sausages

- 1 tsp each ground ginger and nutmeg

SAUSAGES WITH POTATO PUREE

Prick the sausages all over with a fork to allow fat to drain during cooking. ✷ Cook them in a large skillet (frying pan) over medium-high heat until nicely browned. They should produce enough fat to cook themselves. If not, add 1–2 tablespoons of butter or olive oil. ✷ Meanwhile, cook the potatoes in a large pot of salted, boiling water. When tender, mash until smooth. Beat in the butter and enough of the milk to make a soft purée. Season with the nutmeg, salt, and pepper. ✷ Serve the the sausages hot on a bed of steaming puree.

Serves: 4

Preparation: 5'

Cooking: 25'

Level of difficulty: 1

- **8–12 large sausages**
- **2 lb/1 kg potatoes**
- **2 tbsp butter**
- **¹/₂ cup/125 ml milk**
- **salt and freshly ground white pepper to taste**
- **dash of nutmeg**

SAUSAGES & BEANS

Serves: 4

Preparation: 15'

Cooking: 40'

Level of difficulty: 1

- **8 medium highly-flavored pork sausages**
- **¹⁄₂ cup/125 ml hot water**
- **5 tbsp extra-virgin olive oil**
- **2 cloves garlic, finely chopped**
- **4 fresh sage leaves**
- **1 lb/500 g peeled and chopped tomatoes, fresh or canned**
- **salt and freshly ground black pepper to taste**
- **1¹⁄₂ lb/750 g fresh cannellini beans, precooked, or 12 oz/350 g dried cannellini beans, soaked and precooked**

P rick the sausages all over with a fork and put into a skillet (frying pan). Add the water and cook over fairly high heat for 10–12 minutes, turning frequently. ❧ Pour the oil into a large skillet (frying pan) and add the garlic. Cook over low heat with the sage, tomatoes, salt, and pepper for 5 minutes. ❧ Increase the heat and cook for 10 minutes. Add the beans and sausages, cover and cook over medium heat for 15 minutes, stirring occasionally. ❧ Serve hot.

If short of time, use two cans of high quality white kidney or cannellini beans.

597

KIELBASY IN WINE
WITH POTATO SALAD

Place the sausages in a heavy-bottomed pan just large enough to hold them. Add the onions and pour in enough wine to cover the sausages. Bring to a boil over medium-low heat and simmer for about 35 minutes. ❧ Potato Salad: Cook the potatoes in their skins in a large pot of salted, boiling water until just tender. Place under cold running water until cool enough to handle, then slip off the skins. Cut into bite-sized chunks and place in an ovenproof dish. ❧ Add the onion and parsley and toss with the hot oil. Add the cooking liquid from the sausage, and the vinegar. Season with salt to taste. ❧ Serve the sausages with a little of their sauce spooned over the top together with the hot potato salad.

598

Kielbasy are a type of Polish sausage. Their superb flavor is enhanced by slow cooking in the wine.

Serves: 4

Preparation: 10'

Cooking: 45'

Level of difficulty: 1

- **4 large kielbasy sausages**
- **1 large onion, finely chopped**
- **2 cups/500 ml dry red wine**

POTATO SALAD
- **2 lb/1 kg potatoes**
- **4 scallions/spring onions, finely chopped**
- **6 tbsp finely chopped parsley**
- **4 tbsp extra-virgin olive oil, heated**
- **2 tbsp cooking liquid from the sausage**
- **2 tbsp wine vinegar**
- **1 tsp salt**

FRANKFURTERS IN SOUR CREAM ON RICE

Cut the frankfurters in half lengthwise. ❧ Cook the rice in a large pot of salted, boiling water until tender. ❧ In a large skillet (frying pan), sauté the onion in the butter until transparent. Add the frankfurters and chile sauce and cook for 3–4 minutes. ❧ Stir in the sour cream and cook until hot, without allowing it to boil. Season with salt and pepper. ❧ Drain the rice well and toss with the parsley. Place the rice on a large serving dish and spoon the frankfurters and their sauce over the top. ❧ Serve hot.

Serves: 4

Preparation: 15'

Cooking: 20'

Level of difficulty: 1

- **1¹/₂ lb/750 g frankfurters**
- **4 shallots, finely chopped**
- **4 tbsp butter**
- **6 tbsp chile sauce**
- **1 cup/250 ml sour cream**
- **salt and freshly ground white pepper to taste**
- **4–6 tbsp finely chopped parsley**

SPANISH SAUSAGES

Serves: 4

Preparation: 15'

Cooking: 1¼ h

Level of difficulty: 1

- **6 pork sausages**
- **6 rashers bacon**
- **1 onion, thinly sliced**
- **1 carrot, cut in wheels**
- **1 tsp mixed herbs**
- **4 tbsp ketchup**
- **salt and freshly ground black pepper to taste**
- **about ½ cup/ 125 ml water**

Preheat the oven to 300°F/150°C/gas 2. ❧ Wrap each sausage in a rasher of bacon. ❧ Place the sausages in a large skillet (frying pan) over medium heat and fry until the bacon is crisp. ❧ Transfer to a casserole and add the vegetables, ketchup, salt, and pepper. Pour the water over the top. ❧ Bake for 1 hour. ❧ Serve hot.

SAUSAGES WITH BELL PEPPERS

P ut the bell peppers whole under the broiler (grill) at high heat, giving them quarter turns until their skins blacken. This will take about 20 minutes. When the bell peppers are black all over, wrap them in foil and set aside for 10 minutes. Unwrap the bell peppers and remove their skins. ❧ Cut the bell peppers in half and discard the stalks, seeds, and pulpy inner core. Rinse under cold running water. Cut into long strips. ❧ Heat half the oil in a large skillet (frying pan) and sauté the garlic until transparent. ❧ Add the bell peppers and sauté until tender. This won't take long, as their flesh will be almost cooked after broiling. ❧ In the meantime, prick the sausages lightly and poach in a pot of boiling water for 5 minutes. ❧ Drain well and sauté in a separate skillet with the remaining oil until lightly browned and cooked through. ❧ Place the sausages on a serving dish and spoon the bell peppers over the top. ❧ Sprinkle with the parsley and serve hot.

This dish is very good served with rice, polenta, or mashed or boiled potatoes.

602

Serves: 6
Preparation: 15'
Cooking: 30'
Level of difficulty: 1

- **4 large bell peppers/capsicums, mixed colors**
- **6 tbsp extra-virgin olive oil**
- **4 cloves garlic, finely chopped**
- **salt and freshly ground black pepper to taste**
- **12 large sausages**
- **2 tbsp finely chopped parsley**

MIXED SAUSAGE, CHICKEN, & VEGETABLE SKEWERS

Wash and dry the zucchini. Trim the ends and chop in thick wheels. Wash and dry the bell pepper.

These skewers can also be barbecued. Baste with a little extra olive oil while grilling.

Remove the seeds and cores and chop in squares. Rinse the tomatoes and cut in quarters. Chop the sausages into 1-in (2.5-cm) thick slices. Chop the chicken into cubes of about the same size. Combine all the ingredients in a bowl with the sage, rosemary, parsley, salt, pepper, and oil and marinate in the refrigerator for 1 hour. Thread alternate pieces of chicken, sausage, and vegetables onto wooden or metal skewers. Heat the grill pan or broiler (grill) to very hot. Place the skewers in the pan or under the broiler, and cook for 15–20 minutes, or until the meat and vegetables are well-cooked. Serve hot or at room temperature.

Serves: 4

Preparation: 20' + 1 h

Cooking: 15'

Level of difficulty: 1

- 1 large zucchini/courgette
- 1 red or yellow bell pepper/capsicum
- 4–6 salad tomatoes
- 2 Italian pork sausages
- 1 large chicken breast
- 2 tbsp mixed finely chopped sage, rosemary, and parsley
- salt and freshly ground black pepper to taste
- 2 tbsp extra-virgin olive oil

A World of Sausages

Sausages are made from ground meat, fat, and salt and are usually highly-flavored with herbs or spices. Some have more fanciful additions such as whole pepper corns, pistachios, or chilies. They are usually stuffed into casings before cooking, although there are also many recipes for sausage meat. Sausages have been made throughout the world for many centuries. In most cases they are made of pork, although there are also some delicious sausages made using beef, chicken, turkey, game birds, and seafood. Sausages can be bought in a variety of forms, including fresh (usually to be cooked at home), dried (salami, etc), cooked, and smoked.

Some traditional types of sausages from around the world

Andouille: (French) a large smoked, spicy sausage made with neck and stomach meat. Now very popular in Cajun cuisine in the southern United States.

Blood sausage or black pudding: (British) a black sausage made from pork blood, suet, bread crumbs, and oatmeal.

Blutwurst: (German) a dark brown blood sausage made with pork blood, pork, fat, and seasonings. It is smoked or cooked.

Bologna: (USA) term used to refer to a variety of large smoked sausages that are sliced and eaten cold. Also known as baloney.

Boudin blanc: (French) a sausage made from finely ground pork, veal, or chicken, with onions, bread crumbs, and cream.

Boudin noir: (French) a black or blood sausage made with pork blood and fat, onions, and cream.

Bratwurst: (German) a fresh or cooked pork or mixed pork and veal sausage. Fresh bratwurst is often cooked in beer and served with sauerkraut.

Cervelas: (French) a pork and pork fat sausage that is boiled and served with mustard and potato salad.

Chorizo: (Mexican, Spanish) fresh or smoked pork sausage highly

seasoned with garlic. The Mexican version is very flavorful, being seasoned with vinegar, garlic, cumin, and chilies.

Cotechino: (Italian) a large pork sausage flavored with nutmeg and cloves and a variety of other herbs and spices. The sausage meat is forced into a pig's snout and jowl. It is boiled for several hours and served with potatoes, lentils, or polenta.

Crépinette: (French) a small pork, lamb, veal, or chicken sausage shaped into a patty and wrapped in caul.

Frankfurter: (German) general term used for a range of smoked, seasoned, precooked

sausages made from pork, beef, chicken, or turkey. Also known as a hot dog or wiener.

Kielbasy: (Polish) general term (it is actually the Polish word for "sausage,") is usually a smoked, semidry, highly seasoned pork sausage. Can be sliced and eaten cold, but usually poached and eaten with potatoes or sauerkraut.

Knockwurst: (German) a plump beef and pork sausage flavored with garlic. Also known as knackwurst.

Linguiça: (Portuguese, Brazilian) a thin pork sausage flavored with garlic. Often used to flavor eggs, soups, or stews.

Spicy homemade sausages

- 2 lb/1 kg lean ground pork
- 12 oz/350 g kidney suet
- 4 cloves garlic, chopped
- 1 small onion, finely chopped
- 6 fiery chile peppers, finely chopped
- 4 tbsp brandy
- 4 tbsp cider vinegar
- 1 tsp freshly ground black pepper
- 1 tsp cumin seeds
- 1 tsp Tabasco
- salt
- sausage casings

Combine the pork with the suet in a large bowl. Add the garlic, onion, chilies, brandy, vinegar, pepper, cumin, Tabasco, and salt. Stir until well mixed. Stuff the mixture into the casings to make sausages about 3 in (8 cm) long. Hang in a dry place (not in direct sunlight) or in front of an open fire or electric fan for 24 hours. Cover with a clean cloth. These sausages will keep in the refrigerator for up to one week. If you can't get sausage casings, shape the meat into patties and cook it as you would a normal sausage.

Liverwurst: (German) a smooth spreadable sausage meat usually made of pork liver. A similar sausage is known as braunschweiger.

Mortadella: (Italian) a large sausage made in Bologna, Italy. Made from finely ground pork and flavored with pepper corns or pistachios, it is slowly steamed, and has a delicate flavor.

Pepperoni: (USA) an Italian-style American sausage. It is usually spicy and used to flavor pizza.

Salami: general term for a huge variety of air-dried sausages flavored with varying mixtures of herbs and spices.

Saucisson à la cendre: (French) a pork sausage rolled in ashes, which gives it a lovely smoked flavor.

Saucisson de sanglier: (French) an air-dried salami-type sausage made from wild boar meat.

Saucisson sec: (French) a range of dried salami-type sausages made in the various regions of France.

Weisswurst: (German) a delicately-flavored white sausage made from veal, cream, and eggs. Traditionally served with mustard and rye bread, it can also be added to soups and stews.

Zampone: (Italian) a large pork sausage flavored with a variety of herbs and spices. The sausage meat is forced into a pig's trotter. It is soaked and boiled for several hours and served with mashed potatoes or polenta.

CURRIED SAUSAGE & APPLE PIE

Serves: 4–6

Preparation: 25'

Cooking: 1 1/2 h

Level of difficulty: 1

- **2 lb/1 kg potatoes**
- **2 medium onions, thinly sliced**
- **2 lb/1 kg sausage meat**
- **1–2 tbsp curry powder**
- **1 tbsp brown sugar**
- **2 cups/500 ml cooked apple (or one 13 oz/400 g can apple sauce)**
- **1 tbsp butter**
- **freshly ground black pepper to taste**
- **1/2 cup/125 ml milk**
- **4 oz/125 g freshly grated Parmesan cheese**

Cook the potatoes in a pot of salted, boiling water. ❧ Preheat the oven to 350°F/ 180°C/ gas 4. ❧ Place half the onion in the bottom of a large, shallow ovenproof dish. ❧ Flour your hands and shape the sausage meat into walnut-sized balls. Place them on top of the onions in a single layer. Sprinkle with the remaining onion. ❧ Mix the curry powder and brown sugar and sprinkle over the sausages. ❧ Drain the cooked apple thoroughly and spoon it over the sausages. ❧ Drain and mash the cooked potatoes with the butter, pepper, and milk. Spoon the mashed potato over the sausages and spread out in an even layer. If liked, use a fork to roughen the surface attractively. Sprinkle with the grated cheese. ❧ Bake for 1 hour. ❧ Serve hot or at room temperature.

> *If you like sweet spicy dishes, this will become a favorite. Add crushed chilies for even more sting!*

609

SAUSAGES & SHALLOTS IN WHITE WINE

Preheat the oven to 350°F/ 180°C/ gas 4. ❧ Heat the butter in a large skillet (frying pan) and sauté the shallots and parsley until the shallots are transparent. ❧ Prick each sausage in several places with a skewer or fork to allow fat to drain during cooking. ❧ Add the sausages to the skillet with the shallots. Pour the wine over the top and season lightly with salt and pepper. Cook for 5 minutes. ❧ Transfer the sausages, shallots, and cooking juices to a roasting pan. Bake, basting frequently, for 30 minutes. ❧ Serve hot.

The sweet taste of the onions blends with the wine to create a scrumptious sauce for the spicy sausages.

Serves: 4

Preparation: 10'

Cooking: 35'

Level of difficulty: 1

- **12 shallots, finely chopped**
- **2 tbsp finely chopped parsley**
- **2 lb/1 kg spicy pork sausage links**
- **1 cup/250 ml dry white wine**

BAKED SAUSAGES & BREAD

Serves: 4

Preparation: 25'

Cooking: 1½ h

Level of difficulty: 1

- 1 tbsp extra-virgin olive oil
- 1 small onion, finely chopped
- 1 stalk celery, finely chopped
- 1 tbsp finely chopped parsley
- 1 lb/500 g sausages
- 7 oz/200 g day-old bread, cut in cubes
- 4 fresh sage leaves, torn
- 2 eggs
- 1¼ cups/300 ml *Chicken Stock* (see page 140)
- salt and freshly ground black pepper to taste
- 1 tbsp butter

Preheat the oven to 350°F/ 180°C/gas 4. ✿ Heat the oil in a large skillet (frying pan) and sauté the onion, celery, and parsley for 5 minutes. Add the sausages and cook until nicely browned. Chop the sausages into thick slices. ✿ Drain the fat from the skillet, pouring 4 tablespoons into a large bowl and discarding the rest. If there is not this much fat in the skillet, add extra olive oil to the bowl. ✿ Place the fat in a small bowl and mix in the cubes of bread, sage, and sausages. Season with salt and pepper. ✿ Beat the eggs lightly then stir them into the chicken stock. Pour this liquid over the sausage and bread mixture. ✿ Grease a large ovenproof dish and fill with the mixture. ✿ Cover the dish and bake for 40 minutes. Remove the lid and cook for 15 minutes more. ✿ Serve hot.

Serve this hearty dish with a green salad for a complete meal.

613

SAUSAGES WITH APPLE SAUCE

Prick the sausages in several places with a fork to allow fat to drain during cooking. ❧ Heat the butter in a large skillet (frying pan) and sauté garlic for 3–4 minutes. Add the sausages and cook over medium-high heat until nicely browned and cooked through.

Serve this dish with boiled potatoes and a crisp green salad.

Remove the sausages from the skillet and set aside in a warm oven. ❧ Peel and core the apples and chop them into small pieces. ❧ Place the apples in the same skillet with the cooking juices from the sausages. Cook until the apples turn into a smooth sauce. Season with salt and pepper. ❧ Spoon the apples onto a serving dish and arrange the sausages on top. ❧ Serve hot.

Serves: 4

Preparation: 10'

Cooking: 30'

Level of difficulty: 1

- **2 tbsp butter**
- **1 clove garlic, finely chopped**
- **1¹/₄ lb/625 g highly-flavored sausages**
- **6 tart-flavored cooking apples**
- **salt and freshly ground black pepper to taste**

614

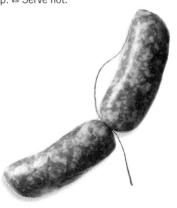

CABBAGE BAKED WITH SAUSAGE & BACON

Prick the sausages lightly with a fork and place them in a bowl with the onion, oil, salt, and pepper. Set aside to marinate for 1 hour. ❧ Preheat the oven to 350°F/180°C/gas 4. ❧ Slice the cabbage into 8–10 same-sized wedges. Blanch in boiling water for 2–3 minutes. Drain well and place in a deep-sided ovenproof dish. ❧ Arrange the sausages and bacon on the cabbage and pour the chicken stock over the top. Season lightly with salt and pepper. ❧ Cover the dish and bake for 50 minutes. ❧ Serve hot.

Serves: 4

Preparation: 5' + 1 h

Cooking: 25'

Level of difficulty: 1

- 1¹/₂ lb/750 g pork sausages
- 1 small onion, finely chopped
- ¹/₂ cup/125 ml extra-virgin olive oil
- salt and freshly ground black pepper to taste
- 2 lb/1 kg white cabbage
- 8 oz/250 g bacon, sliced
- 3 cups/750 ml *Chicken Stock* (see page 140)

VEGETABLES

BAKED ONIONS WITH CHEESE

Serves: 6

Preparation: 10'

Cooking: 1 h

Level of difficulty: 1

- **12 medium white onions**
- **2 tbsp butter**
- **1 cup/250 ml Beef Stock (see page 140)**
- **salt and freshly ground black pepper to taste**
- **8 oz/250 g Cheddar or Gruyère cheese, grated**

Preheat the oven to 350°F/180°C/gas 4. ❧ Butter a 10 in (25-cm) baking dish and arrange the onions in it. ❧ Pour in enough stock to cover the bottom of the dish to about ¹/₂ in (1 cm). Season with salt and pepper. ❧ Cover and bake 1 hour, or until the onions are just tender. ❧ Add more stock as required during cooking. ❧ Sprinkle with the grated cheese and place under the broiler (grill) for 5–10 minutes, or until the cheese is melted and golden brown. ❧ Serve hot.

SPICY COTTAGE CHEESE POTATOES

Serves: 3–6

Preparation: 10'

Cooking: 1 h

Level of difficulty: 1

- **6 medium potatoes**
- **12 oz/350 g cottage cheese**
- **2 tsp tomato paste**
- **1 tsp cumin seeds**
- **1 tsp ground cilantro/coriander**
- **1 tsp red pepper flakes**
- **salt and freshly ground black pepper to taste**
- **1 tbsp extra-virgin olive oil**
- **$\frac{1}{2}$ tsp mixed onion and mustard seeds**
- **3 tbsp water**
- **mixed salad greens**
- **3–4 tomatoes, quartered**
- **slices of fresh lemon, to garnish**

Preheat the oven to 350°F/180°C/gas 4. ❧ Scrub the potatoes under cold running water. Pat dry and cut a slit in the top of each one. Prick with a fork, then wrap each potato in a piece of foil. ❧ Bake for 1 hour, or until tender. ❧ Place the cottage cheese in a heatproof bowl and set aside. ❧ Place the tomato paste, cumin, cilantro, red pepper flakes, salt, and pepper in a bowl. ❧ Heat the oil in a small saucepan and cook the onion and mustard seeds for 1 minute. Add the tomato paste mixture and water to the saucepan and mix well. Cook for 1 more minute, then pour the spicy tomato mixture into the cottage cheese. Mix well. ❧ When the potatoes are cooked, unwrap them and cut them open along the top. Divide the spicy cottage cheese equally among the six potatoes. ❧ Rinse and dry the salad greens and place them on a serving dish. Arrange the potatoes on top and garnish the dish with the tomatoes and lemon. ❧ Serve hot.

TOMATO ASPIC MOLDS

Prepare the gelatin following the instructions on the package and cool to lukewarm. ❧ Plunge the tomatoes into boiling water for 10 seconds, then into cold. Slip off the skins then squeeze gently to remove the seeds. ❧ Blend the tomatoes with the garlic, red pepper flakes, two basil leaves, salt, and the lukewarm gelatin. Set the mixture aside until it begins to set, stirring gently from time to time. ❧ Grease four small molds and fill with the mixture. Refrigerate for at least 2 hours. ❧ Turn out and serve garnished with the remaining basil and, if liked, an extra drizzle of olive oil.

These fresh and flavorful little molds make perfect appetizers.

Serves: 4

Preparation: 20' + 2 h

Level of difficulty: 2

- 1 cup/250 ml prepared gelatin
- 1 lb/500 g ripe plum tomatoes
- 1 clove garlic
- ½ tsp red pepper flakes (or 1 small red chile pepper)
- 4 fresh basil leaves, torn
- dash of salt
- 1 tbsp extra-virgin olive oil

GREEK-STYLE STUFFED TOMATOES

Serves: 3–6

Preparation: 20'

Cooking time: 40'

Level of difficulty: 3

- 6 ripe firm tomatoes
- dash of salt
- 1 onion, finely chopped
- 4 tbsp extra-virgin olive oil
- 11 oz/300 g ground beef
- ²/₃ cup/150 ml dry white wine
- 1 bay leaf
- 3 cloves
- salt and freshly ground black pepper to taste
- 1 quantity Béchamel sauce (see page 950)

Preheat the oven to 400°F/200°C/gas 6. ❧ Slice the tops off the tomatoes. Scoop out the pulp with a teaspoon and set aside. ❧ Sprinkle the shells lightly with salt and place upside-down in a colander to drain. ❧ In a skillet (frying pan), sauté the onion in the oil until soft. ❧ Add the meat and cook briefly. Pour in the wine, then add the tomato pulp, bay leaf, and cloves. Season with salt and pepper. Cook for 5 more minutes. ❧ Fill the tomato shells with the mixture and transfer to an ovenproof dish. Spoon part of the Béchamel Sauce over each tomato. ❧ Bake in a preheated oven at for about 25 minutes, until the sauce is brown and bubbling. Serve hot.

Allow one tomato per person when serving as an appetizer and two or more as a main course.

ALGERIAN-STYLE STUFFED TOMATOES

P eel the eggplants, slice them into $\frac{1}{2}$-in (1-cm) thick slices and sprinkle with salt. Place in a colander and leave for 1 hour to purge. ❧ Preheat the oven to 350°F/180°C/gas 4. ❧ Slice the tops off the tomatoes. Scoop out the pulp with a teaspoon and set aside. ❧ Drizzle the shells with the oil and sprinkle lightly with salt. Arrange them in an ovenproof dish and bake for about 10 minutes. ❧ Rinse the salt off the eggplant and pat dry with paper towels. ❧ Heat the oil in a large skillet (frying pan) and fry the eggplant until tender. ❧ Chop the eggplant coarsely and place in a bowl. Add the garlic, mint leaves, and half the parsley and mix well. ❧ Fill the tomato shells with this mixture. Sprinkle with the remaining parsley. Return to the oven for 5–10 minutes to brown. ❧ Serve hot or at room temperature.

The tang of the mint in this traditional North African dish enhances the flavor of the eggplant.

Serves: 4

Preparation: 30' + 1 h to purge

Cooking: 15'

Level of difficulty: 2

- **3 eggplants/ aubergines**
- **8 firm ripe tomatoes**
- **dash of salt**
- **2 tbsp extra-virgin olive oil**
- **oil for frying**
- **1 clove garlic, finely chopped**
- **10–12 fresh mint leaves, torn**
- **1 tbsp finely chopped parsley**

MEXICAN-STYLE TOMATOES

Slice the tops off the tomatoes. Scoop out the pulp with a teaspoon and set aside. ♣ Sprinkle the shells lightly with salt and place them upside down in a colander to drain. ♣ Place the avocados in a bowl with the eggs, tomato pulp, onion, garlic, lemon juice, cilantro, red pepper flakes, salt, and pepper. Mix well. ♣ Fill the tomato shells with this mixture and refrigerate for at least 30 minutes. ♣ Arrange the lettuce leaves on a serving dish, place the chilled tomatoes on top and serve.

The fresh spicy taste of these tomatoes is the very epitome of Mexican cuisine.

Serves: 4

Preparation: 15' + 30' to chill

Level of difficulty: 2

- 8 ripe tomatoes
- salt and freshly ground black pepper to taste
- 3 small avocados, peeled and diced
- 4 hard-boiled eggs, peeled and chopped
- 1 tsp finely chopped onion
- 1 clove garlic, finely chopped
- juice of 1 lemon
- dash of cilantro/coriander
- $1/2$ tsp red pepper flakes (or 1 small red chile pepper, chopped)
- 1 tbsp extra-virgin olive oil
- lettuce leaves to garnish

TOMATOES BAKED WITH PARMESAN, PARSLEY & GARLIC

Serves: 4–6

Preparation: 30'

Cooking: 35'

Level of difficulty: 2

- **10 medium tomatoes**
- **salt and freshly ground black pepper to taste**
- **5 cloves garlic, finely chopped**
- **10 tbsp finely chopped parsley**
- **6 tbsp bread crumbs**
- **6 tbsp freshly grated Parmesan cheese**
- **6 tbsp extra-virgin olive oil**

Preheat the oven to 350°F/180°C/gas 4. ❧ Cut the tomatoes in half. Squeeze gently to remove as many seeds as possible. Sprinkle lightly with salt and place upside-down in a colander to drain for 20 minutes. ❧ Mix the garlic and parsley together in a bowl, add the bread crumbs and Parmesan, and gradually work in the oil using a fork. Season with salt and pepper. ❧ Using a teaspoon, push the filling mixture into the tomato halves. Press it down with your fingers so that it sticks to the inside of the tomatoes (it will swell slightly in the oven and could overflow). ❧ Place the filled tomatoes in a greased ovenproof dish and bake for 35 minutes. ❧ Serve hot or at room temperature.

INDIAN STUFFED POTATOES

Preheat the oven to 350°F/180°C/gas 4. 🍃 Bake the potatoes in the oven until tender. 🍃 Cut in half and scoop out the flesh. Mash in a bowl and add the nuts, raisins, milk powder, and chilies. Mix well and stuff back into the potatoes. 🍃 Heat the oil in a large skillet (frying pan) and sauté the onion and garlic until transparent. Add the tomatoes and spices and cook over low heat until the oil separates. 🍃 Add the yogurt, water, and salt and cook for 5 minutes. Add the potatoes and simmer for 5 more minutes. 🍃 Serve hot.

Serves: 4

Preparation: 15'

Cooking: 1 h

Level of difficulty: 1

- 6 medium potatoes
- 1 cup/100 g mixed chopped cashew nuts and almonds
- 6 tbsp raisins
- 4 tbsp extra-virgin olive oil
- 1 onion, finely chopped
- 2 cloves garlic, finely chopped
- 3 tomatoes
- 1 tsp cumin
- 1 tsp turmeric
- 2 chile peppers, thinly sliced
- 6 tbsp yogurt
- 1 cup/250 ml water
- salt to taste

POTATOES
WITH MIXED SPICES

Serves: 4

Preparation: 10'

Cooking: 25'

Level of difficulty: 1

- 4 tbsp extra-virgin olive oil
- 1 tsp cumin seeds
- 1 tsp onion seeds
- 1 tsp fennel seeds
- 6 curry leaves
- 2 onions, finely chopped
- 2 cloves garlic, finely chopped
- 1 tsp grated ginger root
- 2 chile peppers, thinly sliced
- salt to taste
- 6 medium potatoes, sliced

Pound the cumin, onion, fennel seeds, and curry leaves with a mortar and pestle. ❧ Heat the oil in a deep skillet (frying pan). and sauté the onion, garlic, ginger, and chile peppers until the onions are transparent. Season with salt. ❧ Add the potatoes and cover the pan tightly with a lid. Cook for about 10–15 minutes, or until the potatoes are tender (stirring often so that the potatoes don't stick to the pan). ❧ Serve hot.

635

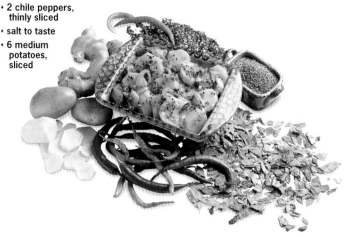

MUSHROOMS COOKED IN FOIL PACKAGES

Preheat the oven to 375°F/190°C/gas 5. ❧ Place the cheese, bread crumbs, anchovies, garlic, parsley, lemon juice, salt, pepper, and oil in a large bowl and mix well. ❧ Place each mushroom cap upside-down on a fairly large piece of oiled foil. ❧ Spread an equal part of the mixture over each mushroom. ❧ Bring two sides of the foil up over each mushroom to make a pleat, leaving plenty of air space inside, and fold the ends over. ❧ When all the mushrooms are packaged, place on a baking sheet and bake for 20–25 minutes, depending on the size of the mushrooms. ❧ If using smaller porcini place two in each package. The small porcini or white mushrooms will take only about 15–20 minutes to cook.

Serves: 4
Preparation: 15'
Cooking: 20–25'
Level of difficulty: 1

- 5 tbsp freshly grated Pecorino cheese
- 3 tbsp bread crumbs
- 2 salted anchovies (rinsed and boned) or 4 anchovy filets, finely chopped
- 2 cloves garlic, finely chopped
- 2 tbsp finely chopped parsley
- 1 tsp lemon juice
- salt and freshly ground black pepper to taste
- 4 tbsp extra-virgin olive oil
- 4 large or 8 small porcini mushroom caps (or large horse, field, or cultivated mushrooms), cleaned

MUSHROOMS
WITH PINE NUTS

Serves: 4

Preparation: 10'

Cooking: 25'

Level of difficulty: 1

- **2 large potatoes, diced**
- **2 cloves garlic, finely chopped**
- **4 tbsp extra-virgin olive oil**
- **1¹/₂ lb fresh or frozen white mushrooms, coarsely chopped**
- **salt and freshly ground black pepper to taste**
- **²/₃ cup/150 g pine nuts**
- **¹/₂ cup/100 g slivered almonds**
- **1 tbsp coarsely chopped mint**

Sauté the potatoes and garlic in the oil in a large skillet (frying pan) for 5 minutes. ❧ Add the mushrooms and season with salt and pepper. Cover and cook for 5 minutes. ❧ Uncover and let some of the moisture evaporate. Stir in the pine nuts and almonds and cook for 10–15 more minutes. ❧ Sprinkle with the mint just before removing from heat. ❧ Serve hot.

BRAISED SAVOY CABBAGE

Discard the tough outer leaves of the cabbage. Take the rest apart leaf by leaf, cutting out the hard ribs and rinsing. Cut the leaves into thin strips. ❧ Chop the pork fat and rosemary leaves together with a heavy kitchen knife. ❧ Sauté briefly in a large skillet (frying pan) with the garlic, discarding the garlic when it starts to color. ❧ Add the shredded cabbage and a dash of salt and cover. Cook over low heat, stirring frequently to prevent the cabbage from burning, for up to 1 hour. ❧ Add the wine, then cover and continue cooking for another hour. ❧ Serve hot.

Serves: 6

Preparation: 15'

Cooking: 2 h

Level of difficulty: 1

- **4 lb/2 kg Savoy cabbage**
- **4 tbsp pork fat/ lard**
- **1 sprig rosemary**
- **1 clove garlic, whole but lightly crushed**
- **salt to taste**
- **$^1/_2$ cup/125 ml dry white wine**

MUSHROOM PARCELS

Preheat the oven to 400°F/200°C/gas 6. ❧ Sauté the onions, garlic, butter, ham and mushrooms in the oil in a large skillet (frying pan) over medium heat for 10 minutes. ❧ Add the parsley, sage, and rosemary and mix well. Season with salt and pepper. Set aside to cool. ❧ Divide the pasty into 4 pieces and roll each one out into 8-in (20-cm) squares. Cut a ½-inch (1-cm) strip from each square. ❧ Spoon a quarter of the mushrooms into the center of each pastry. Gather up the edges to make a parcel and tie each one with the strip of pastry. ❧ Place on a baking sheet and brush with the egg. ❧ Bake for about minutes, or until golden brown. ❧ Serve hot.

Serves: 4

Preparation: 20'

Cooking: 20'

Level of difficulty: 2

- 4 tbsp extra-virgin olive oil
- 1 onion, finely chopped
- 1 clove garlic, finely chopped
- 2 oz/60 g Parma ham, finely chopped
- 1 lb/500 g mixed mushrooms
- 1 tsp parsley, finely chopped
- 2 leaves sage
- 1 tsp rosemary
- salt and freshly ground black pepper to taste
- 2 oz/60 g frozen puff pastry, thawed
- 1 egg, lightly beaten

MUSHROOM CURRY

Serves: 4

Preparation: 20'

Cooking: 25'

Level of difficulty: 1

- **3 oz/90 g cashew nuts**
- **2 cups/500 ml water**
- **2 tbsp oil**
- **1 cinnamon stick, halved**
- **5 cardamons**
- **1 onion, sliced**
- **1 tbsp chopped root ginger**
- **2 cloves garlic, finely chopped**
- **4 tomatoes, chopped**
- **2 tbsp ground cilantro/coriander**
- **1 green chile pepper, seeded and finely sliced**
- **1 tsp turmeric**
- **2 tsp garam masala**
- **1 tsp salt**
- **11 oz/300 g mushrooms, coarsely chopped**

Chop the cashew nuts with ½ cup (125 ml) water in a food processor until smooth. ❧ Warm the oil in a large skillet (frying pan) over medium heat. Sauté the cinnamon and cardamon until fragrant. ❧ Add the ginger and garlic and sauté for 3 minutes. Add the tomatoes, cilantro, chili, turmeric, and garam masala and cook over low heat for 10 minutes, or until the oil begins to separate. ❧ Add the salt and water. Bring to a boil. Stir in the mushrooms, peas, and cashew nut mixture. ❧ Cover and cook, stirring occasionally, for 5 minutes more. ❧ Serve hot.

BAKED MUSHROOMS AND POTATOES

Serves: 4

Preparation: 15'

Cooking: 15'

Level of difficulty: 1

- **4 tbsp extra-virgin olive oil**
- **1 tsp butter**
- **1 small onion, finely chopped**
- **6 large mushrooms, coarsely chopped**
- **1 tbsp each finely chopped fresh thyme, marjoram, and parsley**
- **salt and freshly ground black pepper to taste**
- **4 eggs, lightly beaten**
- **$^1/_3$ cup/90 ml heavy/double cream**
- **13 oz/400 g potatoes, boiled and sliced**

P reheat the oven to 350°F/180°C/gas 4. ❧ Heat the oil and butter in a large skillet (frying pan) over medium heat. Sauté the onions and mushrooms until softened. Add the thyme, marjoram, and parsley. ❧ Beat the eggs and cream in a medium bowl until well mixed.

If you can't get porcini mushrooms, use other wild or cultivated mushrooms in their place.

Season with salt and pepper. Add the potatoes and mushroom mixture. ❧ Butter an ovenproof dish. Pour the mixture into the dish. ❧ Bake for 15 minutes, or until golden brown. ❧ Turn out onto a serving plate. ❧ Serve hot.

SPICY MUSHROOMS

Sauté the the fennel, cardamons, and bay leaf in the oil in a large skillet (frying pan) over medium heat until fragrant. ❧ Add the onions and cook until browned. Stir in all the remaining ingredients, except the mushrooms. Continue cooking over low heat for 15 minutes, or until the oil begins to separate. ❧ Add the mushrooms and mix well. ❧ Cover and cook, stirring occasionally, for 10 minutes more. ❧ Serve hot.

Serves: 4–6

Preparation: 20'

Cooking: 20'

Level of difficulty: 2

- 2 tbsp oil
- 1 tsp fennel seeds
- 5 cardamons
- 1 bay leaf
- 3 onions, finely chopped
- 14 oz/450 g chopped tomatoes
- $1/2$ cup/125 ml water
- 2 tsp ground ginger
- 2 tsp garlic powder
- 1 tbsp sugar
- 2 tbsp vinegar
- salt and freshly ground black pepper to taste
- 2 chile peppers, seeded and finely chopped
- $1/2$ tsp turmeric
- 2 tsp garam masala
- 1 tsp ground nutmeg
- $1/2$ tsp ground cardamom powder
- 11 oz/300 g button mushrooms, cut into quarters

ASPARAGUS
WITH SABAYON SAUCE

Serves: 4

Preparation: 15'

Cooking: 20'

Level of difficulty: 1

- **3 lb/1.5 kg medium green asparagus stalks**
- **4 egg yolks**
- **8 tbsp dry white wine**
- **2 tbsp butter, at room temperature**
- **salt to taste**

Trim off the tough lower parts of the asparagus stalks. Rinse well under cold running water. ❧ Steam the asparagus until the stalks are tender but not mushy. The cooking time will vary depending on the freshness and thickness of the asparagus. ❧ While the asparagus is cooking, beat the egg yolks, wine, butter, and salt until well mixed. Place in a double boiler over barely simmering water and beat constantly with a whisk for 10 minutes, or until thick. ❧ Pour the sauce over the asparagus tips and serve hot.

ASPARAGUS WITH EGG DRESSING

Serves: 6

Preparation: 15'

Cooking: 15'

Level of difficulty: 1

- **3 lb/1.5 kg very fresh, young asparagus**
- **4 hard-boiled eggs**
- **3 tbsp extra-virgin olive oil**
- **2 tbsp white wine vinegar**
- **salt and freshly ground black pepper to taste**

Trim off the tough lower parts of the asparagus stalks. Rinse well under cold running water. ❧ Steam the asparagus until the stalks are tender but not mushy. The cooking time will vary depending on the freshness and thickness of the asparagus. ❧ Take the asparagus carefully out of the saucepan and refresh by rinsing briefly in a colander under cold running water. This will stop them cooking and keep them an attractive fresh green color. ❧ Mash the eggs in a bowl with a fork, blending in the oil, vinegar, salt, and pepper until smooth. ❧ Arrange the asparagus on a serving dish and spoon the dressing over the tips. ❧ Serve hot or at room temperature.

PEAS WITH BACON, GARLIC, & WINE

Wash the peas in a colander under cold water, if fresh. ❧ Sauté the onion, garlic, parsley, and bacon together in the oil over medium heat for 2 minutes. ❧ Add the peas, season with salt and pepper, and stir. ❧ Pour in the wine, cover and simmer gently for 15–20 minutes, stirring occasionally. Moisten with a little stock as necessary. ❧ Serve hot.

Serves: 4

Preparation: 10'

Cooking: 25'

Level of difficulty: 1

- **4 cups/625 g hulled fresh or frozen peas**
- **1 small white onion or shallot, very thinly sliced**
- **1 clove garlic, finely chopped**
- **2 tbsp finely chopped parsley**
- **½ cup/125 g diced bacon**
- **4 tbsp extra-virgin olive oil**
- **salt and freshly ground black pepper to taste**
- **½ cup/125 ml dry white wine**
- **½ cup/125 ml stock (homemade or bouillon cube)**

SUGAR PEAS WITH CREAM

Serves: 4

Preparation: 5'

Cooking: 8–10'

Level of difficulty: 1

- 1 lb/500 g sugar peas/mange-tout
- salt to taste
- 4 tbsp butter
- 6 tbsp heavy/ double cream
- 6 tbsp freshly grated Parmesan cheese

Rinse the sugar peas and string them if necessary. ❧ Place in a saucepan of boiling salted water and cook for 8–10 minutes, or until tender. ❧ When they have about 2 minutes cooking time left, heat the butter in a small saucepan until it turns golden brown. ❧ Drain the sugar peas and place in a heated serving dish. Cover quickly with the cream. Sprinkle with the grated Parmesan. Pour the very hot butter over the top. Serve at once.

POTATO & CABBAGE MIX

Serves: 4

Preparation: 35'

Cooking: 20'

Level of difficulty: 1

- **3 large potatoes**
- **salt to taste**
- **$1/2$ medium Savoy cabbage**
- **2 tbsp extra-virgin olive oil**
- **1 small onion, finely chopped**
- **4 tbsp diced bacon**
- **1 clove garlic, finely chopped**
- **$1/2$ tsp red pepper flakes**
- **freshly ground black pepper to taste**

Cook the potatoes in a large pot of salted, boiling water. Peel and mash them. ❧ Boil the cabbage in another pot of salted water for 10 minutes. Drain well and chop coarsely. ❧ Heat the oil in a large skillet (frying pan) and sauté the onion until pale gold. Add the bacon, garlic, and red pepper flakes. Season with salt and pepper, then add the potatoes and cabbage. ❧ Mix well and then set aside for about 20 minutes to absorb the flavors. ❧ Serve warm or at room temperature.

FAVA BEAN STEW

Put the beans in a bowl and cover with cold water to prevent their skins from toughening. ❧ Sauté the bacon, garlic, and onion in the oil in a large skillet (frying pan) for 5–6 minutes over a moderate heat. ❧ Remove the garlic and add the drained beans, parsley, salt, pepper, and stock. Cover and simmer over medium heat for about 20 minutes, or until the beans are very tender. ❧ Reduce any remaining stock by increasing the heat with the lid removed. ❧ Serve hot.

Serves: 4

Preparation: 15'

Cooking: 30'

Level of difficulty: 1

- **4 cups/500 g freshly hulled fava beans/broad beans (about 5 lb/ 2.5 kg of fresh bean pods)**
- **1/2 cup/75 g finely chopped bacon**
- **2 cloves garlic, whole but lightly crushed**
- **1 onion, thinly sliced**
- **4 tbsp extra-virgin olive oil**
- **2 tbsp finely chopped parsley**
- **salt and freshly ground black pepper to taste**
- **1 cup/250 ml hot *Chicken* or *Vegetable Stock* (see page 140)**

SWEET AND SOUR BABY ONIONS

Serves: 4–6

Preparation: 10'

Cooking: 35'

Level of difficulty: 1

- 1 lb/500 g white baby onions
- 4 tbsp Parma ham, coarsely chopped
- 1 tbsp lard (or butter or extra-virgin olive oil)
- salt and freshly ground black pepper to taste
- 1 tbsp sugar
- 3 tbsp white wine vinegar
- $^1/_2$ cup/125 ml cold water

Clean the onions and place them in a bowl of cold water. ❧ Sauté the Parma ham in the lard. ❧ Drain the onions and add to the pan. Season with salt and pepper and add the sugar. Pour in the vinegar and water. ❧ Cook over a medium-low heat until the onions are tender and the cooking juices have almost all been absorbed. ❧ Serve hot or at room temperature.

651

SALADS

Salad Dressings

The easiest and arguably the tastiest way to dress a salad is to sprinkle it lightly with salt, grind a little pepper over the top, then drizzle it with lemon juice or vinegar, followed by extra-virgin olive oil. The important thing to remember is to always pour the oil on last. This simple, healthy dressing works with most salads. But then there are days when we want something more.... This page has a selection of seven old favorites. Enjoy!

Joy's Cole Slaw Dressing

- 2 eggs
- 7 oz/200 g sugar
- 1 tsp salt
- 1 tsp white pepper
- 1 tsp dry mustard powder
- 2 tbsp flour
- 1 cup/250 ml cider vinegar
- 13 oz/400 g sweetened condensed milk

Beat the eggs lightly and add the sugar, salt, pepper, mustard, and flour. Gradually stir in the vinegar. Place in the top of a double boiler (or in a saucepan placed within a larger pan of simmering water) and cook over low heat until thick. Set aside to cool, then stir in the condensed milk. Store in an airtight jar in the refrigerator for up to one month.

Coconut Cream Dressing

- 8 tbsp sour cream
- 3 tbsp flaked coconut
- 1 tbsp honey
- 1 tbsp lime juice

Use a whisk to beat all the ingredients together. Chill in the refrigerator before serving.

Mustard Vinaigrette

- 1 tsp hot mustard
- 3 tbsp red wine vinegar
- 1 clove garlic, finely chopped
- salt and freshly ground black pepper to taste
- $1/2$ cup/125 ml extra-virgin olive oil
- 1 tbsp capers

Place the mustard, vinegar, garlic, salt, and pepper in a small bowl and whisk well.

Continue whisking while gradually pouring in the oil. Stir in the capers. Store in the refrigerator for up to one week.

Blue Cheese Dressing

- **6 tbsp blue cheese (Roquefort, Gorgonzola)**
- **4 tbsp butter**
- **2 tbsp port wine**

Warm the ingredients gently until softened. Use a whisk to beat all the ingredients together.

Garlic Dressing

- **8 tbsp plain yogurt**
- **5 tbsp extra-virgin olive oil**
- **1 tbsp white wine vinegar**
- **2 tbsp freshly grated Parmesan cheese**
- **1 clove garlic, finely chopped**

Use a whisk to beat all the ingredients together. Chill in the refrigerator before serving.

Orange Poppyseed Dressing

- **²/₃ cup/150 ml safflower or corn oil**
- **2 tbsp orange juice**
- **2 tbsp honey**
- **2 tbsp poppy seeds**
- **4 tbsp lime juice**
- **2 tbsp grated orange zest**
- **2 tbsp minced onion**
- **salt and pepper**

Place all the ingredients in a screw-top jar. Shake vigorously. Chill in the refrigerator before serving. For even better flavor, the seeds can be lightly toasted in a preheated oven at 350°F/180°C/gas 4 for about 5 minutes.

Honey and Garlic Dressing

- **1¹/₂ cups/375 ml mayonnaise**
- **3 tbsp liquid honey**
- **1 tbsp spicy mustard**
- **1 tsp Tabasco**
- **4 tbsp red wine vinegar**
- **2 garlic cloves, finely chopped**
- **1 tbsp Worcestershire sauce**
- **salt and freshly ground pepper to taste**

Use a whisk to beat all the ingredients together. Chill in the refrigerator before serving.

PLATTER OF RAW VEGETABLES WITH OLIVE OIL DIP

Serves: 4

Preparation: 20'

Level of difficulty: 1

- **4 artichokes**
- **juice of 2 lemons**
- **4 carrots (or 8 baby spring carrots)**
- **4 celery hearts**
- **2 large fennels**
- **12 spring onions**
- **12 radishes**
- **1 cup/250 ml extra-virgin olive oil**
- **salt and freshly ground black pepper to taste**

Wash all the vegetables thoroughly under cold running water. ❧ Artichokes: remove all but the pale inner leaves by pulling the outer ones down and snapping them off. Cut off the stem and the top third of the remaining leaves. Cut the artichokes in half lengthwise and scrape any fuzzy choke away with a knife. Cut each artichoke in wedges and soak in a bowl of cold water with the juice of 1 lemon for 10 minutes. ❧ Carrots: scrub with a brush or peel and soak in a bowl of cold water with the remaining lemon juice for 10 minutes. ❧ Celery: trim off the leafy tops and discard the tough outer stalks. Keep the inner white stalks and the heart. ❧ Fennel: slice off the base, trim away the leafy tops, and discard any blemished outer leaves. Divide into 4 or more wedges, depending on the size. ❧ Onions: remove the roots and the outer leaves and trim the tops. ❧ Radishes: cut the roots off and trim the tops. ❧ For the dip: beat the oil with salt and pepper with a whisk or blender until well mixed. Pour into 4 small bowls.

Place the vegetable platter in the middle of the table and give each guest a plate and a small bowl of dip.

WOODLAND SALAD WITH RASPBERRIES & WILD RICE

Cook both types of rice in a pot of salted, boiling water for about 40 minutes, or until tender. ❧ Wash and dry all the salad greens. ❧ Prepare the vinaigrette. Crush about 15 raspberries and add to the dressing. Blend well. ❧ Place the salad greens in a large salad bowl with the mint and parsley and toss well. ❧ Sprinkle with the carrots and drizzle with half the vinaigrette. Garnish with 20 raspberries. ❧ Drain the rice, shaking thoroughly to remove excess moisture. Transfer to a bowl, add the oil and mix well. ❧ Place in a large serving dish and garnish with the remaining raspberries. Drizzle with the remaining vinaigrette, toss lightly, and serve.

Serves: 6–8

Preparation: 20'

Cooking: 40'

Level of difficulty: 1

- 4 oz/125 g brown rice
- 7 oz/200 g wild black or red rice
- 8 oz/250 g mixed wild salad greens (dandelion, wild endives, and green radicchio)
- 1 bunch arugula/ rocket, chopped
- 1 bunch salad burnet
- 2 bunches cress, coarsely chopped
- 2 quantities *Mustard Vinaigrette* (see page 654)
- 2 cups/500 g fresh raspberries
- 1 tbsp each finely chopped fresh mint and parsley
- 4 carrots, finely grated
- 4 tbsp extra-virgin olive oil

CARROT SALAD WITH GARLIC, LEMON, & PARSLEY

Place the carrots, garlic, and parsley in a salad bowl. Add the lemon juice, oil, salt, and pepper and toss well. ❧ Chill in the refrigerator for 30 minutes before serving.

Serves: 4

Preparation: 10'
  + 30' to chill

Level of difficulty: 1

- **4–6 large carrots, coarsely grated**
- **1–2 cloves garlic, finely chopped**
- **¹/₂ cup/30 g finely chopped parsley**
- **juice of 1 lemon**
- **4 tbsp extra-virgin olive oil**
- **salt and freshly ground black pepper to taste**

APPLE & CELERY SALAD

Serves: 4–6

Preparation:

Level of difficulty: 1

- **2 large crisp tangy apples (Granny Smiths)**
- **4 tbsp fresh lemon juice**
- **1 large bunch celery**
- **2 cloves garlic, finely chopped**
- **$1/2$ cup/45 g raisins**
- **1–2 tsp cumin seeds**
- **4–6 tbsp finely chopped parsley**
- **1 cup/150 g toasted, lightly salted nuts (peanuts, almonds, cashews)**
- **salt and freshly ground black pepper to taste**
- **6 tbsp extra-virgin olive oil**

Rinse the apples, dry well, and cut into quarters. Remove the cores and chop into bite-sized pieces. Place in a salad bowl. Drizzle with half the lemon juice to stop them from turning brown. ❧ Rinse the celery, dry well, and remove all the tough outer filaments. Cut into bite-sized pieces. ❧ Add the garlic, raisins, cumin, parsley, and nuts. Season with salt and pepper and drizzle with the remaining lemon juice and the oil. Toss well and serve.

ARUGULA, CORN, & KIWIFRUIT SALAD

Rinse the arugula thoroughly under cold running water and dry well. Place in a large salad bowl and add the corn. ❧ Peel the kiwi fruit and slice. Add to the salad with the garlic and chile pepper, if using. ❧ Season with salt and pepper *For extra color and flavor, add 12 cherry tomatoes cut in half.* and drizzle the vinegar and oil over the top. ❧ Toss well and serve.

Serves: 4

Preparation: 10'

Level of difficulty: 1

- **2 bunches arugula/ rocket**
- **7 oz/200 g canned corn, drained**
- **3–4 kiwifruit**
- **2 cloves garlic, finely chopped**
- **1 fresh chile pepper, chopped in rings (optional)**
- **salt and freshly ground black pepper to taste**
- **3–4 tbsp balsamic (or white wine) vinegar**
- **6 tbsp extra-virgin olive oil**

BLUE CHEESE POTATO SALAD

lace the onions, celery, parsley, mayonnaise, sour cream, lemon juice, salt, and pepper in a bowl and mix well. Stir in the blue cheese. ❧ Cover the bowl and chill in the refrigerator overnight. ❧ Cook the potatoes in their skins in a large pot of lightly salted, boiling water for about 25 minutes, or until tender. Drain and set aside to cool. ❧ Slip the skins off the potatoes (or leave them on, if preferred). Dice the potatoes into bite-sized pieces and place in a salad bowl. Pour the cheese and onion mixture over the potatoes, mix carefully, and serve.

Serves: 6–8

Preparation: 15' + 12' h to chill

Cooking: 25'

Level of difficulty: 1

- **10 scallions/green onions, sliced**
- **5 stalks celery, chopped**
- **6 tbsp finely chopped parsley**
- **1 cup/250 ml mayonnaise**
- **1 cup/250 ml sour cream**
- **1 tbsp lemon juice**
- **salt and freshly ground black pepper to taste**
- **5 oz/150 g blue cheese, crumbled**
- **4 lb/2 kg red or yellow potatoes**

WILD SALAD GREENS WITH BACON & BALSAMIC VINEGAR

Serves: 6

Preparation: 15'

Cooking: 10'

Level of difficulty: 1

- 1 lb/500 g mixed wild salad greens
- 4 oz/125 g bacon, cut in small dice
- 2 cloves garlic, finely chopped
- 2 tbsp butter
- 2–4 tbsp best-quality balsamic vinegar
- salt to taste

Rinse and dry the salad greens. Separate the leaves and arrange them in a ceramic or heatproof bowl. ❧ Sauté the bacon with the garlic in the butter in a small skillet (frying pan) until crisp. ❧ Add the balsamic vinegar and a dash of salt then remove from the heat. ❧ Pour over the endives and serve immediately before the salad greens start to wilt.

SUMMER SALAD GREENS WITH APPLES & STRAWBERRIES

Blend the oil, chives, salt, and pepper with a whisk. Set aside for 20 minutes. ❧ Wash and dry the salad greens. Arrange in the bottom of a large, shallow salad bowl. ❧ Wash the apples thoroughly, divide in half, remove the core and cut in thin wedges, without peeling. ❧ Arrange a ring of apple wedges over the salad greens. ❧ Scatter the sliced radishes over the apples. ❧ Cut the strawberries in half. Garnish the salad by placing a slice of Ricotta between each strawberry (if the Ricotta is too soft to slice, distribute with a teaspoon). ❧ Pour the dressing over the top. ❧ Serve with freshly baked bread or whole wheat toast.

Serves: 4–6

Preparation: 20'

Level of difficulty: 1

- **5 tbsp extra-virgin olive oil**
- **2 tbsp chopped chives**
- **salt and freshly ground black pepper to taste**
- **12 oz/350 g corn salad and green cutting lettuce**
- **6 oz/180 g red and green ryegrass or curly endive hearts**
- **2 Red Delicious apples**
- **10 red radishes, sliced**
- **14 oz/450 g firm ripe strawberries**
- **12 oz/350 g Ricotta cheese, sliced**

GADO GADO (JAVANESE SALAD)

Serves: 6

Preparation: 10'

Cooking: 25'

Level of difficulty: 1

W ash and dry the lettuce and use it to line a salad bowl. Arrange the potato, beans, cabbage, and bean sprouts on top. ♣ Cover with alternate slices of tomato and hard-boiled egg and arrange the onion rings, scallions, and chile pepper on top. Sprinkle with the parsley. ♣ Heat the oil in an omelet pan and pour in the beaten eggs, spreading thinly across the bottom. Cook until firm, then remove and set aside to cool. Cut into thin shreds and pile in the center of the salad. Add the pineapple chunks and shrimp crisps and, if liked, toss all the ingredients gently (otherwise leave them separate). ♣ Sauce: Place all the sauce ingredients in a small saucepan and bring to a boil. Set aside to cool. ♣ Pour over the salad or serve in a separate bowl.

This salad can be a meal in itself. Vary the vegetables according to what you have in the garden or refrigerator.

- 1 crisp lettuce
- 2 large cooked potatoes, sliced
- 7 oz/200 g lightly cooked green beans, sliced
- 7 oz/200 g shredded cabbage, blanched
- 5 oz/150 g fresh bean sprouts
- 15 cherry tomatoes, cut in half
- 3 hard-boiled eggs, sliced
- 1 onion, sliced
- 2 scallions/green onions, chopped
- 1–2 fresh red chile peppers, seeded and shredded
- 2 tbsp finely chopped parsley
- 1 tbsp extra-virgin olive oil
- 2 eggs, beaten
- $1/4$ tsp salt
- $1/2$ cup fresh pineapple chunks
- 1 cup/150 g shrimp crisps

FOR THE SAUCE

- 1 tbsp soy sauce
- 1 tbsp lemon juice
- 6 tbsp crunchy peanut butter

- 1 tsp red pepper flakes
- $^1/_2$ tsp salt
- 2 tsp sugar
- $^3/_4$ cup/180 ml thick coconut milk
- 2 tbsp extra-virgin olive oil

COOKED MIXED VEGETABLE SALAD

ook all the vegetables whole in a large pot of salted, boiling water until tender. If preferred, cook them all together, removing the different vegetables as they are ready. The beets will stain the other vegetables, so it may be better to cook them apart. ❧ Peel the potatoes and beets after cooking. To peel the beets, just press the skin with your fingers and it will slip off easily. ❧ When all the vegetables are cooked, drain well and arrange (either sliced or whole) on a large tray, divided by types. ❧ Serve at room temperature with vinaigrette, mayonnaise, or a little lemon juice and extra-virgin olive oil.

Serves: 6–8
Preparation: 15'
Cooking: 25'
Level of difficulty: 1

- 5 bulbs fennel
- 5 artichokes
- 6 medium carrots
- 6 long zucchini/ courgettes
- 6 medium potatoes
- 6 beets
- 1 lb/500 g green beans
- 1 cup/250 ml mayonnaise or 1 quantity *Mustard Vinaigrette* (see page 654)

CUCUMBER & ONION SALAD

Serves: 4–6

Preparation: 10' + 30' to rest

Level of difficulty: 1

• **5 medium red onions**
• **salt and freshly ground black pepper to taste**
• **4 tbsp extra-virgin olive oil**
• **1 tbsp white wine vinegar**
• **2 medium cucumbers**
• **1 tbsp capers**
• **6 leaves fresh basil, torn**

Peel the onions and slice in thin wheels. ❧ Put the onions in a salad bowl, sprinkle with the salt, pepper, vinegar, and oil. Toss well and set aside for 30 minutes. ❧ Peel the cucumbers and slice very thinly. ❧ Add the cucumbers and capers to the onions and toss well. ❧ Garnish with the basil and serve.

Serve this delicious salad with slices of warm toasted bread and fresh goat ❧ cheese.

673

TABBOULEH (LEBANESE SALAD)

oak the burghul in the boiling water for 5
minutes. Drain, squeeze out excess moisture,
and place in a large salad bowl. ❧ Rinse the
parsley thoroughly under cold running water and
dry well. Chop very finely and add to the burghul.

*Serve with crisp Romaine lettuce leaves. Tear into
pieces and use them to scoop the salad up.* ❧ Add the
remaining
ingredients, toss well, and serve.

676

Serves: 4–6

Preparation: 15'

Level of difficulty: 1

- 4 oz/125 g burghul (crushed wheat)
- 2 cups/500 ml boiling water
- 5 cups/250 g fresh parsley
- 4 scallions/spring onions, chopped
- 20 fresh mint leaves, finely chopped, or 1 tbsp dried mint
- 3 medium salad tomatoes, diced
- salt and freshly ground black pepper to taste
- juice of 1–2 lemons
- 6–8 tbsp extra-virgin olive oil

ORANGE SALAD

Serves: 4

Preparation: 10' + 20' to rest

Level of difficulty: 1

- **3 large fresh oranges**
- **4–6 cups mixed salad greens**
- **2 medium red onions**
- **1 cup/100 g black olives, pitted and chopped**
- **6 tbsp extra-virgin olive oil**
- **2 tbsp red vinegar**
- **salt and freshly ground black pepper to taste**

Peel the oranges, discard any seeds and use a sharp knife to remove all the white part. Cut in thick slices and divide each slice in half. ❧ Wash and dry the salad greens. ❧ Cut the onions in thin slices. ❧ Place the oranges, salad greens, onions, and olives in a salad bowl. ❧

This salad makes an eyecatching appetizer or an excellent side dish with roast meat or fish.

Mix the oil, vinegar, salt, and pepper together in bowl and drizzle over the salad. Toss well. ❧ Set aside for 20 minutes before serving.

EGG, PROVOLONE, APPLE, & RADICCHIO SALAD

Clean the radicchio rosso by discarding the outer leaves and rinsing under cold running water. Dry well and place in a salad bowl. ♣ Season with the lemon juice and half the oil, toss well, and set aside for about 1 hour. ♣ Slice the eggs with an egg cutter. ♣ Peel the apples and dice. Cut the Provolone into cubes. ♣ Add the eggs, apples, Provolone, and olives to the salad bowl. ♣ Mix the mustard, vinegar, remaining oil, salt, and pepper together in a bowl. Beat vigorously with a fork and drizzle over the salad. ♣ Toss well and serve.

To vary this salad, replace the radicchio rosso with the same quantity of fresh spinach.

Serves: 4–6

Preparation: 15' + 1 h to rest

Level of difficulty: 1

- 10 oz/300 g radicchio rosso
- juice of 1 small lemon
- 6 tbsp extra-virgin olive oil
- 3 hard-boiled eggs, shelled
- 3 crisp eating apples
- 7 oz/200 g Provolone cheese
- 16 large black olives, pitted and chopped
- 2 tbsp spicy mustard
- 1 tbsp white wine vinegar
- salt and freshly ground black pepper to taste

SPICY TUNA SALAD WITH MOZZARELLA

lace the tuna, Mozzarella, tomatoes, onion, basil, parsley, and garlic, if using, in a large salad bowl and mix well. Sprinkle with the chile pepper and cover with slices of egg. ♣ Beat the oil, vinegar, salt, and pepper in a small bowl and drizzle over the salad.

Serves: 4

Preparation: 15'

Level of difficulty: 1

- 7 oz/200 g canned tuna, drained and crumbled
- 7 oz/200 g fresh Mozzarella cheese, cut into bite-sized chunks
- 6 firm red salad tomatoes, sliced
- 1 large red onion, finely chopped
- 12 leaves fresh basil, torn
- 4 tbsp finely chopped parsley
- 2 cloves garlic, finely chopped (optional)
- 1 large chile pepper, finely chopped
- 4 hard-boiled eggs, shelled and chopped
- 6 tbsp extra-virgin olive oil
- 2 tbsp balsamic (or plain white-wine) vinegar
- salt and freshly ground black pepper to taste

SPICY SALAD

Serves: 4

Preparation: 20'

Cooking: 30'

Level of difficulty: 1

- 11 oz/300 g green beans
- 1 bunch baby spinach leaves
- 4 oz/125 g bean sprouts
- 1 red onion, thinly sliced
- 1 red bell pepper/ capsicum, chopped
- 1 tsp finely grated ginger root
- 2 cloves garlic, finely chopped
- 2–3 red chilies, finely chopped
- 2 tbsp shredded coconut
- 1 tbsp sugar
- 1 tbsp vinegar
- 6 tbsp water
- salt to taste

Place the beans in a pot of boiling water and cook for 3–4 minutes. Drain and dry. ❧ Place the spinach leaves, bean sprouts, onion, and bell pepper in a salad bowl. ❧ Heat the oil in a small pan and add the ginger, garlic, chilies, and coconut and sauté for 2 minutes. ❧ Add the sugar, vinegar, and water and simmer for 2 more minutes. Set aside to cool. ❧ Drizzle the dressing over the salad and toss well.

FRESH SPINACH & PARMESAN SALAD

T rim the stems and discard any bruised spinach leaves, wash thoroughly, drain, and dry on a clean cloth. ❧ Grate the carrots in julienne strips. ❧ Place the spinach in a large round dish or low, wide salad bowl and sprinkle with the carrots and corn kernels. ❧ Top with the flakes of Parmesan. ❧ In a small bowl, dissolve the salt in the lemon juice, add the oil and pepper, and whisk until well blended. ❧ Dress the salad 5 minutes before serving.

Serves: 4

Preparation: 15'

Level of difficulty: 1

Variations
• Add a small honeydew melon in balls (made with a melon baller) or cubes, and 5 oz/150 g of lean Parma ham, cut in strips.

• **7 cups/450 g dwarf spinach, tender and very fresh**

• **2 carrots, peeled**

• **8 oz/250 g canned corn kernels, or 8 baby corn cobs**

• **8 oz/250 g Parmesan cheese, in flakes**

• **$1/2$ tsp salt**

• **juice of 1 lemon**

• **4 tbsp extra-virgin olive oil**

• **freshly ground black pepper to taste**

FETA CHEESE
& SPINACH SALAD

Trim the spinach and rinse thoroughly under cold running water. Dry well and place in a salad bowl. ❧ Put the oil, vinegar, lemon juice, cinnamon, mustard, salt, and pepper in a small jar with a screw top, and shake well. ❧

Be sure to choose only the most tender and succulent leaves of young spinach for this salad.

Pour half the dressing over the spinach and toss well. ❧ Add the cucumber, tomatoes, Feta, and scallions to the salad. ❧ Pour the remaining dressing over the top, toss gently, and serve.

686

Serves: 6
Preparation: 10'
Level of difficulty: 1

- **2 lb/1 kg fresh spinach**
- **8 tbsp extra-virgin olive oil**
- **2 tbsp white wine vinegar**
- **2 tbsp lemon juice**
- **$^1/_2$ tsp ground cinnamon**
- **$^1/_2$ tsp dry mustard powder**
- **salt and freshly ground black pepper to taste**
- **1 cucumber, sliced**
- **1 lb/500 g cherry tomatoes**
- **8 oz/250 g Feta cheese, crumbled**
- **6 scallions/ spring onions, chopped**

EGG & TOFU SALAD

Serves: 4

*Preparation: 10' +
4 h to chill*

Cooking: 10–15'

Level of difficulty: 1

- 7 oz/200 g firm or hard tofu, cubed
- 4 scallions/spring onions, sliced
- 1 clove garlic, finely chopped
- $\frac{1}{2}$ tsp red pepper flakes
- 1 tbsp light soy sauce
- 1 tbsp lime juice
- 2 tbsp extra-virgin olive oil
- 1 (13 oz/400 g) can baby corn cobs
- 1 stalk celery,
- 1 small red bell pepper/capsicum
- 4 hard-boiled eggs, quartered
- chopped parsley, to garnish

Place the tofu in a ceramic dish. ❧ Combine the scallions, garlic, red pepper flakes, soy sauce, and lime juice in a small bowl. Mix well and pour over the tofu. Cover the dish and chill in the refrigerator for 4 hours. ❧ Drain the tofu, reserving the marinade. ❧ Cut the corn cobs in quarters lengthwise. Cut the celery and bell pepper into long strips. ❧ Heat the oil in a large skillet (frying pan) and cook the tofu until browned all over. Remove from the pan. ❧ Put the corn, celery, and bell pepper in the pan and sauté for 2 minutes. ❧ Add the marinade and tofu and cook until all the ingredients are hot. ❧ Transfer to a serving dish and top with the eggs. Sprinkle with the parsley and serve.

TOMATO & MOZZARELLA CHEESE

Serves: 4–6

Preparation: 10'

Level of difficulty: 1

- **8 large red tomatoes**
- **1 lb/500 g Mozzarella cheese**
- **20 large basil leaves, torn**
- **1 cup/200 g raw vegetables (celery, bell peppers, carrots, etc), cut in small dice**
- **1 tbsp capers**
- **salt and freshly ground black pepper to taste**
- **6 tbsp extra-virgin olive oil**

C ut the tomatoes in thick slices and arrange on a flat serving dish. ❧ Cut the Mozzarella in slices of the same width and alternate with the tomato. ❧ Sprinkle with basil, vegetables, capers, salt, and pepper, and drizzle with the oil. ❧ Serve at once.

RASPBERRIES, FETA, & WALNUT SALAD

Preheat the oven to 350°F/180°C/gas 4. ✥ Place the walnuts in a roasting pan and toast for 15 minutes. ✥ Combine the onions, mustard, and both vinegars in a large bowl. Add the honey and orange juice and whisk well. ✥ Add the olive oil a little at a time, whisking constantly. ✥ Rinse the salad greens under cold running water and dry well. Place them in a large salad bowl and toss with half the vinaigrette. ✥ When the walnuts are cool, chop coarsely. ✥ Divide the salad greens among four serving dishes and top each one with Feta cheese, raspberries, and toasted walnuts. Place the remaining vinaigrette in a small bowl and pass separately at the table.

Serve this eyecatching salad as an appetizer with a basket of freshly baked bread.

Serves: 4

Preparation: 10'

Cooking: 15'

Level of difficulty: 1

- 4 oz/125 g shelled walnuts
- 2 scallions/spring onions, finely chopped
- 2 tsp spicy mustard
- 2 tbsp raspberry vinegar
- 1 tbsp balsamic vinegar
- 2 tbsp honey
- 2 tbsp fresh orange juice
- $^3/_4$ cup/180 ml extra-virgin olive oil
- 4 cups/500 g mixed salad greens
- 6 oz/180 g Feta cheese, crumbled
- 1 cup/250 g fresh raspberries

TOMATO & BASIL SALAD

Wash and dry the tomatoes. ❧ Slice into quarters and arrange in a salad bowl. Dress with the oil, basil leaves (be sure to tear them with your fingers, so that they don't lose any of their superb fragrance), and oregano. Mix well and serve. ❧ The amount of oil and salt can be varied according to taste.

Serves: 4

Preparation: 10'

Level of difficulty: 1

- **2 lb/1 kg firm ripe salad tomatoes**
- **3 tbsp best quality extra-virgin olive oil**
- **10 leaves fresh basil, torn**
- **dash of oregano**
- **salt and freshly ground black pepper to taste**

Variations

• Slice the tomatoes into smaller sections, or dice them, to make the perfect topping for a *bruschetta* (garlic toast with tomatoes). To make the *bruschetta*, toast the bread in the oven or, better still, over an open fire or barbecue, rub each slice with half a clove of peeled garlic and top with the tomato mixture. Serve at once before the toast becomes soggy.

• Slice the tomatoes into smaller sections or dice them. Add a finely chopped clove of garlic with the other ingredients and serve as an uncooked tomato sauce with spaghetti or penne pasta.

• Add a handful of black olives, some chopped cucumber, cubed Feta cheese, and a finely sliced red onion to the mixture for an excellent Greek salad.

TUSCAN BREAD SALAD

Soak the bread in a bowl of cold water for at least 10 minutes. ❧ Use your hands to squeeze out as much water as possible. Crumble the bread into a large salad bowl. ❧ Slice the tomatoes and squeeze gently to remove some of the seeds. Clean the onions and slice in thin wheels. Peel the cucumber and slice thinly. ❧ Add the tomatoes, cucumber, basil, and onions to the bread. Season with salt and pepper and 4 tablespoons of the oil, and mix carefully. ❧ Set aside in a cool place or in the refrigerator for about 30 minutes. ❧ Add the vinegar and remaining oil just before serving.

Serves: 4–6

Preparation: 15' + 30'

Level of difficulty: 2

- **1 lb/500 g day-old bread**
- **5 medium tomatoes**
- **2 red onions**
- **1 cucumber**
- **12 leaves fresh basil, torn**
- **salt and freshly ground black pepper to taste**
- **6 tbsp extra-virgin olive oil**
- **1 tbsp red wine vinegar**

Variations
• This refreshing salad comes from Tuscany, in central Italy, where the ingredients used vary from village to village. The addition of cucumber, for example, is shunned in the area around Siena, while it is always included in Florence. Our recipe can be enriched by adding diced carrots, fennel, celery, hard-boiled eggs, capers, or Pecorino cheese.

CAESAR'S MUSHROOM SALAD

Serves: 4–6

Preparation: 10'

Level of difficulty: 1

- 14 oz/450 g Caesar's (royal agaric) mushrooms
- 1 cup/100 g walnuts, shelled and chopped
- 3 oz/90 g Parmesan cheese, flaked
- 6 tbsp extra-virgin olive oil
- salt and freshly ground white pepper to taste
- juice of 1 lemon

C lean the mushrooms and rinse them carefully in cold water. Pat dry with paper towels. ❧ Slice the mushrooms finely and arrange them on a serving dish. ❧ Sprinkle with the walnuts and Parmesan flakes. ❧ Mix the oil, salt, pepper, and lemon juice in a bowl and pour over the mushrooms. ❧ Serve immediately, before the flavor begins to change.

DESSERTS

VANILLA CREAM

Whisk the egg yolks and sugar in a medium saucepan until pale and creamy. ❧ Bring the milk to a boil with the salt and vanilla, then stir it into the egg and sugar. ❧ Cook over very low heat, stirring constantly, until the cream thickens.

Makes: 2 cups/500 ml
Preparation: 10'
Cooking: 10'
Level of difficulty: 1

- **5 egg yolks**
- **5 oz/150 g sugar**
- **2 cups/500 ml milk**
- **dash of salt**
- **1 tsp vanilla extract**

Variations

• To make Lemon Cream: Boil the very finely grated zest of 1 lemon with the milk and omit the vanilla extract.

• To make Chocolate Cream: Melt 4 oz/125 g grated bittersweet/dark chocolate in the milk.

• To make Liqueur Cream: Add 1–2 tablespoons cognac, run, brandy, or other liqueur into the cream while still hot.

KIWI MERINGUE ROLL

Serves: 4

Preparation: 20'

Cooking: 30'

Level of difficulty: 2

• **3 egg whites**
• **5 oz/150 g sugar**
• **1 tbsp confectioners'/ icing sugar, sifted**
• **1 tsp cornstarch/ cornflour**
• **2 kiwifruit, peeled and sliced**
• **1¹/₄ cups/310 ml heavy/double cream, whipped**

Preheat the oven to 350°F/180°C/gas 4. ❧ Grease a 10 x 6¹/₂ in (26 x 16 cm) baking pan and line with waxed paper. ❧ Beat the egg whites until stiff. ❧ Add the sugar gradually, beating continuously until the mixture is thick. ❧ Fold in the confectioners' sugar and cornstarch and beat again briefly. ❧ Stir in the vinegar. ❧ Transfer the mixture to the prepared baking pan and smooth the surface. ❧ Bake for 30 minutes, or until pale golden brown. ❧ Cool in the baking pan. ❧ Turn the roll out onto a clean tea towel and carefully peel off the waxed paper. ❧ Spread the whipped cream over the upturned surface and sprinkle with the kiwifruit pieces. ❧ Roll up like a jelly roll (Swiss roll) and place on a serving dish.

This makes a very elegant dessert for a party. Try it with raspberries or other fruits too.

SICILIAN RICOTTA CAKE

B oil the sugar, water, and vanilla bean in a saucepan until the mixture turns to syrup. Set aside to cool. ❧ Beat the Ricotta vigorously with a spatula, then add the syrup gradually, stirring until the mixture becomes soft and creamy. ❧ Mix the chocolate and candied fruit (reserving some for decoration) with the Ricotta, then add the nuts and Maraschino. ❧ Cut the sponge cake into thin slices and line a 10 in (25 cm) springform pan with them, adding a little apricot jelly to bind them together. ❧ Fill with the Ricotta mixture, spreading it evenly. ❧ Cover with the remaining sponge and refrigerate for at least 2 hours. ❧ Prepare the glaze by heating the rest of the apricot jelly, vanilla sugar, and orange flower water, stirring until it becomes syrupy. ❧ Remove the cake from the refrigerator, coat evenly with the glaze, and decorate with the reserved pieces of candied fruit.

This cake comes from the beautiful Mediterranean island of Sicily. It is not easy to make, but well worth the effort.

Serves: 6–8

Preparation: 2¼ h + 2 h to chill

Cooking: 10'

Level of difficulty: 3

- 8 oz/250 g sugar
- ½ cup/125 ml water
- 1 vanilla bean/pod
- 1 lb/500 g Ricotta cheese, strained
- 5 oz/150 g semi-sweet/dark chocolate, chopped
- 11 oz/300 g mixed candied fruit
- 2 tbsp pistachio nuts, shelled
- 2 tbsp Maraschino or Kirsch liqueur
- 1 *Sponge Cake* (see page 878)
- 4 tbsp apricot preserves
- 1 tbsp confectioners'/icing sugar
- 2 tbsp orange-flower water

BAKED
COCONUT CUSTARD

Preheat the oven to 325°F/170°C/gas 3. ❧ Beat the eggs, yolk, sugar, and almond extract in a large bowl until pale and creamy. ❧ Heat the coconut milk with the cream or milk in a medium saucepan over low heat until lukewarm. ❧ *This creamy custard is a smooth, delectable taste sensation!* Slowly pour this mixture onto the eggs, whisking continuously. ❧ Pour into an ovenproof dish, then stand in a roasting pan. ❧ Pour in enough water to come halfway up the outside of the dish and bake at for 1 hour, or until the custard is set. ❧ Serve warm or cold with extra whipped cream.

Serves: 4

Preparation: 10'

Cooking: 1 h

Level of difficulty: 1

- 3 eggs + 1 egg yolk
- 4 tbsp sugar
- ¹/₂ tsp almond extract
- 2 cups/500 ml coconut milk
- 1 cup/250 ml cream or milk

RUM RAISIN CHEESECAKE

Serves: 8–10

Preparation: 30' + 4 h to chill

Cooking: 1 h

Level of difficulty: 1

- 2 cups/400 g old fashioned oats, uncooked
- 8 tbsp brown sugar
- 4 tbsp butter, melted
- 1 lb/500 g cream cheese, softened
- 3 oz/90 g sugar
- 2 tbsp all-purpose/plain flour
- 2 large eggs
- ½ cup/125 ml sour cream
- 3 tbsp rum
- 3 tbsp butter, melted
- ½ cup/100 g brown sugar, packed
- 4 tbsp golden raisins/sultanas
- 4 tbsp chopped nuts
- 4 tbsp old fashioned oats, uncooked

Preheat the oven to 350°/180°C/gas 4. ❧ Combine the oats, brown sugar, and first measure of butter and mix well. Press into the bottom and sides of a 9-in (23-cm) springform pan. ❧ Bake for 15 minutes. ❧ Beat the cream cheese, sugar, and 2 tablespoons of the flour in a large bowl until well blended. ❧ Add the eggs, one at a time. ❧ Add the sour cream and rum and mix well. ❧ Spoon this mixture over the crust. ❧ In a mixing bowl, cut the second measure of butter into the remaining flour and second measure of brown sugar until it resembles coarse bread crumbs. ❧ Stir in the raisins, nuts, and second measure of oats. ❧ Sprinkle over the cheesecake and bake for 45 minutes, or until set. ❧ Let cool. ❧ Refrigerate for at least 4 hours before serving.

RICOTTA CAKE WITH BERRIES

Serves: 6–8

Preparation: 40' + 3 h to chill

Level of difficulty: 2

- 1 lb/500 g Ricotta cheese, strained
- 1¹/₄ cups/250 g sugar
- 1 cup/250 ml Greek yogurt
- 1³/₄ cups/450 ml heavy/whipping cream
- 1 lb/500 g mixed berry fruits
- 1 quantity *Sponge Cake* (see page 878)
- juice of 1 lemon

Place the Ricotta with just over half the sugar and the yogurt in a large bowl. ❧ Whip the cream until stiff and fold it carefully into the mixture. ❧ Stir in 3 tablespoons of berries. ❧ Cut the sponge cake in half horizontally. Place one round in the bottom of a 10 in (25 cm) springform pan and spread the Ricotta mixture over it. Cover with the other piece of sponge. ❧ Cook the rest of the berries in the remaining sugar and lemon juice over a high heat until syrupy. ❧ Spread the fruit over the the cake and refrigerate for at least 3 hours before serving.

RASPBERRY WHITE CHOC CHEESECAKE

Preheat the oven to 350°/180°C/gas 4. ❧ Crust: Mix the crumbs, butter, and sugar in a small bowl. Grease and flour a 10-in (25-cm) springform pan and press the mixture into bottom. ❧ Filling: Melt the chocolate in the top of a double boiler over simmering water. Place in a large bowl with the cream cheese and sugar and mix well. Beat in the eggs, one at a time. ❧ Reserve 4 tablespoons of the filling, and spoon the rest over the prepared crust. ❧ Add the melted jelly, raspberry liqueur, and food coloring to the remaining filling. Carefully spread on top of the white filling. ❧ Bake for 1 hour, or until set. ❧ Cool to room temperature, then refrigerate overnight, without removing from pan. ❧ Topping: Melt the chocolate and butter in the top of a double boiler over simmering water. Transfer to a large bowl containing the cream cheese and lemon juice and beat until smooth. ❧ Remove the cheesecake from the pan and spread with the topping. Refrigerate for 1 hour, or until the topping is firm. ❧ Glaze: Melt the jelly in a small saucepan. Cool slightly, then spread over the topping. ❧ Refrigerate for 30 minutes, or until the glaze is set. ❧ Serve at room temperature.

Serves: 8–10

Preparation: 1 h +
13½ h to chill

Cooking: 1 h

Level of difficulty: 3

CRUST
- 8 oz/250 g cookie crumbs
- 6 tbsp melted butter
- 4 tbsp sugar

FILLING
- 1 lb/500 g cream cheese, softened
- ¾ cup/150 g sugar
- 8 oz/250 g white chocolate, melted
- 2 eggs
- 6 tbsp raspberry jelly/ jam, melted
- 3 tbsp raspberry liqueur
- ½ tsp red food coloring

TOPPING
- 13 oz/400 white chocolate
- ¾ cup/200 g butter
- 13 oz/400 g cream cheese, softened
- 2 tbsp lemon juice

GLAZE
- 1 cup/250 ml raspberry jelly/jam

NEW YORK CHEESECAKE

Preheat the oven to 350°/180°C/gas 4. ❧
Crust: Combine the crumbs, butter, and sugar
in a bowl. Grease and flour a 10-in (25-cm)
springform pan and press the mixture into bottom.
❧ Bake for 10 minutes. ❧ Filling: Beat the cream
cheese, sugar, and flour until well blended. Add the
eggs, one at a time, beating well after each
addition. Beat in the sour cream and vanilla. ❧
Spoon the filling over the over crust and bake for 1
hour. Turn the oven off and leave the cheesecake
inside with the door half open until cool. ❧ Let cool
completely in the pan then refrigerate for 1–2
hours. ❧ Serve as is, or with a melted fruit jelly
glaze or with chopped fresh fruit.

Serves: 8–10

Preparation: 15'
+ time to chill

Cooking: 1¼ h

Level of difficulty: 1

CRUST
- **7 oz/200 g cookie crumbs**
- **4 tbsp butter, melted**
- **4 tbsp sugar**

FILLING
- **2 lb/1 kg cream cheese, softened**
- **1 cup/200 g sugar**
- **3 tbsp flour**
- **4 eggs**
- **1 cup/250 ml sour cream**
- **2 tsp vanilla extract**

RICE CAKE

Serves: 6

Preparation: 45'

Cooking: 1 h

Level of difficulty: 2

- 4 cups/1 liter milk
- dash of salt
- 8 oz/250 g Arborio or pudding rice
- 3 oz/90 g sugar
- finely grated zest of 1 lemon
- 3 oz/90 g finely chopped toasted almonds
- 2–3 drops almond extract
- 4 eggs, separated
- dash of salt

Preheat the oven to 350°/180°C/gas 4. 🍃 Bring the milk and salt to a boil in a saucepan. 🍃 Add the rice and simmer over low heat, stirring frequently, until the rice is tender. 🍃 Remove from heat, stir in the sugar and lemon zest. Let cool to room temperature. 🍃 Stir in the almonds, almond extract, and egg yolks. 🍃 Beat the egg whites with a dash of salt until very firm and carefully fold into the rice mixture. 🍃 Grease a 10-in (25-cm) springform pan with butter, then sprinkle with bread crumbs or flour. Spoon the mixture into it. 🍃 Bake for 40 minutes, or until pale golden brown. 🍃 Serve at room temperature.

STRAWBERRY BAVARIAN CREAM

Soak the gelatin in the first measure of cold water and dissolve in the boiling water. ❧ Stir the strawberries into the gelatin and water. Refrigerate until the mixture begins to set. ❧ Cook the sugar and the second measure of cold water in a small saucepan until a few drops form a soft ball in cold water. ❧ Remove from heat and gradually add to egg whites, beating constantly. Continue beating gently until cool. ❧ Combine the egg whites and sugar with the strawberry gelatin and place in a 1½ quart (1.5 liter) pudding mold. Refrigerate until set. ❧ To serve, unmold on a plate and garnish with fresh strawberries.

Serves: 8

Preparation: 15' +
2 h to chill

Cooking: 10'

Level of difficulty: 2

• 2 envelopes/2 tbsp
  unflavored gelatin
  (or 8 sheets leaf
  gelatin)
• 6 tbsp cold water
• 6 tbsp boiling water
• 2 cups/500 g
  strawberries (or
  raspberries),
  crushed, or 1½ lb/
  750 g frozen
  berries
• ¾ cup/150 g sugar
• 2 tbsp cold water
• 4 egg whites

PANNA COTTA
WITH APRICOT SAUCE

Place the cream, 6 cups (1.5 liters) of milk, and the lemon zest in a large saucepan over medium-high heat. Bring almost to a boil, then remove from heat. Cover and set aside for about 1 hour. ❧ Sprinkle the gelatin over the remaining milk and set aside until dissolved. ❧ Return the milk and cream mixture to heat until almost boiling. ❧ Remove from heat and beat in the dissolved gelatin, sugar, and vanilla until smooth. ❧ Strain the mixture into a bowl then pour into 12 ramekins (or other small molds). ❧ Refrigerate for at least 2 hours. ❧ Sauce: Place the apricots and water in a saucepan and bring to a boil. Reduce heat and cook for about 30 minutes, or until the water is reduced by one-third. Transfer to a food processor and mix until smooth. Stir in the sugar. ❧ To remove the panna cotta from the ramekins, dip them briefly in hot water then unmold onto individual serving dishes on which you have already spread 2 tablespoons of the apricot sauce. ❧ Garnish each dish with mint leaves.

Serves: 6–12
Preparation: 15' + 3 h
Cooking: 40'
Level of difficulty: 2

CREAM

• 2 cups/500 ml heavy/double cream
• 7 cups/1.75 liters milk
• zest of 1 lemon
• 1 tbsp vanilla extract
• 4 envelopes/4 tbsp unflavored gelatin (or 16 sheets leaf gelatin)
• 7 oz/200 g sugar
• mint leaves, to garnish

SAUCE

• 1 cup/200 g dried apricots
• 3 cups/750 ml water
• 2 tbsp confectioners'/icing sugar

CUSTARD WITH ALMOND BRITTLE

Serves: 4

Preparation: 20'

Cooking: 20'

Level of difficulty: 1

- **zest of 1 lemon, in one piece**
- **1¼ cups/310 ml milk**
- **4 egg yolks**
- **¾ cup/150 g sugar**
- **4 tsp cornstarch/ cornflour**
- **4 oz/125 g almond brittle, chopped**

Bring the lemon zest and milk to a boil over medium heat. ❧ Place the egg yolks and sugar in a saucepan and whisk until pale and creamy. ❧ Stir in the cornstarch and hot milk, and cook over very low heat until the custard comes to a boil. Cook for 3 more minutes, stirring continuously. ❧ Remove the saucepan from heat and add the almond brittle, reserving a few pieces for decoration. ❧ Serve the custard in small individual dishes garnished with the remaining almond brittle.

FLUFFY EGG DELIGHT

Preheat the oven to 400°F/200°C/gas 6. ❧ Beat the egg whites and salt in a bowl until stiff. ❧ Sift the cornstarch into the egg whites and beat well. ❧ Add the sugar gradually, beating until stiff. ❧ Butter a 1 quart (1 liter) mold and sprinkle with a little sugar. Spoon the mixture into the mold. ❧ Place the mold in a roasting pan half-filled with water and bake for 5 minutes. Turn off heat and leave for 15 minutes in the oven to set. ❧ Unmold on a serving dish and let cool. ❧ Sauce: Simmer the rice and water in a pan for 30 minutes. Strain, reserving the water and discarding the rice. ❧ Cook the sugar with ¹/₂ cup of the rice water over medium heat to make a thin syrup. Remove from heat. ❧ Whisk the syrup into the egg yolks and return to the pan. Cook over low heat, whisking constantly, until thick. Set aside cool. ❧ Spoon over the pudding, sprinkle with the almonds, and serve.

Serves: 4–6
Preparation: 30'
Cooking: 35'
Level of difficulty: 2

- **8 large egg whites**
- **¹/₂ tsp salt**
- **2 tsp cornstarch/ cornflour**
- **¹/₂ cup/100 g sugar**
- **2 oz/60 g flaked almonds**

SAUCE
- **2 oz/60 g short-grain rice**
- **2 cups/500 ml water**
- **1 cup/200 g sugar**
- **8 large egg yolks, lightly beaten**

RICE CREAM

Serves: 4

Preparation: 15' + 2 h to chill

Cooking: 1 h

Level of difficulty: 1

- 2¹/₂ cups/625 ml milk
- 4 oz/125 g short-grain rice
- 2 tbsp sugar
- 4 tbsp blanched, finely chopped almonds
- 2 tbsp butter
- 2 cups/500 ml heavy/double cream
- 1 tsp vanilla extract
- 1 envelope/1 tbsp unflavored gelatin (or 4 sheets leaf gelatin)
- ¹/₂ cup/125 ml cold water

Place the milk in the top of a double boiler and bring to a boil. Add the rice and cook for about 50 minutes. The rice should be very well cooked. ❧ Stir in the sugar, almonds, and butter and set aside to cool. ❧ Beat the cream until stiff and fold into the mixture with the vanilla. ❧ Place the gelatin in a small saucepan with the cold water over low heat and stir until the gelatin dissolves. Set aside to cool. ❧ Fold the gelatin into the mixture. ❧ Pour into a large serving bowl and refrigerate for at least 2 hours. ❧ Serve as is, or with a sauce made with raspberry preserves (jam) heated with a little boiling water.

CRÈME BRÛLÉE

Preheat the oven to 350°/180°C/gas 4. ❧ Beat the eggs and yolks with the sugar until the mixture falls in ribbons. ❧ Warm the cream slightly and beat it into the mixture. ❧ Pour the mixture, through a strainer, into 6 individual ramekins. ❧ Arrange the ramekins in a roasting pan half-filled with water. Bake for about 1 hour, or until golden brown. ❧ Remove from the oven. Let cool, then refrigerate for at least 4 hours. ❧ Sprinkle the ramekins with the brown sugar. Place under a preheated broiler (grill) and broil until the sugar is caramelized. ❧ Serve at once or return to the refrigerator and let cool again before serving.

If liked, serve straight from under the broiler. The hot topping contrasts deliciously with the cold cream.

Serves: 6

Preparation: 30' + 4 h to chill

Cooking: 1 h

Level of difficulty: 1

- 2 eggs
- 7 egg yolks
- ³/₄ cup/150 g sugar
- 2³/₄ cups/625 ml light/single cream
- ¹/₂ cup/100 g firmly packed brown sugar

CHESTNUT CUSTARD CREAM

P lace the egg yolks, sugar, flour, lemon zest, and salt in a small saucepan. Mix with a wooden spoon until pale and creamy. ❧ Add the boiling milk in a very thin stream, stirring continuously. Place over very low heat and continue stirring until the custard

This wonderful dessert comes from the city of Turin, in northwestern Italy.

thickens; this will take only a few minutes. Do not let it boil or it will curdle. ❧ Remove from heat and set aside to cool, stirring at intervals to prevent a skin from forming. If preparing the custard well in advance, cover with a piece of plastic wrap, resting it on the surface of the custard to prevent a skin from forming. ❧ Place a slice of sponge cake in the bottom of each glass or dish. Sprinkle with the rum diluted with 2–3 tablespoons of water. ❧ Cover with a thick layer of cool custard. ❧ Sprinkle with the pieces of marrons glacés and top with little blobs of whipped cream. ❧ Decorate each serving with a candied cherry and serve.

Serves: 4

Preparation: 15'

Cooking: 4–5'

Level of difficulty: 1

- **2 egg yolks**
- **4 tbsp sugar**
- **2 tbsp all-purpose/ plain flour**
- **1 tsp finely grated lemon zest**
- **dash of salt**
- **1 cup/250 ml boiling milk**
- **4 slices sponge cake, $^{1}/_{2}$-in/1-cm thick**
- **6 tbsp rum**
- **6 tbsp broken pieces of marrons glacés/candied chestnuts**
- **$^{1}/_{2}$ cup/125 ml unsweetened heavy/double cream, whipped**
- **4 candied/glacé cherries**

WATERMELON JELLY

ieve or liquidize the watermelon. You should obtain about 4 cups (1 liter) of sieved watermelon flesh. ⚘ Place the prepared watermelon in a large saucepan. Add the sugar and cornstarch and place over low heat, stirring well. ⚘ When it comes to a boil, reduce the heat and simmer for 4–5 minutes, stirring continuously. ⚘ Remove from heat, add the cinnamon, and let cool. Add the candied pumpkin and chocolate. ⚘ Rinse the inside of a 1 quart (1 liter) pudding mold with cold water and fill with the watermelon mixture. ⚘ Refrigerate for at least 4 hours, or until completely set. ⚘ Turn out onto a serving dish, decorate with jasmine flowers, and serve.

This cool, thirst-quenching dessert is a perfect way to finish a hot summer meal.

724

Serves: 4

Preparation: 15' + 4 h to chill

Cooking: 7–8'

Level of difficulty: 1

- 4 lb/2 kg watermelon, peeled and seeded
- 3/4 cup/150 g sugar
- 1/2 cup/75 g cornstarch/corn flour
- dash of ground cinnamon
- 4 tbsp candied pumpkin, or candied lemon peel, diced
- 3 tbsp coarsely grated bittersweet/dark chocolate
- fresh jasmine flowers, for decoration

QUEEN OF PUDDINGS

Serves: 4

Preparation: 10' + 30' to cool

Cooking: 1 h

Level of difficulty: 1

- 2¹/₂ cups/625 ml **full-cream milk**
- 3 oz/90 g fresh **white bread crumbs**
- ³/₄ cup/150 g sugar
- ¹/₂ tsp vanilla **extract**
- 2 eggs, separated
- 3 tbsp raspberry **preserves, warmed**

Preheat the oven to 350°/180°C/gas 4. ❧ Pour the milk into a saucepan and bring to a boil. ❧ Remove from heat and stir in the bread crumbs, half the sugar, and vanilla. ❧ Set aside for 30 minutes to cool. ❧ Beat the egg yolks and add them to the cooled mixture. Pour it into an ovenproof dish. ❧ Bake for 40–45 minutes, or until set. ❧ Spread the jam carefully over the surface of the pudding. ❧ Beat the egg whites until stiff. ❧ Whisk in the remaining sugar and beat until stiff peaks form. ❧ Spread the meringue on top of the jam and bake for 20–25 minutes more, or until the top is set and lightly browned.

RICOTTA MOUSSE WITH PLUM SAUCE

Beat the Ricotta and confectioners' sugar in a large bowl until creamy and well mixed. 🍂 Beat in the egg yolks, lemon zest, and rum. 🍂 Carefully fold in the cream, chocolate, and peel (reserve a few pieces for decoration). Refrigerate for at least 1 hour. 🍂 Meanwhile, cook the plums, brown sugar, and lemon juice over high heat until the mixture thickens. Sieve into a medium bowl. 🍂 Spoon the mousse into individual serving bowls, and pour the hot plum sauce over the top. 🍂 Decorate with flaked chocolate and candied orange peel.

The slightly tart flavor of the plums blends perfectly with the full, bland taste of the Ricotta .

Serves: 6

Preparation: 20' + 1 h to chill

Cooking: 15'

Level of difficulty: 1

- **13 oz/400 g very fresh Ricotta cheese**
- **$^1/_2$ cup/75 g confectioners'/ icing sugar**
- **3 egg yolks**
- **grated zest of 1 lemon**
- **1 tbsp rum**
- **$^2/_3$ cup/150 ml heavy/double cream, whipped**
- **2 oz/60 g semi-sweet/dark chocolate, + extra for decoration**
- **2 tbsp chopped candied orange peel**
- **1 lb/500 g plums, pitted**
- **$^1/_2$ cup/100 g firmly packed brown sugar**
- **juice of $^1/_2$ lemon**

MONT BLANC

Place the pieces of marrons glacés in a bowl. Sprinkle with the rum and let soak for 30 minutes. ❧ Put the rum-soaked pieces of marrons glacés in a large bowl and use a potato masher to mash until smooth (or chop in a food processor). ❧ Shape the chopped marrons glacés into a mound in the center of a serving dish. ❧ Cover the mound carefully with the cream, smoothing the surface, or leaving it uneven, as preferred. ❧ Serve at room temperature or chill for 2 hours before serving.

The original recipe uses raw chestnuts. This much shorter method gives equally good results.

Serves: 4–5

Preparation: 15' + 30' to soak

Level of difficulty: 1

- **2 cups/400 g marrons glacés/ candied chestnuts**
- **3 tbsp dark rum**
- **1 1/4 cups/310 ml heavy/double cream, whipped**

RASPBERRY & PEACH TRIFLE

Rinse the raspberries and drain well. ❧ Slice sponge cake horizontally into three thin layers. Place one layer in the bottom of a crystal or glass serving bowl. It should be flat-bottomed and about 10 in (25 cm) across and 6 in (15 cm) deep. ❧ Sprinkle the cake with one-third of the sherry. Spread about one-third of the raspberries and peaches on top. Spoon one-third of the custard over the fruit. Repeat cake, sherry, fruit, and custard layers, saving a dozen or so raspberries to garnish. ❧ Topping: Beat the cream with the sugar until stiff. ❧ Spoon the cream over the top of the trifle. Garnish with raspberries and toasted almonds. ❧ Refrigerate until ready to serve.

Serves: 6–8

Preparation: 15'
 + time to chill

Level of difficulty: 1

- 8 oz/250 g fresh raspberries
- 1 quantity *Sponge Cake* (see page 878)
- 1 cup/250 ml dry sherry
- 1 cup/250 g peaches, sliced
- 1 quantity chilled *Vanilla Cream* (see page 698)
- 1 cup/250 ml heavy/double cream
- 1 tbsp sugar
- 1/2 cup/75 g toasted slivered almonds

KAHLUA MOUSSE

Melt the chocolate with the butter in a double boiler over simmering water. ❧ In a large bowl, combine the confectioners' sugar, egg yolks, Kahlua, and coffee powder. ❧ Stir the chocolate mixture into the bowl. ❧ Whip the cream until stiff and fold it into the Kahlua-chocolate mixture. ❧ Beat the egg whites until just stiff (do not overbeat). Fold them into the mixture. ❧ Spoon the mixture into a serving dish or individual serving bowls. ❧ Refrigerate for at least 4 hours before serving.

If liked, decorate the mousse with extra whipped cream flavored with vanilla extract or Kahlua.

732

Serves: 8

Preparation: 15' + 4 h to chill

Cooking: 10'

Level of difficulty: 1

- 1 lb/500 g semi-sweet/dark chocolate, cut in pieces
- 3 oz/90 g butter, cut in pieces
- 2 oz/60 g sifted confectioners'/ icing sugar
- 3 eggs, separated
- 4 tbsp Kahlua liqueur
- 1 tsp instant coffee powder
- 2 cups/500 ml heavy/double cream

LEMON CREAM

Serves: 4–6

Preparation: 15'
 + 2 h to chill

Cooking: 10'

Level of difficulty: 1

- ¾ cup/150 g sugar
- 1 cup/150 g all-purpose/plain flour
- grated zest of 2 lemons
- 4 cups/1 liter whole milk

P lace the sugar, flour, and zest of 1 lemon in a heavy-bottomed saucepan. Gradually stir in the milk, making sure that no lumps form. ❧ Place the pan over medium-low heat and, stirring continuously, bring to a boil. ❧ Boil for 1 minute, then remove from heat. ❧ Pour into a mold and leave to cool. When cool, refrigerate for at least 2 hours. ❧ Serve cold sprinkled with the remaining grated lemon zest.

> Replace the lemon zest with 2 tbsp unsweetened cocoa powder to make Chocolate Cream.

CHOCOLATE ORANGE MOUSSE

Melt the chocolate and butter with the Grand Marnier in a double boiler over simmering water. ❧ Set aside to cool. ❧ Beat the egg yolks and sugar until the mixture fall in ribbons. This will take about 10 minutes. ❧ In a large bowl, combine the chocolate sauce with the egg mixture. Beat with a wire whisk until thick. ❧ In another bowl, beat the egg whites until stiff peaks form. ❧ Fold the egg whites into the chocolate sauce until just combined. ❧ Beat the cream until stiff and fold it into the chocolate mixture. ❧ Spoon into one large or four individual serving bowls and refrigerate for at least 3 hours before serving.

This mousse will keep in the refrigerator for up to 2 days before serving.

Serves: 4

*Preparation: 15'
+ 3 h to chill*

Cooking: 10'

Level of difficulty: 1

- 11 oz/300 g semi-sweet/dark chocolate
- 1 cup/250 g butter
- 4 tbsp Grand Marnier or other orange liqueur
- 8 eggs, separated
- ¾ cup/150 g sugar
- 2½ cups/625 ml heavy/double cream

734

ITALIAN RICE PUDDING

Serves: 8

Preparation: 15'

Cooking: 50'

Level of difficulty: 1

- 5 oz/150 g short-grain rice (preferably Italian arborio)
- 4 cups/1 liter milk
- 1 tsp vanilla extract
- 1/2 cup/100 g sugar
- 3 oz/90 g golden raisins/sultanas
- 2 tbsp chopped candied peel
- dash of salt
- 1 tbsp butter
- 2 eggs
- 2 egg yolks
- 1/2 cup/125 ml rum or cognac
- 2 tbsp butter
- 4 tbsp fine dry bread crumbs

Preheat the oven to 350°/180°C/gas 4. ❧ Place the rice, milk, and vanilla over medium heat. Bring to a boil and simmer for 10 minutes. ❧ Add the sugar, raisins, peel, salt, and butter and continue cooking until the rice is tender. Remove from heat and let cool. ❧ When cool, beat in the eggs one at a time, followed by the rum. ❧ Grease the pudding mold with a little butter and sprinkle with bread crumbs. Pour the mixture into it. ❧ Bake for about 35 minutes, or until pale golden brown. ❧ Unmold and serve hot or at room temperature.

Serve this scrumptious pudding with 1 quantity of Vanilla Cream (See page 698).

737

LEMON SOUFFLÉ

Prepare a 1 quart (1 liter) souffle dish with a paper collar. ❧ In a bowl, whisk the lemon zest, juice, sugar, and egg yolks together over a pan of hot water until thick. ❧ Place the water in a small bowl and sprinkle with the gelatin. Let soak, then place over a pan of simmering water and stir until dissolved. ❧ Stir the gelatin into the soufflé mixture; Let cool and and refrigerate. ❧ Whip the cream until thick. Whisk the egg whites until stiff. ❧ Fold half the cream into the soufflé, followed by the egg whites. Pour into a soufflé dish and level the surface. ❧ Refrigerate for at least 4 hours. Remove the paper from around the top of the souffle. ❧ Decorate with the remaining cream and candied lemon zest.

Serves: 4–6

Preparation: 15' + 4 h to chill

Level of difficulty: 1

- **grated zest of 3 lemons**
- **6 tbsp lemon juice**
- **4 oz/125 g sugar**
- **4 eggs, separated**
- **1 envelope/1 tbsp unflavored gelatin (or 4 sheets leaf gelatin)**
- **3 tbsp cold water**
- **1¼ cups/310 ml heavy/double cream**
- **candied lemon zest, to decorate**

AMARETTO MOUSSE

Serves: 4–6

Preparation: 15' + 2 h
  to chill

Level of difficulty: 1

- 6 tbsp amaretto
  (almond liqueur)
- 1 envelope/1 tbsp
  unflavored
  powdered gelatin
  (or 4 sheets leaf
  gelatin)
- 4 eggs
- 3 tbsp confectioners'/
  icing sugar
- 2½ cups/625 ml
  heavy/whipping
  cream
- almond extract, to
  taste
- 5 oz/150 g sliced,
  toasted almonds

P lace the amaretto liqueur in the top of a
double boiler (or in a heatproof bowl placed
in a pan of hot water). Add the gelatin and
stir until it dissolves. Set aside in a warm place. &
Warm the eggs and confectioners' sugar in a
another double boiler over very low heat, whisking
constantly. Remove from heat and whisk vigorously
until very pale and creamy. & Fold the gelatin
mixture into the egg mixture. & Whip the cream
with the almond extract until stiff, then fold it into
the egg mixture. & Spoon the mousse into
individual serving bowls and refrigerate for at least
2 hours. & Garnish with sliced, toasted almonds
just before serving.

MASCARPONE & CHOCOLATE CREAM

B eat the egg yolks and sugar until very pale and creamy. Mix in the Mascarpone gently and flavor with the Marsala. ❧ Melt the chocolate in the milk over very low heat. Set aside to cool. ❧ Mix the chocolate and milk with half of the Mascarpone mixture. ❧ Crumble the meringues in the bottom of 6 ice-cream dishes and pour in the Mascarpone and chocolate mixtures. ❧ Blend the surfaces of the two mixtures with a knife to give a marbled effect, or leave them separate, as preferred. ❧ Refrigerate for at least 2 hours before serving.

Serves: 6

Preparation: 30' + 2 h to chill

Level of difficulty: 1

- **2 egg yolks**
- **$^1/_2$ cup/100 g sugar**
- **11 oz/300 g Mascarpone cheese**
- **1 tbsp dry Marsala wine**
- **4 oz/125 g semi-sweet/dark chocolate, chopped**
- **2 tbsp milk**
- **4 small meringues**

ZUCCOTTO

Cut the sponge cake in half horizontally, then divide it into 8–12 triangular wedges. ♣ Moisten the cake on both sides with the Cointreau or rum and use it to line a 1½ quart (1.5 liter) pudding mold. ♣ Beat the cream until stiff, adding the confectioners' sugar when almost ready. Fold in the grated chocolate, almonds, and candied fruits. ♣ Transfer half this mixture to a separate bowl. ♣ Melt the second measure of chocolate in a double boiler (or in a bowl over boiling water) and mix gently into one half of the cream. ♣ Put the white cream into the mold and spread it over the cake lining. Cover with foil and place in the freezer for 10–15 minutes. ♣ Spoon the chocolate cream into the mold, which it should fill completely. ♣ Cover with foil and freeze for at least 4 hours before serving.

This dessert comes from Florence, Italy, where it has been made for centuries.

Serves: 6

Preparation: 15' + 4 h to freeze

Cooking: 10'

Level of difficulty: 2

- **12 oz/375 g bought fatless sponge cake**
- **½ cup/125 ml Cointreau or rum**
- **2 cups/500 ml heavy/double cream**
- **2 oz/60 g confectioners'/ icing sugar**
- **2 oz/60 g bittersweet/dark chocolate, grated**
- **3 tbsp peeled, finely chopped almonds**
- **2 oz/60 g diced candied orange and lemon peel**
- **3 oz/90 g unsweetened dark chocolate, coarsely chopped**

GRAND MARNIER SOUFFLÉ

P reheat the oven to 350°/180°C/gas 4. ✤ Grease a 2-quart (2-liter) soufflé dish lightly with butter and sprinkle it with sugar. Prepare a collar for the dish. ✤ Melt the butter over low heat in a saucepan. ✤ Remove from heat and stir in the flour and salt until smooth. Add the milk, a little at a time, stirring constantly. ✤ Return to heat, stirring constantly with a whisk, until thick and smooth. Remove from heat. ✤ Beat the 5 egg yolks well. ✤ Add the hot cream sauce, a little at a time, beating constantly. Set aside to cool. ✤ Beat the 8 egg whites until soft peaks form. Add the sugar gradually, beating until stiff. ✤ Stir the lemon juice, zest, and Grand Marnier into the egg yolk mixture, then fold it into the egg whites. ✤ Pour into the soufflé dish. Set the dish in a roasting pan half-filled with hot water. ✤ Bake for 1 hour. Remove the paper collar and serve.

Serves: 6

Preparation: 15'

Cooking: 1 h

Level of difficulty: 2

- **6 oz/180 g butter**
- **²/₃ cup/100 g all-purpose/plain flour**
- **¹/₂ tsp salt**
- **1¹/₂ cups/375 ml milk**
- **5 eggs, separated**
- **3 egg whites**
- **1 cup/200 g sugar**
- **2 tbsp lemon juice**
- **1 tsp grated lemon zest**
- **¹/₂ cup/125 ml Grand Marnier**

PASSIONFRUIT CREAM

Serves: 4

Preparation: 15' + 4 h to chill

Cooking: 15'

Level of difficulty: 2

- **2¹/₃ cups/600 ml heavy/double cream**
- **5 egg yolks**
- **¹/₂ cup/100 g sugar**
- **5 passionfruit**

Place the cream in a small saucepan over low heat and bring to a gentle simmer. ❧ Place the egg yolks and sugar in a double boiler over simmering water and whisk until pale and creamy. ❧ Cut the passionfruit in half and scoop out the pulp. Strain and set the juice aside. Discard the seeds. ❧ When the cream reaches boiling point, pour it into the egg yolk mixture and whisk to combine. Place the bowl over the simmering water and stir constantly until the mixture coats the back of a spoon. ❧ Add the passionfruit juice and cook for 1 minute more. ❧ Remove from heat and pour into a bowl. When cool, refrigerate for 4 hours before serving.

This versatile cream can be served alone, spooned over fresh fruit salad, or used to fill trifles or sponges.

745

STRAWBERRY MASCARPONE MOUSSE

Put the water in a small bowl and sprinkle with the gelatin. Let soften for 5 minutes. ❧ Add half the gelatin mixture to the liqueur and the other half to the wine. Stir both over medium-low heat to dissolve the gelatin. When cool, refrigerate both mixtures. ❧ Mix the Mascarpone with the liqueur. Beat the cream until stiff and fold it into the Mascarpone mixture. ❧ Refrigerate for at least 4 hours. ❧ Slice the strawberries and arrange in individual dishes (reserving a few to garnish). ❧ Pour a little of the jellied wine over the top and fill the dishes with the Mascarpone mousse. Top with the remaining strawberries and serve.

Serves: 4

Preparation: 30' + 4 h to chill

Level of difficulty: 1

- 2 envelopes/2 tbsp unflavored gelatin (or 8 sheets leaf gelatin)
- 3 tbsp cold water
- 4 tbsp strawberry liqueur
- 1 cup/250 ml fruity white wine
- 2 oz/60 g confectioners'/icing sugar
- 8 oz/250 g Mascarpone cheese
- 1¼ cups/310 ml heavy/whipping cream
- 2 cups/500 g strawberries

KEY LIME CHEESECAKE

Mix the crumbs, sugar, and butter in bowl. Press into the bottom and sides of a 9-in (23-cm) springform pan. ❧ Filling: Combine the lime juice and water in a saucepan and sprinkle with the gelatin. Let stand 5 minutes to soften. ❧ Stir the sugar, eggs, and zest into the gelatin mixture. Cook over medium heat until almost boiling, stirring constantly. Do not let it boil. Remove from heat. ❧ Beat the butter and cream cheese in a large bowl until well mixed. ❧ Gradually stir in the lime mixture. ❧ Refrigerate for 45 minutes. ❧ Beat the cream in a chilled bowl until stiff peaks form, then fold it into the lime mixture. ❧ Spoon into the prepared crust. ❧ Refrigerate for 4 hours before serving.

Serves: 8–10

Preparation: 20'
+ 4–5 h to chill

Level of difficulty: 2

CRUST

- 12 oz/350 g graham cracker crumbs
- $^1/_2$ cup/100 g sugar
- $^1/_2$ cup/125 g butter, melted

FILLING

- 1 cup/250 ml fresh lime juice
- 4 tbsp water
- 2 envelopes/2 tbsp unflavored gelatin (or 8 sheets leaf gelatin)
- 11 oz/300 g sugar
- 5 eggs, beaten
- 2 tsp grated lime zest
- $^1/_2$ cup/125 g butter, warmed
- 1 lb/500 g cream cheese
- $^1/_2$ cup/125 ml heavy/double cream, chilled

RICOTTA CREAM

- 1¼ lb/625 g fresh Ricotta cheese
- 6 tbsp confectioners'/icing sugar
- 1 tsp freshly ground cinnamon

Put the Ricotta in a large bowl and stir in the confectioners' sugar and cinnamon. Mix well to obtain a smooth, light cream. ❧ Place in the refrigerator to rest for at least 1 hour before serving.

This recipe calls for the freshest of Ricotta cheese. Don't try to make it with prepacked Ricotta in plastic containers.

749

FRESH FRUIT CHOCOLATE FONDUE

Rinse and dry the fruit. Cut the larger pieces into bite-sized chunks. ❧ If using apple, pear, or banana, immerse the chunks in water and lemon juice for a few seconds to prevent the flesh from browning, then dry carefully. ❧ Arrange the fruit in an attractive bowl or serving dish. ❧ Melt the chocolate in the top of a double-boiler over hot, not simmering water. Dilute with the cream, add the butter and sugar and mix thoroughly. ❧ Pour the chocolate mixture into the fondue bowl and keep warm over the flame. ❧ Place bowls filled with the almonds, hazelnuts, and coconut on the table, so that your guests can dip their pieces of fruit into them, after having dipped them in the chocolate sauce.

This dessert is delicious, eyecatching, and fun — a perfect way to finish a dinner party!

| Serves: 8 |
| Preparation: 15' |
| Cooking: 15' |
| Level of difficulty: 1 |

- 2 lb/1 kg fresh fruit (grapes, figs, strawberries, bananas, apples, apricots, plums, peaches)
- 2 cups/500 ml water
- juice of 1 lemon
- 1 lb/500 g semi-sweet/dark chocolate, chopped
- 1 cup/250 ml cream
- 4 tbsp butter
- 4 tbsp sugar
- 1/3 cup/50 g each chopped toasted almonds and hazelnuts
- 1/2 cup/30 g shredded coconut

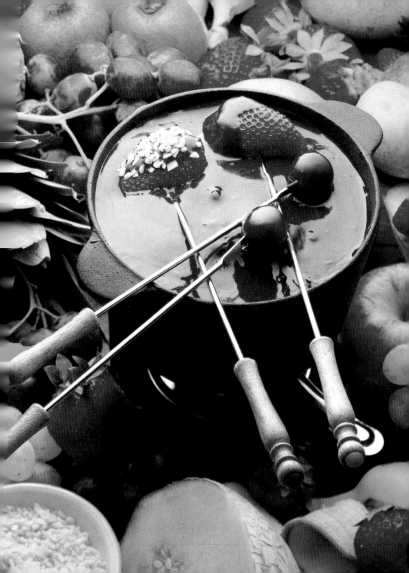

CHOCOLATE RICE PUDDING

Serves: 6

Preparation: 5'

Cooking: 25'

Level of difficulty: 1

- 4 cups/1 liter heavy/double cream milk
- ½ cup/100 g sugar
- 2½ cups/500 g short-grain rice
- 7 oz/200 g semi-sweet/dark chocolate, grated
- dash of ground cinnamon

Heat the milk and sugar in a saucepan over medium-low heat. ✿ When the milk is boiling, add the rice and cook for about 20 minutes, or until the rice is well-cooked and the milk has all been absorbed. Depending on the quality of the rice, you may need to add a little more milk during cooking or strain a little milk off the mixture when the rice is cooked. ✿ Add three-quarters of the chocolate, and the cinnamon, and stir until well mixed. ✿ Remove from the heat and pour into a deep serving bowl. Sprinkle with the remaining chocolate and serve while still warm.

This wonderful dessert is definitely winter fare. It is particularly good served with whipped cream.

753

TIRAMISÙ

Whisk the egg yolks and sugar until the mixture is a very pale color. ❧ Carefully fold in the Mascarpone. ❧ Beat the egg whites and salt until very stiff and then fold into the mixture. ❧ Spread a thin layer over the bottom of a large oval or rectangular dish. ❧ Dip the ladyfingers in the coffee and place a layer over the cream on the bottom of the dish. ❧ Cover with another layer of the cream and sprinkle with a little chocolate. ❧ Continue in this way until all the ingredients are used up. ❧ Finish with a layer of cream and chocolate, then dust with the cocoa powder.

This dessert can be prepared in advance— it needs at least 3 hours in the refrigerator before serving.

Serves: 6

Preparation: 30' + 3 h

Level of difficulty: 1

- **5 eggs, separated**
- **³/₄ cup/150 g sugar**
- **2 cups/500 g Mascarpone cheese**
- **dash of salt**
- **30 ladyfingers/ sponge fingers**
- **1 cup/250 ml strong espresso coffee**
- **7 oz/200 g semi- sweet/dark chocolate, grated**
- **1 tbsp unsweetened cocoa powder**

CHOCOLATE EGG CUSTARD

Serves: 4–6

Preparation: 20'

Cooking: 1 h

Level of difficulty: 2

- 1 cup/200 g sugar
- ½ tsp lemon juice
- 2 tbsp cold water
- 3½ cups/800 ml whole/full cream milk
- 6 eggs
- 2–3 tbsp unsweetened cocoa powder
- 2 oz/60 g amaretti cookies, finely pounded
- 3 tbsp rum

Preheat the oven to 300°/150°C/gas 2. ❧ Place half the sugar in a small saucepan with the lemon juice and water and place over medium heat. ❧ As soon as the sugar caramelizes to golden brown, pour it into a warmed 8-cup (2-liter) ring tube mold. Tip the mold to coat the inside evenly before the caramel hardens. Set aside. ❧ Heat the milk gently until just tepid. ❧ Use a balloon whisk or electric beater to beat the eggs very thoroughly in a bowl with the remaining sugar. Add the cocoa powder carefully and mix well. ❧ Stir in the warm milk, followed by the amaretti cookies and rum. ❧ Pour this mixture into the caramel-lined mold. Cover the mold with a piece of foil and place in a larger ovenproof container half filled with cold water. Bake for 1 hour, or until set. ❧ Take the mold out of the oven and let cool for 15–20 minutes before unmolding carefully onto a dish. ❧ Serve at room temperature, or chill for a few hours in the refrigerator.

PEARS WITH CHOCOLATE SAUCE

P eel the pears, and without removing the cores, place them whole, in a high-sided, narrow saucepan. Cover with cold water, stir in the sugar, and a dash of cinnamon. ✿ Leave on low heat until cooked but still firm. Remove from the saucepan and let cool. ✿ Whisk the egg yolks and sugar until pale in color, then stir in the flour. ✿ Bring the milk to a boil with the salt and vanilla. Stir the milk into the egg mixture, and cook over very low heat, stirring constantly, then pour into an earthenware pot, cover with plastic wrap (cling film) so that it touches the surface, and set aside. ✿ Melt the chocolate in the top of a double-boiler over hot, not simmering water. ✿ Bring the cream to a boil then use it to dilute the liquid chocolate. ✿ Remove the plastic wrap, warm the custard, and pour it into individual dishes. ✿ Serve the pears covered with the melted chocolate, on the bed of custard, and sprinkled with the crumbled amaretti cookies.

These chocolate glazed pears are also delicious served with vanilla or chocolate ice cream.

758

Serves: 6

Preparation: 30'

Cooking: 1 h

Level of difficulty: 1

- **6 large ripe yellow pears (Kaiser or Williams)**
- **1 1/2 cups/300 g sugar**
- **dash of cinnamon**

CUSTARD
- **5 egg yolks**
- **3/4 cup/150 g sugar**
- **1/3 cup/50 g all-purpose/plain flour**
- **2 cups/500 ml milk**
- **1 tsp vanilla extract**
- **dash of salt**
- **4 oz/125 g semi-sweet/dark chocolate**
- **4 tbsp light/single cream**
- **6 amaretti cookies**

ZABAGLIONE

Combine the egg yolks and sugar in a double boiler (not on the heat yet) and whisk until they are pale yellow and creamy. ❧ Add the Marsala gradually, beating continuously, then place the pan in the bottom pan of the double boiler over warm water and cook, beating continuously with the whisk, until the mixture thickens, about 15 minutes. ❧ Keep the heat extremely low so that the zabaglione does not boil or it will curdle. ❧ Serve warm or cold. If serving cold, cover with plastic wrap so that it is touching the surface to prevent a skin from forming as the mixture cools.

Serves: 4
Preparation: 5'
Cooking: 15'
Level of difficulty: 1

• **4 egg yolks**
• $^1/_2$ **cup/100 g sugar**
• $^1/_2$ **cup/125 ml dry Marsala wine**

CHOCOLATE ICE CREAM

Serves: 4–6

*Preparation: 20' + 1 h
  + 2–3 h*

Level of difficulty: 1

- ²/₃ cup/150 ml water
- ³/₄ cup/150 g sugar
- 3 tbsp unsweetened cocoa powder, sifted
- 2 oz/60 g semi-sweet/dark chocolate, chopped
- ¹/₂ cup/125 ml heavy/double cream, whipped

Place the water and sugar in a saucepan and stir over low heat until the sugar has dissolved. ❧ Remove from the heat, stir in the cocoa, and beat well. ❧ Bring slowly to a boil, stirring constantly. ❧ Simmer for 5 minutes. ❧ Remove from the heat and add the chocolate, stirring until it melts. ❧ Allow to cool, then beat vigorously before refrigerating for about 1 hour. ❧ Fold the whipped cream into the chocolate mixture and place in a suitable container. ❧ Freeze for at least 2–3 hours before serving.

RASPBERRY CHOCOLATE PUDDING

Combine the raspberries and sugar and set aside. ✢ Melt the chocolate in a double boiler over barely simmering water. ✢ Gradually beat in the butter. ✢ Remove from heat and let cool before beating in the egg yolks. ✢ Fold in the whipped cream. ✢ Dip each ladyfinger briefly into the coffee and use half of them to line an attractive serving dish. ✢ Cover with half the raspberries and sugar. ✢ Spoon over half of the chocolate mixture. ✢ Repeat, finishing with a chocolate layer. ✢ Refrigerate for at least 2 hours or overnight. ✢ Garnish with the raspberries and serve with whipped cream or creme fraiche.

Amaretti cookies can be used instead of the ladyfingers, or a mixture of the two.

Serves: 8–10

Preparation: 15' + 2 h to chill

Level of difficulty: 2

- 2 cups/500 g raspberries
- 4 tbsp sugar
- 1 lb/ 500 g semi-sweet/dark chocolate
- ½ cup/125 g butter
- 2 egg yolks
- 1 cup/250 ml heavy/double cream, whipped
- 7 oz/200 g ladyfingers/ sponge fingers
- 1–2 tbsp strong cold espresso coffee
- extra raspberries to garnish
- cream or creme fraiche to serve

CHOCOLATE MOUSSE

Melt the chocolate in a double-boiler over barely simmering water, then set aside until tepid. ❧ Whisk the egg yolks and confectioners' sugar until the mixture becomes pale in color, then add the melted chocolate and return to the heat for a few minutes still stirring. ❧ Whip the cream and the egg whites in separate bowls. ❧ Take the egg-and-chocolate mixture, which should be cold at this point, and add the egg whites followed by the cream, taking great care not to let the mixture collapse. ❧ Refrigerate the mousse for about 12 hours before serving.

Serves: 6–8

Preparation: 30' + 12 h to chill

Level of difficulty: 1

- **12 oz/350 g semi-sweet/dark chocolate**
- **6 eggs, separated**
- **4 tbsp confectioners'/icing sugar**
- **³/₄ cup/200 ml light/single cream**

COINTREAU & WHITE CHOCOLATE MOUSSE

Melt the chocolate in a double-boiler over simmering water. ❧ Whisk the egg yolks and sugar until pale and frothy. ❧ Fold in the melted chocolate, followed by the dissolved gelatin. Stir in the Cointreau. ❧ Whip the cream lightly and fold into the cooled chocolate mixture. ❧ Pour into 4–6 small individual dishes or one large serving bowl. ❧ Refrigerate for 3–4 hours before serving. Serve with amaretti or almond tuile cookies.

Serves: 4–6

Preparation: 30'

Level of difficulty: 2

- 4 oz/125 g white chocolate
- 4 egg yolks
- 3 tbsp sugar
- 2 tsp gelatin dissolved in 2 tbsp warm water
- 2 tbsp Cointreau
- 1 cup/250 ml heavy/double cream

EMILIAN TRIFLE

Serves: 4

Preparation: 45' + 3–4 h

Cooking: 15'

Level of difficulty: 1

- ½ **cup/100 g sugar**
- **3 egg yolks**
- ½ **cup/75 g all-purpose/plain flour**
- **3 cups/750 ml warm milk**
- **5 oz/150 g semi-sweet/dark chocolate, grated**
- **12 oz/350 g bought fatless sponge cake**
- **8 tbsp Alchermes liqueur or Jamaica rum**
- ¾ **cup/200 g Morello cherry, or plum preserves/jam**

Beat the sugar and egg yolks in a heatproof bowl until very pale and creamy. ♣ Stir in the flour. ♣ Pour in the milk, stirring all the time. ♣ Place the bowl over a saucepan of gently simmering water. Cook, while stirring, until the mixture begins to thicken. ♣ Remove from heat and pour half the custard into another bowl. ♣ Add the chocolate to the custard remaining in the first bowl. Replace over the simmering water, stirring until the chocolate has melted. Remove from heat. ♣ Lightly grease a springform pan. Line the bottom with thin slices of sponge cake. Dip a pastry brush in the liqueur or rum and moisten the cake. ♣ When the plain custard has cooled, spread it over the cake. Cover with a layer of jam, followed by the chocolate custard. Cover with a final layer of sponge cake, briefly dipped in the liqueur or rum. Refrigerate for 3–4 hours. Turn out onto a plate just before serving.

767

CHOCOLATE MOLD

Preheat the oven to 350°/180°C/gas 4. ♣ Mix the flour in a little of the milk until smooth. ♣ Bring the remaining milk to a boil in a saucepan with the sugar and butter. Add the flour mixture and stir well. Remove from heat and set aside to cool. ♣ Beat the egg yolks until pale in color. ♣ Whisk the egg whites until stiff. ♣ Add the cocoa powder to the cooked milk and mix well. Stir in the egg yolks, then carefully fold in the egg whites. ♣ Butter and flour a ring mold and spoon the mixture into it. Bake for 25 minutes. ♣ Remove from the oven and set aside to cool. Turn out of the ring mold and serve.

Serves: 6

Preparation: 30'

Cooking: 25'

Level of difficulty: 3

- ½ cup/75 g all-purpose/plain flour
- 1 cup/250 ml milk
- ⅔ cup/125 g sugar
- 4 tbsp butter
- 4 eggs, separated
- 5 tbsp unsweetened cocoa powder

CRÊPES

Pancake and Crêpe Basics

Pancakes and crêpes are really a type of quick bread. They are made with varying amounts of liquid (usually milk, water, oil, or melted butter) and flour into pourable batters that can be cooked quickly and easily in a special skillet or frying pan. They make excellent breakfast foods (especially with savory toppings) but can also be served at the end of a lunch or dinner as an elegant dessert. Many countries have their own version of the pancake or crêpe, but most are very similar. The difference between a pancake and a crêpe, for example, is minimal. Pancakes are generally a little thicker and are almost always served as sweets. Crêpes, of French origin, are much thinner and are served as savory dishes just as often as they are sweet. Our basic crêpe recipe can be adapted to savory dishes by omitting the sugar. (Try them spread with a little Béchamel sauce and crispy fried bacon, or grated tasty cheese and a generous grinding of black pepper).

Chocolate Pastry Cream

Makes: 2 cups/500 ml

Preparation: 30'

Level of difficulty: 1

- **2 cups/500 ml Vanilla Cream (see page 698)**
- **7 oz/200 g bittersweet/plain chocolate, coarsely chopped**

Prepare the Vanilla Cream, but do not cool. ❧ Melt the chocolate in a double boiler over barely simmering water. ❧ Stir the chocolate into the cream while still hot. ❧ Press a sheet of waxed paper directly onto the surface to prevent a skin from forming. Refrigerate.

Basic Crêpes

Makes:	about 12 crêpes
Preparation:	20'
Cooking:	30'
Level of difficulty:	1

- **3 large eggs**
- **1 cup/150 g all-purpose/plain flour**
- **2 tbsp sugar**
- **dash of salt**
- **1½ cups/375 ml milk**
- **4 tbsp butter**

1 Beat the eggs in a large bowl with a whisk. Place the flour, sugar, and salt in another bowl and pour the milk in gradually, stirring all the time so that no lumps form. Pour into the eggs and beat until smooth. Cover with plastic wrap and refrigerate for 30 minutes.

2 Beat the batter again before using. Melt 1 tablespoon of the butter in an 8-inch (20-cm) skillet (frying pan). Place a ladleful of batter in the skillet. Rotate the skillet so that it covers the bottom in an even layer.

3 Place over medium heat and cook until the bottom is golden brown.

4 Use a wooden spatula to flip the crêpe. Brown on the other side, then slide onto a plate. Add a little more butter, and prepare another crêpe. Repeat until all the batter is used. Pile the crêpes up until ready to use.

773

CHOCOLATE PANCAKES

lace the dry ingredients in a large bowl.
❧ Beat the eggs and milk and then pour
into the dry ingredients. ❧ Mix to a smooth
batter and pour into a jug. ❧ Heat an 8-in (20-cm) skillet (frying pan) and grease it lightly with
butter. ❧ Pour in enough batter to cover the
base of the skillet. ❧ Cook until set and then flip
to cook the other side. ❧ Repeat until all the
batter is used, stacking the pancakes on a plate.
Cover and keep warm. ❧ Fill pancakes with
desired filling, roll up, and serve with a dollop of
whipped cream or yogurt on top.

Serves: 4–6

Preparation: 5'

Cooking: 25'

Level of difficulty: 1

- 1 cup/150 g all-purpose/plain flour
- 1 tsp baking powder
- 2 tbsp sugar
- 2 tbsp unsweetened cocoa powder
- dash of salt
- 2 eggs
- 1 cup/250 ml milk

PANCAKE LAYER CAKE

repare the crêpe batter and use it to make 7 thick pancakes. ❧ Leave the ice cream at room temperature for about 10 minutes to soften. ❧ Place one crêpe on a serving plate. Spread the crêpe with half the cherry ice cream. Place another crêpe on top and spread with a half the lemon ice cream. Place another crêpe on top and spread the crêpe with half the strawberry ice cream. ❧ Repeat so that all the crêpes and ice cream are stacked. Cover with the remaining crêpe. ❧ Decorate the top of the cake with the fresh strawberries. ❧ Serve at once.

Serves: 6

Preparation: 40'

Cooking: 30'

Level of difficulty: 2

- **1 quantity *Basic Crêpes* (see page 773)**
- **1 cup/250 g cherry or black currant ice cream**
- **1 cup/250 g lemon ice cream**
- **1 cup/250 g strawberry ice cream**
- **6 oz/180 g fresh strawberries**

RASPBERRY RICOTTA CRÊPE PARCELS

Prepare the crêpe batter and use it to make 12 crêpes. ❧ Beat the Ricotta and ⅓ of the sugar in a medium bowl until creamy. ❧ Add the candied peel, chocolate, cinnamon, rum, and 2 tablespoons of orange juice. Mix well. ❧ Spoon 1 tablespoon of the filling into the center of each crêpe. Fold up the corners to make small parcels and tie each one with a piece of orange peel. ❧ Heat the remaining sugar and orange juice in a saucepan over medium heat until the sugar has dissolved. ❧ Place the raspberries in a food processor and process until smooth. ❧ Add the raspberries to the sugar and orange mixture. Cook over low heat for about 5 minutes, or until slightly reduced and thickened. ❧ Press through a sieve to remove the seeds and refrigerate for 1 hour. ❧ Serve the crêpes with the raspberry sauce on the side.

Serves: 6

Preparation: 20'

Cooking: 30'

Level of difficulty: 2

- **1 quantity *Basic Crêpes* (see page 773)**
- **8 oz/250 g Ricotta cheese**
- **¾ cup/150 g sugar**
- **3 oz/90 g candied lemon peel, coarsely chopped**
- **3 oz/90 g semisweet chocolate, coarsely chopped**
- **1 tsp ground cinnamon**
- **1 tsp rum**
- **4 tbsp fresh orange juice**
- **peel of 1 large orange, cut in one long thin strip, then cut in pieces 8-in/ 20-cm long**
- **1 lb/500 g fresh or frozen raspberries**

FRESH FRUIT & JAM CRÊPES

Prepare the crêpe batter and use it to make 12 crêpes. ❧ Stir the marmalade and Grand Marnier in a small saucepan over medium heat until warmed. Set aside to cool. Stir in the strawberries. ❧ Place 2 crêpes on each of 6 individual serving dishes. Spoon 1 tablespoon of filling onto one half of each crêpe and fold over. Sprinkle with the sugar and extra strawberries and serve.

Vary the fruit according to the season and what you have on hand in the pantry or garden.

Serves: 6
Preparation: 20'
Cooking: 30'
Level of difficulty: 1

- **1 quantity *Basic Crêpes* (see page 773)**
- **11 oz/300 g orange marmalade**
- **6 tbsp Grand Marnier**
- **8 oz/250 g strawberries, sliced + few extra to decorate**
- **6 tbsp sugar**

BANANA & LEMON CRÊPES

Serves: 6
Preparation: 20'
Cooking: 30'
Level of difficulty: 1

- 1 quantity *Basic Crêpes* (see page 773)
- 1 cup/250 ml heavy/double cream
- 6 tbsp sugar
- 2–3 large bananas, mashed
- 2 tbsp lemon juice

Prepare the crêpe batter and use it to make 12 crêpes. ❧ Beat the cream and 2 tablespoons sugar together until thickened. ❧ Carefully stir in the banana and lemon juice. ❧ Spread each crêpe with 3–4 tablespoons of filling and roll up. Sprinkle with the remaining sugar. ❧ Serve immediately.

For a different flavor, replace the banana with the same amount of crushed pineapple.

781

WALNUT CRÊPES WITH CHOCOLATE SAUCE

Serves: 6

Preparation: 1 h

Cooking: 45'

Level of difficulty: 1

- **1 quantity *Basic Crêpes* (see page 773)**
- **3 oz/90 g raisins**
- **4 tbsp rum**
- **5 oz/150 g walnuts, coarsely chopped**
- **¹/₂ cup/100 g sugar**
- **³/₄ cup/185 ml heavy/double cream**
- **2 tbsp orange zest**
- **1 cup/250 ml milk**
- **2 oz/60 g confectioners'/ icing sugar**
- **4 oz/125 g bittersweet/dark chocolate, grated**
- **4 tbsp unsweetened cocoa powder**
- **2 tbsp rum**
- **2 egg yolks**
- **1 tbsp butter**
- **¹/₂ tsp vanilla extract**
- **2 tbsp butter, melted**
- **confectioners'/ icing sugar, to dust**

Preheat the oven to 375°F/190°C/gas 5. ⚜ Butter a large baking dish. ⚜ Soak the raisins in the rum for 1 hour. ⚜ Whizz the walnuts and sugar in a food processor until finely chopped. ⚜ Place the walnut mixture, cream, orange zest, raisins and rum in a large saucepan. Bring to a boil over medium heat, and cook, stirring constantly, until thickened, about 5 minutes. Set aside. ⚜ Bring the milk and confectioners' sugar to a boil over medium heat. ⚜ Place the chocolate in a heatproof bowl and pour the hot milk over the top. Set aside for 3 minutes, then whisk until the chocolate is melted. ⚜ Whisk the cocoa and rum in a medium bowl. Beat in the egg yolks. Gradually whisk in the chocolate mixture. Return to the saucepan and stir over medium-low heat until thick enough to coat a spatula or wooden spoon, about 3 minutes. ⚜ Stir in 1 tablespoon of butter and the vanilla. ⚜ Spoon 1 tablespoon of the walnut filling onto one quarter of each crêpe. Fold in half and in half again. ⚜ Place the crêpes, overlapping, in the prepared pan. Brush with the melted butter. Bake for 15 minutes. ⚜ Place 2 crêpes on each of 6 individual serving dishes. Dust half of each crêpe with confectioners' sugar and spoon the chocolate sauce over the other half. ⚜ Serve hot.

CRÊPES SUZETTE

Prepare the crêpe batter, mixing in 1 tablespoon of Grand Marnier, and use it to make 12 crêpes. ❧ Rub the sugar lumps with the orange and lemon and set aside for 15 minutes so that the sugar is perfumed with the zest of the fruit. ❧ Combine the butter with the sugar lumps, orange juice, and orange and lemon zest in a large saucepan. Place over low heat and stir until the sugar is melted. Cook for 5 minutes, then stir in 4 tablespoons of Grand Marnier. ❧ Dip the crêpes into the mixture one by one, then fold each one in quarters and arrange on a warm, heatproof serving plate. ❧ Sprinkle with the sugar and the remaining Grand Marnier. Stand well back and light the alcohol with a long match. ❧ Serve while still burning.

These crêpes were invented by French chef Henri Charpentier for Albert, Prince of Wales.

Serves: 6

Preparation: 30' + 15' to rest

Cooking: 40'

Level of difficulty: 2

- 1 quantity **Basic Crêpes** (see page 773)
- 9 tbsp Grand Marnier
- 12 sugar lumps
- 1 orange
- 1 lemon
- $^1/_2$ cup/125 g butter
- 1 cup/250 ml fresh orange juice
- 1 tbsp finely grated orange zest
- 4 tbsp sugar, for sprinkling

PINEAPPLE CRÊPE LAYER CAKE

Prepare the crêpe batter and use it to make 12 crêpes. ❧ Place a crêpe on a serving dish and spread with a layer of Vanilla Cream. Drizzle with a teaspoon of Grand Marnier and add a little pineapple. Place another crêpe on top and repeat until all crêpes have been stacked. ❧ Syrup: Caramelize the sugar in a saucepan over medium-low heat. When deep gold, stir in the orange juice and cook until reduced. ❧ Add the cream and bring to a boil. Boil for 2–3 minutes, then set aside to cool. ❧ Stir in the remaining Grand Marnier, pour over the crêpes and serve.

Serves: 6
Preparation: 25'
Cooking: 35'
Level of difficulty: 2

- 1 quantity *Basic Crêpes* (see page 773)
- 1 quantity *Vanilla Cream* (see recipe, p. 698)
- 1 cup/250 ml Grand Marnier
- 10 oz/300 g canned pineapple rings, chopped
- ¾ cup/150 g sugar
- 1 cup/250 ml fresh orange juice
- 6 tbsp heavy/ double cream

COCONUT CREAM CHOCOLATE CRÊPES

Serves: 6

Preparation: 25'

Cooking: 30'

Level of difficulty: 1

- 1 quantity *Basic Crêpes* (see page 773)
- 1 cup/250 ml heavy/double cream
- 2 tbsp sugar
- 4 oz/125 g freshly grated coconut
- 4 oz/125 g bittersweet/dark chocolate
- coarsely chopped nuts, to decorate

Prepare the crêpe batter and use it to make 12 crêpes. ❧ Whisk the cream and sugar until thickened then stir in the coconut. ❧ Spread each crêpe with 3–4 tablespoons of coconut filling and roll up. ❧ Melt the chocolate in a double boiler over barely simmering water. ❧ Pour the chocolate over the crêpes and decorate with nuts. ❧ Serve immediately.

CRÊPES WITH CARAMELIZED APPLES

Prepare the crêpe batter and use it to make 12 crêpes. Fold into quarters and set aside in a warming oven. ❧ Place the cider, corn syrup, brown sugar, and lemon juice in a saucepan and bring to a boil. Cook for about 10 minutes, or until the mixture has reduced by half. Remove from heat and gradually add 2 tablespoons butter. Set aside. ❧ Heat the remaining butter in a medium skillet (frying pan) over medium heat until melted. ❧ Add the apples and cook, stirring often, until the fruit is tender but not mushy, about 5 minutes. ❧ Sprinkle with the sugar and cook until caramelized and golden, about 10 minutes. Remove from the pan and place around the crêpes. ❧ Pour the syrup over the top and serve immediately.

For best results, prepare the pastry and filling in advance, and assemble the dessert just before serving.

Serves: 6

Preparation: 30'

Cooking: 30'

Level of difficulty: 2

- **1 quantity *Basic Crêpes* (see page 773)**
- **1 cup/250 ml apple cider**
- **4 tbsp corn syrup**
- **1 tbsp brown sugar**
- **1 tbsp lemon juice**
- **4 tbsp cold butter, cut up**
- **3 firm sweet apples (Golden Delicious are a good choice), peeled, cored, and cut into wedges**
- **2 tbsp sugar**

RUSTIC DATE & RAISIN PANCAKES

Serves: 2–4

Preparation: 1 h

Cooking: 1¹/₂ h

Level of difficulty: 2

- 4 oz/125 g dates, pitted and chopped
- 2 oz/60 g raisins
- 1 tbsp finely grated lemon zest
- 6 tbsp rum (or apple juice)
- 4 eggs, separated
- 4 tbsp sugar
- 1 cup/250 ml milk
- 2 tbsp melted butter
- 1 cup/150 g all-purpose/plain flour
- 1 tsp ground cinnamon
- dash of salt
- 2 tbsp butter, softened
- confectioners'/icing sugar, to dust

Place the dates, raisins, lemon juice, and rum (or apple juice) in a medium saucepan and bring to a boil. Remove from heat and set aside. ❧ Beat the egg yolks and sugar in a medium bowl until pale and creamy. ❧ Beat in the milk, melted butter, flour, cinnamon, and salt until just blended. ❧ Beat the egg whites in a separate large bowl until stiff peaks form. Fold the whites into the egg yolk mixture. ❧ Melt 1 tablespoon of butter in a large skillet (frying pan) over medium heat. Pour half of the batter into the skillet. Use a slotted spoon to scoop the dates and raisins out of the rum and sprinkle over the pancake. Rotate to cover the surface. ❧ Cook until the bottom is light golden brown, about 3 minutes. (The top side will be uncooked.) ❧ With a large metal spatula, cut into quarters, turn over, and cut into bite-size pieces. Cook until just brown. ❧ Place on a heatproof plate in a warming oven. Repeat with the remaining batter. ❧ Dust with the confectioners' sugar and serve.

For a rustic version, replace the white flour with whole-wheat flour and add 2 tbsp of butter.

BAKED APRICOT CRÊPES

Prepare the crêpe batter and use it to make 12 crêpes. ❧ Preheat the oven to 375°F/190°C/gas 5. ❧ Butter a large baking dish. ❧ Spoon 1 tablespoon of the preserves onto one quarter of each crêpe. Fold in half, the fold again. Place the crêpes, overlapping, in the prepared pan. Brush with the butter and bake in a preheated oven at for 15 minutes. ❧ Whizz the walnuts and sugar in a food processor until very finely chopped. ❧ Sprinkle the crêpes with the walnut and sugar mixture and serve immediately.

Replace the apricot preserves with the same quantity of other preserves or chocolate Nutella spread.

792

Serves: 6
Preparation: 30'
Cooking: 30'
Level of difficulty: 2

- **1 quantity *Basic Crêpes* (see page 773)**
- **1 cup/250 g apricot preserves/ jam**
- **2 tbsp butter, melted**
- **4 oz/125 g walnuts, coarsely chopped**
- **4 tbsp sugar**

CRÊPES WITH CHOCOLATE MOUSSE

Serves: 6

Preparation: 20' + 1 h to chill

Cooking: 30'

Level of difficulty: 1

- 1 quantity *Basic Crêpes* (see page 773)
- 4 oz/125 g bittersweet/dark chocolate, coarsely chopped
- 4 tbsp butter, softened
- 2 eggs, separated
- 1 cup/200 g sugar
- ¹/₂ cup/125 ml Grand Marnier
- 2 oz/60 g candied orange peel
- ¹/₂ cup/125 ml water
- 2 oranges, peeled and segmented

Prepare the crêpe batter and use it to make 12 crêpes. ❧ Melt the chocolate in a double boiler over barely simmering water. ❧ Beat the egg yolks and sugar in a medium bowl until pale and creamy. ❧ Stir in the chocolate. Sprinkle with the half of the Grand Marnier and stir in the candied peel. ❧ Beat the egg whites in a separate bowl until stiff peaks form. Fold the whites into the chocolate mixture. Cover with plastic wrap and refrigerate for 1 hour. ❧ Place the remaining sugar and Grand Marnier with the water and oranges in a large saucepan. Cook for about 20 minutes, or until well reduced. ❧ Spoon 1 tablespoon of the chocolate mousse onto one quarter of each crêpe. Fold in half, then in half again. ❧ Spoon the syrup over the top and serve.

BAKED MERINGUE CRÊPES FLAMBÉE

Prepare the crêpe batter and use it to make 12 crêpes. ❧ Preheat the oven to 375°F/190°C/gas 5. ❧ Butter a large baking dish. ❧ Place the sugar and water in a medium saucepan over medium heat and cook until the sugar reaches soft-ball stage. ❧ While the sugar is cooling, beat the egg whites in a heatproof bowl until stiff peaks form. ❧ Gradually pour the sugar and water into the egg whites, beating at high speed. ❧ Fold in the nougat. ❧ Spoon the meringue into the center of each crêpe and roll up. Place the crêpes, overlapping, in the prepared pan. Bake for 15 minutes. ❧ Sprinkle with the Grand Marnier. Stand well back and light the alcohol with a long match. ❧ Serve while still burning.

Serves: 6

Preparation: 45'

Cooking: 30'

Level of difficulty: 2

- 1 quantity *Basic Crêpes* (see page 773)
- 1¹⁄₂ cups/300 g sugar
- 4 egg whites
- ¹⁄₂ cup/125 ml water
- 2 oz/60 g chocolate nougat bars, chopped
- 1 cup/250 ml Grand Marnier

CREAMY CRÊPES WITH CHOCOLATE

Serves: 6

Preparation: 30'

Cooking: 30'

Level of difficulty: 1

- **1 quantity *Basic Crêpes* (see page 773)**
- **4 egg yolks**
- **³/₄ cup/150 g sugar**
- **1 tbsp all-purpose/ plain flour**
- **1 tsp vanilla extract**
- **1 cup/250 ml milk**
- **4 oz/125 g bittersweet/dark chocolate, grated**
- **unsweetened cocoa powder, to dust**

Prepare the crêpe batter and use it to make 12 crêpes. ✿ Whisk the egg yolks and sugar in a heavy-bottomed saucepan until creamy. Add in the flour and vanilla and mix well. ✿ Gradually beat in the milk. Cook over medium heat for about 10 minutes, or until thick. ✿ Spoon the filling onto one quarter of each crêpe and sprinkle with a little chocolate. Fold in half, then in half again. ✿ Place on a serving plate and sprinkle with the cocoa. ✿ Serve hot.

For a different flavor, omit the chocolate and sprinkle the filling with 12–15 crushed amaretti cookies.

797

BLUEBERRY BLINTZES

Place the flour, milk, eggs, and 1 tablespoon each of sugar and butter in a food processor or blender and whizz until smooth. Refrigerate for at least 30 minutes before cooking. ❧ Heat 1 tablespoon of butter in a crêpe pan and add 3 tablespoons of batter. Rotate

Unlike crêpes, blintzes are cooked on one side only. They are then wrapped around a filling and fried.

the pan so that it spreads evenly over the bottom. Cook until the top is dry and set and the underside is light golden brown. ❧ Place half of the blueberries, the lemon juice and zest, sugar, ginger, and cinnamon in a saucepan. Bring to a boil over medium-high heat, stirring constantly. Simmer until the fruit has broken down and the mixture is thick. Stir in the remaining blueberries. Cook, stirring constantly, for 1 minute. Cool to room temperature. ❧ Set out the blintzes on a plate, uncooked-side up. Spoon the filling into the center of each blintz. Fold up the sides to form a rectangle. ❧ Melt the butter in a large skillet (frying pan) over medium heat. Add the blintzes, seam-side-down, and fry until golden brown. Drain on paper towels. Serve immediately.

Serves: 6

Preparation: 30' + 30' to chill

Cooking: 30'

Level of difficulty: 2

- $^2/_3$ **cup/100 g all-purpose/plain flour**
- $^1/_2$ **cup/125 ml milk**
- **2 large eggs**
- **1 lb/500 g fresh or frozen blueberries**
- **juice and grated zest of $^1/_2$ lemon**
- **3 tbsp sugar**
- $^1/_2$ **tsp ground ginger**
- $^1/_2$ **tsp ground cinnamon**
- **4 tbsp butter**

CHOCOLATE AMARETTI CRÊPES

Serves: 6

Preparation: 40'

Cooking: 50'

Level of difficulty: 2

- 1 quantity *Basic Crêpes* (see page 773)
- 1 cup/250 ml milk
- 3 egg yolks
- ¹/₂ cup/100 g sugar
- 2 tbsp all-purpose/plain flour
- 3 oz/90 g semisweet /dark chocolate, coarsely chopped
- 1 tbsp almond liqueur
- ¹/₂ cup/125 ml heavy/double cream
- 2 oz/60 g amaretti cookies
- 2 tbsp butter, melted
- sugar, for sprinkling
- 4 tbsp brandy

Prepare the crêpe batter and use it to make 12 crêpes. ❧ Preheat the oven to 375°F/190°C/gas 5. ❧ Butter a large baking dish. ❧ Bring the milk to a boil in a small saucepan over medium heat. ❧ Beat the egg yolks, sugar, and flour in a medium bowl just until blended. Pour in the hot milk. ❧ Return the mixture to the saucepan and boil gently for 2–3 minutes, stirring constantly. ❧ Remove from heat and stir in the chocolate and liqueur. Set aside to cool. ❧ Whip the cream and add it to the chocolate mixture with the amaretti cookies. ❧ Spoon 1 tablespoon of the chocolate mixture onto one quarter of each crêpe. Fold in half, then in half again. ❧ Place the crêpes, overlapping, in the prepared pan. Brush with the butter and sprinkle with the sugar. ❧ Bake for 15 minutes. ❧ Remove from the oven. Sprinkle with the brandy. Stand well back and light the alcohol with a long match. Serve while still burning.

FRUIT-FILLED CRÊPES WITH MERINGUE TOPPING

Prepare the crêpe batter and use it to make 12 crêpes. ♣ Place the pears, peaches, sugar, and butter in a large saucepan. Cook over low heat for about 30 minutes, or until the fruit has broken down. Set aside to cool. ♣ Chop the fruit mixture in a blender or food processor then stir in the amaretti, pine nuts, egg yolk, and almond liqueur. Mix well. ♣ Spread the fruit filling into one half of each crêpe. Fold over. Place the crêpes in a greased ovenproof dish. ♣ Beat the egg whites in a medium bowl until stiff peaks form. Fold in the confectioners' sugar. ♣ Place the jelly in a small saucepan over low heat until warm. Brush the jelly over the crêpes. Spoon the meringue over and smooth. ♣ Place under a hot broiler (grill) and broil until the meringue is golden. ♣ Serve warm.

For an elegant finish to dinner, prepare the crêpes and filling ahead of time and broil just before serving.

Serves: 6
Preparation: 30'
Cooking: 40'
Level of difficulty: 2

- 1 quantity *Basic Crêpes* (see page 773)
- 1 lb/500 g small sweet pears, peeled and sliced
- 1 lb/500 g ripe yellow peaches, peeled and sliced
- $^1/_2$ cup/100 g sugar
- 4 tbsp butter
- 4 oz/125 g amaretti cookies
- 1 egg yolk
- 2 tbsp almond liqueur
- 3 egg whites
- $^2/_3$ cup/100 g confectioners'/ icing sugar
- 4 tbsp apricot jelly/jam

NOUGAT
APPLE CRÊPES

Prepare the crêpe batter and use it to make 12 crêpes. ❧ Preheat the oven to 375°F/190°C/gas 5. ❧ Place the apples, butter, and sugar in a large saucepan. Cover and simmer over low heat, stirring frequently, until the apples have softened but not broken down. Remove from the heat and cool to lukewarm. ❧ Stir in the cream, jelly, nougat, and rum. ❧ Spread the filling over each crêpe and roll up. Sprinkle with the extra sugar. Place on a cookie sheet and bake for about 10 minutes, or until heated through. ❧ Serve hot.

Serves: 4–6

Preparation: 20'

Cooking: 40'

Level of difficulty: 2

- 1 quantity *Basic Crêpes* (see page 773)
- 8 large apples, peeled, cored, and sliced
- 4 tbsp butter
- $1/2$ cup/100 g sugar
- 6 tbsp heavy/double cream
- 4 tbsp apricot jelly/jam
- 4 tbsp almond nougat, crushed
- 6 tbsp rum
- extra sugar, to sprinkle

YOGURT & FRUIT CRÊPES

Serves: 4–6

Preparation: 15'

Cooking: 30'

Level of difficulty: 2

- 1 quantity *Basic Crêpes* (see page 773)
- 2 oz/60 g raspberries
- 2 oz/60 g strawberries
- 1 ripe kiwifruit, coarsely chopped
- 6 tbsp g sugar
- 2 tbsp Kirsch
- ½ cup/125 g yogurt
- ½ cup/125 g whipped cream
- 2 tsp cinnamon
- 3 oz/90 g bittersweet/dark chocolate, grated
- 4 tbsp honey
- 2 tbsp shredded coconut

Prepare the crêpe batter and use it to make 12 crêpes. ❧ Mix the raspberries, strawberries, kiwifruit, sugar, and Kirsch in a large bowl until well mixed. ❧ Add the yogurt, cream, and cinnamon, then stir in the chocolate. ❧ Spread the filling over each crêpe. Fold up the sides to form a rectangle. Place on a serving plate. Brush with the honey and sprinkle with the coconut. ❧ Serve hot.

COCONUT & MANGO CRÊPES

Combine both flours, coconut, and 2 tablespoons sugar in a medium bowl. Add the eggs and milk and whisk until well mixed. ❧ Place the butter in a medium skillet (frying pan) over medium heat and warm until the butter has melted. Pour 2 tablespoons of batter into the skillet and rotate to cover the surface. Cook until light brown. With a large metal spatula, turn over and cook until just brown. Place on a heatproof plate. ❧ Repeat until all the batter is used up. ❧ Spread each crêpe with mango then roll them up, tucking in the ends. Place on a serving dish. ❧ Stir the coconut cream and remaining sugar in a heavy-bottomed saucepan over medium heat until the sugar has dissolved. ❧ Spoon the coconut sauce over the top and serve hot.

804

Serves: 4

Preparation: 25'

Cooking: 30'

Level of difficulty: 2

- $^2/_3$ cup/100 g all-purpose/plain flour
- $^1/_2$ cup/75 g rice flour
- 2 oz/60 g shredded coconut
- 4 tbsp sugar
- 2 eggs, lightly beaten
- 1$^1/_4$ cups/310 ml milk
- $^1/_2$ cup/125 g butter
- 2 mangoes, peeled and chopped
- 1 cup/250 ml coconut cream

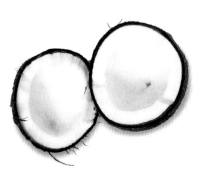

DUSKY CRÊPES

Combine the flour, cocoa, and baking soda in a large bowl. Stir in the sugar and chocolate chips. Make a well in the center and add the milk, cream, egg, and butter until smooth. ❧ Cover and refrigerate for 30 minutes. ❧ Whisk the egg whites until stiff peaks form. Fold into the batter. ❧ Melt the butter in an 8-in (20-cm) skillet (frying pan) over medium heat. Spoon 4 tablespoons of batter into the skillet and rotate to cover the surface. Fry until golden brown. Turn over and fry until just brown. Repeat until all the batter has been made into pancakes. ❧ Stir the sauce ingredients in a saucepan over medium heat until smooth. Spoon over the crêpes and serve hot.

Serves: 4

Preparation: 20' + 30' to chill

Cooking: 35'

Level of difficulty: 2

- 1 cup/150 g all-purpose/plain flour
- 2 tbsp unsweetened cocoa powder
- 1 tsp baking soda
- 2 tbsp sugar
- 4 tbsp chocolate chips
- 1/2 cup/125 ml milk
- 1/2 cup/125 ml heavy/double cream
- 1 egg, beaten
- 1 tbsp butter, melted
- 2 egg whites

SAUCE
- 3 oz/90 g bittersweet/dark chocolate, coarsely chopped
- 1 tbsp butter
- 1 tbsp molasses/treacle
- 2 tbsp brown sugar
- 4 tbsp heavy/double cream

CRÊPES WITH MASCARPONE, RAISINS & RUM

Serves: 6

Preparation: 20'

Cooking: 30'

Level of difficulty: 2

- 1 quantity *Basic Crêpes* (see page 773)
- 1¹/₃ cups/350 g Mascarpone cheese
- ³/₄ cup/150 g sugar
- 3 tbsp dark rum
- grated zest of 1 lemon
- 4 tbsp raisins
- ¹/₃ cup/50 g confectioners'/ icing sugar

repare the crêpe batter and use it to make 12 crêpes. ❧ Combine the Mascarpone, sugar, rum, and lemon zest in a large bowl and beat until soft and creamy. Stir in the raisins. ❧ Fill the crêpes with this mixture, fold them over, and dust with confectioners' sugar. ❧ Serve hot.

CRÊPES WITH CREAM & CANDIED CHESTNUTS

M ix both flours with the eggs, sugar, and melted butter. Add the milk gradually, beating the mixture with a whisk to prevent lumps from forming. ❧ Brush a nonstick skillet (frying pan) with oil and heat to very hot. Pour in a small ladleful of batter, rotating the skillet so that the mixture spreads evenly. Cook the crêpe on both sides without browning. Repeat until all the batter is used. ❧ Whip the cream with the confectioners' sugar and mix the chopped marrons glacés in gently. ❧ Fill the crêpes with this mixture and serve sprinkled with extra confectioners' sugar.

Serves: 8

Preparation: 20'

Cooking: 30'

Level of difficulty: 2

- 1 cup/150 g chestnut flour
- 1 cup/150 g all-purpose/plain flour
- 3 eggs
- 1 tbsp sugar
- 3 tbsp butter
- grated zest of 1 lemon
- 2 cups/500 ml milk
- 1 cup/250 ml heavy/double cream
- 2 tbsp confectioners'/icing sugar
- 1 cup/200 g candied chestnut pieces

DOUBLE CHOCOLATE CRÊPES

Serves: 8

Preparation: 20' + 30'

Cooking: 25'

Level of difficulty: 1

- ²/₃ cup/100 g all-purpose/plain flour
- 3 tbsp unsweetened cocoa powder
- 3 large eggs
- 1¹/₄ cups/310 ml milk
- 4 tbsp sugar
- 2 large oranges
- 2 tbsp Grand Marnier
- ¹/₂ cup/125 g butter

CHOCOLATE SAUCE
- 6 oz/180 g bittersweet/dark chocolate, chopped
- 1¹/₄ cups/310 ml heavy/double cream
- 3 oz/90 g white chocolate, grated
- 8 oz/250 g red or black currants, for decoration

Combine the flour and cocoa in a medium bowl. Make a well in the center and add the eggs, milk, and sugar. Whisk until smooth. Cover and refrigerate for 30 minutes. ❧ Peel and segment the oranges. Place the segments in a medium bowl with the Grand Marnier.

Vary the fruit according to the season. Raspberries and cherries always go well with chocolate.

811

Cover and refrigerate. ❧ Melt the butter in an 8-in (20-cm) skillet (frying pan) over medium heat. Spoon 2 or 3 tablespoons of batter into the skillet and rotate to thinly cover the surface. Fry until golden brown. Repeat until all the batter has been made into crêpes. ❧ With a large metal spatula, turn over and fry until just brown. ❧ Place the orange juice (reserving the oranges), bittersweet chocolate, and ¹/₂ cup (125 ml) of cream in a medium saucepan over medium heat. Cook, stirring constantly, until the chocolate is melted. ❧ Beat the remaining cream until thickened. Place a spoonful of whipped cream in one quarter of each crêpe. Fold in half, then in half again. ❧ Sprinkle with the grated chocolate and drizzle with the sauce. Top with the orange segments and red or black currants. ❧ Serve warm.

SMALL CAKES & COOKIES

CHOCOLATE CHIPS

Preheat the oven to 350°F/180°C/gas 4. ♣ Beat the sugar, butter, flour, salt, and egg yolks in a large bowl with an electric mixer at medium speed until well blended. ♣ Stir in the chocolate chips. ♣ Stir until smooth. ♣ Spoon teaspoonfuls of the mixture onto a buttered baking sheet, pressing down lightly with a fork. ♣ Bake for 12–15 minutes, or until lightly browned. ♣ Cool the cookies on the baking sheet for 3 minutes. Turn out onto racks and let cool completely.

Makes: about 30

Preparation: 10'

Cooking: 12–15'

Level of difficulty: 1

- 1 cup/200 g sugar
- 1 cup/250 g butter, softened
- 1¹/₂ cups/225 g all-purpose/plain flour
- ¹/₂ tsp salt
- 2 egg yolks
- 7 oz/200 g chocolate chips

ALMOND COOKIES

Makes: about 24

Preparation: 10' + 30' to chill

Cooking: 15'

Level of difficulty: 1

- 1²/₃ cups/250 g all-purpose/plain flour
- dash of salt
- ¹/₃ cup/75 g sugar
- ¹/₂ cup/125 g butter, cut up
- 2 egg yolks
- ¹/₃ cup/50 g confectioners'/icing sugar

Preheat the oven to 350°F/180°C/gas 4. ☙ Place the flour and salt into a large bowl. Stir in the sugar. ☙ Make a well in the center and rub in the butter until a dough is formed. ☙ Add the egg yolks and work the dough with your hands until smooth and elastic. ☙ Shape into a ball, wrap in plastic wrap, and refrigerate for 30 minutes. ☙ Discard the wrap and roll the dough out on a lightly floured surface to ¹/₄-in (5-mm) thick. ☙ Use various cookie cutters to stamp out different shapes. ☙ Arrange on a buttered and floured baking sheet ☙ Bake for 15 minutes, or until lightly browned. ☙ Turn out onto racks and let cool completely. Dust with the confectioners' sugar.

FRIED PASTRIES WITH RICOTTA CHEESE

Makes: 12 pastries	
Preparation: 25' + 1 h	
Cooking: 30–40'	
Level of difficulty: 3	

- 1¹/₂ **cups/225 g all-purpose/plain flour**
- **1 egg, separated**
- **3 tbsp sugar**
- **1 tbsp brandy**
- **3 tbsp white wine**
- **2 tbsp shortening, melted and cooled**
- **dash of salt**
- **3 tbsp almond oil**
- **shortening or oil for frying**
- **8 oz/250 g fresh Ricotta cheese**
- **1 cup/150 g confectioners'/icing sugar**
- **6 tbsp chopped mixed candied peel**
- **1 oz/30 g semi-sweet/dark chocolate, finely chopped**

P lace the flour in a bowl and make a well in the center. Add the egg yolk, sugar, brandy, wine, shortening, and salt. ❧ Mix quickly, adding more wine if needed. The dough should be smooth and elastic. ❧ Shape into a ball, wrap in a cloth, and set aside for at least 1 hour. ❧ Roll the dough out thinly and cut into 12 squares. ❧ Rub 12 cannoli tubes with almond oil and wrap the squares diagonally round the tubes, starting with one corner of a square and finishing with the opposite corner. ❧ Lightly beat the egg white and use it to moisten the overlapping surfaces. This will stop them from unwrapping during cooking. ❧ Deep fry, 2–3 at a time, in plenty of very hot shortening or oil, until they are a deep golden brown, with small blisters on the surface. ❧ Lift out with a slotted spoon and drain on paper towels. When cool enough to handle, slide them carefully off the cannoli tubes. ❧ Place the Ricotta in a bowl and beat in the confectioners' sugar until light and fluffy. ❧ Fold in the chocolate and candied peel. ❧ Fill the cases with this mixture. ❧ Sprinkle with extra confectioners' sugar and serve.

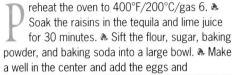

MARGARITA MUFFINS

Makes: about 12 muffins

Preparation: 15'

Cooking: 20'

Level of difficulty: 1

• 2 oz/60 g golden raisins/sultanas
• 2 tbsp tequila
• 2 tbsp freshly squeezed lime juice
• 1²/₃ cups/250 g all-purpose/plain flour
• 3 oz/90 g sugar
• 1 tsp baking powder
• 1 tsp baking soda
• 2 eggs, beaten
• 1 cup/250 ml buttermilk
• 1 tbsp grated lemon zest
• 1 tbsp grated lime zest
• dash of salt

Preheat the oven to 400°F/200°C/gas 6. ❧ Soak the raisins in the tequila and lime juice for 30 minutes. ❧ Sift the flour, sugar, baking powder, and baking soda into a large bowl. ❧ Make a well in the center and add the eggs and buttermilk. Stir in the lemon and lime zest and mix until smooth. ❧ Spoon into greased muffin pans and sprinkle lightly with salt. ❧ Bake for 20 minutes, or until golden brown.

The delicious tang of the lime brings the heady flavors of a thirst-quenching Margarita to mind.

819

CHELSEA BUNS

Use the first 3 ingredients to prepare the yeast as explained on page 250, using 1 teaspoon of the sugar. ❧ In a large bowl, combine the flour with 3 tablespoons of sugar, the salt, nutmeg, cinnamon, and cloves. ❧ Rub 12 oz (350 g) of the butter into the flour. ❧ Make a well in the center and add the yeast mixture and the milk. Mix well, then add the egg. ❧ Knead until smooth and elastic and set aside to rise. ❧ When the rising time has elapsed (about $1^{1}/_2$ hours), transfer the dough to a lightly floured work surface. Knead for 2 minutes, then divide in half. ❧ Working with one portion at a time, roll out on a floured work surface to form a rectangle roughly 10 x 15 in (25 x 38 cm). Sprinkle with half the remaining butter, and half the brown sugar, then half the raisins, and half the candied peel. Then, working from the narrow end, roll up the rectangle of dough. Repeat with the other piece of dough. ❧ Cut each roll into 10 portions and arrange them $^{1}/_2$ in (1 cm) apart on lightly greased baking sheets. Cover with a clean cloth and let rise for 30 minutes, or until the buns are just touching. ❧ Preheat the oven to 400°F/200°C/gas 6. ❧ Bake for about 20 minutes, or until golden brown. ❧ Glaze: Boil 1 tablespoon of the remaining sugar and the second measure of milk until foamy. Brush the hot buns with this glaze. Sprinkle with the remaining sugar.

Makes: about 20 buns

Preparation: 30'

Rising time: $1^{1}/_2$ h

Cooking: 20'

Level of difficulty: 2

- $^{3}/_4$ oz/25 g fresh yeast or $1^{1}/_2$ ($^{1}/_4$ oz) packages active dry yeast
- 6 tbsp warm water
- 6 tbsp sugar
- 4 cups/600 g all-purpose/plain flour
- 1 tsp salt
- 1 tsp nutmeg
- 1 tsp ground cinnamon
- dash of ground cloves
- 2 cups/500 g butter, chopped
- 1 cup/250 ml lukewarm milk
- 1 egg, lightly beaten
- $^{3}/_4$ cup/150 g firmly packed brown sugar
- 3 oz/90 g raisins
- 2 tbsp candied orange or lemon peel
- 2 tbsp milk

PRATO COOKIES

Spread the almonds out in a shallow baking pan and roast at 400°F/200°C/gas 6 for 4–5 minutes. ✿ When cool enough to handle, skin and chop coarsely. ✿ Beat the eggs and sugar together in a large bowl until pale. ✿ Stir in the flour, almonds, and salt gradually, using a fork and then combining by hand. ✿ Knead the mixture quickly but thoroughly on a floured work surface. ✿ Shape the dough into long cylinders about 1/2 in (1 cm) in diameter. ✿ Transfer to a greased and floured cookie sheet. Bake in a preheated oven at 375°F/190°C/gas 5 for 25 minutes. ✿ Remove from the oven and raise the temperature to 400°F/200°C/gas 6. ✿ Slice the cylinders diagonally into pieces 1 1/2 in/4 cm long, and return them to the oven for 10 minutes more, or until pale golden brown.

Makes: about 40

Preparation: 15'

Cooking: 45'

Level of difficulty: 1

• **scant 2 cups/250 g sweet almonds, unpeeled**
• **4 eggs**
• **2 1/2 cups/500 g sugar**
• **4 1/3 cups/500 g all-purpose/plain flour**
• **dash of salt**

ALMOND CRUNCHIES

Makes: about 50

Preparation: 15'

Cooking: 70'

Level of difficulty: 1

• **6 egg whites**
• **7 cups, loosely packed/600 g ground almonds**
• **2¹/₂ cups/500 g sugar**

Preheat the oven to 350°F/180°C/gas 4. ❧ Beat the egg whites in a deep bowl with an electric mixer on high speed until stiff but not dry. ❧ Add the ground almonds and the sugar and fold in carefully. ❧ Transfer to a large bowl over a pan of simmering water. Cover and cook for 20 minutes. ❧ Use a tablespoon to scoop out egg-shaped spoonfuls and place them on a lightly greased and floured cookie sheet. ❧ Bake for 45 minutes, or until golden brown. ❧ Let cool before serving.

CREAM CRESCENTS

These creamy crescents just melt in your mouth!

Preheat the oven to 350°F/180°C/gas 4. ❧ Place the first measure of flour in a bowl and make a well in the center. Add the sugar, butter, lemon zest, egg yolks, and salt. ❧ Work the ingredients together quickly, then add the baking powder. ❧ Roll the dough out to a thickness of ¼ in (5 mm) and cut into rounds using a pastry cutter. ❧ Filling: Whisk the egg yolks and sugar until pale in color, then stir in the flour. ❧ Bring the milk to a boil with the salt and vanilla and stir into the egg mixture. Cook over a low heat and stir constantly until the custard thickens. ❧ Set aside to cool, then cover with a layer of plastic wrap that touches the surface of the custard (to prevent a skin from forming). ❧ Place spoonfuls of the filling on each round of pastry and fold in half to form a crescent-shaped parcel, pressing down on the edges to seal them. ❧ Arrange on a greased and floured cookie sheet and for 20 minutes, or until pale golden brown. ❧ Dust with confectioners' sugar and serve.

Makes: about 20

Preparation: 20'

Cooking: 20'

Level of difficulty: 1

- 3 cups/450 g all-purpose/plain flour
- 1 cup/200 g sugar
- 1 cup/250 g butter, softened
- grated zest of 1 lemon
- 2 egg yolks
- dash of salt
- 3 tsp baking powder

FILLING

- 3 egg yolks
- 3 tbsp sugar
- 3 tbsp all-purpose/plain flour
- 2 cups/500 ml milk
- dash of salt
- vanilla extract
- 6 tbsp confectioners'/icing sugar

MARZIPAN PETITS FOURS

Preheat the oven to 400°F/200°C/gas 6. ❧ Spread the almonds out on a cookie sheet (baking tray) and roast for 3–4 minutes. When roasted, grind in a pestle and mortar and transfer to a bowl. ❧ Lower the oven temperature to 300°F/150°C/gas 2. ❧ Stir in the sugars, orange peel, and almond extract, then carefully fold in the egg white. ❧ Shape the mixture into lozenges or squares and place on rice paper or wafers, trimming off the excess. Place on cookie sheets and let stand in a cool place for about 10 hours. ❧ Bake for 1 hour, reducing the heat if they show signs of browning. They should remain quite soft. ❧ Remove from the oven and dust with extra confectioners' sugar.

Makes: about 20

Preparation: 25' + 10 h to rest

Cooking: 1 h

Level of difficulty: 3

- 1 3/4 **cups/250 g peeled whole almonds**
- 1 cup/200 g sugar
- 1 cup/150 g **confectioners'/icing sugar**
- 2 tbsp **candied orange peel, chopped**
- 1/2 tsp almond **extract**
- 1 **egg white, stiffly beaten**
- **rice paper**

SPICE, HONEY, & NUT COOKIES

Makes: about 25

Preparation: 20'

Cooking: 1¼ h

Level of difficulty: 2

- 1 cup/200 g sugar
- 6 tbsp clear, liquid honey
- 2 cups/300 g all-purpose/plain flour
- ½ cup/60 g chopped walnuts
- 4 tbsp finely chopped candied orange and lemon peel
- 1 tsp freshly ground anise seeds
- freshly ground coriander seeds
- 1 tbsp butter

Preheat the oven to 350°F/180°C/gas 4. ❧ Using a double boiler or a bowl over barely simmering water, heat the sugar and honey together. When a thread of honey forms when a spoonful is lifted above the bowl, remove from the heat and stir in the flour, walnuts, peel, anise, and coriander. ❧ Flour your hands to stop the mixture sticking to them and break off pieces of the dough, rolling them into small cylinders. Cut them into slices about 1-in (2.5-cm) thick and form into curved shapes. ❧ Place on a greased and floured cookie sheet and bake for 1 hour, or until pale golden brown. ❧ Let cool before serving.

ALMOND CRISPIES

Makes: about 20

Preparation: 20'

Cooking: 20'

Level of difficulty: 1

- **1 cup/150 g whole blanched almonds**
- **³/₄ cup/150 g sugar**
- **²/₃ cup/100 g all-purpose/plain flour**
- **4 tbsp butter**
- **1 tsp ground cinnamon**
- **1 egg**
- **grated zest of ¹/₂ lemon**

Preheat the oven to 350°F/180°C/gas 4. ♣ Spread the almonds on a large cookie sheet and toast for around 8 minutes, or until the almonds are just beginning to color. Remove from the oven and set aside to cool. ♣ Lower heat to 300°F/150°C/gas 2. ♣ Combine the cooled almonds with half the sugar in a food processor fitted with a steel blade. Process until the almonds are finely ground. ♣ Place the almonds in a mixing bowl and stir in three-quarters of the flour, the butter, cinnamon, egg, and lemon zest. Mix well to obtain a smooth, firm dough. ♣ Use the remaining flour to lightly flour a clean work surface and shape the dough into a long sausage. Slice crosswise to obtain small, oval cookies. Sprinkle with the remaining sugar. ♣ Transfer the cookies to a greased and floured cookie sheet and bake for 20 minutes, or until the cookies are light golden brown. ♣ Remove from the sheet and set aside to cool on a wire rack. After a few hours they will be crisp. Store in an airtight cookie jar.

These little cookies are good with coffee or tea, or with a sweet dessert wine.

829

FOOLPROOF MERINGUES

Preheat the oven to 200°F/100°C/gas ½. ❧ Place the egg white in a large bowl (or the bowl of your electric beater) and cover it with the sugar. ❧ Add the vinegar and then the boiling water. ❧ Beat with a whisk or electric beater until very stiff. ❧ Pipe or place teaspoonfuls of the mixture onto a greased cookie sheet and bake for 50–60 minutes, or until crisp and dry. Turn off the heat and leave in the oven to cool. ❧ Store in an airtight container.

These meringues are so simple to make and can be served in pairs, filled with whipped cream.

Makes: 12–14
Preparation: 15–20'
Cooking: 50–60'
Level of difficulty: 1

- **1 egg white**
- **¾ cup/150 g superfine/caster sugar**
- **1 tsp vinegar**
- **2 tbsp boiling water**

CHOCOLATE HEDGEHOGS

Preheat the oven to 350°F/180°C/gas 4. ❧ Melt the butter, sugar, and syrup. ❧ Add the baking soda dissolved in the milk. ❧ Sift the flour, baking powder, and cocoa into a large bowl and add the remaining dry ingredients. ❧ Gradually pour in the butter mixture, mixing well. ❧ Place in spoonfuls on a greased cookie sheet and press each one firmly with a fork. ❧ Bake until well cooked and crisp. Cool and store in an airtight container.

Makes: about 35

Preparation: 15'

Cooking: 15'

Level of difficulty: 1

- ¹/₂ **cup/125 g butter**
- ²/₃ **cup/125 g sugar**
- **1 tbsp corn/golden syrup**
- **1 tsp baking soda**
- **1 tbsp milk**
- **1¹/₃ cups/200 g all-purpose/plain flour**
- **1 tsp baking powder**
- **1 tbsp unsweetened cocoa powder**
- **4 oz/125 g corn flakes**
- **2 tbsp rolled oats**
- **2 tbsp dessicated coconut**

MOCHA CHOCOLATE COOKIES

Preheat the oven to 325°F/160°C/gas 3. ❧ Beat the butter and sugar in a medium bowl with an electric mixer until pale and creamy. ❧ Add the coffee and vanilla and mix well. ❧ Sift in the flour, baking powder, and salt and mix again. ❧ Roll into small balls and place on a greased cookie sheet. ❧ Flatten slightly with the heel of your hand and press a piece of chocolate into the top of each cookie. ❧ Bake for 15–20 minutes, or until golden brown. ❧ Cool on a rack and store in an airtight container.

For a different flavor, replace the chocolate with pieces of candied ginger, glacé cherries, or dates.

Makes: about 30

Preparation: 15'

Cooking: 15–20'

Level of difficulty: 1

- ¹/₂ **cup/125 g butter**
- ³/₄ **cup/150 g sugar**
- **2 tsp coffee extract (or 2 tsp instant coffee dissolved in 1 tbsp boiling water)**
- **1 tsp vanilla extract**
- **1 cup/150 g all-purpose/plain flour**
- **1 tsp baking powder**
- **dash of salt**
- **30 thin chocolate squares (or chocolate buttons, dark or white)**

HEAVENLY MOMENTS

Preheat the oven to 325°F/160°C/gas 3. ❧ Beat the butter and sugar in a medium bowl with an electric mixer until pale and creamy. ❧ Add the flour and custard powder, followed by the orange juice. Mix well. ❧ Form into small balls and place on a greased cookie sheet. ❧ Flatten slightly with a fork. ❧ Bake for about 20 minutes, or until pale golden brown. ❧ Cool on a wire rack. ❧ Filling: Place the butter, confectioners' sugar, custard powder, and orange zest in a small bowl and beat until smooth. ❧ Stick pairs of cookies together with a generous amount of filling. ❧ Store in an airtight container.

Heavenly Moments are irresistible!
Forget about the calories and enjoy them!

Makes: about 15

Preparation: 15'

Cooking: 20'

Level of difficulty: 2

- ²/₃ cup/150 g butter
- ¹/₃ cup/50 g confectioners'/icing sugar
- 1¹/₃ cups/200 g all-purpose/plain flour
- ¹/₃ cup/50 g custard powder
- 1 tbsp fresh orange juice

FILLING

- 2 tbsp butter, melted
- ²/₃ cup/100 g confectioners'/icing sugar
- 1 tbsp custard powder
- grated zest of ¹/₂ orange

AFGHANS

P reheat the oven to 350°F/180°C/gas 4. ❧
Beat the butter and sugar in a medium bowl
with an electric mixer until pale and creamy.
❧ Add the flour and cocoa, followed by the
cornflakes. Mix well. ❧ Place spoonfuls of the
mixture on a greased cookie sheet. ❧ Bake for
15 minutes, or until browned. ❧ Cool on a wire
rack. ❧ Icing: Place the butter, water, cocoa,
confectioners' sugar, and vanilla in a small bowl
and beat until smooth. ❧ Ice the cooled cookies
and press a half walnut into the top of each. ❧
Store in an airtight container.

Makes: about 30

Preparation: 15'

Cooking: 15'

Level of difficulty: 1

- ³/₄ cup/225 g butter, softened
- 6 tbsp sugar
- 1¹/₃ cups/200 g all-purpose/plain flour
- 2 tbsp unsweetened cocoa powder
- 1³/₄ oz/50 g corn flakes, crushed slightly

ICING

- 2 tbsp butter
- 1 tbsp boiling water
- 1 tbsp unsweetened cocoa powder
- 1¹/₃ cups/200 g confectioners'/icing sugar
- ¹/₂ tsp vanilla extract

- 30 walnut halves

SHREWSBURY COOKIES

Preheat the oven to 350°F/180°C/gas 4. ❧ Beat the butter and sugar in a medium bowl with an electric mixer until pale and creamy. ❧ Add the egg and almond extract and beat again. ❧ Add the flour and baking powder. ❧ Roll out on a floured board and cut into rounds with a pastry cutter. ❧ Make a small hole (an apple corer is good for this) in the center of half of them. ❧ Place on a greased cookie sheet and bake for 15–20 minutes, or until pale golden brown. ❧ When cool, stick the pairs together with the raspberry preserves. ❧ Store in an airtight container.

Shrewsbury Cookies, as the name implies, come from the English town of Shrewsbury.

Makes: about 15
Preparation: 15'
Cooking: 15–20'
Level of difficulty: 2

- ¹/₂ **cup/125 g butter**
- ²/₃ **cup/125 g sugar**
- **1 egg**
- ¹/₂ **tsp almond extract**
- 2¹/₂ **cups/225 g all-purpose/plain flour**
- **1 tsp baking powder**
- **6 oz/180 g raspberry preserves/jam**

SHORTBREAD

P reheat the oven to 300°F/150°C/gas 2. ☙
Beat the butter and sugar in a medium bowl
with an electric mixer until pale and creamy.
☙ Add the flour and cornstarch and beat until well
mixed. ☙ Roll out on a floured board and cut into

Shortbread, originally from Scotland, is now enjoyed all over the world. It is not hard to make.

squares. ☙ Place
on a cookie sheet
and prick all over with a fork. ☙ Bake for 20–25
minutes, or until golden but not browned. ☙ Cool
on a rack and store in an airtight container.

Makes: about 30

Preparation: 10'

Cooking: 25'

Level of difficulty: 1

- 1 cup/250 g butter
- 1 cup/150 g
  confectioners'/
  icing sugar
- 2½ cups/225 g all-
  purpose/plain flour
- 1 cup/150 g
  cornstarch/
  cornflour

GINGERNUTS

P reheat the oven to 350°F/180°C/gas 4. ✿
Beat the butter, sugar, and corn syrup in a
medium bowl with an electric mixer until
pale and creamy. ✿ Add the egg and beat again. ✿
Add the flour, ginger, baking soda, and cinnamon

Everyone loves a crunchy ginger cookie, so make a batch of these before a holiday weekend.

and mix well.
✿ Place in
teaspoonfuls on a greased cookie sheet, and
flatten slightly with a fork. ✿ Bake for 10–12
minutes, or until golden brown. ✿ Cool on a rack
and store in an airtight container.

Makes: about 30

Preparation: 15'

Cooking: 10–12'

Level of difficulty: 1

- ¹/₂ **cup/125 g butter**
- 1¹/₄ **cups/250 g sugar**
- 1 tbsp corn/golden syrup
- 1 egg, beaten
- 2¹/₂ **cups/225 g all-purpose/plain flour**
- 2 tsp ground ginger
- 1 tsp baking soda
- ¹/₂ **tsp ground cinnamon**

ANZAC COOKIES

Preheat the oven to 350°F/180°C/gas 4. ❧ Place the oats, coconut, flour, and sugar in a large bowl. ❧ Stir in the butter. ❧ In a small bowl, combine the corn syrup, water, and baking soda and pour into the dry ingredients and butter.

These cookies from Down Under are named after the 1918 Australian and New Zealand Army Corps.

Mix well. ❧ Place teaspoons of the mixture on a cookie sheet, leaving room for spreading. ❧ Bake for about 15 minutes, or until pale golden brown. ❧ Cool on a rack and store in an airtight container.

Makes: about 40
Preparation: 10'
Cooking: 15'
Level of difficulty: 1

- 4 oz/125 g rolled oats
- 4 oz/125 g dessicated coconut
- 1 cup/150 g all-purpose/plain flour
- ¹/₂ cup/100 g sugar
- ²/₃ cup/150 g butter, melted
- 1 tbsp corn/golden syrup
- 2 tbsp boiling water
- 1 tsp baking soda

BRAN COOKIES

Makes: about 30

Preparation: 15'

Cooking: 15'

Level of difficulty: 1

- ¹/₂ cup/125 g butter
- 6 tbsp sugar
- 1 egg
- ²/₃ cup/100 g all-purpose/plain flour
- 1 tsp baking powder
- dash of salt
- 1 cup/100 g bran
- ²/₃ cup/100 g whole-wheat flour

Preheat the oven to 350°F/180°C/gas 4. ❧ Beat the butter and sugar in a medium bowl with an electric mixer until pale and creamy. ❧ Add egg and beat well. ❧ Add the all-purpose flour, baking powder, and salt, followed by the bran and whole-wheat flour. ❧ Mix very well, using your hands to knead the mixture. ❧ Roll out on a floured board and cut into thin rounds with a pastry cutter. ❧ Place on a cookie sheet and bake for 15 minutes, or until pale golden brown. ❧ Cool on a rack and store in an airtight container.

Spread the bran cookies with butter, a slice of cheese, or just enjoy them as they are.

SUGAR COOKIES

Preheat the oven to 350°F/180°C/gas 4. ♣ Beat the butter and sugar in a medium bowl with an electric mixer until pale and creamy. ♣ Add the egg and beat again. ♣ Add the flour and cocoa and mix well. ♣ Form into small balls and roll *Children of all ages will love these cookies with their sugary coating.* in the second measure of sugar. ♣ Place on a greased cookie sheet and flatten slightly with a fork. ♣ Bake for 15–20 minutes, or until golden brown. ♣ Cool on a rack and store in an airtight container.

Makes: about 30
Preparation: 15'
Cooking: 15–20'
Level of difficulty: 1

- ¹/₂ **cup/125 g butter**
- ³/₄ **cup/150 g sugar**
- **1 egg**
- **2¹/₂ cups/225 g all-purpose/plain flour**
- **1 heaped tbsp unsweetened cocoa powder**
- **6 tbsp sugar**

JAM-FILLED TURNOVERS

Makes: about 14

Preparation: 1 h + 1 h to rest

Cooking: 30'

Level of difficulty: 2

- 3 cups/450 g all-purpose/plain flour
- 1 cup/200 g sugar
- dash of salt
- ²/₃ cup/150 g butter, cut up
- 3 eggs
- 3 tbsp Jamaica rum
- 1¹/₂ cups/450 g Morello cherry or plum jam
- 4 tbsp confectioners'/icing sugar

Preheat the oven to 350°F/180°C/gas 4. 🍒 🍒 Combine the flour, sugar, and salt in a bowl. Make a well in the center and add the butter, eggs, and rum. Combine well, without working the dough too much; it should be just smooth. 🍒 Shape into a ball, cover with plastic wrap, and let rest for 1 hour. 🍒 Roll the dough out to just under ¹/₄ in (5 mm) thick. Use a pastry cutter to cut out 3 in (8 cm) disks. 🍒 Place a teaspoon of jam in the center of each and fold it in half to form a half-moon shape. Press the edges together to seal. 🍒 Place the filled turnovers on a greased and floured cookie sheet. 🍒 Bake for 30 minutes. 🍒 Cool on a rack, dust with confectioners' sugar, and store in an airtight container.

CORNMEAL, PINE NUT, & RAISIN COOKIES

Preheat the oven to 400°F/200°C/gas 6. ✿ Soak the raisins in water, drain well, and squeeze out excess moisture. ✿ Sift the cornmeal and flour into a large bowl. Combine with the sugar, salt, and lemon zest. ✿ Make a well in the center and add the butter and milk. ✿ Gradually combine these ingredients with the flour, adding a little more milk if necessary. The dough should be firm. ✿ Work the dough, incorporating the raisins and pine nuts. ✿ Break off pieces of dough about the size of a large walnut. Shape into balls, then flatten slightly. ✿ Place them, well spaced out, on a greased and floured cookie sheet (baking tray). ✿ Bake for 15 minutes, or until pale golden brown. ✿ Cool on a rack. Dust with sifted confectioners' sugar and store in an airtight container.

These tasty delicacies made with cornmeal are an old specialty of central Italy.

Serves: 6

Preparation: 40'

Cooking: 15'

Level of difficulty: 1

- ¹/₂ cup/100 g golden raisins/sultanas
- 2 cups/300 g yellow cornmeal
- 2 cups/7 oz/200 g all-purpose/plain flour
- ¹/₂ cup/100 g sugar
- dash of salt
- grated zest of 1 lemon
- ²/₃ cup/150 g butter
- 4 tbsp milk
- 4 tbsp pine nuts
- confectioners'/icing sugar for dusting

SWEET RINGS

Serves: about 45

Preparation: 15' + 1 h
to rest

Cooking: 25'

Level of difficulty: 1

- **2 cups/300 g all-purpose/plain flour**
- **1 cup/200 g sugar**
- **2–3 drops vanilla extract**
- **1 tsp ground cinnamon**
- **finely grated zest of 1 lemon**
- **1 tsp baking powder**
- **3 tbsp extra-virgin olive oil**
- **2 eggs**

Preheat the oven to 400°F/200°C/gas 6. ✿ Place the flour, sugar, vanilla, cinnamon, lemon zest, and baking powder in a mixing bowl. Stir in the oil and eggs and mix for about 5–8 minutes with a wooden spoon. Cover with a clean cloth and let rest for 1 hour. ✿ Lightly flour a clean work surface and shape pieces of dough into long, thin sausages. Cut into lengths of about 4 in (10 cm) and press the ends of each length together to form a ring. ✿ Transfer the rings to a greased and floured cookie sheet. ✿ Bake for 25 minutes, or until pale golden brown. ✿ Cool on a rack and store in an airtight container.

These simple and delicious little cookies are Italian biscotti popular in the area around Rome.

AMARETTI COOKIES

Preheat the oven to 450°F/230°C/gas 7. ❧ In a food processor fitted with a steel blade, combine the almonds and a little of the sugar and process until the almonds are ground to a powder. ❧ Place the ground almonds in a bowl and add half the remaining sugar, then one of the egg whites. Mix well then add the remaining sugar, the second egg white, and the almond extract. Mix until smooth. ❧ Roll the dough into sausage shapes about 2 in (5 cm) in diameter. Cut these into slices about ½-in (1-cm) thick, form into balls and squash them slightly. ❧ Place on a greased cookie sheet, dust with confectioners' sugar and bake for 30 minutes, or until pale golden brown. ❧ Cool on a rack and store in an airtight container.

The original recipe includes a small quantity of bitter almonds, but these are not available everywhere.

Makes: *about 30*
Preparation: *20'*
Cooking: *30'*
Level of difficulty: *2*

- **1½ cups/180 g sweet almonds toasted**
- **2 cups/300 g confectioners'/icing sugar**
- **2 egg whites**
- **½ tsp almond extract**

PEANUT BUTTER COOKIES

Preheat the oven to 325°F/160°C/gas 3. ♣ Sift the flour and baking soda into a large bowl. ♣ Add the sugars and combine. ♣ Stir in the peanut butter, butter, and egg, and mix well. ♣ Form into small balls and place on a greased cookie sheet . ♣ Flatten slightly with a fork. ♣ Bake for 15 minutes, or until pale golden brown. ♣ Cool on a wire rack and store in an airtight container.

Lovers of peanut butter will relish these cookies. Use the crunchy kind for a coarser texture.

Makes: about 30 cookies

Preparation: 15'

Cooking: 15'

Level of difficulty: 1

- 1 ¹/₃ cups/200 g all-purpose/plain flour
- 1 tsp baking soda
- ¹/₂ cup/100 g sugar
- ¹/₂ cup/100 g firmly packed brown sugar
- 4 tbsp peanut butter
- 4 tbsp butter, melted
- 1 egg, beaten

SWEET CRISPS

Makes: about 60 cookies

Preparation: 40' + 2½ h + 2 days'

Cooking: 20'

Level of difficulty: 3

- 3 cups/450 g all-purpose/plain flour
- ¾ cup/200 ml milk
- ½ oz/15 g fresh yeast or 1 (¼ oz) packets active dry yeast
- 4 tbsp sugar
- dash of salt
- 6 tbsp butter, softened
- 1 egg white, stiffly whisked

Preheat the oven to 350°F/180°C/gas 4. ❧ Place a quarter of the flour in a bowl and make a well in the center. ❧ Heat half the milk until tepid and mix with the yeast in a small bowl until it dissolves. ❧ Pour the yeast and milk into the flour and mix to obtain a fairly firm dough. ❧ Knead the dough on a floured work surface and shape into a ball. Place in a floured bowl, covered with a cloth, for 30 minutes. ❧ Sift the remaining flour into a bowl and stir in the sugar and salt. Place the risen dough in the center, then add the butter and egg white. Knead, adding as much milk as required to form a soft dough. ❧ Divide the dough in four and shape into small sausages. Transfer to lightly floured cookie sheets. Cover with a clean cloth and let rise for 2 hours. ❧ Bake for 10 minutes, or until golden brown. ❧ Cover and set aside to rest for 2 days. ❧ Cut into slices ⅛-in (3-mm) thick. Bake in a preheated oven at 325°F/160°C/gas 3 for 10 minutes. Turn after 5 minutes. The cookies should be pale golden brown. ❧ Cool on a wire rack and store in an airtight container.

UNCOOKED CHOCOLATE SLICE

P lace the cookies in a large bowl and crush until they are fine crumbs. ❧ Melt $^1/_2$ cup (125 g) of butter in a saucepan over low heat. ❧ Stir in the sugar, 1 tablespoon of cocoa, and the egg. ❧ Cook for 2 minutes over low heat stirring all the time. ❧ Pour the chocolate and egg mixture into the crushed cookies and mix well. ❧ Lightly butter a shallow rectangular dish, about 8 x 12-in (20 x 30-cm). ❧ Spoon the mixture in the dish and press down evenly with your fingers. ❧ Refrigerate for at least 2 hours. ❧ Place the confectioners' sugar and remaining butter and cocoa powder in a small bowl. ❧ Pour in the water and stir well until smooth and creamy. ❧ Spread the icing over the chocolate slice, cut into squares, and decorate with the walnut pieces.

Makes: 18 squares

Preparation: 20' + 2 h

Level of difficulty: 1

- 8 oz/250 g plain sweet cookies/ biscuits
- $^2/_3$ cup/150 g butter
- 6 tbsp sugar
- 3 tbsp unsweetened cocoa powder
- 1 egg
- $1^1/_4$ cups/180 g confectioners'/ icing sugar
- 1 tbsp boiling water
- $^1/_2$ cup/60 g coarsely chopped walnut pieces

DOUBLE CHOCOLATE BROWNIES

Makes: 20 squares

Preparation: 20'

Cooking: 25'

Level of difficulty: 2

- **4 oz/125 g semi-sweet/dark chocolate**
- **$^1/_2$ cup/125 g butter**
- **$1^1/_4$ cups/250 g sugar**
- **1 cup/150 g all-purpose/plain flour**
- **1 tsp baking powder**
- **2 large eggs, beaten**
- **3 oz/90 g semi-sweet/dark chocolate, grated**

P reheat the oven to 325°F/160°C/gas 3. ❧ Grease a shallow, rectangular baking pan, about 8 x 12-in (20 x 30-cm), and line with waxed paper. ❧ Melt the first measure of chocolate with the butter in a double-boiler over simmering water. ❧ When melted, remove from the heat and add the sugar, flour, baking powder, and eggs. ❧ Mix until smooth. ❧ Pour into the prepared pan and bake for 25 minutes, or until a skewer inserted into the center comes out clean. ❧ Remove from the oven and sprinkle with the grated chocolate, so that the chocolate melts. ❧ Leave to cool then cut into 20 squares with a serrated knife.

CHOCOLATE TRUFFLES

B eat the butter and confectioners' sugar until pale and creamy. ✤ Beat in the egg yolks one at a time. ✤ Bring the cream to a boil in a small saucepan, add the sugar and stir until dissolved. ✤ Pour the boiling cream into the butter mixture, stir in the grated chocolate, and nuts, and refrigerate for at least 2 hours. ✤ Use a tablespoon to form the mixture into balls and roll these in the cocoa powder. ✤ Refrigerate for at least 2 more hours before serving.

Makes: 30 truffles

Preparation: 30' + 4 h to chill

Level of difficulty: 1

- **4 tbsp butter**
- **$^1/_3$ cup/50 g confectioners'/ icing sugar**
- **2 egg yolks**
- **$^1/_3$ cup/100 ml light/single cream**
- **2 tbsp sugar**
- **11 oz/300 g bittersweet/dark chocolate**
- **4 tbsp unsweetened cocoa powder**

CANDIED GRAPEFRUIT

C ut off the top and bottom of the grapefruit, leaving about $1/2$-in (1 cm) of the flesh attached. Cut off the remaining rind in four parts, leaving about $1/2$-in (1 cm) of the flesh attached. ❧ Cut the pieces of rind and fruit into $1/2$-in (1 cm) pieces. ❧ Place them in a large saucepan and cover with cold water. Bring to a boil. Drain well and repeat twice. This will remove the bitterness. ❧ Return the grapefruit to the saucepan. Pour in the water and 1 cup (200 g) sugar. Place over medium heat and, stirring constantly, bring to a boil. Continue cooking for about 30 minutes, or until the grapefruit is opaque and the liquid has evaporated. ❧ Set aside to cool and dry. ❧ Place the remaining sugar on a small plate and dip the grapefruit in to cover.

Makes: about 60
Preparation: 30'
Cooking: 30'
Level of difficulty: 2

- **4 grapefruit**
- **4 cups/1 liter water**
- **1$1/2$ cups/300 g sugar**

MINI RASPBERRY TARTS

Serves: 6–8

Preparation: 25' + 30' to rest

Cooking: 15'

Level of difficulty: 2

- 7 oz/200 g frozen puff pastry, thawed
- 1 cup/250 ml heavy/double cream
- 1 tbsp confectioners'/icing sugar
- 7 oz/200 g raspberries
- 2 tbsp apricot jelly/jam
- 1 tbsp water

Rinse 8–10 2½-in (6-cm) tartlet pans with cold water. ❧ Roll the pastry to ⅛ in (3 mm) thick on a lightly floured work surface. Using a pastry cutter, cut out rounds to fit the pans. Prick the pastry with a fork. Set aside for 30 minutes. ❧ Preheat the oven to 400°F/200°C/gas 6. ❧ Bake for 15 minutes, or until golden brown. Cool on a rack. ❧ Whisk the cream and confectioners' sugar in a medium bowl until thick. Spoon into a pastry bag and pipe into the tarts. ❧ Place the raspberries on top. ❧ Place the apricot jam and water in a small saucepan. Bring to a boil. Remove from the heat and brush over the raspberries.

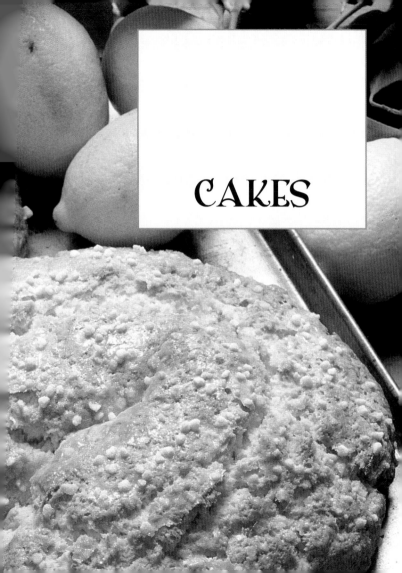

CAKES

MIMOSA CAKE

Prepare the Sponge Cake and the Vanilla Cream. ❧ When the sponge has cooled, cut it crosswise into three layers, one slightly thinner than the others. ❧ Carefully cut the outer crust off the thinnest layer and either crumble into large crumbs or cut into tiny cubes. ❧ Mix the Grand Marnier with the sugar and water and soak one of the thicker layers in this. Place on a serving dish and spread with half the Vanilla Cream, mounding it up slightly in the center. ❧ Cover with the remaining layer of sponge cake and spread the remaining pastry cream over the top and sides. ❧ To finish, sprinkle the cake with the crumbs or tiny cubes to achieve the classic mimosa effect.

Serves: 6–8

Preparation: 10'

Level of difficulty: 2

- 1^{1}/$_{2}$ quantities *Sponge Cake* (see page 878)
- 1 quantity *Vanilla Cream* (see page 698)
- ^{1}/$_{2}$ cup/125 ml Grand Marnier
- ^{1}/$_{2}$ cup/100 g sugar
- ^{3}/$_{4}$ cup/200 ml water

POOR MAN'S CAKE

Serves: 6

Preparation: 15' + 1 h to soak

Cooking: 30'

Level of difficulty: 1

- **¹/₂ cup/125 ml dark Jamaica rum**
- **7 oz/200 g golden raisins/sultanas**
- **12 oz/350 g stale white bread**
- **4 cups/1 liter milk**
- **¹/₃ cup/100 g butter**
- **1¹/₄ cups/250 g sugar**
- **5 eggs**
- **grated zest of 1 lemon**
- **butter and fine dry bread crumbs for the cake pan**

Preheat the oven to 350°F/180°C/gas 4. ❧ Place the rum and raisins in a bowl and soak for 30 minutes. ❧ Cut the bread into small pieces and place in a large bowl. ❧ Bring the milk to a boil, add the butter and sugar, and stir briefly. Pour over the bread. ❧ When the bread has absorbed all the milk (this will take about 30 minutes), add the lightly beaten eggs, the drained raisins, and lemon zest. ❧ Mix well and transfer to a 10 in (25 cm) springform pan. ❧ Bake for 30 minutes, or until pale golden brown. ❧ Serve hot or at room temperature.

This cake comes from Italy, where it was popular with poor people who could afford its simple ingredients.

HAZELNUT CAKE

Preheat the oven to 325°F/160°C/gas 3. ❧ Place both flours and the baking powder in a large bowl. ❧ Chop the hazelnuts finely in a food processor, then add to the bowl with the salt. ❧ Beat the eggs with the sugar in a separate bowl with an electric beater until pale and creamy. ❧ Continue beating while gradually adding the butter, a piece at a time. ❧ Gradually add the mixed flours, beating them in 1 tablespoon at a time. ❧ Beat in the rum. ❧ Grease and lightly flour a 9-in (23-cm) springform pan. ❧ Spoon the batter into the prepared pan. ❧ Bake for 35–40 minutes, or until a skewer inserted into the center comes out clean. ❧ Let cool in the pan for 10 minutes, then turn out onto a wire rack.

Serves: 6–8

Preparation: 25'

Cooking: 35–40'

Level of difficulty: 2

- 1 cup/150 g all-purpose/plain flour
- 1 cup/150 g cornstarch/corn flour
- 2¹/₂ tsp baking powder
- 7 oz/200 g shelled hazelnuts
- dash of salt
- 3 large eggs
- 1 cup/200 g sugar
- ²/₃ cup/150 g butter, chopped in small pieces
- 3 tbsp rum

PIEDMONTESE CHOCOLATE CAKE

Serves 6

Preparation: 30'

Cooking: 45'

Level of difficulty: 3

- ◆ 4 eggs, separated, whites beaten to stiff peaks
- ◆ 1 cup/150 g confectioners'/icing sugar
- ◆ 1 cup/150 g all-purpose/plain flour
- ◆ 5 tbsp cocoa powder
- ◆ 4 tbsp butter, melted

CREAM
- ◆ 2 egg yolks
- ◆ ³/₄ cup/150 g sugar
- ◆ ¹/₂ cup/75 g all-purpose/plain flour
- ◆ 7 tbsp butter
- ◆ 4 oz/125 g semi-sweet/dark chocolate, grated
- ◆ ¹/₂ tsp vanilla extract
- ◆ 2 cups/500 ml milk
- ◆ 4 tbsp toasted, shelled almonds

Preheat the oven to 350°F/180°C/gas 4. ❧ Beat the egg yolks and confectioners' sugar in a large bowl until pale and creamy. ❧ Add the flour and cocoa powder and mix well. ❧ Fold in the egg whites, followed by the melted butter. ❧ Grease and flour a 9 in (23 cm) springform pan. Spoon the batter into the prepared pan and bake for 35–40 minutes, or until a skewer inserted into the center comes out clean. ❧ Cool on a rack. ❧ Cream: Beat the egg yolks with the sugar until pale and creamy. ❧ Stir in the flour, butter, chocolate, and vanilla, then gradually add the milk. ❧ Place over low heat and stir continuously until thick and creamy. The mixture must not boil. When thick, set aside to cool a little. ❧ When the cake is cool, cut in half horizontally and cover one half with half the chocolate cream. Place the other half on top and cover with the remaining chocolate cream. ❧ Sprinkle with the almonds and serve.

CAKES

CHEWY FRUIT & SPICE CAKE WITH CHOCOLATE GLAZE

Preheat the oven to 325°F/170°C/gas 3. ❧ Coarsely chop the walnuts, almonds, and hazelnuts. ❧ Place in a large bowl and add the pine nuts, candied peel, raisins, cocoa, chocolate, cinnamon, nutmeg, coriander, and pepper. Mix well, then add the honey, flour, and fennel seeds. ❧ Lightly butter and flour a 10-in (25-cm) springform pan. Spoon the mixture into the pan and bake for 30 minutes, or until nicely browned. ❧ Leave in the pan for 30 minutes, then turn out onto a cake rack to cool. ❧ Glaze: Melt the chocolate in a double boiler over simmering water. Set aside to cool for 10 minutes, then spread over the top of the cake.

This old Italian recipe is similar to Siennese panforte, with the addition of a chocolate glaze.

Serves: 12

Preparation: 15'
+ 40' to cool

Cooking: 30'

Level of difficulty: 1

- 2 oz/60 g each shelled walnuts, almonds, hazelnuts
- 1 oz/30 g pine nuts
- 2 oz/60 g mixed candied orange and lemon peel, cut in small cubes
- 1 oz/30 g raisins
- 2 oz/60 g cocoa powder
- 4 oz/125 g semi-sweet/dark chocolate, coarsely chopped
- 1/2 tsp each ground cinnamon, nutmeg, coriander, black pepper
- 6 tbsp honey, warmed
- 2 1/3 cups/350 g all-purpose/plain flour
- 1/4 tsp fennel seeds
- 12 oz/350 g semi-sweet/dark chocolate

SACHERTORTE

Preheat the oven to 325°F/170°C/gas 3. ❧ Melt the first measure of chocolate in a double boiler over simmering water. Remove from heat and let cool. ❧ Bea the butter and sugar together until pale and creamy. ❧ Beat the egg yolks in one at a time. Add the chocolate. Gradually beat in sifted flour. ❧ Beat the egg whites until stiff but not dry and fold them into the mixture. ❧ Spoon the batter in an ungreased 9-in (23-cm) springform pan. ❧ Bake for 1 hour, or until a skewer inserted into the center comes out clean. Cool the cake in the pan. ❧ Slice horizontally and fill with jam. ❧ Icing: Melt the butter and chocolate in a double boiler over simmering water. Add the coffee and beat well. Stir in the confectioners' sugar and vanilla. Ice the top and sides of the cake.

Serves: 6–8

Preparation: 15'

Cooking: 1 h

Level of difficulty: 2

- 5 oz/150 g semi-sweet/dark chocolate
- 6 tbsp butter
- ½ cup/100 g sugar
- 5 eggs, separated
- ⅔ cup/100 g cake flour
- ⅔ cup/100 g apricot jelly/jam

ICING

- 1 tbsp butter, softened
- 4 oz/125 g semi-sweet/dark chocolate
- 6 tbsp strong brewed coffee
- 2 cups/300 g confectioners'/icing sugar
- 1 tsp vanilla extract

CHOCOLATE BUTTERMILK CAKE

Serves: 6–8

Preparation: 30'

Cooking: 25'

Level of difficulty: 2

- 11 oz/300 g semi-sweet/dark chocolate chips
- 4 tbsp water
- 2 cups/300 g cake flour
- 1 tsp baking soda
- ¹/₄ tsp salt
- ²/₃ cup/180 g butter, softened
- 1¹/₄ cups/250 g sugar
- 2 tsp vanilla extract
- 3 eggs
- 1 cup/250 ml buttermilk
- 4 tbsp honey
- 2 tbsp water
- ¹/₈ tsp salt
- 2 cups/500 ml heavy/double cream, whipped

Preheat the oven to 375°F/190°C/gas 5. ❧ In a small saucepan over low heat, combine half the chocolate chips with the water. Stir until the chocolate has melted. Set aside to cool. ❧ Sift the flour, baking soda, and salt together. ❧ In a large bowl, beat the butter, sugar, and vanilla until pale and creamy. ❧ Beat in the eggs one at a time. ❧ Add the chocolate mixture, followed by the flour and buttermilk. ❧ Butter and flour three 9-in (23-cm) cake pans. ❧ Divide the batter evenly among the pans and bake for 25 minutes, or until a skewer inserted into the center comes out clean. ❧ Cool the cakes in the pans for 15 minutes, then turn onto racks. ❧ In a small saucepan over low heat, melt the remaining chocolate chips with the honey and second measures of water and salt. Set aside to cool. ❧ Fold the cream into the chocolate mixture and use it to fill and frost the cake.

COUNTRY APPLE BAKE

Preheat the oven to 350°F/180°C/gas 4. ❧ Beat the butter, sugar, and lemon zest in a medium bowl with an electric mixer until pale and creamy. ❧ Beat in the eggs, one at a time, followed by the flour, baking powder, and salt, alternating with the milk. ❧ Spoon the batter into a greased and floured 10-in (25-cm) springform pan. ❧ Peel the apples, cut them in half, and core. Cut a grid pattern into the rounded sides, and sprinkle with lemon juice. ❧ Place the apples, rounded side up, in the top of the cake. ❧ Bake for 45 minutes, or until a skewer inserted into the center comes out clean. ❧ Brush the top with a little of the warmed, strained apricot jelly and serve hot or at room temperature.

Serves: 6-8

Preparation: 30'

Cooking: 45'

Level of difficulty: 1

- $^1/_2$ **cup/125 g butter**
- $^1/_2$ **cup/100 g sugar**
- **grated zest of 1 lemon**
- **2 eggs**
- **1$^2/_3$ cups/250 g all-purpose/plain flour**
- **2 tsp baking powder**
- **dash of salt**
- **6 tbsp milk**
- **4 medium cooking apples**
- **2 tbsp lemon juice**
- **2 tbsp apricot jelly/jam**

BLACK FOREST CAKE

Preheat the oven to 350°F/180°C/gas 4. ❧ Sift the flour, cocoa, baking soda, and salt into a bowl and set aside. ❧ Cream half the butter with the sugar until light and fluffy. Beat in the eggs and 1 teaspoon of vanilla. ❧ Beat in the flour mixture, alternating with the buttermilk. ❧ Line the bottoms of two 8-in (20-cm) springform pans with waxed paper. Spoon the batter into the pans. ❧ Bake for 35–40 minutes, or until a skewer inserted into the center comes out clean. Turn out onto racks to cool. ❧ Remove the paper from the cakes. Cut each layer in half, horizontally, making 4 layers total. Sprinkle the layers with the first measure of cherry brandy. ❧ In a medium bowl, beat the remaining butter with the confectioners' sugar until pale and creamy. Add the coffee and beat until smooth. ❧ Spread one layer of cake with one-third of the filling. Top with one-third of the cherries. Repeat with the remaining layers. ❧ In a separate bowl, whip the cream to stiff peaks. Beat in the remaining vanilla. Use this mixture to frost the top of the cake.

This famous cake comes from the Black Forest region in southern Germany.

876

Serves: 6–8

Preparation: 30'

Cooking: 35–40'

Level of difficulty: 2

- 1²/₃ cups/250 g all-purpose/plain flour
- ²/₃ cup/100 g unsweetened cocoa powder
- 1¹/₂ tsp baking soda
- 1 tsp salt
- 1 cup/250 g butter
- 1¹/₂ cups/300 g sugar
- 2 eggs
- 1 tsp vanilla extract
- 1¹/₂ cups/375 ml buttermilk
- ¹/₂ cup/125 ml kirsch
- 13 oz/400 g confectioners'/icing sugar
- 1 tbsp strong brewed coffee
- 2 (13 oz/400 g) cans pitted Bing cherries, drained
- 2 cups/500 ml whipping cream

SPONGE CAKE

Preheat the oven to 325°F/170°C/gas 3. ❧ Place the eggs and sugar in a double boiler and whisk until frothy. Remove from heat and add the lemon zest and continue to whisk until cool. ❧ Fold in the sifted flours and salt, using slow movements and keeping the blade of the spatula pointing downward. ❧ Spoon the batter into a greased, floured 10-in (25-cm) springform pan and bake for 35–45 minutes, or until golden brown, and a skewer inserted into the center comes out clean.

Serves: 6

Preparation: 30'

Cooking: 35–45'

Level of difficulty: 1

- **6 eggs**
- **³/₄ cup/150 g sugar**
- **2 tsp grated lemon zest**
- **²/₃ cup/100 g all-purpose/plain flour**
- **²/₃ cup/100 g cornstarch/corn flour**
- **dash of salt**

ALMOND POLENTA CAKE

Serves: 6

Preparation: 20'

Cooking: 40'

Level of difficulty: 1

- 8 oz/250 g almonds, blanched
- ³/₄ cup/150 g sugar
- 1¹/₃ cups/200 g all-purpose/plain flour
- 8 oz/250 g yellow cornmeal, coarsely ground
- grated zest of 1 lemon
- 1 tsp vanilla sugar
- dash of salt
- ¹/₂ cup/125 g butter, cut in small pieces
- 3¹/₂ oz/100 g lard, cut in small pieces
- 2 egg yolks, beaten

Preheat the oven to 375°F/190°C/gas 5. ❧ Chop the almonds in a food processor with two-thirds of the sugar. ❧ Transfer to a work surface and add the flour, cornmeal, lemon zest, remaining sugar, vanilla sugar, and salt. Shape into a mound and make a well in the center. ❧ Combine the butter and lard with the egg yolks, and add to the flour mixture. Working quickly, use your fingertips to combine the mixture until it is smooth and crumbly. ❧ Place the dough in a buttered and floured 10-in (25-cm) springform pan, pressing down lightly with your fingertips to make an uneven surface. ❧ Bake for 40 minutes. ❧ If liked, dust with confectioners' (icing) sugar before serving.

SANDY CAKE

Preheat the oven to 350°F/180°C/gas 4. ❧ Beat the butter and sugar in a medium bowl with an electric mixer until pale and creamy. ❧ Beat in the egg yolks, one at a time, making sure each is fully incorporated before adding the next. ❧ Mix the two types of flour thoroughly with the baking powder. Sift them into the egg, butter, and sugar mixture. Stir until evenly blended. ❧ Whisk the egg whites with a dash of salt until stiff but not dry and fold carefully into the cake mixture. ❧ Grease a 10-in (25-cm) springform cake pan with butter and dust with flour. Spoon the batter into the prepared pan, tap the bottom on a work surface, and gently smooth the surface level. ❧ Bake for 45 minutes, or until a skewer inserted into the center comes out clean. ❧ Cool on a rack.

Serves: 6

Preparation: 30'

Cooking: 45'

Level of difficulty: 2

- 1¹⁄₄ cups/300 g butter, cut into small pieces
- 1¹⁄₂ cups/300 g sugar
- 3 eggs, separated
- 1 cup/150 g cornstarch/corn flour
- 1 cup/150 g all-purpose/plain flour
- 1 tsp baking powder
- dash of salt

TURKISH CAKE

Serves: 6

Preparation: 20'

Cooking: 40'

Level of difficulty: 1

- **4 cups/1 liter milk**
- **³/₄ cup/150 g sugar**
- **11 oz/300 g short-grain pudding rice**
- **3¹/₂ oz/100 g very finely chopped almonds**
- **2¹/₂ oz/75 g Muscatel raisins, seeded**
- **4 tbsp pine nuts**
- **10 dates, preferably fresh, torn into small pieces**
- **2 eggs + 2 extra egg yolks**
- **1 tbsp citron water or rose water**
- **dash of salt**

P reheat the oven to 350°F/180°C/gas 4. ❧ Bring the milk to a boil in a medium saucepan. ❧ Stir in the sugar, then the rice and salt. Cook while stirring continuously for 10 minutes, then drain off any milk that has not been absorbed and transfer the rice to a bowl. ❧ Mix the rice with the almonds, raisins, pine nuts, dates, and the 2 whole eggs plus the yolks. Mix well, adding the citron or rose water. ❧ Spoon the batter into a turban ring mold previously greased with butter and dusted flour. ❧ Bake for 30 minutes, or until pale golden brown. ❧ Serve warm.

MODENA CAKE

Preheat the oven to 350°F/180°C/gas 4. ♣ Sift the flour into a large bowl. ♣ Mix in the sugar, salt, lemon zest, and baking powder. ♣ Turn out onto a pastry board and heap up into a mound. Make a well in the center and fill with the butter and eggs (reserving 1 tablespoon of beaten egg to glaze the cake). ♣ Work these ingredients together, gradually combining them with the flour, and adding 2–3 tablespoons of milk. Knead the dough until only just smooth. ♣ Grease a baking sheet and dust with flour. ♣ Shape the dough into a long, thick sausage and arrange it in an S-shape on the baking sheet. ♣ Brush the surface with the reserved egg and sprinkle with the roughly crushed sugar. Using a sharp, pointed knife, make an incision along the center of the entire length of the cake. ♣ Bake for 40 minutes, or until a skewer inserted into the center comes out clean. ♣ Let cool on a rack for 10 minutes before serving.

884

Serves: 6–8

Preparation: 25'

Cooking: 40'

Level of difficulty: 1

- 3$\frac{1}{3}$ cups/500 g cake flour
- $\frac{3}{4}$ cup/150 g sugar
- dash of salt
- finely grated zest of 1 lemon
- 3$\frac{1}{2}$ tsp baking powder
- $\frac{1}{2}$ cup/125 g butter, chopped in small pieces
- 3 eggs, lightly beaten
- 2–3 tbsp milk
- 3 oz/90 g roughly crushed sugar (grains/crystals/ nibs)

CHOCOLATE ORANGE CAKE

Preheat the oven to 350°F/180°C/gas 4. ♣ Beat the butter and sugar in a medium bowl with an electric mixer until pale and creamy. ♣ Beat in the eggs one at a time. Stir in the orange zest. ♣ Stir the orange juice and brown sugar in a small saucepan over low heat until the sugar has dissolved. ♣ Sift the flour, baking powder, and cocoa into the butter and sugar mixture gradually, alternating it with the orange juice and brown sugar mixture. ♣ Butter an 8-in (20-cm) square cake pan and line with waxed paper. ♣ Spoon the batter into the pan and smooth the surface. ♣ Bake for 45 minutes, or until a skewer inserted into the center comes out clean. ♣ Invert onto a cake rack and leave to cool. ♣ Icing: Combine the cream cheese in a large bowl with the confectioners' sugar, orange juice and zest, and beat until smooth and creamy. ♣ When the cake is completely cool, spread the top and sides with the icing. Decorate the top with strips of orange zest and, if liked, very thin slices of fresh orange.

Serves: 8–10
Preparation: 35'
Cooking: 45'
Level of difficulty: 1

- ²/₃ cup/180 g butter
- ¹/₂ cup/100 g sugar
- 2 eggs
- finely grated zest of 1 orange
- ¹/₂ cup/125 ml fresh orange juice
- 6 tbsp brown sugar
- 2 cups/300 g all-purpose/plain flour
- 1¹/₂ tsp baking powder
- 3 oz/90 g cocoa powder

ICING

- 11 oz/300 g cream cheese, softened
- 2 oz/60 g confectioners'/icing sugar
- 2 tsp finely grated orange zest
- 6 tbsp fresh orange juice
- strips of candied orange zest, to decorate

POLENTA & CANDIED FRUITS CAKE

reheat the oven to 350°F/180°C/gas 4. ❧ Place the almonds in a bowl with the candied peel and cherries, figs, raisins, fennel seeds, and grappa. Mix well and let stand for at least 15 minutes. ❧ Heat the milk to boiling point in a nonstick saucepan or double boiler and then gradually sift the cornmeal and flour into it while stirring continuously with a wooden spoon over low heat. Cook for 15 minutes, stirring continuously. Add the butter, shortening, sugar, and salt, and cook for 10 minutes more. ❧ Remove from heat. Add the fruit, nuts, and grappa mixture, and stir well. ❧ Grease a shallow 11-in (28-cm) cake or pie pan with butter and dust lightly with flour. Fill with the batter, tapping the bottom on a work surface to settle and smoothing the surface until level. ❧ Bake for 1 hour, placing a sheet of foil on top of the cake after 30 minutes to prevent it drying out too much. ❧ Serve at room temperature.

Place a small roasting pan filled with water in the oven while baking to keep the cake moist.

Serves: 6

Preparation: 1 h

Cooking: 1¹/₂ h

Level of difficulty: 2

- 2 oz/60 g almonds, blanched, skinned, and coarsely chopped
- 1 oz/30 g chopped candied peel and cherries
- 2 tbsp chopped dried figs
- 3 tbsp seedless white raisins/ sultanas
- 1 tsp fennel seeds
- 4 tbsp grappa or eau de vie
- 4 cups/1 liter milk
- 11 oz/300 g fine yellow water-ground cornmeal/ very fine polenta
- ²/₃ cup/100 g all-purpose/plain flour
- 6 tbsp butter
- 6 tbsp shortening
- ¹/₂ cup/100 g sugar
- dash of salt

CHOCOLATE HAZELNUT CAKE

Serves: 6

Preparation: 40'

Cooking: 50'

Level of difficulty: 3

- ²/₃ cup/150 g butter, cut up
- ³/₄ cup/150 g firmly packed brown sugar
- 4 eggs, separated
- 1 cup/150 g all-purpose/plain flour
- 1 tsp baking powder
- 1 cup/100 g toasted hazelnuts, chopped
- 7 oz/200 g semi-sweet/dark chocolate, chopped
- dash of salt

FILLING
- ¹/₂ cup/125 ml heavy/double cream

ICING
- 5 oz/150 g semi-sweet/dark chocolate
- vanilla extract
- 2 tbsp light/single cream
- 2 tbsp chopped hazelnuts

reheat the oven to 350°F/180°C/gas 4. ❧ Beat the butter and sugar in a medium bowl with an electric mixer until pale and creamy. ❧ Beat in the egg yolks one at a time. ❧ Add the flour and baking powder. ❧ Add the nuts and chocolate. ❧ Beat the egg whites with the salt until stiff and then fold them into the mixture. ❧ Spoon the batter into a 9-in (23-cm) springform pan and bake for 50 minutes, or until a skewer inserted into the center comes out clean. ❧ Remove from the pan and place on a rack to cool. ❧ Melt the chocolate in a double boiler over simmering water. Use a wooden spoon to stir in vanilla and the cream ❧ Whip the cream until stiff. ❧ When the cake is cool, split it in two horizontally. ❧ Spread the cake with whipped cream and cover with the chocolate icing. ❧ Decorate with the hazelnuts.

APPLE STRUDEL

Melt the butter in the water over low heat. Set aside to cool. ❧ Sift the flour onto a work surface and shape into a mound. Make a well in the center and fill with salt, sugar, egg, and butter-and-water mixture. ❧ Combine the ingredients well and knead vigorously for 20 minutes, until a soft, elastic dough forms. Roll into a ball. Cover and let rest in a warm place for 30 minutes. ❧ Preheat the oven to 350°F/180°C/gas 4. ❧ Peel and core the apples and slice thinly. ❧ Let the raisins soften in warm water for 10 minutes. ❧ Mix the sugar with the cinnamon and lemon zest. ❧ Toast the bread crumbs in half the butter. ❧ Place the dough on a large, floured cloth and roll it out partially with a rolling-pin. Then stretch the dough out as much as possible, placing your fists underneath with your knuckles upward and pulling gently outward from the center. The dough should be as thin as a sheet of paper. Brush it with melted butter. ❧ Sprinkle half the dough with the bread crumbs, followed by the apples, raisins, and sugar mixture. Spread with the apricot jelly. ❧ Roll up the strudel, sealing the edges well so that no filling escapes during cooking. Place on a baking sheet covered in waxed paper. ❧ Brush with the remaining butter (melted) and bake for 1 hour, or until golden brown. ❧ Serve hot or warm dusted with confectioners' sugar.

Serves: 4–6

Preparation: 30' + 30' to rest

Cooking: 1 h

Level of difficulty: 3

- **4 tbsp butter**
- **6 tbsp water**
- **1²/₃ cups/250 g all-purpose/plain flour**
- **dash of salt**
- **1 tsp sugar**
- **1 egg**

FILLING

- **8 cooking apples**
- **4 oz/125 g golden raisins/sultanas**
- **¹/₂ cup/100 g sugar**
- **1 tsp ground cinnamon**
- **grated zest of 1 lemon**
- **1 cup/150 g fine dry bread crumbs**
- **6 tbsp butter**
- **¹/₂ cup/125 g apricot jelly/jam**
- **confectioners'/icing sugar**

BERRYFRUIT CAKE

Preheat the oven to 375°F/190°C/gas 5. ❧ Beat the butter and sugar in a medium bowl with an electric mixer until pale and creamy. ❧ Beat in the egg yolks one at a time. ❧ Beat the egg whites with the salt until stiff and fold them into the mixture. Fold in the flour. ❧ Spoon the batter into a buttered and floured 10-in (25-cm) springform pan. Cover with the berries (some may sink into the batter), reserving plenty for decorating. ❧ Bake for 1 hour, or until a skewer inserted into the center comes out clean. ❧ Cool in the pan for 10 minutes, then turn out onto a rack to cool completely. ❧ Sprinkle with the confectioners' sugar and decorate with the reserved berries just before serving.

Serves: 8–10

Preparation: 30'

Cooking: 1 h

Level of difficulty: 2

- ³/₄ cup/200 g butter, melted
- 8 eggs, separated
- 1 cup/200 g sugar
- dash of salt
- 1²/₃ cups/250 g all-purpose/plain flour
- 14 oz/450 g mixed berry fruit (wild strawberries, raspberries, blackberries)
- 2 oz/60 g confectioners'/icing sugar

JAMS &
PRESERVES

QUICK TOMATO CHUTNEY

P lace the tomatoes, ginger, raisins, and sugar in a large saucepan over medium heat. Simmer for about 20 minutes, then add the turmeric and cook for 5 minutes more. ❧ Toast the fennel seeds with the cumin in a small skillet (frying pan). Grind the seeds in a pepper grinder or using a pestle and mortar and add them to the chutney mixture. Season with salt and pepper. ❧ Stir in the lemon juice and transfer the chutney to a small bowl. Let cool for 1 hour before serving.

Spicy or bland, Indian chutneys are good with meat and a wide range of other dishes.

Makes: about 1 cup/ 250 ml

Preparation: 10' + 1 h to cool

Cooking: 25'

Level of difficulty: 1

- **6 ripe tomatoes, coarsely chopped**
- **1-in/2.5-cm piece fresh ginger root, peeled and grated**
- **$^1/_2$ cup/90 g seedless raisins, soaked briefly in water**
- **4 tbsp sugar**
- **$^1/_2$ tsp ground turmeric**
- **1 tsp fennel seeds**
- **1 tsp cumin seeds**
- **salt and freshly ground black pepper to taste**
- **juice of $^1/_2$ lemon**

GREEN TOMATO JAM

Makes: 3 cups/
  750 ml

Preparation: 15'

Cooking: 40'

Level of difficulty: 2

- 1 lb/500 g green tomatoes
- 1½ cups/300 g sugar
- grated zest and juice of 1 waxed lemon

Sterilize three ½-pint (two ½-liter) screw-top jars as described below. ❧ Roughly chop the tomatoes and place in a large saucepan. Add the sugar, lemon zest, and juice and cook for 40 minutes, or until 1 teaspoon of jam sets in a cold saucer within 2 minutes. ❧ Cool to lukewarm. Ladle into the sterilized jars, leaving a ½-in (1-cm) headspace. Fasten the caps. ❧ Replace the jars in the large saucepan. Cover completely with water and boil for 10 minutes. Allow the water to cool completely. ❧ Store in a cool, dark place for 90 days before use.

These slightly tart-tasting preserves have an unusual but very pleasant flavor.

To sterilize the jars: *place a cotton cloth in a large saucepan (to prevent the jars from breaking during boiling), stand the jars on top, fill the pan with water, and simmer for 20 minutes. Leave in the water until ready to fill. Boil the flat caps for 5 minutes to sterilize.*

GREENGAGE PLUM PRESERVES

Sterilize six $1/2$-pint (three $1/2$-liter) screw-top jars as described on page 899. ❧ Cook the plums and water in a large saucepan over medium heat for 15–20 minutes, or until the fruit has softened. ❧ Stir in the sugar and lemon zest. Cook, stirring often, over medium-low heat for 30 minutes, or until 1 teaspoon of the preserves sets in a cold saucer within 2 minutes. ❧ Cool to lukewarm. Ladle into the sterilized jars, leaving a $1/2$-in (1-cm) headspace. Fasten the caps. ❧ Replace the jars in the large saucepan. Cover completely with water and boil for 10 minutes. Allow the water to cool completely. ❧ Store in a cool, dark place.

Makes: about 3 pints/ 1.5 liters

Preparation: 30'

Cooking: 50–55'

Level of difficulty: 2

- 3 lb/1.5 kg greengage plums, pitted
- 2 cups/500 ml water
- 3$1/2$ cups/750 g sugar
- finely grated zest of 1 lemon

PLUM CHUTNEY

Makes: 3 quarts/
3 liters

Preparation: 30'

Cooking: 1¼ h

Level of difficulty: 3

- 2 lb/1 kg firm ripe plums, quartered and pitted
- 2 lb/1 kg cooking apples, peeled, cored, and coarsely chopped
- 1 lb/500 g onions, thinly sliced
- 2 cloves garlic, finely chopped
- 1 tbsp fresh ginger root, peeled and finely grated
- 1 tbsp mustard seeds
- 1 tbsp salt
- 2 cups/500 ml red wine vinegar
- 2¼ cups/450 g brown sugar

Sterilize six 1-pint (six ½-liter) screw-top jars as described on page 899. ❧ Place the plums, apples, onion, garlic, ginger, mustard seeds, and salt in a large saucepan. Bring to a boil over low heat. Simmer for 30 minutes, or until softened. ❧ Stir in the vinegar and brown sugar. Cook for 45 minutes, or until thick and the vinegar has been absorbed. ❧ Cool to lukewarm. Ladle into the sterilized jars, leaving a ½-in (1-cm) headspace. Fasten the caps. ❧ Replace the jars in the large saucepan. Cover completely with water and boil for 10 minutes. Allow the water to cool completely. ❧ Store in a cool, dark place for at least 6 weeks before eating.

STRAWBERRY PRESERVES

Sterilize six $^1/_2$-pint (three $^1/_2$-liter) screw-top jars as described on page 899. ❧ Place the strawberries and lemon juice and zest in a large bowl and mix well. ❧ Heat the sugar and water in a large saucepan over medium heat, stirring constantly, for 5 minutes. Stir in the strawberry mixture, followed by the brandy. Remove from heat and set aside for 2 hours. ❧ Bring to a boil over medium heat, stirring constantly, for 20 minutes, or until 1 teaspoon of jam sets in a cold saucer within 2 minutes. ❧ Cool to lukewarm. Ladle into the sterilized jars, leaving a $^1/_2$-in (1-cm) headspace. Fasten the caps. ❧ Replace the jars in the large saucepan. Cover completely with water and boil for 10 minutes. Allow the water to cool completely. ❧ Store in a cool, dark place.

Try this recipe using tiny wild strawberries — their flavor makes the preserves really special.

Makes: 3 pints/ 1.5 liters

Preparation: 30' + 2 h to rest

Cooking: 25'

Level of difficulty: 2

- 2$^1/_2$ lb/1.25 kg firm ripe strawberries, washed
- juice and zest of 1 lemon
- 4$^1/_2$ cups/900 g sugar
- 4 tbsp water
- 2 tsp brandy

GINGER & LIME MARMALADE

Sterilize six 1-pint (six ½-liter) screw-top jars as described on page 899. ❧ Place the limes and water in a large bowl. Cover and set aside overnight. ❧ Pour the lime mixture into a large saucepan. Bring to a boil over low heat. Cover and simmer for about 1½ hours, or until the rinds are tender. ❧ Place the fresh ginger in a cheesecloth (muslin) bag and secure tightly. Add to the lime mixture. ❧ Add the sugar and stir until dissolved. ❧ Cook for 20 minutes, or until 1 teaspoon of marmalade sets in a cold saucer within 2 minutes. ❧. Remove from heat and discard the cheesecloth bag. Pour in the brandy and ginger. Set aside for 10 minutes, then stir. ❧ Cool to lukewarm. Ladle into the sterilized jars, leaving a ½-in (1-cm) headspace. Fasten the caps. ❧ Replace the jars in the large saucepan. Cover completely with water and boil for 10 minutes. Allow the water to cool completely. ❧ Store in a cool, dark place.

A full rolling boil is indicated when stirring with a spoon does not distort the liquid surface.

Makes: 3 quarts/3 liters

Preparation: 30'

Cooking: 2 h

Level of difficulty: 1

- 2 lb/1 kg limes, thinly sliced
- 8 cups/2 liters water
- 7½ cups/1.5 kg sugar
- 1 tbsp fresh ginger root, peeled and finely grated
- 4 tbsp brandy
- 4 oz/125 g candied ginger, coarsely chopped

GRAPE CHEESE

Sterilize six $^1/_2$-pint (three $^1/_2$-liter) screw-top jars as described on page 899. ❧ Place the grapes in a large saucepan over low heat and bring to a boil. Simmer for about 20 minutes, or until the grapes are softened. ❧ Press through a sieve to remove the skins. ❧ Place the lemon juice, sugar, and grape pulp in a large heavy-bottomed saucepan over low heat. Stir until the sugar has dissolved. Simmer, stirring occasionally, for about 15–20 minutes, or until thick. ❧ Cool to lukewarm. Ladle into the sterilized jars, leaving a $^1/_2$-in (1-cm) headspace. Fasten the caps. ❧ Replace the jars in the large saucepan. Cover completely with water and boil for 10 minutes. Allow the water to cool completely. ❧ Store in a cool, dark place.

Makes: 3 pints/ 1.5 liters

Preparation: 30'

Cooking: 50'

Level of difficulty: 2

- **2 lb/1 kg seedless black grapes**
- **juice of 4 lemons**
- **2$^1/_2$ cups/500 g sugar**

MANGO CHUTNEY

Sterilize six 1-pint (six ¹/₂-liter) screw-top jars as described on page 899. ❧ Place the mangoes, currants, and lime juice in a large bowl. ❧ Heat the oil in a large saucepan over low heat. Add the onion and chile. Sauté for about 10 minutes, until the onion is soft. ❧ Stir in the mango mixture, vinegar, sugar, mustard seeds, ginger, cinnamon, and salt. Continue cooking, stirring constantly, until the sugar has dissolved. ❧ Bring to a boil over medium-high heat. Cook until the mango has softened but not broken down, about 15 minutes. ❧ Remove the chile. ❧ Cool to lukewarm. Ladle into the sterilized jars, leaving a ¹/₂-in (1-cm) headspace. Fasten the caps. ❧ Replace the jars in the large saucepan. Cover completely with water and boil for 10 minutes. Allow the water to cool completely. ❧ Store in a cool, dark place.

Makes: 3 quarts/ 3 liters

Preparation: 30'

Cooking: 30'

Level of difficulty: 2

- 3 lb/1.5 kg firm ripe mangoes, peeled and seeded
- 3 oz/90 g currants
- ¹/₂ cup/125 ml fresh lime juice
- 2 tbsp vegetable oil
- 1 large onion, finely chopped
- 1 large fresh red chile pepper, seeded
- 1¹/₂ cups/450 ml white wine vinegar
- 1 cup/200 g sugar
- 2 tsp mustard seeds
- 4 tbsp minced preserved stem ginger
- 1 tsp ground cinnamon
- 1 tbsp coarse sea salt

SAUERKRAUT

Makes: 4 quarts/
4 liters

Preparation: 30' + 3
weeks to ferment

Level of difficulty: 3

- 8 lb/4 kg firm white cabbage, discard the outer leaves
- 4 tbsp coarse sea salt for each 5 lb/2.5 kg shredded cabbage
- 2 tbsp caraway seeds
- 1 tbsp juniper berries

Core and shred the cabbages. Weigh the cabbage. ❧ Place the cabbage and salt in a large bowl. Set aside for 15 minutes, or until softened. ❧ Place the cabbage mixture, caraway seeds, and juniper berries in layers in a large (4-quart/4-liter) crock. Pour any juices over. ❧ Cover the crock with a double thickness of cheesecloth (muslin) and a plate that seals the opening. Fill a large jar with water and place on the plate, pressing down on the cabbage. Set aside at room temperature for 1 week, or until frothing at the edges. ❧ Remove the water, plate, and cheesecloth. Skim off the froth. ❧ Repeat the fermenting process with a clean cheesecloth, changing the cheesecloth every few days for a 2-week period, or until the frothing stops. ❧ Sterilize eight 1-pint (eight $^1/_2$-liter) screw-top jars as described on page 899. ❧ Ladle into the sterilized jars, leaving a $^1/_2$-in (1-cm) headspace. Fasten the caps. ❧ Replace the jars in the large saucepan. Cover completely with water and boil for 10 minutes. Allow the water to cool completely. ❧ Store in a cool, dark place.

909

RED CURRANT JELLY

Sterilize four 1-pint (four ½-liter) screw-top jars as described on page 899. ❧ Place the cranberries in a large saucepan. Bring to a boil over low heat. Let simmer until the fruit has broken down. ❧ Strain the cranberries. ❧ Return to the saucepan over low heat and add the sugar. ❧ Mix well and simmer until thickened. ❧ Cool to lukewarm. Ladle into the sterilized jars, leaving a ½-in (1-cm) headspace. Fasten the caps. ❧ Replace the jars in the large saucepan. Cover completely with water and boil for 10 minutes. Allow the water to cool completely. ❧ Store in a cool, dark place.

Makes: 2 quarts/ 2 liters
Preparation: 30'
Cooking: 30'
Level of difficulty: 3

• 2 lb/1 kg black and red cranberries
• 2 cups/500 ml water
• 2½ cups/500 g sugar

RASPBERRIES IN EAU‑DE‑VIE

Makes: 3 quarts/
3 liters

Preparation: 30'

Level of difficulty: 1

- **2 lb/1 kg raspberries**
- **14 oz/400 g sugar**
- **4 raspberry leaves, (optional)**
- **4 cups/1 liter raspberry eau-de-vie**

Sterilize three 2-pint (three 1-liter) screw-top jars as described on page 899. ❧ Place the raspberries, sugar, and 2 raspberry leaves, if using, in layers in the jars. Pour the eau-de-vie over the raspberries, leaving a ¹/₂-in (1-cm) headspace. Fasten the caps. ❧ Store in a cool, dark place for at least 1 month before using.

911

PASSIONFRUIT BUTTER

Cut the passion fruit in half and scoop out the pulp. ❧ Place the pulp, sugar, butter, and eggs in a double boiler over simmering water. Stir until the sugar has dissolved and the butter has melted. ❧ Continue cooking, until the mixture is thick enough to coat the back of a spoon, about 25 minutes. ❧ Ladle into small jars and store in the refrigerator for up to 1 week.

Makes: about 2 cups/ 500 ml

Preparation: 15'

Cooking: 30'

Level of difficulty: 1

- **10 large passionfruit**
- **2^1/$_2$ cups/450 g sugar**
- **3 tbsp butter**
- **4 eggs, lightly beaten**

PICKLED ONIONS

Makes: 2 quarts/ 2 liters

Preparation: 30'

Cooking: 10'

Level of difficulty: 2

- 4 lb/2 kg pickling onions
- 2 quarts/2 liters white vinegar
- 1 tbsp sugar
- 5 pepper corns
- 4 cloves
- 2 laurel leaves
- ½ cup/125 ml extra-virgin olive oil

Sterilize four 1-pint (four ½-liter) screw-top jars as described on page 899. ❧ Bring a large saucepan filled with water to a boil and plunge in the onions for 1 minute. Set aside to cool, then peel. ❧ Pour the vinegar into a large saucepan and bring to a boil. Add in the sugar, pepper corns, cloves, and laurel leaves. Stir in the onions, mixing well. Simmer for 3 minutes. Remove from the heat. Set aside to cool for a few hours. ❧ Ladle into the sterilized jars, leaving a 2-in (5-cm) headspace. Top up the space with oil. Fasten the caps. ❧ Replace the jars in the large saucepan. Cover completely with water and boil for 10 minutes. Allow the water to cool completely. ❧ Store in a cool, dark place.

BELL PEPPERS IN OIL

Place the bell peppers on a clean cloth in the hot sun for a few hours. ❧ Sterilize six 1-pint (six ¹/₂-liter) screw-top jars as described on page 899. ❧ Place the vinegar, sugar, pepper, 1 teaspoon salt, and 2 tablespoons oil in a large saucepan over medium heat, until the vinegar begins to boil. Add the peppers. Bring to a boil over high heat. Remove from heat and leave to cool for 4 hours in the vinegar. ❧ Drain the peppers and wrap in a clean cloth. Set aside for 4 hours. ❧ Spoon the pepper mixture, garlic (if using), and oregano (if using) in layers into the sterilized jars. Pour in the oil leaving a 2-in (5-cm) headspace. Sprinkle with the remaining salt. Set aside overnight. ❧ Check the level of the oil. If it has reduced, top up with more oil. Fasten the caps. ❧ Store in a cool, dark place.

Makes: 3 quarts/ 3 liters

Preparation: 30' + 8 h to cool

Cooking: 15'

Level of difficulty: 2

- 4 lb/2 kg yellow, red or green peppers, washed, seeded, and cut into strips lengthways
- 2 quarts/2 liters white vinegar
- freshly ground white pepper to taste
- 2 tsp salt
- 6 cups/1.5 liters sunflower oil
- 10 cloves garlic, thinly sliced (optional)
- oregano (optional)

BABY VEGETABLES IN OIL

Sterilize three 1-pint (three $^1/_2$-liter) screw-top jars as described on page 899. ♣ Place the onions, carrots, celery, cauliflower, zucchini, and peppers in a large saucepan. Pour in enough vinegar to cover the vegetables. Add the sugar, oil, salt, cloves, bay leaves, cinnamon, and pepper. Stir in the peppers, mixing well. Bring to a boil over high heat. Cook for 5 minutes, then leave to cool in the vinegar. ♣ Drain the vegetables and ladle into the sterilized jars, leaving a 2-in (5-cm) headspace. Top up the space with oil. Fasten the caps. ♣ Replace the jars in the large saucepan. Cover completely with water and boil for 10 minutes. Allow the water to cool completely. ♣ Store in a cool, dark place.

Peel the onions after plunging them in boiling water and allowing them to cool.

Makes: 3 pints/ 1.5 liters

Preparation: 30'

Cooking: 15'

Level of difficulty: 2

- **16 pickling onions**
- **7 large carrots, peeled and thinly sliced**
- **$^1/_2$ bunch celery, cut into small sticks**
- **$^1/_2$ small cauliflower, broken into small florets**
- **3 small zucchini/ courgettes, coarsely cut into small slices**
- **4 green and 4 yellow peppers, seeded, and cut into small pieces**
- **5 quarts/5 liters white vinegar**
- **1 tbsp sunflower oil**
- **2 tbsp sugar**
- **2 cloves**
- **dash of white pepper**
- **1 cinnamon stick**
- **2 bay leaves**
- **dash of salt**

ARTICHOKES PRESERVED IN OIL

S terilize four ¹/₂-pint (two ¹/₂-liter) screw-top jars as described on page 899. ❧ Clean the artichokes by trimming the tops and stalks. Remove all the tough outer leaves so that only the pale, tender hearts remain. Place in a bowl of cold water with the lemon juice for 15 minutes. ❧ Bring the water, vinegar, and salt to a boil in a large saucepan. Drain the artichokes and add to the saucepan. Cook for 10 minutes. ❧ Drain the artichokes and dry well with paper towels. Transfer to clean preserving jars and cover with oil. Seal the jars and set aside in a cool, dark place for at least 2 months before serving.

Makes: 2 pints/1 liter

Preparation: 30' + 15' to stand

Cooking: 10'

Level of difficulty: 1

- **8–12 fresh globe artichokes**
- **juice of 1 lemon**
- **2 quarts/2 liters cold water**
- **¹/₂ cup/125 ml white wine vinegar**
- **salt to taste**
- **extra-virgin olive oil**

TOMATO PASSATA

Makes: 6 quarts/
  6 liters

Preparation: 30'

Cooking: 3¹/₂ h

Level of difficulty: 3

- **14 lb/7 kg firm ripe tomatoes, seeded and coarsely chopped**
- **2 lb/1 kg onions, peeled and coarsely chopped**
- **2 lb/1 kg carrots, peeled and coarsely chopped**
- **14 oz/400 g celery, coarsely chopped**
- **7 oz/200 g fresh parsley, sage, or basil**
- **1 clove garlic**
- **1 cup/250 ml extra-virgin olive oil**
- **1 tsp salt**

Sterilize four 3-pint (four 1¹/₂-liter) screw-top jars as described on page 899. ❧ Place the tomatoes, onions, carrots, celery, herbs, and garlic in a large saucepan over low heat. Bring to a boil, stirring constantly. Cover and simmer for 2¹/₂ hours, stirring occasionally. ❧ Stir in the oil and sprinkle with the salt. Cook over medium heat for 1 hour. ❧ Cool to lukewarm. Ladle into the sterilized jars, leaving a ¹/₂-in (1-cm) headspace. Fasten the caps. ❧ Replace the jars in the large saucepan. Cover completely with water and boil for 10 minutes. Allow the water to cool completely. ❧ Store in a cool, dark place.

OLIVE PÂTÉ

S terilize two ¹/₂-pint (one ¹/₂-liter) screw-top jars as described on page 899. ❧ Finely chop the olives using a knife or food processor. Stir in enough of the oil to make a creamy paste. ❧ Ladle into the sterilized jars, cover with oil, and seal. ❧ If liked, add herbs or spices, such as garlic or parsley, to the olive before chopping them. ❧ Serve this pâté on slices of warm toast or as a pasta sauce.

Serve this exquisite pâté on slices of warm toast or with pasta.

Makes: 1 pint/500 ml
Preparation: 30'
Level of difficulty: 1

- **13 oz/400 g pitted green or black olives**
- **6 tbsp extra-virgin olive oil**
- **salt and freshly ground white pepper to taste**

SUN-DRIED TOMATOES

Makes: 1 pint/500 ml

Preparation: 15'

Cooking: 8'

Level of difficulty: 1

- **13 oz/400 g dried tomatoes**
- **extra-virgin olive oil to cover**
- **4 anchovy fillets**
- **1 tbsp capers**
- **salt and freshly ground black pepper to taste**

Sterilize two ¹/₂-pint (one ¹/₂-liter) screw-top jars as described on page 899. ⟡ Blanch the tomatoes in a little lightly salted boiling water for 4–5 minutes. ⟡ Drain and dry on a clean cloth. Place the tomatoes in sterilized jars, alternating them with the anchovies, capers, and oregano. Pour in enough oil to cover the tomatoes and seal. ⟡ Store for at least 1 month before serving.

ZUCCHINI IN OIL

S terilize four ¹/₂-pint (two ¹/₂-liter) screw-top jars as described on page 899. ❧ Clean and rinse the zucchini, dry well, and cut lengthwise in thin slices. Sprinkle lightly with salt and place in a colander to drain for about 3 hours. ❧ Boil for 1 minute in the vinegar seasoned with the peppercorns and bay leaves. Drain well and dry on a clean cloth. ❧ Ladle into the sterilized jars, alternating slices of zucchini with bits of basil leaves and oregano. Cover with the oil and seal. ❧ Store for at least 1 month before serving.

Makes: 2 pints/1 liter

Preparation: 15' + 3 h to drain

Cooking: 1'

Level of difficulty: 2

- 1³/₄ lb/750 g zucchini/ courgettes
- 3¹/₄ cups/750 ml white wine vinegar
- extra-virgin olive oil to cover
- 4 leaves fresh basil
- ¹/₂ tsp dried oregano
- 2 bay leaves
- 3 black peppercorns

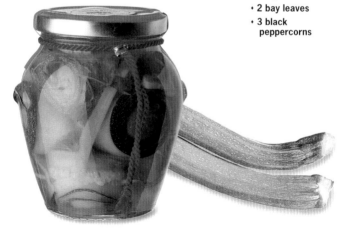

EGGPLANTS IN OIL

Makes: 3 pints/
1.5 liters

Preparation: 30'

Cooking: 2–3'

Level of difficulty: 1

- 2 lb/1 kg
  eggplants/
  aubergines
- 2 cups/500 ml
  white vinegar
- 2 cloves garlic,
  peeled
- 2 tbsp finely
  chopped parsley
- 1 tsp dried oregano
- salt and freshly
  ground black
  pepper to taste
- 1–2 tsp red pepper
  flakes
- extra-virgin olive oil
  to cover

Sterilize six ½-pint (three ½-liter) screw-top jars as described on page 899. ✿ Rinse the eggplants and slice or dice them into cubes. Boil for 2–3 minutes in the vinegar flavored with the garlic. Drain and dry on a clean cloth. ✿ Place in a large flat dish and season with the parsley, oregano, salt, pepper, and red pepper flakes. ✿ Ladle into sterilized jars and pour in enough oil to cover. ✿ Seal and store for at least 1 month before serving.

TUNA PRESERVED IN OIL

Bring a large pan of water to the boil over medium heat. Add the tuna and salt and cook for 1¹/₂ hours. ❧ Drain the tuna and dry carefully with paper towels. Let stand for 12 hours. ❧ Sterilize four ¹/₂-pint (two ¹/₂-liter) screw-top jars as described on page 899. ❧ Remove the skin and bones from the tuna, then flake the fish into pieces with your hands. ❧ Divide the pieces evenly among the sterilized jars. Cover with oil and seal.

Serve the tuna with a bean salad, accompanied by coarsely chopped red onions.

Makes: 2 pints/1 liter

Preparation: 30' + 12 h to stand

Cooking: 1¹/₂ h

Level of difficulty: 2

• 1¹/₂ lb/750 g fresh tuna, sliced
• 4 oz/125 g salt
• 4 cups/1 liter extra-virgin olive oil

CHILE‑PEPPER OIL

Rinse the chile peppers under cold running water. Dry well with paper towels. ❧ Finely chop and add to the olive oil with the bay leaf. Transfer the oil to a sterilized bottle and seal. ❧ Let infuse in a cool, dry place for about 30 days. Filter the oil. Add 2 or 3 whole chile peppers to make it look more attractive. ❧ Use to dress pasta, rice, fish, meat, and homemade pizzas. For a more delicate flavor, add fresh oil to the infused oil. For a spicier oil, let infuse for about 45 days.

Makes: 2 cups/500 ml
Preparation: 10'
Level of difficulty: 1

- **1 oz/30 g spicy small red chile peppers**
- **2 cups/500 ml extra‑virgin olive oil**
- **1 bay leaf**

SPICED OIL

Makes: 4 cups/1 liter

Preparation: 30' + 12 h to stand

Level of difficulty: 2

- **4 cups/1 liter extra-virgin olive oil**
- **2 bay leaves**
- **2 cloves**
- **6 mixed pepper corns**
- **1 sprig rosemary**
- **4 juniper berries**
- **1 stick cinnamon**
- **20 dried chile peppers**

Place all the ingredients in one or two sterilized bottles and cover with the oil. Seal and let infuse in a cool, dry place for about 30 days. ❧ Filter the herbs and spices from the oil (adding a few fresh ones to make it look attractive) and use for salads, boiled meats, or to marinate game. Vary the spices and herbs to suit your taste and the seasons.

SAUCES

BASIC TOMATO SAUCE

I f using fresh tomatoes, plunge into boiling water for 10 seconds and then into cold. Slip off their skins and cut them in half horizontally. Squeeze gently to remove most of the seeds and chop the flesh into small pieces. ⚘ Sauté the onion, carrot, celery, and garlic in a skillet (frying pan) with the oil for 5 minutes. ⚘ Add the tomatoes, parsley, basil, salt, and pepper, and sugar, if using. Partially cover and cook over medium-low heat for about 45 minutes, or until the sauce has reduced. ⚘ For a smoother sauce, put the mixture through a sieve or chop in a food processor.

This recipe makes a fairly large quantity of classic pasta sauce. Store in the refrigerator.

932

Makes: about 4 cups/ 1 liter

Preparation: 15'

Cooking: 50'

Level of difficulty: 2

- 4 lb/2 kg tomatoes
- 1 large onion, 1 large carrot, 1 stalk celery, 1 clove garlic, all coarsely chopped
- 4 tbsp extra-virgin olive oil
- 1 tbsp finely chopped parsley
- 8 fresh basil leaves, torn
- salt and freshly ground black pepper to taste
- 1 tbsp sugar (optional)

ORANGE &
WINE SAUCE

Place the butter in a large saucepan over medium heat until melted. 🍂 Pour in the wine and mix well. Cook until the wine has reduced and the mixture thickens. 🍂 Gradually stir in the orange juice and salt. Continue cooking until the mixture is thick. Stir in 2 tablespoons orange zest, mixing well. 🍂 Serve immediately.

This sauce is a delicious accompaniment to boiled or roast meat and fish dishes.

Makes: about 1 cup/ 250 ml

Preparation: 10'

Cooking: 20'

Level of difficulty: 2

- ¹/₂ **cup/125 g butter**
- ³/₄ **cup/175 ml dry white wine**
- **juice of 6 oranges**
- **dash of salt**
- **1 tbsp finely grated orange zest**

GORGONZOLA CHEESE SAUCE

Makes: about 2 cups/
  500 ml

Preparation: 10'

Cooking: 15'

Level of difficulty: 1

- **4 tbsp butter**
- **1 small onion, very finely chopped**
- **8 oz/250 g Gorgonzola cheese, chopped**
- **4 oz/125 g Mascarpone cheese**
- **³/₄ cup/185 ml heavy cream**
- **freshly ground black pepper to taste**

Stir the butter in a large saucepan over medium-low heat until melted. ♣ Add the onion and sauté for 3–4 minutes. ♣ Add the Gorgonzola, Mascarpone, and cream and stir carefully until blended and creamy. ♣ Remove from the heat and season with pepper to taste.

This superb Italian sauce comes from Piedmont, where it is served with gnocchi di patate (potato dumplings).

935

INDONESIAN SHRIMP PASTE SAMBAL

P lace the chilies, shrimp paste, tomato, brown sugar, and lime juice in a medium bowl and mix well. ❧ Set aside for 2 hours before serving.

Dried shrimp paste, or terasi, can be found in Asian food stores or the ethnic food aisle of your supermarket.

Makes: about 1 cup/ 250 ml

Preparation: 15' + 2 h to stand

Level of difficulty: 1

- **12–15 fiery red chilies, seeded and thinly sliced**
- **1–2 tbsp dried shrimp paste (terasi)**
- **1 large tomato, seeded and finely chopped**
- **2 tbsp soft brown sugar**
- **1 tbsp lime juice**

SPICY PEANUT SAUCE

Makes: about 1½
cups/375 ml

Preparation: 15'

Cooking: 5'

Level of difficulty: 1

- 1 cup/250 ml
  coconut cream
- 6 tbsp peanut
  butter
- 1 tsp
  Worcestershire
  sauce
- 1–2 tsp red pepper
  flakes
- fresh coconut
  (optional)

Warm the coconut cream in a large saucepan over low heat for 2 minutes. Stir in the peanut butter, mixing well. ✿ Add the Worcestershire sauce and red pepper flakes. Remove from heat and transfer to a serving bowl. ✿ Decorate with shavings of fresh coconut, if desired. ✿ Serve warm.

This spicy sauce can be served with kebabs or spooned over mixed stir-fried vegetables.

937

WARM RED SAUCE

Plunge the tomatoes into boiling water for 1 minute, then peel. Cut in half and squeeze gently to remove the seeds. Drain for 15 minutes in a colander, cut-side downward. ❧ Prepare the other vegetables while the tomatoes are draining. ❧ Cut the tomatoes into small pieces and place them in a saucepan with the other vegetables, garlic, and parsley. Add the chile pepper and cook over a low heat, uncovered, for 1½ hours, stirring frequently. ❧ Sieve the contents of the saucepan (or reduce them to a puree in a food processor), then blend in the oil, mustard, and vinegar. Add salt to taste and serve hot. ❧ This sauce can be prepared in advance and reheated just before serving. Served with boiled or roast meats.

Variations
• To give the sauce an agreeable sweet-sour taste, add more vinegar (scant ½ cup/100 ml) and 1 tablespoon sugar after the other ingredients have cooked for 1 hour.

• Use more or less chile pepper depending on how hot you like your sauce.

Makes: about 2 cups/ 500 ml

Preparation: 25'

Cooking: 1½ h

Level of difficulty: 1

- 1¼ lb/625 g ripe tomatoes
- 1 small onion, coarsely chopped
- 1 tender stalk celery (with leaves), coarsely chopped
- 1 small carrot, coarsely chopped
- 1 clove garlic, finely chopped
- 2 tsp finely chopped parsley
- 1 chile pepper
- 3–4 tbsp extra-virgin olive oil
- 1 teaspoon Dijon-type mustard
- 1 tbsp red wine vinegar
- salt to taste

BOLOGNESE MEAT SAUCE

Sauté the pancetta, onion, carrot, and celery in the butter in a skillet (frying pan) for 10 minutes. ❧ Add the pork and beef and cook for 5 minutes more. ❧ Gradually add half the wine and stock and simmer until reduced, about 10–15 minutes. ❧ Add the tomato paste, tomatoes, salt and pepper and simmer, gradually stirring in the remaining wine and stock. This will take at least 2 hours.

The longer you cook this sauce, the better it will taste. Two hours is the minimum time you should allow.

940

Makes: about 4 cups/ 1 liter

Preparation: 20'

Cooking: 2¹/₂ h

Level of difficulty: 1

- 4 tbsp butter
- 4 tbsp diced pancetta (or bacon)
- 1 small onion, 1 small carrot, 1 stalk celery, all finely chopped
- 8 oz/250 g ground beef
- 4 oz/125 g lean ground pork
- 1 cup/250 ml dry red wine
- 1¹/₄ cups/375 ml *Beef Stock* (see page 140)
- 1 tbsp tomato paste
- 12 oz/375 g peeled and chopped fresh or canned tomatoes
- salt and freshly ground black pepper to taste

AROMATIC HERB SAUCE

Makes: about 1 cup/
250 ml

Preparation: 10'

Level of difficulty: 1

- 1 soft-boiled egg,
  shelled and very
  finely chopped
- 1 tbsp finely
  chopped parsley
- 1 tbsp finely
  chopped tarragon
- 1 tbsp finely
  chopped thyme
- 1 tbsp finely
  chopped basil
- 1 clove garlic,
  finely chopped
- ½ cup/125 ml
  extra-virgin olive
  oil
- 4 tbsp white wine
  vinegar
- salt and freshly
  ground black
  pepper to taste

AROMATIC HERB SAUCE

Makes: about 1 cup/
250 ml

Preparation: 10'

Level of difficulty: 1

P lace the egg in a large bowl. Add the parsley, tarragon, thyme, basil, and garlic and mix well. Pour in the oil and vinegar. ❧ Season with salt and pepper. ❧ Transfer to a serving dish.

- 1 soft-boiled egg, shelled and very finely chopped
- 1 tbsp finely chopped parsley
- 1 tbsp finely chopped tarragon
- 1 tbsp finely chopped thyme
- 1 tbsp finely chopped basil
- 1 clove garlic, finely chopped
- 1/2 cup/125 ml extra-virgin olive oil
- 4 tbsp white wine vinegar
- salt and freshly ground black pepper to taste

This fragrant sauce is delicious served with boiled or roast fish. It is also good with egg dishes.

941

WALNUT SAUCE

Makes: about 1 cup/
250 ml

Preparation: 15'

Level of difficulty: 1

Crumble the bread and place it in a small bowl. Sprinkle with the vinegar. ♣ Place the walnuts and parsley in a blender or food processor. Process until very finely chopped. ♣ Add the bread to the blender and chop until smooth. ♣ Gradually add in the oil until well mixed. Season with salt and pepper. ♣ Serve with fish or poultry.

- 2 slices day-old bread
- 3 tbsp white wine vinegar
- 30 blanched walnuts
- 2 tbsp parsley, coarsely chopped
- 8 tbsp extra-virgin olive oil
- salt and freshly ground black pepper to taste

AGRESTO SAUCE

- ½ cup/125 ml sour grape juice
- 1 tbsp onion, finely chopped
- zest of 1 orange
- 4 tbsp extra-virgin olive oil
- 1 slice day-old bread
- salt and freshly ground black pepper to taste

Boil the grape juice until about two-thirds of it has evaporated, removing the foam that forms on top. ❧ Soak the bread in the hot juice. ❧ In a food processor or blender, finely chop the onion and orange zest. Add the soaked bread and chop again. ❧ Transfer to a bowl and gradually add the oil while whipping the mixture by hand with a fork. Season with salt and pepper. ❧ Serve with meat, poultry, or game.

943

POOR MAN'S SAUCE

Melt the butter in a small saucepan over a low heat. Add the garlic and cook very slowly until pale gold (if browned the garlic will give the sauce a bitter flavor). ❧ Mix the flour and vinegar in a small bowl and season with salt and pepper. Add the eggs and egg yolk and beat very lightly with a fork, making sure the mixture doesn't become frothy. ❧ Remove the garlic from the butter and add the egg mixture gradually while stirring continuously over a very low heat. Continue stirring until the mixture thickens to a smooth, creamy consistency. ❧ Serve with boiled vegetables and meats.

*Makes: about 1 cup/
  250 ml*

Preparation: 5'

Cooking: 7–9'

Level of difficulty: 1

- **3 tbsp butter**
- **1–2 whole cloves garlic, lightly crushed**
- **1 tsp all-purpose/ plain flour**
- **2 tbsp red wine vinegar**
- **salt and freshly ground white pepper to taste**
- **2 eggs + 1 egg yolk**

HONEY SAUCE

Makes: about 1 cup/
250 ml

Preparation: 20'

Level of difficulty: 1

- **20 walnut halves, shelled**
- **³/₄ cup/150 ml mild-flavored honey**
- **2 tbsp mustard**
- **1–2 tbsp hot water**

Chop the walnuts finely in a food processor. ♣ Mix the honey and mustard in a small bowl. Add the water and then the walnuts. Stir thoroughly. ♣ Serve with Pecorino cheese or boiled beef.

945

LEEK SAUCE

Cut the leeks into ⅛ in (2–3 mm) thick slices. ❧ Melt the butter in a saucepan over medium heat, then add the leeks. Cover and cook gently for 5 minutes, or until the leeks have wilted. ❧ Season with salt and pepper. Add the cream and milk and cook for 20–25 minutes. ❧ Serve with polenta or rice.

Makes: about 2 cups/ 500 ml

Preparation: 20'

Cooking: 25–30'

Level of difficulty: 1

- **12 oz/350 g leeks, cleaned (white part only)**
- **3 tbsp butter**
- **salt and freshly ground white pepper to taste**
- **1½ cups/300 ml light/single cream**
- **4–5 tbsp whole/full cream milk**

BELL PEPPER SAUCE

Makes: about 2 cups/
500 ml

Preparation: 15'

Cooking: 40'

Level of difficulty: 1

- **3 large bell peppers/capsicums, seeded and very finely chopped**
- **2 cloves garlic, finely chopped**
- **3 tbsp parsley, finely chopped**
- **1 onion, finely chopped**
- **1 tbsp sugar**
- **1 tbsp white wine vinegar**
- **4 tbsp extra-virgin olive oil**
- **salt to taste**

P lace the peppers, garlic, parsley, and onion in a large saucepan over medium heat. Pour in enough water to cover. Bring to a boil and simmer for 30 minutes. ❧ Stir in the sugar, vinegar, and oil and mix well. Season with salt. Cover and continue cooking for about 5–10 minutes, or until thick. ❧ Serve with baked vegetables or fish.

This sauce is really tasty if set aside overnight and served the following day.

949

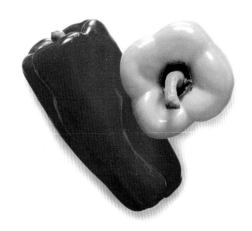

BÉCHAMEL SAUCE

Heat the milk in a small saucepan over low heat until almost boiling. Remove from heat. ❧ Place the butter and flour in a small saucepan over low heat. Cook for 1 minute, stirring constantly. ❧ Remove from heat and pour in half of the hot milk. Return to the heat and warm until the mixture thickens. Gradually mix in the remaining milk, stirring constantly. Bring to a boil and remove from the heat. ❧ Season with salt.

Béchamel sauce is used in a wide variety of dishes, including pasta and many baked specialities.

Makes: about 2 cups/ 500 ml

Preparation: 5'

Cooking: 10'

Level of difficulty: 1

- **2 cups/500 ml milk**
- **4 tbsp butter**
- **¹⁄₃ cup/50 g all-purpose/plain flour**
- **salt to taste**

ONION SAUCE

P our the oil into a medium saucepan over low heat and add the onions. ❧ Season with salt and pepper. ❧ Cover and cook, stirring often, for 3 hours, or until creamy and golden. Gradually add the stock during the cooking period, keeping *This sauce tastes best when made with fresh beef stock.* the onions moist. ❧ Serve with baked vegetables or roast meats.

Makes: about 1¹/₂ cups/375 ml

Preparation: 15'

Cooking: 3 h

Level of difficulty: 1

- **6 medium white onions, thinly sliced**
- **6 tbsp extra-virgin olive oil**
- **salt and freshly ground black pepper to taste**
- **1 cup/250 ml *Beef Stock* (see page 140)**

PARSLEY SAUCE

Makes: about 1 cup/ 250 ml

Preparation: 20' + 1 h to stand

Level of difficulty: 2

- $^{1}/_{2}$ cup/60 g fresh bread crumbs
- 4 tbsp red wine vinegar
- 1 hard-boiled egg yolk
- 8 tbsp finely chopped parsley
- 2 cloves garlic, finely chopped
- 2–3 anchovy fillets (optional)
- $^{1}/_{2}$ cup/125 ml extra-virgin olive oil
- salt and freshly ground white pepper to taste

Soak the bread crumbs in the vinegar for 5 minutes. Drain the excess. ❧ Place the egg yolk in a medium bowl and mash with a fork. Stir in the parsley, garlic, anchovies (if using), and bread crumbs and mix well. ❧ Pour in enough oil to make a thick sauce, stirring constantly. Season with the salt and pepper. ❧ Set aside for 1 hour. ❧ Serve with boiled meat or boiled or baked fish.

FRUIT MUSTARD SAUCE

Place the fruit, lemon juice and zest, and honey in a large saucepan over medium heat. Pour in enough water to cover. ❧ Place the honey and wine in a small saucepan over medium heat. Bring to a boil. Simmer for 10 minutes. Stir in the mustard and mix well. Continue cooking until the mixture thickens. ❧ Pour the sauce over the fruit and mix well. ❧ Serve with boiled and roast meats.

Makes: about 2 cups/ 500 ml

Preparation: 30'

Cooking: 1 h

Level of difficulty: 2

- **2¹/₂ lb/1¹/₂ kg mixed fruit (grapes, apples, pears, or cherries), peeled and cut into large pieces**
- **juice and zest of 1 lemon**
- **1¹/₂ cups/375 ml dry white wine**
- **¹/₂ cup/125 ml honey**
- **4 tbsp powdered mustard**

NEAPOLITAN MEAT SAUCE

Place the beef, lard, and oil in a large saucepan over medium heat. ❧ Stir in the onion, carrots, and celery and mix well. Cook until the vegetables are transparent. ❧ Pour in the wine and continue cooking until it reduces. ❧ Season with salt. Cover and cook over low heat for 30 minutes. ❧ Stir in the tomatoes. Cover and continue cooking for 2 hours. ❧ Remove the beef and serve the sauce with pasta.

This makes a delicious pasta sauce. Serve the beef separately after the pasta.

Makes: about 2 cups/ 500 ml

Preparation: 30'

Cooking: 2½ h

Level of difficulty: 2

- 2 lb/1 kg lean beef
- 4 tbsp lard, cut up
- 4 tbsp extra-virgin olive oil
- 2 onions, finely chopped
- 2 carrots, peeled and finely chopped
- 1 stalk celery, finely chopped
- 1 cup/250 ml dry red wine
- salt to taste
- 1 (15 oz/400 g) can tomatoes

TARTARE SAUCE

Place the egg yolk and vinegar in a small saucepan over low heat. Cook, stirring constantly, until the mixture begins to bubble. ℀ Remove from heat. Set aside to cool for 5 minutes. ℀ Transfer to a blender or food processor. Gradually pour in the oil and process until thick and smooth. ℀ Pour the mixture into a medium bowl. ℀ Stir in the gherkins, onions, capers, and mustard and mix well. ℀ Serve with boiled meat or fish dishes.

Makes: about 1 cup/ 250 ml

Preparation: 15'

Cooking: 5'

Level of difficulty: 2

- **1 egg yolk**
- **2 tsp white vinegar**
- **6 tbsp extra-virgin olive oil**
- **salt to taste**
- **2 pickled gherkins, finely chopped**
- **2 pickled white onions**
- **1 tbsp capers (in vinegar)**
- **1 tsp hot mustard**

INDEX

A

Almonds
- Almond cookies, 815
- Almond crispies, 829
- Almond crunchies, 823
- Almond polenta cake, 881
- Custard with almond brittle, 717

Anchovies
- Anchovies with mint, 454
- Fresh anchovy pizza, 351
- Medallions of ham with broccoli & anchovies, 579
- Tomato, caper & anchovy pizza, 327

Appetizers, see **Starters**

Apples
- Apple strudel, 892
- Country apple bake, 874
- Crêpes with caramelized apples, 788
- Curried sausage & apple pie, 609
- Egg, Provolone, apple, & radicchio salad, 678
- Filet of pork with apple, 570
- Nougat apple crêpes, 802

Apricots
- Baked apricot crêpes, 792
- Chicken-in-a-hurry, 475
- Panna cotta with apricot sauce, 714
- Pecan & apricot focaccia, 313

Artichokes
- Artichoke omelet, 425
- Artichoke pizza, 344
- Artichoke risotto, 213
- Artichokes preserved in oil, 920
- Beef rolls with artichokes, 536
- Lamb & artichoke fricassee, 552
- Rice with peas & artichokes, 211
- Tagliatelle with artichoke sauce, 161

Arugula
- Arugula, corn & kiwifruit salad, 662
- Prosciutto & arugula pizza, 339
- Swordfish steaks with arugula & basil sauce, 452
- Tomato & arugula focaccia, 308

Asparagus
- Asparagus cream, 107
- Asparagus with egg dressing, 645
- Asparagus & egg lunch dish, 428
- Asparagus pie, 377
- Asparagus risotto, 204
- Asparagus with sabayon sauce, 643

Avocado
- Guacamole, 72

B

Banana
- Banana & lemon crêpes, 781

Beef
- Bari-style beef rolls, 540
- Beef rolls with artichokes, 536
- Boiled beef in leek & tomato sauce, 535
- Club steaks with green pepper, 538

INDEX

- Glazed topside with mushrooms sautéed in garlic, 532
- Indonesian beef stew, 526
- Meatballs with tomato, 530
- Pan roasted beef with mushrooms, 529
- Sliced steak with salad greens, 541

Bell peppers
- Bell pepper sauce, 949
- Bell peppers in oil, 916
- Calamari, bacon, & bell pepper kebabs, 578
- Chicken balls with bell peppers & black olives, 482
- Chicken & bell pepper stew, 490
- Focaccia with summer vegetables, 298
- Hard-boiled eggs with bell peppers, 9
- Pizza with bell peppers, 347

Bread
- Baked sausages & bread, 613
- Bread & cheese soup, 131
- Bread soup with tomato, 136
- Bread, making at home, 250

- Breadsticks, 264
- Bruschetta with tomato & basil, 48
- Cumin bread, 272
- Deep-fried seafood sandwiches, 448
- Empanada with clams, 301
- Empanada with pork, 300
- Florentine liver toasts, 50
- Fresh cheese & olive toasts, 57
- Fried Mozzarella sandwiches, 43
- Fruit bread, 283
- Herb rolls, 267
- Honey whole-wheat bread, 273
- Irish soda bread, 260
- Mediterranean corn bread, 258
- Mousetraps, 53
- Naan, 268
- Neapolitan filled bread, 394
- Nun's toast, 10
- Oregano bread, 274
- Parmesan bread, 263
- Quick cheese and beer bread, 280
- Romagna-style flatbread, 277
- Rosemary and raisin rolls, 279
- Rye bread, 254
- Sesame seed bread, 270
- Spicy tomato bread, 276
- Sweet raisin bread, 266

- Walnut and rosemary bread, 257
- Wheatgerm bread, 261
- White bread, 253
- Whole-wheat chapatis, 281

Broccoli
- Broccoli & leek pie, 374
- Medallions of ham with broccoli & anchovies, 579

C

Cabbage
- Braised Savoy cabbage, 636
- Cabbage & cheese soup, 141
- Cabbage baked with sausage & bacon, 616
- Potato & cabbage mix, 649
- Sauerkraut, 909

Cakes
- Almond polenta cake, 881
- Apple strudel, 892
- Berryfruit cake, 894
- Black forest cake, 876
- Chewy fruit & spice cake with chocolate glaze, 870
- Chelsea buns, 820
- Chocolate buttermilk cake, 873

- Chocolate hazelnut cake, 891
- Chocolate orange cake, 886
- Chocolate truffles, 858
- Country apple bake, 874
- Double chocolate brownies, 857
- Hazelnut cake, 868
- Margarita muffins, 819
- Mimosa cake, 864
- Mini raspberry tarts, 861
- Modena cake, 884
- Piedmontese chocolate cake, 869
- Polenta & candied fruits cake, 888
- Poor man's cake, 867
- Rice cake, 711
- Ricotta cake with berries, 707
- Sachertorte, 872
- Sandy cake, 882
- Sicilian ricotta cake, 702
- Sponge cake, 878
- Turkish cake, 883

Carrots
- Carrot salad with garlic, lemon & parsley, 660

Calzone, *see* **Pizza**

Capon
- Roast stuffed capon, 478

Cheese
- Baked onions with cheese, 621
- Baked tomatoes with cheese, 23
- Béchamel sauce, 950
- Blue cheese dressing, 655
- Blue cheese potato salad, 664
- Blue cheese savories, 407
- Blue cheese snacks, 60
- Bowtie pasta in summer sauce, 151
- Bread & cheese soup, 131
- Bresaola with fresh cheese, 49
- Cabbage & cheese soup, 141
- Cheese and almond puffs, 31
- Cheese biscuits or straws, 36
- Cheese, cream & bacon pie, 405
- Cheese croquettes, 35
- Cheese egg dip with crudités, 19
- Cheese flatbread, 401
- Cheese focaccia, 293
- Cheese fondue, 28
- Cheese fritters, 62
- Cheese & ham croquettes, 38
- Cheese soufflé, 431
- Cheddar onion dip, 16
- Cream cheese with fresh herbs, 56

- Fava beans with Pecorino cheese, 26
- Feta cheese & spinach salad, 684
- Focaccia filled with creamy cheese, 297
- Focaccia with Ricotta stuffing, 361
- Fresh cheese & olive toasts, 57
- Fried Mozzarella sandwiches, 43
- Fried pastries with Ricotta cheese, 817
- Fusilli salad with tomato, garlic, & Mozzarella cheese, 167
- Gorgonzola cheese sauce, 935
- Gorgonzola & cream focaccia, 306
- Gorgonzola risotto, 224
- Ham & cheese pizza, 352
- Hot cheese and herb appetizer, 33
- Leek & Fontal country pie, 398
- Mousetraps, 53
- Mozzarella & tomato focaccia, 310
- Neapolitan filled bread, 394
- Parmesan bread, 263
- Parmesan ice cream, 32
- Pasta with ricotta & eggplant, 153
- Pear, walnut, & Gorgonzola pizza, 355

- Penne with Ricotta cheese, 171
- Prickly cheese and celery balls, 20
- Quick cheese and beer bread, 280
- Rice with four cheeses, 246
- Ricotta cheese with fresh herbs, 17
- Ricotta pastry, 370
- Risotto with Mozzarella, 220
- Saffron cheese pie, 402
- Salami & cheese skewers, 93
- Sesame & cheese focaccia rolls, 318
- Spicy egg & cheese soufflé, 429
- Stuffed celery stalks, 27
- Walnut & cheese focaccia rolls, 320
- Wild salad greens with warm Caprino, 22

Chicken
- Braised chicken with mushrooms, 485
- Chicken balls with bell peppers & black olives, 482
- Chicken & bell pepper stew, 490
- Chicken & celery salad, 494
- Chicken with fennel seeds, 507
- Chicken galantine, 481
- Chicken-in-a-hurry, 475
- Chicken & lentil patties, 484
- Chicken Maryland, 474
- Chicken risotto, 241
- Chicken satay, 95
- Chicken in a spiced peanut sauce, 472
- Chicken stew, 495
- Chicken stew with tomato sauce & green olives, 488
- Chicken stock & Parmesan croutons, 118
- Chicken vindaloo, 496
- Chicken with yogurt, 497
- Fijian coconut cream chicken, 476
- Ground chicken satay, 504
- Hunter's chicken, 506
- Mixed sausage, chicken, & vegetable skewers, 604
- Roast chicken with lemon, 493
- Simple chicken salad, 491
- Spicy Spanish chicken, 498
- Spring chicken cooked in sea salt, 487
- Sweet & sour chicken salad, 471

Chicken livers
- Cracked pepper pâté, 77
- Florentine liver toasts, 50

Chocolate
- Afghans, 838
- Chewy fruit & spice cake with chocolate glaze, 870
- Chocolate amaretti crêpes, 799
- Chocolate buttermilk cake, 873
- Chocolate egg custard, 757
- Chocolate hazelnut cake, 891
- Chocolate hedgehogs, 832
- Chocolate ice cream, 761
- Chocolate mold, 768
- Chocolate mousse, 764
- Chocolate orange cake, 886
- Chocolate orange mousse, 734
- Chocolate pancakes, 774
- Chocolate pastry cream, 772
- Chocolate rice pudding, 753
- Chocolate truffles, 858
- Coconut cream chocolate crêpes, 787
- Cointreau and white chocolate mousse, 766
- Creamy crêpes with chocolate, 795
- Crêpes with chocolate mousse, 793
- Double chocolate crêpes, 811

- Fresh fruit chocolate mousse, 750
- Mascarpone & chocolate mousse, 740
- Mocha chocolate cookies, 834
- Pears with chocolate sauce, 758
- Piedmontese chocolate cake, 869
- Raspberry chocolate pudding, 762
- Raspberry white choc cheesecake, 708
- Sachertorte, 872
- Uncooked chocolate slice, 856
- Walnut crêpes with chocolate sauce, 783

Coconut
- Baked coconut custard, 704
- Coconut cream chocolate crêpes, 787
- Coconut cream dressing, 654
- Coconut & mango crêpes, 804
- Fijian coconut cream chicken, 476

Cookies
- Afghans, 838
- Almond cookies, 815
- Almond crispies, 829
- Almond crunchies, 823
- Amaretti cookies, 852
- Anzac cookies, 846
- Bran cookies, 847

- Candied grapefruit, 860
- Chocolate chips, 814
- Chocolate hedgehogs, 832
- Cornmeal, pine nut & raisin cookies, 850
- Cream crescents, 824
- Double chocolate brownies, 857
- Gingernuts, 844
- Heavenly moments, 836
- Jam-filled turnovers, 849
- Marzipan petits fours, 826
- Mocha chocolate cookies, 834
- Peanut butter cookies, 854
- Prato cookies, 822
- Shortbread, 842
- Shrewsbury cookies, 840
- Spice, honey & nut cookies, 827
- Sugar cookies, 848
- Sweet crisps, 855
- Sweet rings, 851

Crêpes
- Baked apricot crêpes, 792
- Baked meringue crêpes flambée, 794
- Banana & lemon crêpes, 781
- Basic crêpes, 773
- Blueberry blintzes, 796
- Chocolate amaretti crêpes, 799

- Chocolate pancakes, 774
- Coconut & mango crêpes, 804
- Coconut cream chocolate crêpes, 787
- Creamy crêpes with chocolate, 795
- Crêpes with caramelized apples, 788
- Crêpes with chocolate mousse, 793
- Crêpes with cream & candied chestnuts, 808
- Crêpes with Mascarpone, raisins & rum, 807
- Crêpes Suzette, 784
- Double chocolate crêpes, 811
- Dusky crêpes, 806
- Fresh fruit & jam crêpes, 780
- Fruit-filled crêpes with meringue topping, 800
- Nougat apple crêpes, 802
- Pancake layer cake, 776
- Pineapple crêpe layer cake, 786
- Walnut crêpes with chocolate sauce, 783
- Yogurt & fruit crêpes, 803

Cucumber
- Cucumber & onion salad, 673
- Tzatziki, 68

D

Desserts
- Amaretto mousse, 739
- Baked coconut custard, 704
- Chestnut custard cream, 722
- Chocolate egg custard, 757
- Chocolate ice cream, 761
- Chocolate mold, 768
- Chocolate mousse, 764
- Chocolate orange mousse, 734
- Chocolate pastry cream, 772
- Chocolate rice pudding, 753
- Cointreau and white chocolate mousse, 766
- Crème brûlée, 720
- Custard with almond brittle, 717
- Emilian trifle, 767
- Fluffy egg delight, 718
- Foolproof meringues, 830
- Fresh fruit chocolate mousse, 750
- Fried pastries with Ricotta cheese, 817
- Grand Marnier soufflé, 744
- Italian rice pudding, 737
- Kahlua mousse, 732
- Key lime cheesecake, 748
- Kiwi meringue roll, 701
- Lemon cream, 733
- Lemon soufflé, 738
- Mascarpone & chocolate mousse, 740
- Mont Blanc, 728
- New York cheesecake, 710
- Panna cotta with apricot sauce, 714
- Passionfruit cream, 745
- Pears with chocolate sauce, 758
- Queen of puddings, 725
- Raspberry and peach trifle, 730
- Raspberry chocolate pudding, 762
- Raspberry white choc cheesecake, 708
- Rice cream, 719
- Ricotta cream, 749
- Ricotta mousse with plum sauce, 726
- Rum raisin cheesecake, 705
- Strawberry Bavarian cream, 712
- Strawberry mascarpone mousse, 746
- Tiramisù, 754
- Vanilla cream, 698
- Watermelon jelly, 724
- Zabaglione, 760
- Zuccotto, 742

Dressings
- Blue cheese dressing, 655
- Coconut cream dressing, 654
- Garlic dressing, 655
- Honey and garlic dressing, 655
- Joy's cole slaw dressing, 654
- Mustard vinaigrette, 654
- Orange poppyseed dressing, 655

E

Eggplant
- Algerian-style stuffed tomatoes, 626
- Eggplant dip, 70
- Eggplant pizza, 340
- Eggplants in oil, 925
- Pasta with ricotta & eggplant, 153

Eggs
- Artichoke omelet, 425
- Asparagus with egg dressing, 645
- Asparagus & egg lunch dish, 428
- Asparagus with sabayon sauce, 643
- Baked herb omelet, 421
- Baked meringue crêpes flambée, 794
- Cheese egg dip with crudités, 19

- Cheese soufflé, 431
- Country-style eggs, 15
- Crabmeat omelet, 415
- Curried eggs, 418
- Egg, Provolone, apple, & radicchio salad, 678
- Egg & tofu salad, 685
- Egg, vegetable, & bacon pâté, 78
- Eggs fairy-style, 12
- Fluffy egg delight, 718
- Foolproof meringues, 830
- Hard-boiled eggs with bell peppers, 9
- Nun's toast, 10
- Plain omelet, 420
- Polenta crêpes with spicy spinach, 84
- Salmon quiche, 388
- Scotch eggs, 417
- Scrambled eggs, Mexican style, 424
- Spaghetti with egg & bacon, 163
- Spicy broccoli omelet, 422
- Spicy egg & cheese soufflé, 429
- Stuffed eggs, 11

F

Fava beans
- Fava bean purée, 117
- Fava bean stew, 650
- Fava beans with Pecorino cheese, 26

Fish
- Baked plaice with capers, 455
- Fish risotto, 233
- Fried tuna balls, 460
- Mixed deep-fried fish, 456
- Pasta with sardines, 176
- Plaice rolls with peas, 438
- Rigatoni with fish sauce, 180
- Risotto with wine and smoked salmon, 236
- Roasted sea bass, 450
- Salmon burgers, 464
- Salmon quiche, 388
- Shark steaks with savory topping, 467
- Sicilian anchovies, 466
- Spaghetti with tuna fish & tomato, 178
- Stockfish cream, 461
- Swordfish steaks with arugula & basil sauce, 452

Focaccia
- Basic focaccia, 286
- Cheese focaccia, 293
- Focaccia filled with creamy cheese, 297
- Focaccia with black olives, 291
- Focaccia with green olives, 292
- Focaccia with potatoes, 307
- Focaccia with red onions, 303
- Focaccia with summer vegetables, 298
- Focaccia with zucchini, 299
- Fruity focaccia, 314
- Garbanzo bean focaccia, 316
- Gorgonzola & cream focaccia, 306
- Mozzarella & tomato focaccia, 310
- Onion focaccia, 288
- Pecan & apricot focaccia, 313
- Rosemary focaccia, 286
- Sage focaccia, 292
- Sesame & cheese focaccia rolls, 318
- Walnut & cheese focaccia rolls, 320
- Whole-wheat focaccia, 294

G

Garbanzo beans
- Falafel, 67
- Florentine soup, 102
- Garbanzo bean focaccia, 316
- Houmous, 69

H

Ham
- Cheese & ham croquettes, 38
- Ham & cheese pizza, 352

– Ham & walnut potato gratin, 399
– Medallions of ham with broccoli & anchovies, 579

J

Jellies/Jams
– Red currant jelly, 910
– Ginger & lime marmalade, 904
– Green tomato jam, 899
– Greengage plum preserves, 900
– Strawberry preserves, 902

L

Lamb
– Braised lamb, 556
– Braised lamb with lemon, 546
– Breaded lamb chops, 550
– Broiled lamb chops, 557
– Hot & spicy lamb stew, 544
– Koftas, 531
– Lamb & artichoke fricassee, 552
– Lamb & potato casserole, 554
– Pan-roasted lamb, 548
– Pilotas, 586

– Roast lamb with olives, 547

Leeks
– Broccoli & leek pie, 374
– Boiled beef in leek & tomato sauce, 535
– Leek & Fontal country pie, 398
– Leek pie, 372
– Leek & potato soup, 110
– Leek sauce, 946

Lemons
– Angel hair pasta with oil & lemon sauce, 193
– Banana & lemon crêpes, 781
– Braised lamb with lemon, 546
– Lemon cream, 733
– Lemon risotto, 223
– Lemon soufflé, 738
– Roast chicken with lemon, 493
– Spaghetti with lemon & chile pepper, 150

Lentils
– Chicken & lentil patties, 484
– Hearty lentil soup, 112

M

Mushrooms
– Austrian gnocchi, 199
– Baked mushrooms and potatoes, 641

– Braised chicken with mushrooms, 485
– Caesar's mushroom salad, 695
– Fettuccine with mushroom sauce, 183
– Fried polenta with mushrooms, 59
– Garlic mushrooms, 86
– Glazed topside with mushrooms sautéed in garlic, 532
– Hazelnut and mushroom risotto, 219
– Mushroom curry, 639
– Mushroom crisps, 87
– Mushroom lasagne, 196
– Mushroom parcels, 638
– Mushroom pie, 379
– Mushroom pizza, 343
– Mushroom risotto, 217
– Mushrooms with pine nuts, 635
– Mushrooms cooked in foil packages, 634
– Mushroom & truffle toasts, 61
– Pan roasted beef with mushrooms, 529
– Pasta with bacon, mushrooms & peas, 179
– Porcini mushroom soup, 123
– Spicy mushrooms, 642

Mussels
– Mussels in pepper sauce, 443

– Mussels in white wine, 447

N

Nuts
– Cheese and almond puffs, 31
– Chicken in a spiced peanut sauce, 472
– Corn & peanut fritters, 82
– Ham & walnut potato gratin, 399
– Hazelnut and mushroom risotto, 219
– Pear, walnut, & Gorgonzola pizza, 355
– Pecan & apricot focaccia, 313
– Walnut & cheese focaccia rolls, 320
– Walnut and rosemary bread, 257

O

Oil
– Chile-pepper oil, 928
– Spiced oil, 929

Olives
– Chicken balls with bell peppers & black olives, 482
– Chicken stew with tomato sauce & green olives, 488
– Country-style eggs, 15

– Focaccia with black olives, 291
– Focaccia with green olives, 292
– Fresh cheese & olive toasts, 57
– Hot and spicy olives, 64
– Olive, onion & anchovy pizza, 348
– Roast lamb with olives, 547
– Spaghetti with olives & tomatoes, 156
– Spaghetti with spicy olive sauce, 155
– Stuffed fried olives, 63

Onions
– Baked onions with cheese, 621
– Cheddar onion dip, 16
– Cucumber & onion salad, 673
– Focaccia with red onions, 303
– Focaccia with summer vegetables, 298
– French onion soup, 120
– Onion focaccia, 288
– Onion fritters in balsamic vinegar, 45
– Onion pie, 386
– Onion sauce, 952
– Onion supreme calzone, 366
– Pickled onions, 915
– Sweet and sour baby onions, 651
– Whole wheat spaghetti with onions, 192

Oranges
– Orange-flavored shrimp cocktail, 444
– Orange risotto, 210
– Orange salad, 677
– Orange & wine sauce, 934

P

Pancakes, see **Crêpes**

Pasta
– Angel hair pasta with oil & lemon sauce, 193
– Baked tomatoes with pasta filling, 168
– Bowtie pasta in summer sauce, 151
– Fettuccine with mushroom sauce, 183
– Florentine soup, 102
– Fusilli salad with tomato, garlic, & Mozzarella cheese, 167
– Garganelli with meat sauce & peas, 186
– Homemade tortellini, 106
– Hot & spicy spaghetti, 162
– Mushroom lasagne, 196
– Pasta with bacon, mushrooms & peas, 179
– Pasta with ricotta & eggplant, 153

- Pasta with sardines, 176
- Pasta, homemade, 142
- Penne with Ricotta cheese, 171
- Rigatoni with fish sauce, 180
- Spaghetti with cherry tomatoes, 170
- Spaghetti with clams, 175
- Spaghetti with egg & bacon, 163
- Spaghetti with lemon & chile pepper, 150
- Spaghetti with olives & tomatoes, 156
- Spaghetti with seafood sauce, 172
- Spaghetti with simple tomato sauce, 146
- Spaghetti with spicy olive sauce, 155
- Spaghetti with tomato & crumb sauce, 157
- Spaghetti with tuna fish & tomato, 178
- Spaghettini with garlic, oil & chile, 149
- Sweet and sour bucatini, 158
- Tagliatelle with artichoke sauce, 161
- Tagliatelle with prosciutto & peas, 189
- Tagliatelle with shrimp & white wine, 190
- Tortellini with meat sauce, 185
- Trenette with pesto, 164
- Whole wheat spaghetti with duck sauce, 194
- Whole wheat spaghetti with onions, 192

Pastry
- Plain pastry, 370
- Puff pastry, 371
- Ricotta pastry, 370
- Special pastry, 370

Pâtès
- Cracked pepper pâté, 77
- Egg, vegetable, & bacon pâté, 78
- Liver pâté, 80
- Olive pâté, 922

Pearl barley
- Pearl barley soup, 99
- Pearl barley & vegetable soup, 114

Peas
- Creamy pea soup, 109
- Garganelli with meat sauce & peas, 186
- Pasta with bacon, mushrooms & peas, 179
- Peas with bacon, garlic, and wine, 646
- Plaice rolls with peas, 438
- Rice & pea soup, 132
- Rice with peas & artichokes, 211
- Rice with peas & pesto, 247
- Sugar peas with cream, 647
- Tagliatelle with prosciutto & peas, 189

Pheasant
- Truffled pheasant, 502

Pizza
- Artichoke pizza, 344
- Eggplant pizza, 340
- Deep-crust pizza, 330
- Four-seasons pizza, 335
- Fresh anchovy pizza, 351
- Fresh tomato & garlic pizza, 329
- Fried pizzas, 360
- Ham & cheese pizza, 352
- Lebanese pizzas, 74
- Lilliput pizzas, 356
- Mushroom pizza, 343
- Olive, onion & anchovy pizza, 348
- Onion supreme calzone, 366
- Pear, walnut, & Gorgonzola pizza, 355
- Pizza with bell peppers, 347
- Pizza with chicory topping, 341
- Pizza in a hurry, 359
- Pizza margherita, 333
- Pizza, making at home, 324
- Pizza with mixed topping, 336

- Pizza with Ricotta stuffing, 361
- Spicy salami & cheese calzone, 362
- Swiss chard calzone, 365
- Tomato, caper & anchovy pizza, 327

Polenta
- Fried polenta with mushrooms, 59
- Polenta & candied fruits cake, 888
- Polenta crêpes with spicy spinach, 84
- Pork & polenta stew, 564

Pork
- Filet of pork with apple, 570
- Glazed spareribs, 580
- Mixed pork stewed in red wine, 574
- Pan Roasted pork, 562
- Pork goulash, 563
- Pork loin with prunes, 572
- Pork & polenta stew, 564
- Pork with strawberries, 587
- Roast pork with apple cider, 588
- Roast pork in orange sauce, 582
- Roast pork with red wine, 593
- Roast pork shanks with mixed vegetables, 576

- Roast spareribs, 560
- Roast suckling pig with vegetables, 567
- Spareribs with honey & herbs, 584
- Spicy pork stir-fry, 590
- Stuffed pig's foot with lentils, 569
- Sweet & sour pork, 591

Potatoes
- Baked mushrooms and potatoes, 641
- Blue cheese potato salad, 664
- Focaccia with potatoes, 307
- Ham & walnut potato gratin, 399
- Indian stuffed potatoes, 632
- Kielbasy in wine with potato salad, 598
- Lamb & potato casserole, 554
- Leek & potato soup, 110
- Mediterranean fritters, 41
- Potato, bacon, & cheese pie, 393
- Potato & cabbage mix, 649
- Potato dumplings, 198
- Potato pie, 391
- Potato & rice soup, 138
- Potatoes with mixed spices, 633

- Spicy cottage cheese potatoes, 623

Preserves
- Artichokes preserved in oil, 920
- Baby vegetables in oil, 918
- Bell peppers in oil, 916
- Eggplants in oil, 925
- Grape cheese, 906
- Mango chutney, 908
- Passionfruit butter, 912
- Pickled onions, 915
- Plum chutney, 901
- Quick tomato chutney, 898
- Raspberries in eau-de-vie, 911
- Sauerkraut, 909
- Sun-dried tomatoes, 923
- Tuna preserved in oil, 926
- Zucchini in oil, 924

Prosciutto
- Neapolitan filled bread, 394
- Prosciutto & arugula pizza, 339
- Risotto with pancetta & prosciutto, 238
- Tagliatelle with prosciutto & peas, 189

Pumpkin
- Rice & pumpkin pie, 395

R

Rice
- Brown rice with uncooked tomato sauce, 245
- Filled rice fritters, 40
- Frankfurters in sour cream on rice, 600
- Herb and rice bouillon, 104
- Italian rice pudding, 737
- Minestrone with rice, 100
- Rice & pea soup, 132
- Rice & pumpkin pie, 395
- Rice cake, 711
- Rice cream, 719
- Rice patties, 237
- Rice with four cheeses, 246
- Rice with peas & artichokes, 211
- Rice with peas & pesto, 247
- Rice-stuffed tomatoes, 242

Risotto
- Artichoke risotto, 213
- Asparagus risotto, 204
- Basil and parsley risotto, 207
- Chicken risotto, 241
- Creamy lentil risotto, 230
- Curried egg risotto, 227
- Fish risotto, 233
- Gorgonzola risotto, 224
- Hazelnut and mushroom risotto, 219
- Lemon risotto, 223
- Milanese risotto, 202
- Milanese risotto – the day after, 203
- Mushroom risotto, 217
- Orange risotto, 210
- Oriental pork risotto, 226
- Pea risotto, 218
- Risotto with beans, 228
- Risotto with fennel, 208
- Risotto with ink squid, 234
- Risotto with John Dory, 232
- Risotto with Mozzarella, 220
- Risotto with pancetta & prosciutto, 238
- Risotto with wine and smoked salmon, 236
- Spinach risotto, 214

S

Salads
- Apple & celery salad, 661
- Arugula, corn & kiwifruit salad, 662
- Caesar's mushroom salad, 695
- Carrot salad with garlic, lemon & parsley, 660
- Chicken & celery salad, 494
- Cooked mixed vegetable salad, 670
- Cucumber & onion salad, 673
- Egg, Provolone, apple, & radicchio salad, 678
- Egg & tofu salad, 685
- Feta cheese & spinach salad, 684
- Fresh spinach & Parmesan salad, 682
- Gado gado, 668
- Orange salad, 677
- Platter of raw vegetables with olive oil dip, 657
- Raspberries, Feta & walnut salad, 688
- Simple chicken salad, 491
- Spicy salad, 681
- Spicy tuna salad with Mozzarella, 680
- Summer salad greens with apples & strawberries, 666
- Sweet & sour chicken salad, 471
- Tabbouleh, 674
- Tomato & basil salad, 690
- Tomato & Mozzarella salad, 687

- Tuscan bread salad, 692
- Wild salad greens with bacon & balsamic vinegar, 665
- Wild salad greens with warm Caprino, 22
- Woodland salad with raspberries & wild rice, 658

Sauces
- Agresto sauce, 943
- Aromatic herb sauce, 941
- Basic tomato sauce, 932
- Béchamel sauce, 950
- Bell pepper sauce, 949
- Bolognese meat sauce, 940
- Fruit mustard sauce, 954
- Gorgonzola cheese sauce, 935
- Honey sauce, 945
- Indonesian shrimp paste sambal, 936
- Leek sauce, 946
- Neapolitan meat sauce, 956
- Onion sauce, 952
- Orange & wine sauce, 934
- Parsley sauce, 953
- Poor man's sauce, 944
- Salsa pico de gallo, 73
- Spicy peanut sauce, 937
- Tartare sauce, 958
- Tomato passata, 921
- Walnut sauce, 942
- Warm red sauce, 938

Sausages
- Baked sausages & bread, 613
- Cabbage baked with sausage & bacon, 616
- Curried sausage & apple pie, 609
- Frankfurters in sour cream on rice, 600
- Homemade sausage meat, 594
- Kielbasy in wine with potato salad, 598
- Mixed sausage, chicken, & vegetable skewers, 604
- Sausage rolls, 54
- Sausages with apple sauce, 614
- Sausages & beans, 597
- Sausages with bell peppers, 602
- Sausages with potato puree, 596
- Sausages & shallots in white wine, 610
- Sausage toasts, 52
- Spanish sausages, 601
- Spicy homemade sausages, 607

Savory pies
- Asparagus pie, 377
- Bacon & egg pie, 406
- Blue cheese savories, 407
- Broccoli & leek pie, 374
- Cheese flatbread, 401
- Cheese, cream & speck pie, 405
- Curried sausage & apple pie, 609
- Fried vegetable pies, 381
- Green pie, 382
- Ham & walnut potato gratin, 399
- Leek & Fontal country pie, 398
- Leek pie, 372
- Macaroni pie, 408
- Mushroom pie, 379
- Neapolitan filled bread, 394
- Onion pie, 386
- Potato, bacon, & cheese pie, 393
- Potato pie, 391
- Rice & pumpkin pie, 395
- Saffron cheese pie, 402
- Salmon quiche, 388
- Spinach pie, 378
- Sweet & sour calamari pie, 410
- Tomato & Mozzarella pie, 392
- Tomato quiche, 389
- Vegetable pie, 385

Seafood
- Baked cockles, 459
- Calamari, bacon, & bell pepper kebabs, 578
- Clams with white wine, 437
- Crabmeat omelet, 415
- Deep-fried seafood sandwiches, 448
- Empanada with clams, 301
- Octopus salad, 462
- Orange-flavored shrimp cocktail, 444
- Seafood morsels, 90
- Seafood salad, 89
- Spaghetti with clams, 175
- Spaghetti with seafood sauce, 172
- Spicy calamari with parsley, 441
- Spicy prawn coconut curry, 434
- Squid, bacon, & bell pepper skewers, 92
- Sweet & sour calamari pie, 410
- Tagliatelle with shrimp & white wine, 190

Snacks, *see* Starters

Soufflé, *see* Desserts

Soups
- Basic stock with pasta, 140
- Cabbage & cheese soup, 141
- Chicken stock & Parmesan croutons, 118
- Chunky zucchini soup, 103
- Cream of squash, 127
- Creamy pea soup, 109
- Dumpling soup, 134
- Florentine soup, 102
- French onion soup, 120
- Hearty lentil soup, 112
- Herb and rice bouillon, 104
- Leek & potato soup, 110
- Minestrone with rice, 100
- Pearl barley soup, 99
- Porcini mushroom soup, 123
- Potato & rice soup, 138
- Rice & pea soup, 132
- Savoy cabbage & salami soup, 111
- Spelt & bean soup, 116
- Vegetable & bread soup, 128
- Vegetable soup, 8
- Winter minestrone, 124

Spinach
- Feta cheese & spinach salad, 684
- Fresh spinach & Parmesan salad, 682
- Polenta crêpes with spicy spinach, 84
- Spinach & rice soup, 130
- Spinach pie, 378
- Spinach pies, 75
- Spinach risotto, 214

Starters
- Baked tomatoes with cheese, 23
- Blue cheese snacks, 60
- Bresaola with fresh cheese, 49
- Bruschetta with tomato & basil, 48
- Cheddar onion dip, 16
- Cheese and almond puffs, 31
- Cheese biscuits or straws, 36
- Cheese croquettes, 35
- Cheese egg dip with crudités, 19
- Cheese fondue, 28
- Cheese fritters, 62
- Cheese & ham croquettes, 38
- Country-style eggs, 15
- Cream cheese with fresh herbs, 56
- Eggs fairy-style, 12
- Fava beans with Pecorino cheese, 26
- Filled rice fritters, 40
- Florentine liver toasts, 50
- Fresh cheese & olive toasts, 57
- Fried green tomatoes, 46

- Fried mortadella, 39
- Fried Mozzarella sandwiches, 43
- Fried polenta with mushrooms, 59
- Hard-boiled eggs with bell peppers, 9
- Hot cheese and herb appetizer, 33
- Hot and spicy olives, 64
- Mediterranean fritters, 41
- Mousetraps, 53
- Mushroom & truffle toasts, 61
- Nun's toast, 10
- Onion fritters in balsamic vinegar, 45
- Parmesan ice cream, 32
- Prickly cheese and celery balls, 20
- Ricotta cheese with fresh herbs, 17
- Sausage rolls, 54
- Sausage toasts, 52
- Savory pastry fritters, 44
- Stuffed celery stalks, 27
- Stuffed eggs, 11
- Stuffed fried olives, 63
- Tomatoes with Caprino cheese, 24
- Wild salad greens with warm Caprino, 22

Swiss chard
- Green pie, 382
- Swiss chard calzone, 365
- Swiss chard omelet, 426

T

Tomatoes
- Algerian-style stuffed tomatoes, 626
- Baked tomatoes with cheese, 23
- Baked tomatoes with pasta filling, 168
- Basic tomato sauce, 932
- Boiled beef in leek & tomato sauce, 535
- Bowtie pasta in summer sauce, 151
- Bread soup with tomato, 136
- Bruschetta with tomato & basil, 48
- Chicken stew with tomato sauce & green olives, 488
- Focaccia with summer vegetables, 298
- Fresh tomato & garlic pizza, 329
- Fried green tomatoes, 46
- Fusilli salad with tomato, garlic, & Mozzarella cheese, 167
- Greek-style stuffed tomatoes, 625
- Hunter's chicken, 506
- Meatballs with tomato, 530
- Mexican-style tomatoes, 628
- Mousetraps, 53
- Mozzarella & tomato focaccia, 310

- Neapolitan filled bread, 394
- Quick tomato chutney, 898
- Rice-stuffed tomatoes, 242
- Spaghetti with cherry tomatoes, 170
- Spaghetti with olives & tomatoes, 156
- Spaghetti with simple tomato sauce, 146
- Spaghetti with tomato & crumb sauce, 157
- Spaghetti with tuna fish & tomato, 178
- Spicy tomato bread, 276
- Sun-dried tomatoes, 923
- Tomato & arugula focaccia, 308
- Tomato aspic molds, 624
- Tomato & basil salad, 690
- Tomato, caper & anchovy pizza, 327
- Tomato & garlic focaccia, 304
- Tomato & Mozzarella salad, 687
- Tomato & Mozzarella pie, 392
- Tomato passata, 921
- Tomato quiche, 389
- Tomatoes baked with Parmesan, parsley & garlic, 631
- Tomatoes with Caprino cheese, 24

INDEX

Turkey
– Turkey mole, 501

V

Veal
– Hot veal carpaccio,
  Mediterranean style,
  524
– Milanese-style stewed
  veal shanks, 518
– Veal & artichoke rolls,
  525

– Veal roll with cheese
  & Prosciutto filling,
  512
– Veal scaloppine with
  lemon, 521
– Veal scaloppine with
  Parmesan & fresh
  tomatoes, 516
– Veal scaloppine with
  savory topping, 514
– Veal slices with
  Prosciutto & sage,
  510

– Veal stew with parsley,
  522

Z

Zucchini
– Filled zucchini, 83
– Focaccia with zucchini,
  299
– Zucchini in oil, 924